ECCE HUMANITAS

INSURRECTIONS: CRITICAL STUDIES IN RELIGION, POLITICS, AND CULTURE

Slavoj Žižek, Clayton Crockett, Creston Davis, Jeffrey W. Robbins, Editors

The intersection of religion, politics, and culture is one of the most discussed areas in theory today. It also has the deepest and most wide-ranging impact on the world. Insurrections: Critical Studies in Religion, Politics, and Culture will bring the tools of philosophy and critical theory to the political implications of the religious turn. The series will address a range of religious traditions and political viewpoints in the United States, Europe, and other parts of the world. Without advocating any specific religious or theological stance, the series aims nonetheless to be faithful to the radical emancipatory potential of religion.

For a complete list of titles, see page 319

ECCE HUMANITAS

Beholding the Pain of Humanity

BRAD EVANS

FOREWORD BY JAKE CHAPMAN

Columbia University Press

New York

Columbia University Press
Publishers Since 1893
New York   Chichester, West Sussex
cup.columbia.edu
Copyright © 2021 Columbia University Press

Library of Congress Cataloging-in-Publication Data
Names: Evans, Brad, author.
Title: Ecce humanitas : beholding the pain of humanity / Brad Evans; foreword by
    Jake Chapman.
Description: New York City : Columbia University Press, 2021. | Includes index.
Identifiers: LCCN 2020056216 (print) | LCCN 2020056217 (ebook) | ISBN 9780231184625
    (hardback) | ISBN 9780231184632 (trade paperback) | ISBN 9780231545587 (ebook)
Subjects: LCSH: Victims—Social aspects. | Sacrifice—Social aspects. |
    Violence—Social aspects. | Civilization, Western. | Aesthetics.
Classification: LCC HV6250.25 .E88 2021 (print) | LCC HV6250.25 (ebook) |
    DDC 362.88—dc23
LC record available at https://lccn.loc.gov/2020056216
LC ebook record available at https://lccn.loc.gov/2020056217

Columbia University Press books are printed on permanent
    and durable acid-free paper.

Printed in the United States of America

Cover image: Auguste Rodin, *Le Penseur (The Thinker)*, la Porte de l'Enfer, Musée Rodin
Cover design: Noah Arlow

A number of the sections in this book have previously featured in a revised and
    adapted form in the following published essays: Brad Evans and Henry A. Giroux,
    "Intolerable Violence," *Symploke* 23, no. 1 and 2 (2015); Brad Evans, "Liberal Violence:
    The Benjaminian Divine to the Angels of History," *Theory and Event* 19, no. 1 (2016);
    Brad Evans, "Dead in the Waters," in *Life Adrift: Critical Reflections on Climate Change
    and Migration*, ed. A. Baldwin and G. Bettini (Lanham, MD: Rowman & Littlefield,
    2017); Brad Evans, "The Shame of Being Human," *Frame: The Journal of Literary Studies*
    32, no. 2 (2020); Brad Evans, "Violence in a Post-liberal World," in *Humanitarianism and
    Liberal Order*, ed. J. Fiori et al. (London: Hurst, 2021). All reproduction rights have
    been granted.

For Chantal. Every letter written is an expression of the courage you have brought to my world. Every word written is shadowed by the tender fury your poetic fire carries across the oceans of time. And every page is still an empty canvas or an opening into the beckoning void, for you have taught me this is only just a beginning . . .

Chantal Meza, "The Void," no. IV, from the *State of Disappearance* project. 2019. Charcoal on paper. Copyright Chantal Meza. Permission granted by artist.

"Incontinent the void. The zenith. Evening again. When not night it will be evening. Death again of deathless day. On one hand embers. On the other ashes. Day without end won and lost. Unseen."

Samuel Beckett

"He who jumps into the void owes no explanation to those who stand and watch."
Jean-Luc Godard

"Man's deepest glances are those that go out to the void. They converge beyond the All."

Paul Valéry

Contents

Illustrations

Foreword

An Obituary for the Liberal

Jake Chapman

Nietzsche tells us that "it is only as an aesthetic phenomenon that existence and the world are eternally justified."[1] Only through our experience of art can the incomprehensible cruelty of a murderous world be made bearable. The law can neither curtail evil any more than science can resist mimicking the ambitions of a God it so eagerly banished. Existence is justified aesthetically, since the world is infinitely cruel, and humanity cannot reasonably claim any righteous place on the surface of the planet. Only pitiful aggregations of small comfort—art, music, poetry, can compensate the tragedy of our cosmic insignificance.

Ecce Humanitas tells us that "humanity is bound to the sacrificial model of existence. And such sacred harm continues to bring us to the point of our annihilation," and so "countering annihilation requires liberating the political imagination from the scene of the sacrificial, for it is precisely our allegiance to a sacred claim on life where the memory of violence is inscribed with the logics of violence to come."

This poses quite a paradox, since "if through horror we find freedom," then the logic of catastrophism might find some kind of millenarian conclusion, say, in the prospect of the impending ecological extinction, as if the logical solution to the end of violence would be the end of man. Evans suggests that "instead of looking with confidence toward a postliberal society in which we commit ourselves to transforming the living conditions of the world of peoples, what has taken its place is an intellectually barren landscape offering no alternative other than to live out our catastrophically fated existence with ever greater speed and intensities." This infertile plain, scorched by false promises, deserves at the very least "an obituary for the liberal" before a new theory of humanity can be conceived.

In *Beyond the Pleasure Principle*, Freud contends that "unpleasure corresponds to an increase in the quantity of excitement and pleasure to a diminution."[2] We might speculate upon the (albeit reductive) dynamics of human evolution, where unpleasure presumably corresponds to outbursts of profligate violence, and a diminution in the quantity of excitement to the more sedentary forms of modern civility; this liberalizing of the base instincts would concede to a more favorable affection for the arts and humanities, and come to define "what it means to live a valued life."

Staying loyal to Freud's view of human teleology, we might be encouraged to imagine how our cowering ancestors were teased out from the safety of the dark, lured by a vision of the luminous, giving valorization to an enlightened truth lying beyond. Emerging into the light, leaving the congealed wake of primal violence behind, this elevation from bloodshed has come to define the mythical nature of our struggle. Each heroic move forwards is accompanied by a slip back into war and genocide, upon which the various ontotheological versions of humanity return to contest their sectarian claims with unbridled violence, each relapse bringing into question the very validity of the conjecture "humanity."

In striving to eliminate "man's inhumanity to man" in favor of a more liberal world, we each time unwittingly concede to the sequence man/inhumanity/man, which structures the promissory mythology of progress, since each fall is memorialized with the injunction "lest we forget." Inscribed in the institutionalized memory of past violence is a renewed violence that acquires its retaliatory force from the symbolic power of the dead. It's as if also implicit in the process of memorializing violence is a form of amnesia, so that we experience each outrage afresh. Pierre Klossowski describes how the threat of transgression is intimately tied to the sacred, in a sequence which ensnares violence to a ritual repetition: "a transgression must engender another transgression. . . . its image is each time represented as though it had never been carried out."[3]

For Evans, "the psychic life of violence" describes the process by which violence is returned to utility, transformed by the necessity of prohibition, and absorbed into the immanent rule of law. He writes: "The sacrificial is precisely that which allows for the unbearable to become tolerable. And in the process of its consecration, it allows the intolerable to become an act of symbolic importance. It enables the exceptional event to appear as something altogether necessary, all the while it keeps hold of the exceptional act in order to normalize the violent will to rule." Consecrated symbolic power demands a unity of response, a univocality of sorrow; for the individual to be humane, they must aspire to humanity. And, for Evans, implicit in such an obligation is the fact that "humanity is ultimately a mythical claim, demanding its own sacrifices. Indeed, not only does humanity remain promissory and yet to be fully realized, it has for the past few decades grammatically justified the most devastating forms of global violence in the name of this promise. Humanity was meant to be realized through the wars fought to prove its very existence." The sacred memorializes the event of transgression, sublimating a deep reverence for violence in the body of atonement. Such tensions hold the earth together, binding raw energy to matter, primed for volatile release in spontaneous eruptions of sacrifice, cruelty, and holocaust, since it is catastrophe that gives equilibrium its temporary coherence. It is the renunciation of violence and the function of atonement that draws us forwards toward the next encounter with relapse and the new specter of sacralized blood.

Evans suggests that "the aesthetic secularization of life begins with the raw realities of degradation, torture, and human suffering—an image of life reduced to its abstract nakedness." Hans Holbein's *The Body of the Dead Christ in the Tomb* (1522) is arguably one of the most powerful representations of Christ's death (fig. F.1), since it is also one of the most heretical. Dostoyevsky's Prince Myshkin refers to it by stating, "Why, some people may lose their faith by looking at that picture!"[4] Holbein's painting shows Christ simply laid out after crucifixion. The stark horizontality of the painting and close-cropped framing has the effect of stretching the body beyond reasonable proportion, until one realizes that the cross has monstrously elongated Christ's body by the sheer force of gravity, redemption denied by the dead weight of his mortal incarnation. His face is gaunt, the skin livid and discolored, the body wracked with rigor mortis—this is an image at once painful and beautiful, embodying what Evans refers to as "the conditions of vulnerability so endemic to liberal subjectivity." But what exactly is being asked of us, as we take in the sight of Christ petrified in grotesque human

Fig. F.1 Hans Holbein, *The Body of the Dead Christ in the Tomb.* 1522. Oil on panel. Public domain.

form? It seems that implicit in Holbein's humanized corpse—this forensic husk, with the painter's cruel compassion for its ruined flesh and dislocated bone—is the appalling realization that this man is dead. It is the abject power of such a blasphemous spectacle, and of the shocking sight of Divinity so transgressed, that compels us (even us atheists) to repudiate the banal violence of the scene, to restore to Christ's sacrifice its proper and sacred value. After all, Christ died for our sins, but ultimately, in the awful vision of Christ's broken anatomy, here so belittled by mortal violence, it is violence itself that must be redeemed.

With Holbein's Christ, there is an extraordinary presentiment of modern secularization, since, for a religion nucleated by the originary murder of the son of God, the guilty deficit would eventually reach its sell-by date . . . In a cursory view of Western secular society, the sacred has ostensibly taken sanctuary in derelict places of worship, where simple caretakers of the faith are to be found abandoned to their obscure rituals—composing ordained relics upon their altars with the perseverance of madmen, endlessly rearranging the fragments of their sanity. Evans cites Nietzsche's notorious proclamation: "God is dead. God remains dead. And we have killed him. How shall we comfort ourselves, the murderers of all murderers? . . . must we ourselves not become gods simply to appear worthy of it?" With God dead, what need is there of the sacred to enforce its superstitious prohibitions once scientific rationality has overcome superstition?

Liberal society would invent its sacred games and claim that it has engendered less violence. The idea of humanity has remained intact, as the promissory genus under which the humane individual subscribes to the myth of progress. We are no longer at liberty to squander life since it is literally all we have, and the mindfulness of life surely gives rise to a quantifiable diminution of violence by dint of the secular respect for the here-and-now. Life is paramount, since the non-existence of God has made each of us a god in our own right, each a species-of-one, an identitarian monad; and yet, paradoxically, our religion is still *humanity*.

Evans's argument, then, is that the "modernist tendency to reduce life to questions of pure materiality devoid of any spiritual or metaphysical claims" withdraws the sacred from superstition only to embed it at a juridico-political level—painless lethal injection may have replaced the barbarity of the public square, where the condemned was ritualistically dismembered, in order to save them from their petty mortal protestations, before being subjected to further torture to extract confession. Their authentic pain would salvage their souls from damnation and deliver them to the mercy of God—the sacred was thus made public. Lethal injection condemns its subject to the full weight of the law in strict medical isolation, separated as if in possession of a contagion. A barbiturate paralytic and potassium solution are administered for the express purpose of causing rapid death, so that the purposefully violent component in execution complies instead with the humane—corresponding to this decrease in the quantity of excitement and pleasure, violence itself is liberalized and execution civilized. Despite execution by lethal injection lacking a visible subject, the mythologizing modes of speculation make millions captive to its sacralizing power: the hopeless death-row documentaries, the agonized relatives, the impotent prison vigils, the state pardon rejected on live TV as the moment of execution is broadcast live. With death subtracted from the visible, spectacle acquires a new intensity—humanity frenzied by the very absence of sacred violence. Absence only seems to heighten the libidinal economy of the spectacle—as Freud notes, "This pleasure in looking [scopophilia] becomes a perversion . . . if, instead of being preparatory to the normal sexual aim, it supplants it."

The challenge set by Brad Evans in *Ecce Humanitas* is to locate where the "eschatological mastery of life" occurs in a secular society that claims to eschew the sacred. Regarding the mass transcendentalization of the dead, he asks: "What would it mean, for instance, to feel the pain and suffering of every single of victim of Hiroshima?" What would it mean to deny Hiroshima's mushroom cloud its silver lining?

When in the wake of the 9/11 attacks President Bush threatened to bomb the Taliban back into the dark ages, a secular line was drawn between forms of violence putatively categorized as the divine and the systemic, the *blunt* and the *precise*, the archaic and the modern. The subtraction of Western troops from distant war zones is consistent with a secular timeline, in which the investment in technology marks the divergence from God. Specifically, the unmanned drone is the symbolic sublimation of the Omnipotent, the all-seeing eye of the soldier who is no longer required to sacrifice themselves to a heroic death. Unmanned drones do the military's dirty work, except there's nothing very dirty about operating a drone—the most likely threat looming over the operator is the drowsy drive home after a long shift. One imagines the posthumous medal awarded as a sacralization of the fatal car crash.

Stating his motives for writing *Ecce Humanitas*, the author explains, "If liberalism was a globally ambitious project aimed at governing planetary life through its sacred wars, this ambition was over. And, like all dying projects, its myths had been exposed, its violence revealed, and its remaining advocates increasingly vicious in their desperation to cling on to whatever entitlements its violence once permitted. Hence—while the book had become an inquiry into the triangulation between violence, the sacred, and the void, it also needed to confront the end of liberal times."

Nothing is too sacred for Evans, since "to critique the sacred is precisely to critique the hierarchization of power—the metaphysical compulsion to give rise to some higher unity that had already been there—which then continues to alienate and draws upon violence to make its claims visible." With the appearance of "a new dark age" and the rise of a new, fascistic "monstrous myth-making machine," *Ecce Humanitas* draws us to the urgency of our times, reminding us that "the genocide of millions has brought together in ethical tension the nihilistic logics of disposability with the attempts to render life meaningful by inscribing sacred values onto the mass graves of the annihilated."

Nothing could embody the apogee of the liberal project better than a recent announcement by the U.S. army in its commitment to make war more environmentally sustainable—suggesting it will load its munitions with engineered plant seeds to enable the re-wilding of its battlefields. It is as if liberal virtuosity had found a perfect vehicle for world peace in the machinery of warfare. In a return to the scene of original sin, where humanity was first condemned to suffering and the dominion of death—and endless sacrifices, war, and violence pursued in the concessionary name of the sacred—for Evans, "the Fall, in the end, proved itself more potent as a secular tale of man's potential to bring about his own destruction." And once the bombs stop falling and the dust settles, the horror of war will give rise to a second Garden of Eden, fertilized by violence and the enriched soil of the dead, a truly verdant flora will flourish, with trees to populate the earth after humanity has wiped itself from the surface of the planet in a rather touching sacrifice to planetary ecology.

Holbein's *Dead Christ* is laid out, hooked up to life support. Humanity gathers, hushed, anxious for even the faintest glimmer of life, aghast at the sight of the respiratory bellows reaching an optimistic peak only to collapse with a hollow wheeze. It's difficult not to recall the rotten corpse in David Fincher's *Se7en*, as, to our utter horror, the victim unexpectedly gasps alive. This what Brad Evans is calling out in *Ecce Humanitas*. The resuscitation of the manhandled corpse of the sacred, which violently revives after supposedly breathing its last breath to pose the terminal question: how do we bring a possible future back from the dark gravity of memorialization?

Preface

Encountering the Void

I t is always difficult to explain when exactly the idea for any critical inquiry or intellectual project first began. Though, looking back, it seems clear to me that the impetus for this manuscript can be traced to 2010. During the summer I spent a number of months on the Greek island of Kefalonia and in the city of Florence. Being in close proximity to the place that inspired one of the greatest myths of all—the Odyssey—one learns the importance of light and color, which in turn allows us to make sense of the historical political imagination of the region. Greek mythology was always far more vivid than the pious dullness of Christianity that followed many of its vibrant tales. My intellectual companions at the time of my travels were René Girard's *Violence and the Sacred*,[1] Giorgio Agamben's *Homo Sacer*,[2] along with Walter Benjamin's *Reflections*, which featured his remarkable and challenging essay "Critique of Violence."[3]

My intention was to write a short meditation on the theme of "extreme violence," to be presented at a workshop on "politics after the death of God" when I returned. My hope was to submit it to a journal afterward. I never managed to complete this paper, for reasons I couldn't quite understand at the time. While I now recognize I was perhaps too intimidated by the topic, notably by coming to terms with the thought of Agamben and Benjamin, I had also reached a certain limit insomuch as I felt that when it came to explaining the worst, the most extreme, the most intolerable, there was seemingly nowhere left to go after Agamben's ruminations. I felt I was simply repeating what he had already said about the "unspeakable" violence done to fellow humans, and I feared that my explanation had nothing original to contribute. I now see my problem was that I was too constrained by my own methods. Biopolitically allegiant, I was too focused on bodies rather than on the psychic life of violence and what this might have revealed about the aesthetics of annihilation.

Being in Florence didn't help my predicament, though it did give me the time to properly read Dante's *Inferno*[4] and try to make sense of its significance to the world at the time of its writing. I certainly appreciated that back then, as now, any serious critique of sacred violence needed to account for Dante's poetic reverie and its lasting images of thought. It is hard not to feel inspired in Florence. The entire place is like an open-gallery testament to the power of art. That's its enduring claim. But that was also the problem. Florence is a living testimony to the power of figurative art. Bodies in all their most perfect and monstrous forms appear everywhere. Indeed, while I walked through the Florentine plazas, gazing upon giant figures straight from some Classical Greek tale—expecting at any moment for one of them to come alive, step down off its concrete plinth, and walk through its narrow streets—I reflected on how the eternal memory of this City is all about embodiment.

And yet it was during this period that I did at least come to better appreciate the violence of the sacred. I had already accepted the idea that to understand violence one must first understand its sacred claims. This was equally true in the present day, as the legacy of just war was being countered by the most savage spectacles of human sacrifice. But I also understood, like racial persecution, this to be simply another chapter in the history of sacred violence. Modernity I accepted was nothing more than a continuation of pronounced theological notions, which continued to demand their own sacrifices. Not only this, I also felt completely dismayed by the positivism of political science, its secular claims of reason and objectivity, along with how its engagements—especially with violence—might become so much more compelling if it simply attended more to the power of art, aesthetics, and the literary imagination. Furthermore, I also recognized how some critical theory was opening up to new "poetic" terrains, where it was at least possible to consider alternative grammars in our inquiries. This might allow for a rethinking of the history of violence in more purposeful and all too human ways.

Mindful of this, and in light of the ongoing slaughter and other acts of violence perpetrated on a daily basis around the world, I came to think more about the relationship between humanity and violence, which I increasingly saw in theological terms. A number of questions would become of notable concern to me, and would actually form the basis of the initial book proposal, which I discussed with Wendy Lochner at Columbia University Press (to whom I owe an infinite debt for her patience with my endless delays for submission) back in 2015 when the contract was signed. Recognizing the importance of sacred motifs in the continuation of violence, I felt compelled to investigate how metaphysical claims to violence needed to appropriate suffering in order to justify its enactment in the name of some mythical project. Just as the violence of Christianity, for example, needed the body of Christ, so the Nation needed the body of the hero, while claims to Humanity needed the suffering body of the victim. This need to turn victims into sacred objects was, I believed, the poetic truth of humanitarian war, which, resurrecting theological notions of just violence, also presented humanity before us as an endangered and violated form. The questions guiding the initial research were therefore as follows:

1. What is the relationship between violence and sacrifice?
2. What do we actually mean when we say the word "humanity" (which includes the concept of race as a chapter in the history of sacred violence)?
3. How do we make sense of the ways in which liberal conceptions of humanity have justified violence in its name?
4. Why has the victim appeared so central to this drama?
5. What does this tell us about the order of the sacred in the contemporary world?

In the years that followed, I wrote a number of other books which dealt with ideas on the poetic,[5] while pursuing the idea of intolerable violence.[6] And yet something was still preventing me from completing this project. I kept coming up against limits in my own thinking and found that I simply didn't have the language or conceptual tools to really say what I wanted to convey. In truth, I found myself in a state of intellectual limbo, no doubt haunted by the intellectual anxieties of 2010, still trying to say something more than just a final chapter in the theological history of biopolitics and the violence enacted because of some sacred claim. But all was not lost. I had admittedly made a number of breakthroughs in my thinking as a result of columns I was invited to lead in both the *New York Times* and the *Los Angeles Review of Books*,[7] which gave me the freedom to engage more openly in conversation with critical theorists, artists, and writers, to whom I owe a considerable intellectual debt with regard to my reconceptualizing violence and rethinking aesthesis.

Still, it was only after meeting the Mexican abstract painter Chantal Meza (who is now my wife) that I truly recognized the nature of my problem. Or, to put it more explicitly, my problem was that I literally couldn't *see the problem*. Yes, I recognized that our understating of sacred violence needed a more critical exposition, especially given the return of all too archaic forms of sacrifice across the world. And yes, I also recognized there was an urgent need to rethink more deeply the conceptual crises of humanity, especially if we were to counter the emergence of new forms of fascism that were evidently resurrecting older mythical claims. That book would have been completed in 2017. While I have no idea how it might have been received, I do strongly believe that the waiting has taken the project in a far more important and considered direction. For in the time that's followed I have realized the problem behind the problem. Blinded by the appearance of bodies wrapped in blood-soaked mythical shrouds, I hadn't seen what actually gives rise to the sacred, giving true justification to its importance in response to political animality. If violence was something original in the order of sacred meaning, then I needed to properly consider what lay behind in the absence of its appearance. It took somebody with a brilliant aesthetic eye to make this clear to me, moving forward.

Engaging with Chantal's art and discussing aesthetics from the artist's perspective with her allowed me to recognize more attentively and with greater appreciation the importance of abstraction and how it provides a point of entry into the intimate depths of suffering. I was notably taken by the circularity of the violent lines she painted, which tore into the canvas, allowing me to rethink the violence of movement and the flight from history. Then, in 2018, Chantal and I went to visit the Tate Modern gallery in London. The gallery was notably full of people who spent a few brief seconds marvelling at whatever exhibit appeared before them, without any time for critical reflection. As we weaved through the madding crowds, our wandering eventually led us into the thankfully empty room housing Mark Rothko's Seagram Murals. We spent an afternoon immersed in the intensity of his brilliant works, commenting on the violence and the pain they conveyed, the internal suffering and the depths of despair, the subtle light and the darkened vortexes, the eternal optimism and the worldly tragedies yet to come.

Our conversation continued in the evening as to the reasons why we still haven't properly understood the power of his intervention, how the sacred is present and disrupted in his cathedrals of the mind, about the historical crisis of the figurative and the need to take more seriously the abstract in thought. While constantly thinking about this project as the discussion developed, I was also learning how to appreciate the world—especially the aesthetic world of violence—through an artist's gaze. Not to simply appropriate some aesthetic point in order to reaffirm my own theoretical premise but to become a learned student, taking aesthetic notes on how to reimagine the power of critique. Then, finally, it became clear. Not only did Rothko paint the violence of the world in such an intimate way it brought into focus its sacred mediations and claims. Rothko painted "the void." This was the problem that was really haunting this project. And, armed with this understanding, I began to see what needed to be written in this book.

One afternoon, a few weeks later, I returned home after giving a lecture at the university on the importance of Hannah Arendt. Chantal had been working on a series of paintings titled "Obscure Beasts" which were part of her *State of Disappearance* series.[8] I entered the apartment (where she was working) at the moment she was just finishing the final piece that day. She didn't even know I had entered the room. As Chantal lifted herself off the floor where the works were placed, she fell back into the armchair, her hands covered in deep-red and black paint. Her eyes were completely absent of any expression, and her face looked completely exhausted. While admittedly unsettled by this sight, I realized in that moment something else that was deeply significant about the book's problematic and how we might find an escape. The reason we don't like to confront the void is precisely because of the immensity of its terror. The unknown can be atrocious. And there is nothing more terrifying than nothingness. Yet, here was an artist painting about disappearance, the absence of absence, the voiding of existence, looking out after the creative process with such an absent gaze. It was as if she had willfully fallen into the void in order to imagine and create the world anew. This was a powerful realization. For if extreme violence results in us being thrown into void, which in itself is the absence which haunts and underwrites all forms of sacred meaning, this same void can also be a space of pure creation, where the immensity of terror and the affirmation of life collide.

There is, however, an inherent danger. How can one understand what's truly at stake if one can only confront the void with either torturously daemonic or artistic eyes? And how does one return without becoming a monstrous beast, seduced by the power of nihilism and its will to nothing? What had become clear was that in order to do justice to the idea, I must explore such a phenomenon as the pain of humanity; it wasn't sufficient to simply write about the sacred. More searching, there was a need to account for the pure potentiality of the void, which in turn affirmed the need for a more poetic understanding of the political in the face of annihilation, and the hope that we might finally break free from the myths that bind us.

My first reaction was to return to the works of Agamben and engage once again with his sacred mediations. While I had the same admiration for this thinking, what I found notable about his corpus—including *Homo Sacer*, *State of Exception*, *Stasis*, *The Sacrament of Language*, the *Kingdom and the Glory*, and his devastating *Remnants of Auschwitz*—was that it all contained rather fleeting reference to the void.[9] The concept does appear in a subtitle in *State of Exception* (though it is not conceptually developed beyond that one particular headline announcement), and is used very fleetingly elsewhere to describe a mere absence in law, language, or representation. There was also a brief moment in *Kingdom and Glory* where he suggested "the void is the sovereign figure of glory," but he only invoked the word to make a more considered point on the idea of the empty throne.

This same fleeting attention to the concept of the void was also apparent in Jean-Paul Sartre's *Being and Nothingness*,[10] reserved for a very few mentions in respect to the voiding or absence of meaning. Wanting more, I eventually turned to the work of Georges Bataille, whose entire investigations centred on the void.[11] Like Yves Klein, Bataille seemed to picture himself at the edge of the abyss. Welcoming the ineffable and the limits of the sacred calling, Bataille would find his freedom through horror. This led him to develop a theory of nothingness, which literally took nothing to be its object. That is, the object was to confront the dreadful apprehension of death and put oneself before the emptiness of the void. To achieve this, Bataille would find his escape through a return to sacrifice and the power of the sacred. But was this as radical as it appeared? My understanding already led me to believe that the history of Western metaphysics was defined by its allegiance to the sacred: the giving of oneself over to whatever myth appealed. And hence what needed to be accounted for was precisely how critics felt the need to fall back onto sacred ground, which for Bataille meant imagining one's own sacrifice in the name of radical alterity—quite literally pushing the sacred to its limits and over the edge. Although less provocative, this allegiance to sacrifice has since been apparent with many "post-secular" thinkers, who in their search for a more poetic understanding of the human condition only deepen further sacred claims. This added a number of further questions to the project:

6. What is the relationship between sacred violence and the void?
7. How might we conceptualize the void in terms of its destructive and creative potentialities?
8. How might this allow us to provide a more meaningful critique of violence adequate to our times?

In the decade which had passed since the book's thesis was initially conceived, there were also notable political changes that needed to be accounted for in the intellectual body of the work. Just as global politics needed to come to terms with the devastating failures of liberal internationalism and its humanitarian wars, which had exposed most fully the racial violence at the heart of the European idea of modernity, so was the very idea of liberalism put into crisis. I had already written about this crisis in the context of the normalization of terror and the onset of the doctrine of resilience,[12] which I argued was the final resting place for liberal subjectivity. Still, the tumultuous political events of the past few years made it increasingly clear that it was now possible to write an obituary for the liberal. If liberalism was a globally ambitious project aimed at governing planetary life through its sacred wars, this ambition was over. And, like all dying projects, its myths had been exposed, rendering its remaining advocates increasingly vicious in their desperation to cling onto whatever entitlements its violence once permitted. Hence—while the book had become an inquiry into the triangulation between violence, the sacred, and the void—it also needed to confront the end of liberal times:

9. How might we free the concept of humanity from its liberal chains?
10. How might we rethink the very idea of humanism after the death of liberalism?
11. What new mythical claims and sacred games will now be invented, and what violence will this permit?
12. How might we reimagine the future of the political without falling back upon some notion of sacred space?

Each of these questions had largely been dealt with upon completion of the first draft in early April 2020. But I felt that I perhaps hadn't gone far enough in my critique. Then, within a week, the world started to become aware of the tragic significance of the COVID-19 pandemic. As I watched the epicenter of the pandemic move from China to Italy, I was reminded once again of Florence and the bubonic plague, which occurred shortly after Dante's death. Surreptitiously imagined though probably just purely coincidental, as readers of this book will come to appreciate, while the poet would have a marked influence on my thinking, from its inception right through to the very end, so its year of publication also corresponds to the 700th anniversary of Dante's death. As the response to the pandemic unfolded, it became increasingly apparent that the postliberal order was already in the making. That is to say, while at the level of individual people there were remarkable displays of humanism witnessed, at the national level one could recognize the eerily familiar dominance of war narratives and their sacrificial rites.

But there was something different taking place. As every single metropolitan city became engulfed in a humanitarian crisis, it was increasingly apparent who were positioning themselves to be the new rulers in this state of emergency. We had known for some time about the marked separation between politics (at the level of nations) and power (into the global space of flows). But as the forces of militarism and state policing were now being matched by the tremendous acceleration of digital technology, and its involvement in our daily lives, what became crystal clear was that we were entering a new age that could be defined as a *global techno-theodicy*. And if this techno-theodicy accelerated the crisis of the victim, it also showed that the scapegoats would be precisely those who had the temerity to question the sacredness of technocratic reasoning and its post-political vision for a lasting planetary lockdown. Populist leaders were merely a sideshow, and in the end, showed to be just as disposable and expendable to the new technocrats of reason as anyone else. With this in mind, I needed to revise the manuscript in order to more fully address a problem that was already detected but not in focus enough prior to the pandemic.

The lockdown of 2020 didn't come to an end through some shared agreement on social responsibility and a new planetary awakening. The lockdown was torn apart by the brutal killing of George Floyd in Minneapolis, which once again revealed the deeply engrained racial violence present within Western societies. While the riots that followed seemed to speak to a population that was simply exhausted by the prejudice it faced, this event was also significant for a number of no less compelling reasons: 1) liberalism was never able to come to terms with the problem of race other than to violently police its existence. The birth of liberalism in fact corresponds with the birth of race as a lived reality and a political problem. The violence therefore showed how liberalism was no longer able to conceal this history, as 2) the Black Lives Matter movement started tearing down statues, notably in the United States and United Kingdom; it was clear that a new way of doing politics was being sought.

But even here it seemed that narratives of victimhood fell back upon notions of the sacred victim: 3) ostensible radical sympathies were often channeled primarily through rage-filled social media posts, which expressed the fight by highlighting the persistence of old symbols of power rather than the new dominating paradigm—namely the emerging techno-theodicy. Meanwhile, 4) while the question of race remained deeply important for rethinking the direction humanity might take, much of the debate was still all too predictable. Like the mythical assumption that violence was simply natural to the human species, so the question of racial intolerance also appeared timeless. Hence, while my understanding of violence was that it was only naturalized through its being bound to the sacred order of things, as I watched the Black Lives Matter drama unfold I especially felt that it was even more important that the lines of racial persecution were understood to be a distinct colonial invention. Racial violence, in short, was never timeless but in fact a more recent chapter in the history of sacred violence. And unless we understand how the sacred order has already transformed into something new, what is presented as resistance can so easily be appropriated.

Not unrelated to the question of race, there is another issue that must be acknowledged from the outset here. What I am referring to as the sacred order of politics does work within a distinct Eurocentric frame. Indeed, the move from the sacrificial violence of the Greeks to the body of Christ takes us on the road to Jerusalem, which would literally become the center of the earth in many early forms of worldly mapping and representations of power. Moreover, the moves from Christianity to colonization, and onto the nation-state and liberalism, operate within the European framework for sacred thinking. This is not, however, incidental. It is precisely this order of the sacred which has come to dominate the structure for power and violence in the world.

In contrast, it is my contention that "the void" is by definition aterritorial. Indeed, as early Japanese paintings such as Sesshū Tōyō's *Haboku Sansui*—literally "Broken Ink Landscape"—(1495) show (fig. I.1), the concern with the abstract and the question of absence, along with how it relates to presence, have a poetic history that far predates the European invention of the aesthetic terms. The dominant signifiers for the sacred in their current form represent a continuation of

Fig. I.1 Sesshū Tōyō, *Haboku Sansui*. 1495. Ink on paper. Public domain.

the European imaginary, which is able to rework its mythical binds as the forces of history bring the particularities of the sacred into question. However, the creative potential of the void is anti-identarian in the sense that it disavows any authentic claim to righteously call upon the fire from its alluring black sun.

This book certainly doesn't claim to answer all of these questions outlined above to satisfy the doubters. And I have no doubt some will criticize it for being too general, while others will self-righteously insist that I don't see the wider picture. I wrote this book in solitude. That was my curse, and I will have to reckon with its limitations. But once I began to see the problem, I was always more than one, especially when staring into the void. That was my comfort, to realize that I was never alone. And this has been truly instructive in terms of how I have rethought poetics as an ethical sensibility that's counter to the sacred in thought. Striking like a lightning bolt from wounded skies, this sensibility catalyzes an unexpected encounter with a love that demands no sacrifice. A love that accompanies and asks nothing in return. So if this book at least provokes some debate on the history of violence, its sacred claims, the meaning of the void, and why there's an urgent need to imagine a different image of the world to the one that is continuing to annihilate us, then that will be more than any author could have ever asked. In the words of Gaston Bachelard, "The repose of the night does not belong to us. It is not the possession of our being. Sleep opens within us an inn for phantoms. In the morning we must sweep out the shadows."

ECCE HUMANITAS

PART I

The Sacrifice

CHAPTER 1

Humanity Bound

H umanity is bound to the sacrificial model of existence. And such sacred harm continues to bring us to the point of our annihilation. What began in the Western political imaginary with the sacrifice of Iphigenia—the original cut into the innocent flesh of the earth—would be later rewritten in the story of Cain and Abel, and further consecrated and atoned in full brutal glory with the body of Christ. Nietzsche's subsequent proclamation of the death of God would then rework the mythical into the body of the state. Military heroes would offer up their lives for our collective freedoms. And yet, the myth of nations would eventually prove to be truly devastating in its territorial markings and violent divisions, forcing us to shamefully look upon life in its most raw and abstractly naked forms. Through the cracks in the mythical foundations of the state, however, the hero appeared to be just as vulnerable and fragile as everybody else. So eventually we turned to the metaphysical play of victims, foregrounding the sacredness of the vulnerable, replacing their silent screams with a call to save strangers by carrying out justice in their name. The sacredness of life thus begins to author planetary forms of violence borne of human denial.

Hence, what appeared to be a crisis in the order of the sacred would be more revealing of its liberalization, underwritten by a mythical claim to be the true and righteous embodiment of humanity made complete. There was, however, a painful lesson the prophets of catastrophe failed to heed. All sacred violence produces monstrous shadows, which would return in the form of literal sacrifice in new theaters where every type of victim enacted its revenge. All the while, the myth that bound humanity together—the sanctity of the victim—would be further undone by broken communities who occupied internal colonies within former colonial homelands. What remained then was a defeated notion of togetherness, a notion of a humanity brutally ravaged by its own narcissism—humanity in chains—continuously shackled and further tormented by the daily appearances of yet more wretched bodies on the shores of history. But there was already a new sacred order in the making, whose ghostly traces are now coming more into focus. A vision based upon the operations of a new global techno-theodicy, which speaks in planetary terms as it segregates and divides in the most intimate of ways.

This is a far cry from the picture of humanism painted by Raphael in his famous *The School of Athens* (fig. 1.1), which captured the romantic idealism of the European Renaissance.[1] With Aristotle and Plato reinvented in a romanticized scene of tranquil intellectual civility, debating among their fellows the differences between the metaphysical stars and the earthly depths, so the very idea of the human as a being at the center of its mortal universe, endowed with the critical faculty for human inquiry, is dragged out of the gothic brutalism and slumber of reason that defined the "Dark Ages" of Western civilization.[2]

And yet, while the Renaissance would undoubtedly instigate a cultural revolution in Europe, reimagining the legacy of Greece and the importance of the

Fig. 1.1 Raphael, *The School of Athens*. 1510-1511. Oil on canvas. Public domain.

arts and humanities for what it means to live a life of value, the striptease of that enlightened image made so romantic by Raphael would be slowly and surely laid bare. The European model for discovery would increasingly have to come to terms with its inherent contradictions, its denials, its subjugations, and its colonial violence that had to confront its own mimetic returns.[3] Dante was certainty onto something when he insisted upon the need to both venture into the depths of human suffering—to look more intently at the tormentors and tormented, perpetrators, victims, and their witnesses—while recognizing the importance of the poets of antiquity who become watchpersons to the wretchedness of human existence. We cannot but look upon the painful suffering and despair of others. Dante Alighieri's important role in this drama will be revisited throughout this book.

Despite the violence, the sacrificial is precisely that which allows for the unbearable to become tolerable. And in the process of its consecration, it allows the intolerable to become an act of symbolic importance. It enables the exceptional event to appear as something altogether necessary, even regulatory to the power of violence itself, keeping in check our base-level animal instincts while also keeping hold of the exceptional act and its excessive meaning in order to normalize the violent will to rule. The exceptional here appears precisely as a symbolic force that exists on the threshold between life and death—the force of death that gives meaning to life in its sacrificial wake. It *remains* that which has transgressed, so that others might be spared a similar fate. But this is by no means the only theory of the exceptional opened to us. Why should we let it be appropriated by the sovereign gaze? Or even more critically, why do we need to think of it as a transgression to a morality already set, something that is necessarily beyond—and hence violently fated—in order to regulate what remains within? To echo the words of Jean-Luc Godard who, in perhaps his most poetic rumination on violence in his film on Sarajevo, narrates fully the silent shrouds that cover the exception:

In a sense, fear is the daughter of God, redeemed on Good Friday. She is not beautiful, mocked, cursed, or disowned by all. But don't be mistaken, she watches over all mortal agony, she intercedes for mankind; for there is a rule and an exception. Culture is the rule, and art is the exception. Everybody speaks the rule; cigarette, computer, t-shirt, television, tourism, war. Nobody speaks the exception. It isn't spoken, it is written: Flaubert, Dostoyevsky. It is composed: Gershwin, Mozart. It is painted: Cézanne, Vermeer. It is filmed:

Antonioni, Vigo. Or it is lived, then it is the art of living: Srebrenica, Mostar, Sarajevo. The rule is to want the death of the exception. So, the rule for cultural Europe is to organise the death of the art of living, which still flourishes.[4]

To make sense of this commitment to the violence of the exception to the point where its ends are the very annihilation of everything imaginable, what I present constitutes its purposeful regulation to ward off such a time—the violence of the symbolic order that becomes altogether normal and part of the everyday fabric of a violently enframed existence. There is thus a need to understand the amalgamation of intellectual forces, which render the sacred *the* condition of possibility for a meaningful life at the point of this annihilation. This requires addressing the ways in which life is bounded to a distinct philosophical persuasion, appearing meaningful in a world which had no reason to have or ever want us. A world that is still symbolically cloaked by a theology that promises some kind of immortality in the face of death. Such a reckoning demands accounting for the way violence is mobilized on the backs of millions from an account of politics bounded to the question of human survival. One whose very conditions make it possible to atone for every earthly sin. Only after such a reckoning can we bring into sharp relief the links between violence and techno-scientific fetishization. This latter, especially following the death of the Promethean man, promises to be our only salvation from the excesses of our own destructive behaviors, even as it increases with devastating speed our willful nihilistic capacity to separate ourselves from the world.

This is not to say the context and content of these forces don't change over time. What remains a constant, however, is precisely our allegiance to sacred principles, which have now put us into a particular bind. With this in mind, there is no comfort in merely looking upon or even recognizing the plight of unnecessary victims within a juridical frame if what passed for justice can only be realized through a recourse to righteous force. To outlive the violence of the sacred, there is a need to look behind that scene to what truly terrifies us: the fateful absence from which we emerged and into which we will surely return. We are still, it seems, incapable of confronting the unbearable void, even if it is in doing so that we can truly reimagine what it means to be freed from sacred chains.

The politics of the sacred have always been dependent upon the mastery of eschatological time.[5] Having now foregrounded the sacredness of the victim, so our attentions have willfully turned to excavating the past, giving ourselves over to the forensic model for ethical justice, while analytically surveying the ashes of history so that we might retrospectively interrogate the crimes that have befallen our now endangered humanity. Like archaeologists in search of the hidden truth about the meaning of our self-inflicted downfall, we tirelessly work our way back to address every injustice, every claim of victimization that might just hold the key to human togetherness. We dig through the ruins of the modern period in search of the disappeared of recent history to insist upon the need for collective responsibility. We return to when Europe colonized itself and millions were sacrificed by fire as black rain fell over wounded skies, and back further to the pillage and rape of entire continents in the name of savage enlightenment. We go back to the abduction and enslavement of peoples of a different color, when the Atlantic was turned into a vast graveyard of disposable human cargo; to the pre-modern empires of Europe, Hernán Cortés landing on the shores of Veracruz and the subsequent decimation of the indigenous populations; to the exploits of Alexander and the incident of the Sabine women abducted from the streets of Rome. We impose retrospective judgments on humanity's worst crimes, from Herod to Pilate who both brought with lawful intent a massacre of innocence. We may even venture back further to the original violence of Agamemnon and the slaughter of his innocent daughter, or even to the dawn of time itself, so that every blow, every laceration, every scar is another mark on the tortured flesh of this humanity now complete. This history is important. That is not being denied here. The wretchedness of humans needs to be understood. The intolerable needs to be confronted. But such history only matters if we can use it to insist upon a fundamental break with the past, to behold the pain of humanity so that we might steer history in a different direction.

Nietzsche famously said we need art in order to not die from the truth.[6] But we also construct realities, give sacred meaning to tragedies that in the act of revealing their sacrificial qualities are temporally suspended between past and future, so that we don't die from the truth. Our reality—the world we have chosen to construct within a sacred frame—in all its various forms makes bearable the unbearable truth of existence so that we don't have to suffer the sacrificial first-hand. This is its mediating function: to show us the tragic so that we may at least be thankful for living another day. That is why the power of the image has proved enduring. The image is always concerned with conveying and regulating the flesh of the world.[7] Images don't simply appear before us like figurative reference points, signaling how we may trace back to the original meaning of the word. The image is the original scene. It is the realm of (in)visibility, the milieu of (dis)appearance, which through its apparition allows us to recognize that which is possible by opening up the "flesh of the imagination."[8]

But empires are as manipulative as they are studious, especially in their capacity to regenerate the authenticating vision for the truth of power and of rule. What always concerns the imperial mind is mastery over the symbolic or iconic image, which, tasked with consecrating a particularly anesthetizing "image of thought"[9]—the image of the world—asks us to look further than we have ever done before, into the beckoning twilight. This is not so that we might find true affinity with the speculative realism of the metaphysical beyond, but so that we are ultimately struck down with metaphysical awe, looking without truly seeing—and learning in the process to willfully give ourselves over to its sacred promises. Indeed, it is precisely in the regulated act of "looking beyond"—what we might recognize as coming face-to-face with the glory of the exceptional—that we understand the importance of the mythical as a truly devastating construct, capable of binding together the transcendental with the immanent. Christ carries the unbearable weight of the cross so that we don't have to die for our sins. The hero carries the unbearable weight of democratic violence so that we don't have to carry out the task upon which all modern systems are sustained. And the victim carries the unbearable weight of a death experienced in full public gaze so that we don't have to confront the realization that all life is capable of disappearing without a trace.

Every life has the possibility of being denied any meaning whatsoever, much less care for its existence, from a world that never asked it to appear. But what would happen if we merely dispensed with God for a moment while still recognizing a sacrificial claim? What comes into focus then is the unbearable weight of absence—the unbearable weight of history, the unbearable weight of nothing. That is why we uphold the sacred: it offers a bearable witnessing to the reality of a life whose existence is a fluke.[10] But this is not a response to violence. It is allegiance by deferral, until the next sacrifice. What is more, our trouble is not simply what is being deferred; rather, what ultimately passes for the myth of progress is consecrated through the creation of Gods more terrifying still.

Our task then is to look more critically at the sacred realms of the intolerable and feel the weight of the unbearable, to gaze more intently at the tortured figures of history while confronting the exhausting weight of this absence. Our task is to insist upon a break with the sacrificial model and all mythical claims for meaning, which in the process of realizing their mission continually ask for violence enacted in their names. Finally, our task is to insist upon the need for the abstract in thought, to love without the need to give over to sacrifice, to meld one's life with a truly liberated humanity—*Ecce Humanitas*—in the most poetic sense. What is envisaged here is a collective notion of life that is able to stare into the void without becoming a monstrous adaptation of what was once defeated. To imagine such a possibility, we must ask why we are so unsettled when the sands of time that swirl around the vortex of existence stop falling down to earth? What, in other words, do life and meaning truly mean in the face of their annihilation, especially from the perspective of those who are already dead and soon to be forgotten, regardless of what they brought to this world? These questions require us to confront the very idea that life only has meaning if it conforms to a metaphysical demand which insists that a life worth living must, in the end, prove itself worthy of the sacrifice—that it must somehow live up to the sacred order of things, even if that means compromising with violence and accepting conditions that create the most artificial and suffocating forms of love. Ecce Humanitas demands a rethinking of the relationship between love, violence, and sacrifice. We will only achieve this by appreciating in more intimate and poetic detail the wounds of history so we can journey into the depths of the void and still retain our love for humanity, regardless of the violence that continues to make its sacred calling.

THE PROMISE OF HUMANITY

Human. Anti-human. Humanism. Dehumanization. Humanitarian. These terms are part of the everyday political lexicon and central to how we have come to think and write about the concept of "humanity." But what do we actually mean by the concept of humanity, and does it have any meaning in the world today? We could invariably begin with a more positive genealogy and map out the altruistic and culturally enlightened move from the humanist tradition—as it first appeared in Renaissance Europe, with its promotion of arts and culture—to the idea of universality and the ways in which humanity in its liberal guise would suggest the highest stage of human completion. As members of a learned species (at least as this story suggests), some humans have undergone a process of self-realization, becoming more ethically and culturally appreciative of the rich fabric of a shared togetherness, and have eventually learned to live in peaceful cohabitation.

Central here would be the moral demands to uphold individual claims to rights, dignity, and prosperity as enshrined in social contracts and declarations that reveal the best of our ethical deliberations and commitments. Humanity in this sense resembles a true figurative embodiment of reason, rationality, and progressive wisdom which, creating a democratic union among the world of people, will ultimately banish warfare, hunger, poverty, and all other injustices from our shared planet. While this conception of humanity derives from the simple biological fact of being, it has been marked out as philosophically unique insomuch as its realization proves we possess a natural evolutionary tendency, which could eventually result in the most flourishing community ever established. To imagine humanity in these ambitious terms is to reach for the highest state of human development: a humanity that has finally realized its political potential and revealed its true ethical calling. A truly formidable reckoning, as Carl Schmitt was right to insist upon.

None of this wholly liberal concept of humanity is fictitious, despite the fiction of "human completeness" that binds it together. And none of it has been divorced from the realms of the real, even if political realism remains the greatest impediment to its appearance and lasting settlement. Humanity as presented here has always been more than a simple calling to "get along with each other" or an imagined ethical possibility for the type of lasting peace even Immanuel Kant thought was ultimately impossible. Humanity has in fact been colonized within a particularly inclusive political imaginary for thought and action, which has bound the concept to the authenticating demands of its lived presence, which have appeared as ethically and morally determined.

We know, for instance, the very term "humanity" has a fraught and contested political history, and has been invoked both in the justification for slavery and also the expansion of twentieth-century fascism. We know it has also been successfully appropriated to justify war and destruction in the name of humanitarian principles. This violence is not incidental. Humanity has not been galvanized by the constant push to create the most vibrant of political communities—even if the enlightenment would truly run with the notion of a higher consciousness to justify colonial violence and the subjugation of less developed societies. Indeed, while there is a notable genealogy to the universal idea of suffering that takes us directly back to the birth of Christianity and the advent of the universal witness (see chapter 2), what we might call the *liberal conception of humanity* arises out of the ethical devastation of World War II. Humanity in this context moves from being a political ideal to becoming an imperative concept for a world that needs to come to terms with the worst of what humans are capable of doing to one another. In the process, humanity becomes here the dominant myth for the liberal will to rule, which, turning victims into the sacred object for power, allows for the most violent political forms of intervention to be delivered in their names.

This brings us directly to Hannah Arendt, to whom a great deal is owed in terms of how humanity as a political and philosophical concept was rethought and rearticulated in the wake of the horrors of World War II.[11] Arendt was deeply concerned with the most heinous crimes inflicted upon those who were denied their claim to worldly belonging and their very status of humanity. This made her notably attentive to the question of powerlessness, which she saw embodied most clearly in the figure of the refugee and refugees' lived condition of "worldlessness"—to literally be denied a world that they could claim as their own and share with others. Influenced by her own experiences of internment and flight from the ideological forces of fascism, Arendt addressed the crisis in thought which she believed made such a condition possible—the state of thoughtlessness that allowed dehumanization to flourish, which she famously termed "the banality of evil."[12] Connecting the systemic with the personal, the political with the psychological, Arendt also understood how modern violence spoke directly to grand metaphysical claims while reaching into every household through the grammars of life necessity. In doing so, she sought to address how the very order of this violence was able to legitimize its appearance by liberating thoughtless behavior through an active manipulation of instrumentalized reasoning, which always justified violence in the name of modernization.

But Arendt was no apologist for automation; she did not hold that humans were devoid of agency and responsibility. Totalitarianism was rife, she understood, with liberated agencies of nihilistic prejudice, albeit deluded by myths fabricated by those skilled at deception. As she noted, the idea that "everything is possible" can also be translated to mean that "everything can be destroyed" including the very "idea of humanity itself."[13] This manifested itself in the most appalling ways with the return of the concentration camp from overseas colonies (an effect referred to as the "colonial boomerang"), which not only made us realize the true depths of our inhumanity, but ultimately gave rise to a humanitarian imperative the very moment the concept of humanity appeared to be in permanent crisis. As Arendt further wrote:

The conception of human rights, based upon the assumed existence of a human being as such, broke down at the very moment when those who professed to believe in it were for the first time confronted with people who had indeed lost all other qualities and specific relationships except that they were still human. The world found nothing sacred in the abstract nakedness of being human.[14]

It is precisely this crisis of the sacred, as it was revealed by coming face to face with the abstract nakedness of the human condition, which resulted in the emergence of a particular concept of humanity bound to the idea of the universal sacredness of the victim. This concept would also be irrevocably bound to a juridical claim that the rights of humans are guaranteed and protected by law (see chapters 3 and 7). This would necessarily translate into the idea that dehumanization was ultimately a failure of the legal protections and moral certitude guaranteed by international juridical proclamations. However, while this liberal conception of humanity became more visible in the aftermath of World War II, as will be shown, it nevertheless represents less of a departure and more a continuation of Western metaphysics and their allegiance to the sacrificial (see chapter 2).

In fact, what really changes are the biopolitical contours for planetary rule, which, speaking the language of universality, still operate in a highly contingent fashion in order to segregate and forcefully contain global life-forms.[15] Hence, while directly appealing to the human as an endangered form, this concept of humanity would be tied in a real and yet all too promissory way to an emerging system of liberal power, which was still undergoing a violent genesis. This promissory claim to humanity should not be underestimated. As Jacques Derrida observed:

Humanity (still the "promise"), the humanity of mankind, is still a very new concept for philosophers who aren't sleepwalking. The old question about what is specifically human needs to be entirely reworked. Not only in relation to the life sciences, not only in relation to what is called by that general, homogeneous, and confused word, "the animal," but also in relation to all the traits that metaphysics restricted to humans.[16]

Our task is to inquire into this restricted metaphysics, for it is here we discover how, like all political terms that have the power to capture the imagination and mobilize war machines. It is to question how humanity is ultimately a *mythical* claim, demanding its own sacrifices. Indeed, not only does humanity remain promissory and yet to be fully realized, it has for the past few decades grammatically justified the most devastating forms of global violence in the name of this promise. Humanity was meant to be realized through the wars fought to prove its very existence. And yet, as we have learned, it was precisely such violence, notably tied to liberal claims of peace and justice, which has ultimately brought the term into conceptual crisis. This raises a whole number of critical questions: how, for instance, are we to make sense of the violence of humanity? And what has happened to make humanity come to represent, through an appropriation of the witnessed suffering of victims, a continuum in the sacred order of things? What we can say is that since humanity has been presented in an evolutionary way, part of its strength has been to retrospectively open the wounds of history, from the body of Iphigenia to children washed up on the shores of the Mediterranean. This at least provides us with a critical point of entry. Such retrograding of the failures of a humanity yet to be realized allows us to undertake our own metaphysical autopsy on the bodies of its sacred victims—not to simply follow the path laid out by the unromantic Schmitt, but to more purposefully critique the shameful weight of history, and assess how it might be mobilized to bring about its sacred completion.

It should be stressed here that the reintroduction of the sacred as a metaphysical category in direct response to the crisis of sovereign power—that was made apparent after the era of Nazi Germany is not understood as something that is "banned" in the Agambenic sense. The sacred arrived in its liberal guise as a transcendental force to willfully overcome the limits of sovereign power through its modes of inclusion. Thus, it created the crisis of its crisis, which provided yet another entry point into the conditions of vulnerability so endemic to liberal subjectivity.

What the liberalization of the sacred permitted was the promotion of a vision for humanity, which attempted to complete the history of Western metaphysics by rewriting the narrative of an endangered existence through its own sacred lens. This ultimately bound planetary life to scenes of the sacrificial and the forced witnessing of its widespread violence and segregation. Although still limited in terms of definition, this understanding of the sacred does allows us to provide a partial response to Georges Bataille's dilemma. "Across time," Bataille wrote,

the blood sacrifice opened [our] eyes to the contemplation of the vexing reality completely outside daily reality, which is given in the religious world this strange name: the *sacred*. We can give no justifiable definition of this word. But some of us can still imagine (try to imagine) what *sacred* means. . . . [and] try to relate this meaning to the image of what the bloody reality of sacrifice represents to them, the bloody reality of the animal's death in sacrifice.[17]

The vexing reality for liberalism has always been its lack of self-evident realization. That is why the concept of humanity proved particularly useful, as it allowed liberal regimes to intervene without warrant or mediation. In doing so, liberalism was able to overcome the crisis of the sacred by reimagining the figure of the victim, by opening our eyes to the wretched of history so that the world's pain could be felt and its injustices addressed. Yet it was precisely the construction of humanity as a promissory mythical demand, bound to the sacredness of the victim, which would ultimately create the conditions for the flourishing of sacrificial violence. Thus, ontologizing vulnerability would in turn open up the space for the appearance of the new fascisms that exist in the world today. If history is our guide, it is for this reason alone that the concept of humanity needs to be freed from its sacred liberal chains, for its binds have brought it to the point of conceptual ruination.

A RENAISSANCE FOR HUMANITY?

Some of the most evident tensions of recent times—and the so-called "post-secular" turn in critical thought and society—have been the renewed engagements and ongoing concerns with the theological.[18] Critical thinkers of many persuasions have provided a certain opening here by purposefully reacting to the modernist tendency to reduce life to questions of pure materiality devoid of any spiritual or metaphysical claims. However, this has conversely been accompanied by the return of "old religions" and the advent of new forms of violence in which bodies have been brutally sacrificed in arcane and seemingly pre-modern ways. Our forced witnessing to sacrificial violence has in fact become one of the defining features of the present moment.[19]

Let's begin here by dealing with the first of these developments. One of the outcomes of "post-modernism" has been a return to the ineffable as a way not only to rethink the meaning of life beyond crass scientific reductionism, but through this opening to allow for a new understanding of poetics by which the sacred—indeed, a resurrected (albeit much weaker and battle-scared) faith—might return anew.[20] The sacred in these terms has appeared like a new discursive weapon and a more meaningful ethical promise; better attuned to the past and more open to new interpretation, it reveals more fully to us the abstract in thought, especially as it is narrated by the poets of history who are more attentive to the lived reality of suffering, and the tragedy of human existence. While the turn to the poetic in order to critique the suffocating onslaught of modernity has been welcomed, this has nevertheless resulted in a tense and often disjointed contest on the meaning of the sacred, including its key referents. Moreover, the term itself has not been truly problematized in full appreciation of its literal and figurative qualities and affects.

Indeed, while this has been matched by a recognition of the appearance of a new Dark Age marked by sacrificial forms of violence whose theological drivers appear unsettlingly puritanical, too often there has ultimately been a demand to appreciate a more radical hermeneutic position, for a faithless faith, as exemplified in the poetics of a truly sublime critique that recasts the theological order of things. This just might hold the key, it is said, to opening up thinking on the sacred meaning of life after the death of God. Such mysticism is a far cry from the atheism of the twentieth century. Indeed, not only is humanity's search for a new religion in the lived presence of sacred violence proving to be one of the key battle lines in an age of postliberal reason, it shows how the sacrificial destruction of life and ongoing search for sacred meaning in the most elusive of places can occupy an eschatological time.

Today, some of the more purposeful investments in seeing the liberating potential for the sacred have explicitly bound their theological calling to the poetics of catastrophe (what John Caputo terms the *theopoetic*) and the ability to resurrect new meaning out of the ashes of ruination.[21] The act of suffering here becomes the starting point for rethinking the limits of language and our grammatical responses in a way that just might save us. My contention is not with poetics, nor is it with the way the poets of history have provided far richer testimonies on the tragedy of the human condition than any self-identifying political scientist armed with their less-than-objective swords of reason. Their battles too have always been a religious war. How we might rethink subjectivity in more poetic ways still remains a challenge for our times.

What is of concern, however, is the conflation of poetics and the sacred, as if the ineffable or the imagined beyond and its multiple grammars—which create

a powerful symphony with the art of the possible and the abstract in thought—
ultimately represent (however meekly) the rearticulating of a religion by another
name: a true religion for humanity, guided, like Dante, by the best of them in
the worst of times. What's decried as the absence of the sacred in humanitarian
ethics, notably in respect to secular liberal humanism, instead reveals its hidden
capacities for reconceptualization and strategic application in the order of political affairs. The advent of just war in the name of the desecrated bodies of victims (notably women and children) has been more than instructive over the past
two decades in trialing its potential.[22] What becomes a call for "reimagining" the
political by recognizing the suffering of others and to carry their silent screams,
offers to resurrect poetic voices from history to provide a sacred reading of the
present. This, despite its invocation of love and friendship, nevertheless fails to
break out of the sacrificial model, thereby enforcing a concept of love that is
forever indebted to sacrifices made and in turn laying the foundations for further
violence to be authored in its name.

It now seems almost trite to argue that the advent of the "post-modern sublime" in the late 1960s coincided with the "return to religion" in more orthodox
ways. As societies became increasingly suspicious of the role of big government,
their lives increasingly hollow as they became reduced to simple material plea-
sures, so there came to be a political and theological reawakening. With both
of these spheres invariably concerned with the infinite and their shared suspicions of positivism, it became more fashionable to seek out new spiritual meaning while simultaneously the foundation stones to truth and certainty were
being destroyed. Or, as Dostoyevsky might say, true faith "comes forth from
the crucible of doubt." Despite all our science, all our epistemic triumphs, all
our improvements for the human species, the sacred continued to belong to the
unknowable excess.

In order to substantiate these claims, it was important to mark out clear distinctions between the sacred and the secular, thereby allowing for the reworking of the sacred itself into either a more ethical or more familiar religiosity. As
both presented secular modernity to be devoid of sacred claims, the political
could be rethought in more intimate metaphysical ways. It is perhaps no coincidence that during this time both Catholicism (in the guise of liberation theology)
and Islam (in advent of Islamic governance) also became increasingly concerned
with earthly suffering and the role of the victim. Late liberal rule would learn to

overcome the limits of its own positivism by embracing the complexity sciences, which also allowed it to scientifically verify the notion that all things were fundamentally insecure by design.[23] However, it would be remiss to suggest that the sacred (like theology more generally) ever went away, unless one adopted the crudest and most reductive teleological schematic to traverse a bracketed history from the theocratic to the secular, and onward to the post-modern and the religious comeback. The problems of the twentieth century did not arise out of a failure of the sacred imagination. Rather, its devastation and successive atrocities show more fully its terrifying and annihilating potentialities.

And yet it still remains a common and compelling position to argue for a need to "reimagine the sacred" for the present day, in direct response to the perceived absence of a meaningful life.[24] Notable here is the embracing of the more existential qualities of art, poetry, and literature as an attempt to fight back against radical alienation and recover the long-lost mythical art of reading between the lines of human tragedy.[25] In many agreeable ways, this can be said to correspond to a new period of creative flourishing and cultural awakening for our endangered humanity—a second renaissance, where Dante's concern with trans-humanization (*transhumanar*) is seen in the context of a new literary imagination, which in the process of creating a more magnificent transcendental humanism with a love for the stranger, proceeds in full appreciation of the crosses others have carried and the sacrifices they have made in order to survive in the trenches of existence.

In this regard, history as a form of sacred unfolding is further presented as open to literal and aesthetic reinterpretation beyond the merely accessible or immanently comprehensible. This attempt to reclaim the forgotten idea of the sacred as a humane concept (with its all too theological resonance) is poignantly illustrated by Gerry Judah's sculpture *Twin Crosses* (2013), which is situated in the main hall of St. Paul's Cathedral.[26] Commissioned to mark the centenary of World War I, these two white symmetrical crosses literally double the order of the sacred, consciously mirrored and yet set apart. The image of the white cross became synonymous with the marked graves of the glorious dead of this brutal war in cemeteries around the world. Commenting on his work, the artist explained that the "wantonness and wastefulness they represent should also remind us of the ravaged earth of the First World War, of the millions of young men sacrificed defending or attacking mere yards of mud."[27]

This linking of sacrifice to needless suffering is important. But, as the Chapter of the Cathedral further insisted, despite this violence, the order of the sacred needs to be recovered when faced with a legacy of suffering:

> Placed where they are, we are invited to walk through them, and the failure and pain they represent, into a sacred space of hope where people in all our diversity are invited to come together to worship, to respect and to learn from each other. It is a work that starkly asks of us what it must now mean for us to be loyal to our shared future.[28]

What is on trial then is a particular chapter of history, not sacrifice itself as foundational to our histories of violence, nor the idea that the sacred is essential to any viable notion of shared humanity.

Doubtless, the turn in post-Heidegger continental philosophy toward "the event" as a principal concept, notably featured in works of Gilles Deleuze and Alain Badiou, has also been implicit in this so-called return to religion, as the conditions of the new appear like a revelationary force.[29] The actualization of the unknowable—the event of something coming into this world—is proof of a certain beyond, which takes us back into the realm of faith (without the armies of the faithful necessarily in attendance every Sunday). This has been matched by the messianic nature of radical politics more generally, from the late writings of Derrida and his concerns with both hauntology[30] and the question of what-is-to-come onto Agamben's potentiality.[31] But when exactly does this return to religion actually take place? What of Immanuel Kant's demand for a theory of radical evil, Adam Smith's glorious invisible hand, Max Weber's spirit of capitalism, Benjamin's messianic critique, Jacob Taubes's mediations on the Occidental, Hannah Arendt's banality of total moral collapse, Carl Schmitt's theological paradigmatic framing of sovereignty, Heidegger's questioning the notion of *Dasein* in favor of the event to come? What of the realization that most secular leaders and wielders of power since the beginning of the twentieth century have continually appealed to religious motifs whenever the occasion demands—and not just in the Middle East, but in every so-called "liberal democracy" of the West. In truth, religion never went away or vacated the scene.[32] And it could never be left waiting at the door. There was never the full triumph of secular reason. Hobbes already knew that much when domesticating the beast of the waters. In fact, if we use violence as the surest diagnostic of any political system, we see how the most technocratic and nihilistic regimes are inexorably bound to the politics of myths and their sacred demands. The secular has demanded its piety, just as the order of progress has become a giant providential machine tasked with a biopolitical mandate to promote and enslave, affirm and deny, protect life and destroy it in the very same sacrificial movement of its predecessors. There is, however, a caveat. These points of contest regarding religion are possible precisely because of the ambivalence of the sacred, especially as it relates to questions of truth and human affairs.[33] The following passage from Bataille's essay "War, Philosophy and the Sacred" proves to be particularly instructive in this regard:

> Take the example of the corpse; it can be dissected and treated as an object of science only to the extent that it passes—even if this scandalises the devout or superstitious—from the domain of the sacred to that of the profane ... the dead body [is], something which as a rule is considered to be sacred everywhere, but which ceases to be so on a dissecting table, where it has a status of a profane object, an abstract object, an object of science. From the first, therefore, it appears that the same object can be both sacred and profane, depending on the situation in which it is located. Let us now consider this dead body of a child upon which the scientist works and for whom it is an anatomical object presented to scholarly observation in its concrete totality. If I wish to extend the whole range of possibilities, I cannot leave things there, but must move on from the scientist's reactions to those of the mother, if we can imagine here in the same room. For the mother, what is at stake at that moment is the totality of being. . . . And, without any doubt, her grief will accuse the scientist of placing her child's totality of being at risk. She would, nevertheless, be wrong: the scientist has nothing before him but an abstract object. Only the philosopher has, if not the opportunity, then the obligation to experience what the child represents for the mother through her grief (even dearer and more sacred because of the death which has for ever separated him from the banal and futile objects by which, when he was alive, he escaped the empty horror—which is totality, which is time—in the gulf into which everything is thrown in advance and confounded).[34].

This image of the empty horror of the gulf is important for understanding the true terror at work. Agamben has done important work in his attempt to open up this threshold between life and death, and how the sacred appears from the perspective of victims, who can be killed with impunity and without meaningful sacrifice. Still, his analysis remains too wedded to the juridical concept of sovereignty.[35] Indeed, it is reasonable to also be suspicious of Bataille's attempts to rescue sacrifice as a ritualistic gift, integral to notions of communication and political communion, that revels in divine ecstasy and extreme horror. However, the importance he gives to how the sacred and the profane can be altered through a mere change in perspective cannot be emphasized enough. Indeed, whereas Agamben purposefully brings together the meaning of a sacred life with the nihilistic violence of the state, which is shown to act with impunity and indifference to its victims, Bataille reminds us that for the sacred to be qualified as such, it matters: "The *sacred* cannot simply be what it expresses as an object to which I would remain as remote and indifferent as I am to the banal parquet floor. On the contrary, the *sacred* is offered as an object which always matters intimately to the subject: the object and the subject, if I speak of the sacred, always interpenetrate, or exclude each other, but always, whether in association or in opposition, complete each other."[36]

Nevertheless, Bataille's sacrificial claims are still unsatisfactory in their apparent radicality and innermost meaning. Everything, in fact, seems to be reduced to the literal and the explicitly visible nature of the wound. Indeed, what might it mean to his ambivalent fable, for example, if we added further context? What if we now said the dissecting table in question was located at Auschwitz and the scientist in question was Joseph Mengele? The young child would surely still appear like a dehumanized abstract object. But the science would not be in any way devoid of myth. On the contrary, it is the myth of supremacy which gives value beyond the abstract to the surgeon's knife. Fascism is a monstrous myth-making machine. And no science is objective, nor value neutral, however nihilistic its outcomes.

While mindful of the appropriation of sacrifice in the service of banal destruction, Bataille nevertheless sees something potentially liberating in the sacred, as its original gesture points to the violation and transgressive nature of the terrifying taboo (which so preoccupied Freud, and subsequently Girard, in his belief in the regulatory power of the sacred to keep our mimetic desires in check). But Bataille ultimately saw the sacred as being in painful decline, or overtaken (as identified by Nietzsche) by the exhilaration of war and statist revolution. Such is the profanity of man and his failure to grasp the sacred in its true phenomenological form. Sacrifice in these radical terms appears like a violent rupture. It breaks free of taboo in a sort of sacrilegious alliance that reveals the hidden horror and the unspoken of the sacred bind, and which becomes the expression of our ultimate freedom and desires.[37]

Without becoming too anthropomorphic, my explicit concerns with Bataille here specifically concern his claims regarding the "absence of myth" (hence the mediating and communicative nature of the sacred as literally conceived), the apparent uselessness of the victim in the economy of production, along with the ways taboo itself might function in the service of power. While the continuation of myth-making in the process of rendering things sacred, notably through violence, will be dealt with in later chapters (including in its modernist and scientific variants), we should note here the altogether taboo nature in questioning the memory of the fallen of all wars as seen by the victors of history. How much of the horror of this sacrifice can be reclaimed as radical? What is more, it is important to recognize how the figure of "the victim" (including the humanitarian soldier as a vulnerable and traumatized form) would assume a privileged position, which even in death would be sacralized so that the living may go on living. The necro-political proved to be alive and well in the sacred order of liberal politics, deployed by virtue of its own transgressions and then in turn consecrating the limits of prohibition so that a particular concept of the sacred might prevail. Transgressing against a prohibition is not exceptional if the prohibition merely returns in another form and makes an appeal to the same logics, albeit in a reworked fashion.

SUFFERING INTO TRUTH

One question still remains: why do we need the sacred at all? Our thesis concerns how the sacred appears in and through the attempts to consecrate a higher meaning to truth in the face of its potential absence. We also explore how the nature of this truth continues to thwart a particular concern with meaning. In short, the foundational stone for this philosophical reckoning is based upon a direct correlation between the absence of the sacred and the absence of all meaning. Let's not forget that within the Christian tradition it was easier and more acceptable to imagine Hell than nothing at all. For at least in its harrowing depths the condition of life may continue, however torturous the experience. If there was Hell, then at least there was meaning to everything, and even the possibility for escape. But we cannot simply be content to ask questions concerning the absence of meaning by drawing solely upon familiar theological paradigms.

To understand the sacred order of truth and why we have continued to fall back upon the recurring motif of sacrifice, there is a need to look behind the curtain to understand what truly troubles us. Only then might we begin to recognize the ways our metaphysical claims to meaning have been continuously and exclusively bound to the sacred across the ages. And only then might we be able to understand why it is only through our continued attempts to appeal directly to some higher power and purpose, it seems, that we can imagine the bonds that hold us together. To critique the sacred is precisely to critique the hierarchicalization of power—the metaphysical compulsion to give rise to some higher unity that had already been there—which then continues to demand allegiance and draws upon violence to make its claims visible. What's more, to critique the sacred is to ask why its extreme opposite is presented as nothing incarnate, why the concept of this "nothingness" is deemed horrific, and how we might escape from this binary distinction between the sacred and the nothing so that absence becomes the infinitely possible. This critique is to look directly into the abyss, or to call it by its proper name—the void of existence.

The Greek playwright Aeschylus, who penned the original sacrifice of Iphigenia, proposed the now well-established idea that humans learn to "suffer into truth." As he wrote in *Agamemnon*:

> Zeus has led us on to know,
> the Helmsman lays it down as law
> that we must suffer, suffer into truth.
> We cannot sleep, and drop by drop at the heart
> the pain of pain remembered comes again,
> and we resist, but ripeness comes as well.
> From the gods enthroned on the awesome rowing-bench
> there comes a violent love.[38]

We shall return to this violent love in the final chapter. It wasn't any coincidence that this military general, who saw the brutalities of warfare and violence firsthand, would also come to write about sacrifice in a way which still dominates and frames our notions of justice and its symbolic ordering (see chapter 2). While the Greeks would take this mantra of suffering and continually reinvent its meaning through their literary tragedies, offering in the process sites of poetic resistance, it was with Christianity and the body of Christ that suffering became a doctrine.[39] The body that suffered, though never quite reaching the extreme painful heights as the original victim—he who would become the exemplary sacred object for power—showed its pious devotion and willingness to sacrifice this life in order to be rewarded with something better in what was understood to be "there-and-after." Suffering in this regard was always relational and temporal: relational to bodies and relational across time. Committed to earthly suffering, the Christian subject would thus avoid eternal damnation in the fiery or icy pits of Hell—depending upon which circle of Hell the transgressor's sins condemned them to occupy.

Modernity took hold of this theological proposition and reworked it through a secular adaptation of the Fall.[40] Modern life continued to hold onto the suffering as it frantically searched for some contingent meaning to make sense of the sheer finitude of its existence. While traces of the theological therefore remained, as the sacred would be reworked with its competing objects for hierarchical power—each of which would be morally armed with the sacredness of their claims—what marked a notable shift was a fracturing in the logics of eschatological time. Moving away from a determinable metaphysical journey with its definitive "beginnings" and "endings," modernity looked toward a more open horizon, or what we might call the time that remained.[41] But soon this horizon would also be weaponized. Time offered no redemption. Instead it appeared like some independent force, propelling us all into the future and into the eventual nothingness from which we all emerged. This was a fate worse than Hell. And it would require a truly formidable reworking of the sacred to overcome the sheer terror of the realization and suspicion, if not outright conviction, that there just might be no plan, no reason, and ultimately no meaning whatsoever to existence. So, while from time to time the curtain would be drawn back, the performance was already written, and its secular chorus insisted upon the need to write another sacred drama. The word we now give to properly designate this perceived condition of absence is the void. But how are we even to begin imagining such absence? What is being described here doesn't lack meaning. Like looking onto the surface of a black sun, whose mirrored appearance in the heavens would threaten, in its very act of revealing, the true nature of the eclipse and begin to turn entire worlds around. The presence of the void is at the heart of the tragedy of human life. It is the external rupture in the wounded skies above, mirroring the pain felt in the most intimate depths of the uncertain soul left alone to wander in the wilderness of doubt.

Though they seldom voice their awareness, the doubting theologian and secularist alike are ever mindful of the presence of the void. It is the original scene
behind the scene. Life begins from nothing, it is said. How could it be any other
way? And back into nothing, eventually, everything returns. So, if the topos of
the encounter after the death of God is to be thrust upon the world without any
surety, with humanity desperately believing in anything universal in particular,
then, as Kant originally maintained, humans are always, due to their freedoms,
capable of falling through the cracks. They are plagued by the guilt of their own
potential (un)making. Such is the radicality of evil the world needs to confront.
There is no divine plan or any direct correlation between those who adhere to a
sacred life—even if the allegiance to the sacred is underwritten by the search for
a foundation to meaning and truth, for a security of knowledge—and those who
seek a protected existence. Still, life teaches us to accept that the ground could
open up at any moment and pull anybody into its depths. There doesn't need to
be any reason. Though reason is its true mastery. Often it appears to defy rationality. Yet the rational mind is its greatest advocate.

What is being described here opens onto a non-terrestrial plane, the depths
where all subalternity resides, which might consume us all at any given moment.
Such a potential eclipse of all meaning has been integral to the sacred appeal.
Without it, where is the higher truth? But, why don't we all go collectively insane
in light of this ominous total absence? But this is why the progress of humanity
remains illusionary. If we come from nothing, and are destined to return to nothing, how can true meaning ever be truly secured? That has been one of the greatest of political fictions, save the petty gestures of those driven by an immortality
complex, whose achievements are enshrined on a stone plinth, only to be subjected eventually to the realm of memorialized forgetting and the dust of history.
And yet still they scramble, driven by vanity. Why else does so much investment
go into annual "remembrance," if not to perpetually mobilize the armies of the
dead, recruiting their ghosts to justify war in the present? Still yet the general
knows better than anyone the ease with which all materiality can be reduced to
nothing, mercilessly sent with all reason and strategic efficiency into oblivion
with little care for its return.

We know that true absence and potential nothingness is truly terrifying. It
has given rise to a sense of responsibility, by which we try to find some meaning
and purpose beyond the journey into death, and even try to annihilate the idea
of death itself.[42] Foundational thinkers of all kinds remain unable to come to

27

Caridad.

Fig. 1.2 Francisco de Goya, *Caridad (Charity)*, Plate 27 of *Disasters of War*. 1863. Etching. Public domain.

terms with this absence, as they cling to their fantasy of eternal grounding to a political order that can "secure somewhere." Representationally, we might think here of Anish Kapoor's eco-spherical "descension" into a swirling vortex of water that mysteriously opens in the ground and threatens to swallow up all that stand before it.[43] Or, more brutally still, those naked bodies literally thrown into the abyss in Goya's disastrous testimonies (fig. 1.2). While such descents are important, in our concern with absence we also need to avoid being too territorially determined in our understanding. Indeed, while the appearance of the black sun is also a compelling image we shall return to in the final chapter, we need to be more attuned at this point to the intimate depths of suffering and how this connects to the sacred as it temporally appears in response to the absence of meaning.

The most sensitive thinkers on violence know that the spatial is always of secondary importance. How can we account for the fact that two people can occupy the same space, and yet one walks around in blissful ignorance and the other sees only bleeding skies? *What constitutes the void then is a wound in time.* That is why the void is everywhere and nowhere. In fact, it is no place at all.

The void is a non-place, borne of a different logic, and whose traumas cannot be tamed and psychological scars cannot be healed by merely returning to the scene of the crime. And so, just as every act of violence has a spatial intensity that surgically cuts a singular line into the flesh of the earth, so the void overwhelms all the senses, leaving behind tormented silences and aesthetic traces while dragging past, present and future into the spirals of the most violent torrents. It is carried on the winds of change, sweeping all things before it, casting aside carcasses without any consideration for those qualities which designate the human as human and thus demand respect and dignity borne of their very "presence" in the world.

The void is the *pre-existing* extinction of humanity. It is the non-place humanists most fear and yet continually opened with the most devastating purpose—a barren terrain not defined by its limits but by its depths. This is what the progressive mind failed to understand. The void's rhythms and frequencies can't be mapped on an X-Y axis. Yet the progressives persisted, with more advanced technologies at their disposal as they attempted to overcome the lines in the sand that bound them to insecure lands. But as they looked across the planes, deluded in their belief that the void was something only others must consign themselves to, that the black sun would never appear on their own horizon, so they were blinded to the internal depths into which they were wilfully jumping with ever-greater force and intensity.

But how can we imagine this as real? Consider the artist sitting in her studio, having witnessed too much of the world's suffering. She is guided by the questions: how do we visualize unseen feelings? And how do we express the abstract in thought? She knows that the shape of feelings is of primary concern. Still, what remains within is ungraspable. She no longer desires to think about the world's anguish. She willfully goes to another place, whose door is opened as she enters a semi-neurotic state. She knows the black sun that marked the wounded skies was never simply "out-there," and that it always resided in the hearts of those wounded by a concept of time that never heals. Taking hold of a pencil and a plain sheet of paper, she begins liberating the violence contained within her already brutalized senses (fig. 1.3). Its textural borderland appears before the naked eye like the surface of the earth. She anticipates the violence that she knows has already taken place. It is a space without limits, where everything is possible. And so, it begins with a point, whose exact location will soon be forgotten. Everything is when it comes to violence. With a light touch, slowly she starts to mark the paper, leaving the faintest carbon traces. Delicate lines appear like

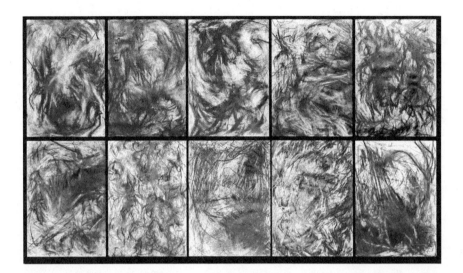

Fig. 1.3 Chantal Meza, *The Void*. 2019. Charcoal on paper. Copyright Chantal Meza. Permission granted by artist.

the pencil is choreographing a beautiful dance. But then the intensity increases, and the violence manifests itself. The pressure builds as the lines cut deeper into the paper, a physical marking of the traces of despair. The pencil is now embodied with forceful intent, and it is the artist who has become an instrument, embodying the pain and terror that comes from simply being human.

She works the paper for hours in this orchestra of expressive emotion. A symphony of terror, rage, and sorrow, which cuts as it cuts and overlays as it destroys. The overtures of Beethoven comfort her as she dances with the realities of human misery. From a distance, the work starts to take on many different shapes, though people will project onto the composition what is already subconsciously embedded in their visual archives. Hope and despair. Upon closer inspection, the work takes on a different appearance, confounding any attempt at forensic certainty. Even aesthetics can be reduced, once it is colonized, and appropriated by science. The artwork is full of lines of miscommunication, which, subtly revealing tortured bodies and disfigured forms, draw the viewer into the scene like some unwitting accomplice. The shame of being human starts to take hold. What might the viewer have done to prevent this violence and devastation? They inevitably withdraw from the intimacy. The most brutal landscapes of devastation are always proven easier to view than the murder of an individual. Upon seeing the work again from a distance, the viewer eventually glimpses the void through the deep overlays and concentrated efforts. It appears here on this paper, as if by a turn of fate. But the void was always there, waiting to appear. The wounds existed before the artist made the lines visible for all to see.

But might we ask what the artist actually achieves with all this abstract expressionism? Is anything being communicated? Can anything be meaningfully translated? If she is merely reflecting the violence of the world, does that not simply make her a passive witness to the pain of others? Documenting the atrocious for the purpose of some aesthetic remembrance or even some guilty pleasure? Such a reading only makes sense if we condemn aesthetics to the predilections and curious desires of a reactionary mind, regardless of how ethically responsible the creative act was. Countering the void demands multiple forms of expression. Indeed, ascending from its depths has always demanded a new image of thought to counter the one which continually annihilates us. This demands a transgressive witnessing, which the artist embodies by her journey into the void and her willingness to confront the intolerable. She appreciates how its unpredictable movements define the violence, and how it flows through the body in ways that overcome the senses. She knows the exhaustion. She feels the thin line between the pencil that creates and the pointed instrument, which is simply a tool used on the most nihilistic lines of flight. She asks herself what if she didn't have the canvas to overcome the trauma? She yells at the world a silent scream, deafening to those who can hear those images imprinting themselves onto the pages of historical denial. And still she is committed to express an uncertain knowledge whose domain remains the irreducible in thought.

Humanity has been forever plagued by the shadow of the non-locatable void; it just became more palpable once God abandoned the scene and left us to our own devices. The black sun that threatens to eclipse all life remains our greatest adversary, the summation of all our darkest fears, far greater than any Hell we could imagine. And so, the sacred made its calling. While the religious man sought to overcome worldly sin as a means of evading that nightmare, the humanist—the modern secularist of technological reason, armed with a mythical belief in the God of himself—merely ran from another terrifying deity: its own divine justice.

But we have also learned that humanity is not a spatial concept. Of course, it is bound to the terrestrial surface of the earth, but humanity as a proposed conceptual union has always been a humanity-to-come. It waits, suspended, before the law, in the mechanisms of its own complex timepiece. This is why its adversary—the specter of the void—remains a problem bound up with the violence of time. A defining feature of the modern man was his habit of fleeing from his own persecutions. And yet, as the world became more populated, he also learned that no sanctuary came with any lasting peace or security. Still, it has always been easier to flee from a terrifying place than escape the entrapments of the mind and the violence of its time. How can you leave behind such a brutal and dehumanizing past, weighing so heavily on the consciousness of humanists in search of peaceful cohabitation? What remains of the concept of the sacred when it is eternally tormented by its own history? And how can we escape the future when violence and worldly catastrophe is all we know?

The force of the void is dramatized through humanity's secular fall as we atone for the death of God. Caught in the historical moment and committing their judgment and reason to its progressive visions, how the masses expressed their desire to feel part of something, even if it proved, in the end, to be their enslavement and undoing. They wanted to live the future in the present, so they devised plans, constructed symbols of triumphant mastery, and showed allegiance to the grand idea backed up by a formidable school of scientific thought and knowledge production. The ideology may have appeared in many different guises, but ultimately it rested upon sacrificing oneself to the logics of order and progress. Countless lives have fallen in service of this ideology, and still more are demanded, for in these lands of quantitative reason, there is always another revolution in time.

There is always another sacred object to be claimed and fought over. But this is not the eternal return. It is the infinite regress back into the void as a space of total extinction and pure annihilation. This is why its ends are ultimately about *the violence of disappearance*, the evisceration of presence and meaning. Often those who have fallen into the depths of the void are incapable of seeing its presence, let alone of thinking beyond its immersions. Still, they are aware that time has collapsed, which in turn shapes every experience. Every spatial arrangement becomes disorientating, lacking in familiar coordinates as the conflicted forces of time pull them in different directions. Days upon days blend together as the temporal nature of tragedy induces a trauma borne of absence. But exactly who or what is absent remains open to question. Once-familiar household rooms are now full of uncertain memories, saddened by absent smiles, full of debilitating cries which rage against the memories of laughter. This haunting is as much about projecting memories onto the future as it is about confronting the tormented past, an era never realized, as it is this very absence that denies resolution to those living with the continued absence of others.

That is the ultimate violence of the void: absolute contingency. Everything proves nothing. It is not simply about robbing humankind of any purposeful value as it is violently torn from the earth. The void also denies life a meaningful death. This is why disappearance is the most brutal demon to emerge from the void. It shows us how the violence of the void turns the logic of worlds inside out; the complete absence to which its victims are consigned reminds us all of our ultimate collective fate. The demon of disappearance weaponizes time and shatters every spatial comfort, while shifting the order of sacrifice—whatever earthly and metaphysical significance we might ascribe to death—onto the fatigued shoulders of those who bear the violence of self-inflicted doubts, both about their own part in the memory of loss and the continued absence of the unfounded.

The demon of the void is the antichrist for our modern theological paradigm as much as it was for times past, however technically secular we may interpret it today. If the mattering of existence is found in its very materiality, the will to nothing bequeaths a realm of absolute denial, which is anti-material and devoid of all meaning. But this demon is beyond the realm of familiar political animality and its modes of human approximation and subtraction. We know how the rendering of lives less than human has resulted in devastating disfigurements and substitutions as the body has been reduced to the animal in the most demeaning ways. However, the demon of the void is anti-figurative. It belongs, in fact, to the realm of pure abstraction and can only be seen through the wounds in time. It cannot, therefore, be countered by drawing upon some authentic figurative ally—especially one that claims to embody the "spirit of humanity" in whatever heroic or sacrificial form. After all, this myth of an essential being has proved time and time again to be the metaphysical screen behind which the demon of annihilation mobilizes its most violent concealments. The act of killing has most often been delivered with an authenticating smile. Countering the purity of annihilation and the eradication of all significance requires a more poetic sensibility, which in turn demands a more intimate relationship with the aesthetics of thought beyond the realms of the figurative and of idealized communicative actions. This is not a call for the "aestheticization of politics," which we know leads to propaganda and the creation of perfectible, fascistically conceived images of thought. Politics is aesthetic, and the liberating potential of the abstract in thought never universalizing.

Armed with a more poetic sensibility, how then might we think and act against the violence of the void without simply clamoring for a more considered sacred claim to life? Or, to put it another way, how can we rethink in critically astute and ethically sensitive ways what it means to be human, beyond the forces of nihilism and its ultimately meaningless sacrifices? Let us take here the two dominant and reinforcing regimes of truth, which have come to define the veri-fiable political order of things: discourse and aesthetics. From Foucault onward, we have known that power depends upon upholding formidable regimes of truth, which, underwriting the ontological and epistemological conditions for life, give purposeful meaning in the most authenticating and yet wholly reductive ways. How we narrate and picture the human condition is always filtered through these reductive schematics, and how we contribute to their ongoing developments is always judged in terms of contributions to manifest claims placed upon us as pro-ductive agents. But any serious consideration of the discursive/aesthetic matrix proves to be meaningless without any prior conception of the senses. *No better reason exists for human expression than to feel the world's beauty and pain.* Through our sensory experiences, their awakenings, excitements, disappointments, and devastations, we are compelled into action.[44] We feel thought into existence, just as we feel all other forms of creation into being through the liberation of ener-gies which are continually bound to the guilt and shame of our very existence. Thought as such is never merely "contemplative," just as art is never merely "rep-resentative." The expressions of thought are always momentarily caught in the act, like the artist who is absent until they release onto the canvas their sense of the world through the visually attesting medium of color. Such expression is all about having the capacity for movement. But what does it mean for a human to be *moved into action* in ways that do justice to their humanity? And how might we better tap into the senses—to feel, perceive, and think—in more affirmative ways, such that the future no longer seems predestined?

The answer is to be found in a reconceptualization of what it means to be human beyond our biological conditioning. More specifically, it is to remind us that the terror of the void is less about a spatial than a temporally controlled disorder of things. Sense itself is bound up with and shaped by the politics of time.[45] We only have to think here about suffering to recognize how it is defined by its duration—[46]to suffer is to en*dure*. Hence the body that suffers is one which, pained by time, longs for a resolution to the torment. "To suffer" in this regard is always about a futurity, which comes from the past and takes the victim down unknown paths. So, while the pious willfully embraced suffering and looked toward the day of redemption, the modernist took refuge in their insufferable utopian dreams, deceiving themselves within technological machines in hope that they could stave off the pain of being human and become immortal within time itself, even if tomorrow the reality of their mortality inevitably returns.

Of course, nobody today believes in the idea of lasting security, or any other form of permanence. Insecurity and vulnerability have been normalized to the point where the mercenary can exploit the internalized reality of our suffering and the nihilism of our dystopian realisms to profiteer off of our anxieties. And yet still we learn to suffer *into* truth—the long duress of humanity—and look in vain for some technologically determinable answers, while being thrown ever deeper into the nihilism of distinctly modern ways of perceiving the world. There is no suggestion here that power is not attuned to the politics of the senses or its emotional reach. Wilhelm Reich taught us that much.[47] Through the psychic life of power, the world is regulated by manipulating and blocking sensation, mobilizing and destroying human desires. Life is categorized into quantifiable sensory groups, especially with regard to its annihilation. But such desire to explain is often really about the desire to explain away. What would it mean, for instance, to feel the pain and suffering of every single victim of Hiroshima? Why is this beyond our individual capacity for perception? And why do we continue to structure the order of suffering in ways that deny the human of its very humanity, by either turning it into a statistic or an embodiment of the sacred?

We can understand the families of those disappeared from history (quite literally this is what is at stake when humanity is forced upon us) as being the most tragic examples of those who endure violence in perpetuity, with no prospect for a resolution to the pain, no way to overcome the temporal horrors of the vanishment from existence. All that remains for the survivors at the altar of this sacrifice are *artifacts in time*. We often encourage ourselves to retain items symbolic of the deceased as part of the intimacy of memorialization, to conjure feelings and memories of persons lost to the inevitable passing of mortal time. However, items kept by families of the disappeared are not simply about holding onto memories or recalling the joys of their existence. A t-shirt or pair of sneakers becomes a painful memory projection, the illusion of a loving embrace that we might otherwise have experienced tomorrow, or the next day. And yet, harrowing testimonies leave us in no doubt about the despair and the life-shattering reality of its violating and stressful disorders.

We cannot know what it truly means to look through the eyes of those living with disappearance. What must it feel like to wake each morning, exhausted by doubts and unending suffering? To strip a human of all meaning, to the point that it vanishes completely from the face of the earth, opens up the most fatalis-tic wound, whose vicious and dehumanizing nihilism takes us into the depths of the void. This wound is unnatural, even though the elements of nature are often weaponized and wielded as an accomplice. It is made real when the conscious choice to determine what can be exorcized from all existence enacts violence on both the past and the future. The importance of time here has been stressed by Joan Cocks, who observes:

> "Appearance/disappearance" bears a distant evocative resemblance to "appear-ance/ darkness," in that what disappears can be understood as entering into an all-obliterating darkness . . . Despite these points of contact with the other two dichotomies, appearance/disappearance is unlike both of them in indi-cating, at least in its purest form, a relationship in time rather than in space: between the "here" and the "gone," the "is" and the "was," or the "soon to be" and the "soon not to be." It also is unlike them in indicating a distinction not between a visible presence and an obscured presence, but between that which is or is soon to be a visible presence and that which has become, or is doomed to become, an absence, relegated to invisibility for that reason.[48]

Countering this requires a new art of thinking, which entails the active pro-duction of a new image of thought to the one that plunges us into the depths of the void. But this is not about jumping into the enlightened stratosphere, with the hope of coming back down to earth safely. Such a retreat into foundational-ism would lead to a reinvestment in bygone sacred claims, blinded by their alle-giance to security and spatial ordering, unable to comprehend the devastation of the world. One must look more intently at the fire that engulfs the wilderness of the black sun. And, like Yves Klein, suspended between life and death, one must jump with ethical consideration into the void to become a transgressive witness to the violence of our times. Flying into the ephemeral space between affirma-tion and the continued fall of humanity, Klein willed the void to appear, like the wounded skies have opened up so many times before, in order to deny claims to absolute certainty and question the will to nothing. Philosophy then is tasked with the creation of new concepts. And the political is all about the creation of people to come. Such is the art of thinking, which feels itself into the world by producing new perceptions of what it means to be human. Resistance in this context is always in the affirmative. It puts itself on the side of the human, the side of life, as a powerful and expressive gesture, reimagining the very notions of justice and freedom.

We can see the void is disorientating. Such disorientation is not, however, about a sense of spatial disruption. In a state of hypersensitivity borne of some traumatic encounter, our sense of space becomes all too aware, the sound of every movement overwhelming. It is all about the disruption in time. There is a notable contradiction here. As time becomes more intensive in its depth of feeling, so the wounds in time slow everything down. We are weighed down by the burdens of time put out of joint. Time places the world on our backs, a Sisyphian burden, although we have committed no crime. We suffer under its weight and just carry on. The void in this annihilating state is the negative adaptation of what Nietzsche called the "untimely," and the wound is the proper name for this untimely event that rips apart the logic of worlds. Voids appear through these wounds in time. They tear apart the fabric of the world, which is woven by the temporal order of things. There is no doubt a powerful, dark ecology at work here too, which focuses directly on the winds of change. The void is a swirling vortex of devastating force that appears to have put time in the most intensive state of flux. That is why it is all about the heights and the depths of its unpredictable columns, which, seemingly without any summit or base, defy the logics of gravity and neat forensic mapping. It is to be caught in the eye of the non-locatable storm.

The movements of the void often appear unstoppable, like some elemental fury sweeping everything before it, flowing through bodies and casting them aside. But it manages to replenish itself on the energies of those it absorbs, and who are willfully seduced by its toxic and yet unrelenting pull. But being immersed within this windswept ecology of life and its creative capacities for worldly change can also engender new critical thought and expression. Ideas dance in the ephemeral and uncaptured space between human connections. Such thought feels the presence of the void all around, and yet refuses its depths. This is why air is the substance of our very freedom. It elevates itself to the sounds and rhythms of the world's beauty, counteracting its torment. Such a dreamscape, no less real for being imaginary, as Gaston Bachelard poetically observed,[49] depends upon the movement of images that add meaning and feeling to a life which refuses any claims to inevitability.

Aesthetics in this sense always must be open to the future of the image.[50] If there is an aesthetic imperative, then it concerns how we venture into the vortex of the visual. And as we venture, we overcome the limits of all representation to reimagine the aesthetic field of possibility and the sensorial awakenings of a time, yet to appear, but which is already feeling its way, through landscapes of beauty and pain, into existence. Our discourse too always has to remain open to these encounters—that is, open to the future of language. One must listen to the senses and try to speak with courage to truth as the journey into vortex forces thought to confront the possibility of its very denial.

This is no doubt a perilous journey. The affirmative flight into the void can easily turn into one of resignation or appropriation. The art of thinking after all enters into the same non-place where nihilism purports to end. But while the poetic imaginary seeks the effacement of aesthetics and discourse in order to bring forth a new image of thought, the nihilistic imaginary demands their ultimate effacement through the production of sacrificial narratives, which in the end destroy all difference. This leaves us with a difficult question: what does a poetic image of the world actually look like? Or maybe it is better to ask how the creative modes of a poetic sensibility might be perceptibly felt? Let's recall here the words of the brilliant fashion designer Alexander McQueen, who once observed, "I hate throwaway images." There is a need to insist upon the exceptional in thought. The fleeting should not mean the banal. And the transgressive should not imply the forgettable. One transgresses to produce something memorable, to alter the mode of perception and the critical frame of reference. One transgresses to immerse oneself in the chaotic center, which elevates and descends between the forces of elemental joy and elemental fury.

Hence, if we can say that critical aesthetics is all about the effacement of the image in order to reimagine the world anew, then critical discourse becomes all about the effacement of language so we might liberate the potentiality words possess to rearticulate how we feel and sense a shared existence. We become more attuned to the logic of sense, and we recognize how aesthetical and discursive practices are affirmative strategies deployed in the trans-valuation of what it means to be human. There is nothing to be negated here, except nothingness itself through the emancipating movements of human potentiality. It is constantly to be undone, in hope of a more liberated time to come. There is an infinite world beyond discourse. Language continues to fail us.

THINKING AGAINST VIOLENCE

We are mortal beings trying to make sense of the insecure sediment of our individual lives and our shared capacity to live together by overcoming a wounded
existence. This much is clear. Painfully aware of our own mortal finitude, as social
creatures still we like to reason beyond ourselves. We mark upon the fabric of
life powerful symbolic resonances, loading our actions with metaphysical meaning, while longing for something more than mere survival. Once carried out in
the name of collectivization, such ascriptions serve to sever the human from
itself, placing definitive markers into the earth signifying who is to be included
and excluded. Such limit conditions continually reduce the poetic qualities of
all human life, essentializing its presence, pre-inscribing certain character traits
based upon assumed potentialities determined by the tyranny of scientific reasoning, while committing barbaric forms of civic violence upon those who defy
categorization. To know a life means to render it figurative. It is to construct a
regime of truth—aesthetically and discursively—that works by connecting images
of bodies to pre-conceived and "naturally ordained" images of the world.

Theodor Adorno was right to insist that an essential condition of truth is to allow
suffering to speak.[51] But to allow suffering to speak also requires us to consider how
it appears before us, or come face to face with what Jacques Rancière calls the "figures of history,"[52] so we might be more open to its violent appearances, its subaltern
traces, the lines of flight by which humans escape the slaughterhouses of history,
and the routine enactments of disfigurement which, beating to a humanist pulse,
routinely deprive the human of those very qualities that make it human as such.
We must look directly at the figurative as a scene of great violence, and yet ask how
we might imagine better what it means to be human. While we will deal more with
Rancière's contribution on this later, we should end here with his important provocation on the "unrepresentability" of extreme suffering. As he passionately writes:

> So we have to revise Adorno's famous phrase, according to which art is
> impossible after Auschwitz. The reverse is true: after Auschwitz, to show
> Auschwitz, art is the only thing possible, because art always entails the pres-
> ence of an absence; because it is the very job of art to reveal something that
> is invisible, through the controlled power of words and images, connected or
> unconnected; because art alone thereby makes the human perceptible, felt.[53]

Rancière's return to the "Adorno question" (which we will specifically revisit later) should be taken seriously. It asks how we might rethink the political function of art as a poetic form of expression, and, in doing so, start the process that will allow us to reimagine a more artistic conception of the political that is not simply tied to perceptions of endangerment, human survival, and its sacred claims.

With the figurative in mind, we can end this chapter by turning to two of Auguste Rodin's most famous sculptures—*The Thinker* and *The Kiss*—which are among the most famous embodiments of the human form in classical Western artistic tradition. Let's begin with *The Thinker*. The symbolic form given to Rodin's isolated and contemplative sculpture should raise a number of critical concerns for us—not least the ways in which its ethnic, masculine, and athletic form speaks to evident racial, gendered, and biopolitical grammars. However, also of concern is its attempt to engage the viewer in some form of conversation with the work. In its presence, we are invariably asked to contemplate what the eponymous Thinker is actually contemplating. From the familiar depiction, we might suggest the Thinker could be thinking about anything in particular. We just hope that it is something serious! However, it was not originally intended to be so ambiguous in terms of its subject matter.

Inspired by Dante, *The Thinker* in fact appeared above the gates of Hell. We might read this as significant for a number of reasons. First, it is the "scene of violence," and its theatricality gives specific context to Rodin's Thinker. Thought begins for the Thinker in the presence of the raw realities of violence and suffering. The Thinker is being forced to suffer *into* truth. The Thinker's physical posture is in fact determined by a scenic multiplicity of performances, whose brutalities are often obscured or hidden in the now more familiar isolated depictions. Second, there is an interesting ambiguity here in terms of the Thinker's relationship to violence. Has the Thinker turned away from the intolerable scene behind him to contemplate the violence it entails? This response to violence is unfortunately all too common in our contemporary world, as well as the world of Dante.

Third, according to Museum Rodin, the Thinker is actually meant to be Dante himself contemplating the circles of Hell as he witnesses them in the Divine Comedy. This is significant. Rather than looking away, might the figure actually be staring *into* the abyss below? In this interpretation, the Thinker is consciously facing the intolerable, thus symbolizing the ethical problem of witnessing violence. Fourth, even more problematic, as Edward Said noted, is that with Dante Orientalism truly had its origins as a monumental intellectual force.[54] Seeing others as a problem to be solved begins from certain claims to violence, borne of a particular narrative of witnessing violent events, something Frantz Fanon understood all too well. Fifth and finally, and not in any way incidental, in the original commission *The Thinker* is actually called "The Poet." This, we can argue, is deeply significant for rethinking the future of the political. The Thinker was initially conceived as a being with a tortured body, almost a damned soul, as well as a freethinking human, determined to transcend his suffering and bring about earthly change through poetry.

In keeping with his *Inferno* theme, Rodin worked on *The Gates of Hell* as part of a commission granted in 1880 to create a set of ornate doors for a new museum on the site of the Palais d'Orsay, which had been destroyed during the Paris Commune. It is well documented that the artist struggled to complete this piece, working on it for some 37 years, putting particular effort into the figures which were to appear directly above the gates. In the initial designs, *The Thinker* was in fact to be accompanied by two sculptures that provided commentary on love and its challenges. For reasons that remain unknown, these figures were never included in the final design.

One of these would have been inspired by the story of Francesca and Paolo and the sexual love for which they were punished. The design for that sculpture instead became Rodin's famous *The Kiss*, which literally began life in hell. Why did Rodin initially consider including these lovers alongside *The Thinker*—Dante the poet—instead of being punished in the scene below? And why did he then recast them in a more torturous setting? Whatever reason, it is perhaps symbolic that the museum for which the gates were commissioned was never built; it remains a non-place, and the gates themselves, which were cast in bronze a full decade after Rodin's death, can't be opened. This threshold upon the most violent of ecologies can thus never be passed over.

But if they happened to be forced apart, on which side of the divide are we, exactly? And does the permanent closure not provide a necessary comfort, as we can fall back upon theological certainties of belonging without seeing the void for what it truly is in respect to the voiding and disappearance of all existence? What, after all, does it mean to come face to face with the realization of being alone, confronting the prospect of the total annihilation of the self and the journey into nothingness?

CHAPTER 2

The Sacred Order of Politics

"**A**nd that each life is sacred." This claim is often made by those who are committed to an account of life which, seeking to offer some form of earthly redemption from an unnecessary crime marked by violence against innocence, gives itself over to the sacred order of politics and its secularized eschatological pronouncements. Such an order of politics has emerged out of the crises of sacrifice, wherein the giant sacrificial machine of nihilism presented us with the raw realities of a life in all its abstract nakedness. A life stripped bare of any metaphysical claim. A life denied its right to exist in the world of recognized forms. To redeem something of the human from this bestial state has meant inscribing a certain universal meaning upon the body of the victim, to give it value in death so that an intolerable act might become the ethical catalyst for the living to go on living with the unbearable weight of history. And yet, in doing so, not only has the victim's body become an abstract object devoid of context and critical purpose, this allegiance to the sacrificial and its metaphysical claims has given rise to new sacred orders. These orders, in the name of life necessity, have taken the imperfections of humanity as just cause to author violence in their own name. Moreover, monstrously doubled, it has been through competing sacred claims of victimization—the particular versus the universal, the once-great versus the promise of those persecuted—that further contemporary battle lines have been drawn, which ultimately have sought to authenticate the endangered meaning of life and contest the very sanctity of humanity's condition.

The idea that the sacred is some original act in the formation of political order has been well made.[1] It is widely known how Mesoamerican beliefs held that civilization and life itself were dependent on sacrifices made to the gods.[2] And from the tragedies of the Greeks—notably the sacrifices of Oedipus, Iphigenia, and Antigone (see below)—to the sacrifice of Dionysus, who was violently torn apart by the Titans for his transgressions;[3] on to God's demand that Abraham sacrifice his son Isaac, a story which has been integral to three monotheistic religions; to the sacrifice of Christ, the primacy of the sacred is well established. Taking it back to antiquity, modern psychoanalysis has returned to the tale of Oedipus as symptomatic of the power of psychic life throughout the ages. The notion that it's worth giving over a material life for some abstract claim is thus sanctified by formidable schools of power and their claims to truth and wisdom. In fact, it is fair to say that we live within a "sacrificial image of thought," which continues to sacralize and objectify in the name of a selected notion of a life worthy of its place in history. This is evident in how we moderns too have learned to die within a loving sacrificial embrace for a righteous cause. Advocates for just violence aside, even those who proffered the most radical philosophical alternatives, from Nietzsche to Bataille, have sought to rework the meaning of sacrifice (and notably where it lies between the sacred and the profane) rather than break with the sacred order of politics itself.

Like all expressions, the word "sacrifice" could undoubtedly be presented in both a literal and figurative sense. We might consider the physical act of taking a life in the name of some sacrificial claim, or in reference to a more metaphorical aspiration, a righteous or sacred calling. Indeed, building on the idea from the Augustinian tradition that sacrifice could be a force for good, worthy of the highest praise,[4] Hegel, among others, claimed that in life "the highest representation of the Idea in Nature is just this: to sacrifice itself and to become Spirit." In fact, seeing the world as an arena of sacrifice, constantly battling over the need to "make life sacred" through a renunciation of the individual will so that one follows a more redemptive path, belongs as much to secular idealism as it does to theological dogma—even if there are tensions between the cosmic imaginary of the sacred and its actual violence.[5] In its modern guise, this concept often brings us back to the reworking, proposed by Emilie Durkheim, of the separation between the sacred and the profane, which has been adapted in some quarters, along with the Kantian idea of the "sublime," as something more phenomenologically acceptable to the secular liberal humanist, who is still able accommodate the incomprehensible.[6]

And yet, from the perspective of power, the lines between the literal and the figurative, the real and the imaginative, are never so separate. While there may be points of tension in terms of definition, the two realms—the sacred and the sacrificial—are mutually reinforcing, and their lines of articulation often blur into one another. What is more, "the prohibitions" imposed upon life are often far more obscure and complex than even the most principled like to suggest. Let's take the edict "thou shall not kill," which is easily turned into "thou shall" on the battlefield and slaughterhouses of the world. In the language of sacrifice, we often see both "thou shall" and "thou shall not" put to the service of actual violence and its imagined possibilities, in order to further political rule in the name of righteousness and justice. Segregating the imaginative from the real then only leads us to wrongly insist that the abstract in thought merely belongs to the realm of pure abstraction, and that aesthetics only come after the creation of regimes of power. We are thus incapable of recognizing how the very act of sacrifice is imagined as real, which, further consecrated in the process of its symbolic representations, has sacred and profane effects. Just as there is no realm of the sacred without the production of allegiant subjects who pour out their reverence to the machine, there is no realm of the sacred without the production of sacred objects worth sacrificing for by the subjects in question.

But what does it mean to sacrifice a life? And how does the sacred appear through the violence of its sacrificial offerings? Nothing in itself is sacred. A thing becomes sacred by being consecrated through the bestowing of metaphysical qualities as revealed through sacramental grammars. And in this regard we can agree with Emmanuel Levinas when explaining that "speech cuts across vision."[7] An image may be violent, but this violence only carries across the ages if it is accompanied by a sacred language and discourse which attributes meaning and historical purpose, adding new depth and further imaginings to the sacrificial image of thought, making it so that the object in question is greater and more eternal than its material form.

Let's take the story of Cain and Abel here as being instructive of this sacrificial play between the immanent and the metaphysical.[8] While the story of Genesis introduces into life the very concept of time—with the duration of existence inextricably and, we might say, irredeemably bound to those attempts to come to terms with suffering and toil—it is with the introduction of these brothers where the sacrificial claim is truly writ large and yet brought crashing down to earth. These very first humans born of flesh and blood are given directly over to God's command. And that command is inscribed through the demand that they prove their allegiance through sacrifice, which in turn exposes more fully the links between the sacred, its judgments and its sentencing. But, more than simply expressing some dutiful obligation, what also appears in this fable is the idea that the future can be enriched by sacrifice in the present.

This is the most powerful realization that we have come to know. It also gave rise to the envy of Cain and the first recorded homicide in the universalizing monothetic tradition—the sacrifice of his brother, catalyzed by envy of his favored position resulting from his intuitive mastery of the sacrificial demand set before him. So, a triangulation between man and metaphysics is established as the violence of man in exile is bound to a sacrifice borne of God's command for sacrificial purity. But humanity couldn't be left to wander for all eternity. Mankind needed to atone for the violent act that soaked the wretched earth in the primordial brother's blood. The sacrificial could in fact be reclaimed by immersing it even further in the depths of the soul: by sacrificing the very concept of love as born of the soul's violent expression. But in order for this to be achieved, the ultimate price had to be paid, that ultimate expression of love being the sacrifice of Jesus on the cross.

Christ shows that what is denied and cast aside by some can be resurrected as sacred by others. Just as his body was violently killed by the Romans and discarded without any sacrificial qualities in mind, it would become the definitive object for sacred understanding, its suffering the ultimate embodiment of a crime against innocence. We see this played out across the ages, as the genocide of millions has brought together in ethical tension the nihilistic logics of disposability with the attempts to render life meaningful by inscribing sacred values onto the mass graves of the annihilated. But what we can also say is that without the sacrifice and the sacred claim, there would be no reason to kill. Homo sapiens might still massacre each other in brutal ways, but without the metaphysical attribution of meaning, there would be no reason behind it, except for the sake of killing. What we call metaphysics, or the "greater good," in this instance is the willingness to sacrifice a life as a certain proof of the importance of a political unity. The sacred always has this attribute in mind, especially within the minds of the perpetrators of violence. To render sacred is to render unto Caesar, God, or whatever unifying force, which mimetically rival each other in their righteous claims to human completion. That is why the sacred is never of the order of difference; for even as it differentiates from the dominant standard in order to cast aside particular forms of life, what remains is the desire for a forced unification—a monstrous shadowing—in the order of things so violently declared.

As mentioned above, it is important to keep hold of the idea that the sacred is first and foremost an image of thought. It is a way of seeing and relating to the world. It looks upon history as beginning with some "dark event," which is central to its foundational myths and becomes a parable for shaping and authenticating existence.[9] Hence, the sacred is about projecting into the metaphysical stars the mystery of experience, while in the same moment reducing the metaphysical claim to suffering through the consecration of earthly sacred objects. In this way, the "greater than" in all its fictitious capacities can at least be imagined and represented as somehow real, even if it retains something of the mysterious, as it remains untouchable and beyond question—the very nature of the taboo. The sacred thus begins by imagining humans in an original scene of violence, where the very existence of the sacred as a meaningful form is wagered against the sacrificial quality of the violent act, following which the success of the vision can be rightly judged.

While the referent of sacred value may change over time, what remains constant are the ways in which the sacred brings together the political, philosophical, and psychoanalytical to create a symbolic realm of the sensible as an aesthetic and lived experience. This, in the process of mediating what is taken as being excessive (the sacred and the sacrifice), consecrates the logics of the real. In this regard, it is possible to glimpse the sacred through the dominant "scenes" out of which its prevailing referents emerge, without ever needing to engage in positivist reductionism. With this in mind, in order to make sense of the sacred we must attend to the theatricality of the sacred image and its performative effects. We might call this the "aesthetico-theologica," as it points to the sacred power of aesthetics and the metaphysical as the mode of experience, or aisthesis,[10] by which we claim to access the abstract nature of being. Aisthesis is to draw upon the multiple grammars of expression to ask how the sacred mystery of the world is revealed to us through its sacrificial violence.

THE TRAGEDY OF THE GREEKS

Greek tragedies provide us with the surest examples of lasting scenes of political sacrifice.[11] No one understood this better than René Girard, who recognized the importance of sacrifice in the original formation of historic and contemporary political orders.[12] Girard's thesis begins by offering a theory of violence that is exclusively bound to human tragedy and the unmediated ethos of competition over power and wealth at the base level of human desire. To develop this theory, Girard refers to the Classic Greek play by Sophocles, *Oedipus Rex*, which illustrates the relationship between unruly competition, tragic dispossession, and a cycle of violence and revenge. We uncover in the tale of Oedipus, born of violence, and his return to his birthplace and ascent to its throne, a genesis of sacrificial violence that is linked to some past tragedy. Oedipus thus epitomizes the motif of the lost prince whose modes of contestation can be understood through competing claims to the same object of desire.

The story follows that when two uncompromising entities vie over the same object, violence necessarily erupts. Through Girard's decoding of the Oedipus myth, we encounter the idea that any attempt to repossess the object of desire, power, and wealth necessarily requires the guilt of the one currently in possession—they must become a sacrificial victim. Thus, to overcome the tragedy one personally feels, the disenfranchised must come from the "outside" and come back into the fold. What we witness then is a violent, predestined journey that can only be justified by making a claim to the original sin, or what Girard rightly terms a return to the "original scene." However, as Sophocles tells it, such violence is more than simply a reclamation of that which has been taken. The violence of the already dispossessed seeks to find its very meaning and purpose through a recovery of what had been falsely appropriated—what Milton would have referred to as being the paradise lost. Hence, the cycle of violence continues unabated.

Importantly, for Girard, such primordial violence is not a relation of difference but rather is more defined by the logic of mimesis: "At first, each of the protagonists believes that he can quell the violence; at the end each succumbs to it. All are drawn unwittingly into a violent reciprocity—which they always think they are outside of, because they all initially came from outside and mistake this positional and temporary advantage for a permanent and fundamental superiority."[13] Plunging into an opposition which "reduces the protagonists into a uniform condition of violence," all claims to "difference" are effectively "eclipsed" by "a resurgence of reciprocity." This is perhaps what Jacques Derrida had in mind when he said, "The rapport of self-identity is always a rapport of violence with the other; so that the notions of property, appropriation and self-presence, so central to metaphysics, are essentially dependent on an oppositional relation with otherness."[14] Or, putting it in more Girardian terms, everybody effectively becomes "the double" inasmuch as they become the "sole object of universal obsession and hatred."[15] And yet, for Girard, such violence does not do away with all hope, especially following Christ's crucifixion, because the appearance of the sacred works to limit violence by giving meaning to humanity's otherwise animalistic state.

Girard is an unashamed religious thinker, but his reflections are equally applicable to the secular. While primal violence is the original scene for Girard, it actually does us a great service once it is mythologized in sacred terms by actually preventing us from tearing each other limb from limb in worthless abandon. What is more, sacred violence confirms the necessity for myth, which as a result of the violence not only gives rise to culture and civil order, but is also the basis for humanity as a regulatory idea. And the remnants of the tragic contain within them the idea that hope, redemption, and salvation may yet be found.[16] Sacred violence thus provides the very opening for meaning to enter, and in doing so it pushes extreme violence to the margins as the exceptional taboo that cannot be transgressed.

Humans need the sacred in order to limit themselves. This position has been recently extended by Jean-Pierre Dupuy, who insists that since the sacred ultimately allows us to make peace with the other, it is humanity's gift.[17] Inspired by Freud's mediations,[18] both Girard and Dupuy give the sacred a clear value in its regulation of suffering. The sacred refers us specifically to something of exceptional value, reserved in fact for the excess that is owed a certain debt to a restrained violence, which only kills when it's meaningful. When everything is touchable or within reach, that's when the real violence occurs! Given this account, it is therefore understandable why Bataille saw an opportunity to link radical politics to sacrifice; doing so was by definition transgressive, and hence truly exceptional. But what if we don't accept that in order for something to be meaningful it has to be sacred? And what if we further show that far from limiting violence, it was precisely through a reworking of the sacred that violence became annihilation?

It would be tempting, as Nietzsche might insist (though rather more optimistically), to see all this as the continuation of two dominant models for thought: the sacrificial violence of Apollo versus the sacrificial violence of Dionysus, the ruler versus the resistive, the one versus the many, the universal versus the particular. This would certainly account for why some critical theorists have been so taken by Benjamin's idea of "divine violence" and how it relates to the messianic (see chapter 4). And yet, far from being incommensurable, both these claims to sacred violence have ultimately proved to need each other in order to justify their very existence; the positioning of each would lose all meaning were it not for the existence of the other.

We also see this played out in the brotherly rivalry between Cain and Abel[19] (which, although foundational to Christianity, we might situate after the Greeks). We might even claim that the story of their fratricide inaugurates the idea of universal rivalry, as it connects to the broader philosophical plane and the reworking of sacrifice in relation to the death of the Other, the lesser sibling, the "one who is less than myself." This rivalry is borne of envy and greed, whose very alliance becomes integral to both the religious and political mind, which first speaks of surrogate victims, and later writes about them using more technical language, such as "dialectics." Only then can enmity be seen as key to understanding any viable notion of politics.[20] Though it is important to note here, while Freud would read this rivalry in psychoanalytical terms, for Girard, who was notably keen to distinguish between early mimetic rivalry and the later arrival of Christ, what really matters are the subjective attributes. Hence, despite his anthropological sentiments, what truly matters to Girard with regard to the violence of Cain against Abel are not some natural attributes; rather, it is the structure of culture which shapes human interactions and ethical relations to the Other.[21] In short, since it is possible to ontologically differentiate between sacred claims, then what matters is how we go about the necessary task of "making sacred." What is it exactly that we give exceptional meaning toward? And how might this allow us to minimize violence on earth by renouncing our primal desires and giving ourselves over to some greater good?

While Oedipus would become a dominant signifier for both psychoanalysis and critical understandings of power by those who sought to overcome the violence of the patriarchal embrace, alternative figures from the history of tragedy would also be drawn upon and their continued relevance rethought. Sophocles's *Antigone* would be notable in this regard, instigating widespread debate in terms of the meaning of self-sacrifice and her apparent resistive fire in the act of refusal when confronted with patriarchal authority. Debates have also centered on whether Antigone's gender had any influence on her empathetic response to her brother's death, along with how her position can be understood in relation to the violence enacted by the sovereign king.[22]

Whilst the often-underappreciated importance of Tiresias in these mediations has already been noted,[23] there is another figure we should not lose sight of here in terms of her dramaturgical relevance to our understanding of violence and the sorrowful lament of the victim. The killing of the innocent virgin Iphigenia at the hands of her father Agamemnon is one of the most brutal and horrifying in all the Greek tragedies. Agamemnon sacrificing his daughter to win the Gods' favor in the Trojan War then instigates a violent doubling when his wife, Clytemnestra, avenges Iphigenia by murdering her husband. She then initiates a regime of terror in which the sacrificial motif is played over and over, until her death. While the sacred claim underwriting the violence speaks to the heavenly forces, including the winds that allow Agamemnon's vessels to set sail, the act of killing this innocent child reveals to us the basest of qualities. As Simon Critchley writes, "The sacrifice of Iphigenia was not dutiful obedience to Artemis but the guilty weakness of an ambitious man, and the capture of Troy was not a just war against a foreign aggressor but a brutal act of destruction, violence, and rape."[24]

Commenting on the exemplary nature of this killing, Nicole Loraux notes how the practice of human sacrifice allowed for the flouting of "pious precautions and, obedient to the myth, to deliver young girls to the slaughterer's knife."[25] Hence, the sacrifice of the virgin allows the unthinkable to be thought, and although the "real life of the city did not sacrifice its young girls" (at least in this way), the performance causes "the double satisfaction of transgressing in imagination the taboo of *phonos* (murder) and of dreaming about virgins blood." This taboo is particularly haunting. "Iphigenia's Sorrow" has been reenacted continuously through the ages, with the innocent child becoming a victim of violence at the hands of disregarding men who claim to be performing sacrificial rites for the sake of bringing glory and favor. As recounted in the words of the young Helena Wanda Blazusiakowna, whose words written on the walls of Cell 3 of the Gestapo headquarters in Zadopane would be taken by Henryk Górecki for his unrivaled Symphony of Sorrows: "No, Mother, do not weep."

While these narratives belong to the realm of mythmaking, they nevertheless offer a poignant insight into the belief systems and the violence of the times with beautiful descriptive reverie. The poetic has always proved to be far more real and compelling than any dogmatic realism. That has been its strength, but also its point of entry for sacred forms of appropriation. Undoubtedly, when these narratives collide with the conditions of the real, we see more fully the power of their dramatic potency and influential effects upon the body politic. And it is in this setting that art and the poetic imagination make their most powerful calling to firmly challenge all claims to pure innocence, which is a favorite claim by high priests of many moral persuasions in the bestowing of sacred qualities in the play of a less than poetic sense of justice.

As Critchley again puts it:

> Take another example, Euripides *The Trojan Women*: it takes place just after the destruction of Troy—the "rape of Troy," as it was called—and a cluster of women gather with Cassandra to lament their fate. Cassandra is given an amazing speech, where she prophesies that they will be sold off as house slaves and used as concubines, and she says that in this lies their legacy and history—to be people who remember Troy because what the Greeks did to us. They are the barbarians, not us. So, this is the greatest thing that could have happened—to be able to remember. In this way, the Greeks used their art to celebrate who they were and, at the same time, critically reflect on their own culpability, on their self-implication in their own historical narratives.[26]

There is, in short, always ambiguity when it comes to tragedy, and this is precisely what the poetic reveals, as opposed to the historic, and why its contemporary appeal is far greater than that of historicism.

ECCE HOMO

He was found guilty and would now face the true force of their law. Paraded through the streets, his recalcitrance and dangerous words would be severed with each painful cut into his violently torn flesh. Betrayed by one of his own, his existence could no longer be tolerated. The angry mob joined in the procession, shouting, screaming, punching, and kicking his exhausted body, reducing it to a worthless piece of meat. The torture lasted for hours. It was unforgiving. He was forsaken. Those who had sentenced him disregarded everything he stood for, except for what they could use to justify what they did to him that day. Nobody should have to suffer like this. How could you rationalize such cruelty, such barbarity, in the name of protecting a vision of peace in colonized lands? And yet, the symbolic message was all too clear: if you defy an empire, you had better be ready to face the cross.

The story of Jesus of Nazareth and his violent fate still remains the most famous tale of human suffering.[27] But if the story of this sacrifice made by God not been rewritten and retold countless times, is it possible that it would have no resonance whatsoever in terms of its transcendental mediations? It's not merely that this man was selected and killed in this way that proves to have any lasting meaning. He was certainly not the only person to have died in such a brutal way. The meaning that is attributed to his life comes from the act of being sacrificed by his father for some greater political good. Just as the death of Christ gave rise to a formidable regime of political power—arguably the most formidable discursive and aesthetic regime of truth ever known, which went by the name of Christianity—, so the notion that his death gave meaning to our imperfect lives offers up the most sacred of qualities. We are the redemption. And we are the salvation, for we could never truly suffer in the same way, though suffer we must in our everyday lives. And how soon the sacrificial atonement, which moved from the Golgothic hilltop to cavalry of the trenches, would recast the mantra "he died for our sins" into the command "they died for our freedom."

Unlike the tragedies of the Greeks, the lived power of the suffering experienced by Jesus of Nazareth resonates in factual realism. And it was such truth concerning his mortal pain at the hands of the most formidable empire that allowed for a reimagining of the sacred in a more universal guise. His suffering would become part of a collective consciousness, and the ultimate proof of the existence of something we may call divine. This would have a marked impact on the image of sacrifice and the body-in-pain. As Hegel realized, you could not use earlier Greek forms of aesthetics to portray the blood-soaked Christ—scourged, crowned with thorns, dying on the cross—with the required potency demanded to reach beyond the Aegean Sea.

Still there was no agreed-upon blueprint for representing this sacred claim. The body of Christ would in fact undergo a number of transformations as dictated by the political mandate concerning the true message and its courted artistic styles. Over time, the Passion would nevertheless become more realistic, and visceral, life-like crucifixion scenes would reach their apogee in the Renaissance as verisimilar depictions of suffering were to be translated into "the humanity of Christ."[28] Before the Renaissance, the body of Christ was largely pacified, and the raw realties of his suffering downplayed, or at least not expressed with the aesthetic potency its truly humanistic appeal allowed.[29]

Hegel once observed: "The real turning point in this life of God is the termination of his individual existence as *this* man, the story of the Passion, suffering on the cross, the Golgotha of the spirit, the pain of death."[30] It was in the act of "sacrificing subjective individuality" that "the spirit attains its truth and its Heaven." While the image of Christ would undoubtedly dominate the sky-lines with its crucified form, becoming one of the most iconic images the world has ever known, it is important to recognize that other images of sacrifice still remained and competed for attention. These include depictions of the suffering of martyrs—including St. Sebastian, who was a notable favorite among the Renaissance elite—as well as scenes from Greek mythology. These other incidents of suffering and martyrdom are exemplified in the works of Caravaggio and Artemisia Gentileschi, both of whom managed to entwine the sacred with the profane, as their stark images of sacrifice were inseparable from their own life experiences.[31]

The power in Christianity lay in its ability to dramatize the crucifixion and render visible "the torture to which Christ is led."[32] It was able to communicate that pain so that followers could encounter the suffering and relate to the self-sacrifice whose catastrophic violence was done in the name of love. It would reach down into the intimate depths of the soul as the exceptional nature of the violence would be transformed into a symbolic act, which was unquestionably sacred. Jesus was not, of course, the only person to have died on the cross. What marked out the singularity of this event, however, was precisely the way his isolation was collectivized and operationalized through sacrificial motifs. And this is where our concern with Bataille's radical claims becomes clearer. Yes, there was a transgressive prohibition (as retrospectively conceived through the unimaginable suffering) and abandonment. But the possibility of a meaningful death through the sacrificial act is not exceptional or radical. It is part of the lived fabric of everyday life. It is the knife, the cross, the gun, the bomb, which continues to cut deep into the flesh of history. Its appearance may be unsettling, but that is why the intolerable image and its unbearable weight are heavily policed and mediated.

A true prohibition would be upon the sacred itself, to render it intolerable and to expose the sacrificial as being at the heart of the burdens of history. This would require moving away from the intimacy of the sacred encounter, which continues to rule over life through the violence of an artificial love—the violent love that Aeschylus already understood—which imposes guilt as it rejoices, languishes while it loves, and continues to terrify life as it opens the judgmental doors to a freedom already imagined. We find traces of this in the artworks of Francis Bacon, who was taken by the image of Christ. Indeed, what he saw as a true revelation was the elevation and how this perspective was integral to the sacred imperative it demanded. "One of the things about Crucifixion," he explained, "is the very fact that the central figure of Christ is raised into a very pronounced and isolated position, which gives it, from a formal point of view, greater possibilities than having all the different figures placed on the same level. The alteration of level is, from my point of view, very important."[33] Hence, for Bacon, it was important to disrupt this image and turn it more into a "physiological scandal." While this was a radical move in itself, the genius of Bacon was to leave open the question about what exactly is being crucified. As Milan Kundera inquires: "What essential is revealed when all the social dreams have evaporated, and man sees 'religious possibilities . . . completely cancelled out for him': The body. The mere Ecce Homo, visible, moving, concrete."[34] So, what becomes of the nail is precisely the mortifying attempt to nail the subject down.[35]

The importance of blood here as a political category loaded with symbolic and sacred purpose should not be understated.[36] It is the tie which binds and the nourishing river which replenishes the claim over lost and emerging souls across time. The sacred moves from the blood that runs from throat of the sacrificed virgin into the hands nailed to the cross. And it would later flow through the artificial veins of what Hobbes called "Leviathan." This would be the start of its domesticity, and while the Great Wars of the twentieth century would continue to witness torrents of red seeping deep into European soil, the shift toward liberal conceptions of the victim would result in an expressed mediation where blood would be removed from the scene of the crime. This "bloodless violence of the victim" would, however, prove to be no less sacrificial in its rites and onto-theological claims—for "bloodless violence" would not refer here to a distinction between the figurative or the literal, but rather to the aesthetic mediation of suffering, as blood would be the marker of intolerability (see chapter 5).

Blood circulates, as William Harvey discovered,[37] and it would become the basis for imagining communities as being bound by some abstract, yet no less real, elemental fact, reproducing its own motives in the name of god, family, tribe, nation, and eventually the victims of history as conceived problematically.[38] It is the truly vital element to a life which is biopolitically conceived, the life that suffers on account of its mortality and yet can open its veins and connect to the channels of history. Blood is the currency through which the body spills its meaning beyond the injured self, and it's the excess in an open wound turned into an aesthetic event—without clear beginning or end—in the psychic life of power. There is no flesh to the sacred image without some relationship to blood. Indeed, we could map out the history of aesthetics and humanist concerns by attending explicitly to its (non)appearance.

But what does this mean in terms of the aesthetics of the crime? When Pilate stood before the masses and uttered the immortal words "Ecce Homo"—behold the man—so began the age of the universal witness to a violence whose thunderous cry would be heard for centuries. "The trial of Jesus" represented, as Agamben observed, "one of the key moments of human history, in which eternity has crossed into history at a decisive point."[39] When confronted with the man, Pilate would be compelled to ask: "What is truth?" Our question is what becomes of this truth once the act of violence turns into a sacred act? The implications, for Agamben, are telling: "To testify, here and now, to the truth of the kingdom that is not here means accepting that what we want to save will judge us. This is because the world, in its fallenness, does not want salvation but justice. And it wants it precisely because it is not asking to be saved. As unsavable, creatures judge the eternal: this is the paradox that in the end, before Pilate, cuts Jesus short. Here is the cross; here is history."[40]

What becomes of these concerns with judgment and justice is where the scene discussed next leads, because it is here that we learn how the sacred enacts its revenge: not solely upon those who put an end to a life, but upon the bodies of those who do not recognize the sacred as such. There is no greater moral affront to any political project than to bring into question its sacred objects. And it is in that political body's response to such an act of transgression that we then witness the full force of its law, and the violence it is willing to carry out to uphold its unquestionable truth.

A SACRED EARTH

If Christ represented the ultimate tragedy, the purely innocent crucified for his righteous beliefs, his story also elevated the question of the sacred to the transcendental plane. The body of Christ soon became an image we had to continually look up toward from the depths. It represented a suffering of the highest revelatory order. No life could be sacrificed in the same way. The sacred, in fact, might have remained a singularity. Or at least one of various singularities, like the murdered John the Baptist or Paul, both part of an exclusive club where the unimaginable suffering of its members linked the sacred to the martyrdom of saints were it not for this unrivalled transcendental ascription.

All of this held true until Dante, who in his *Divine Comedy* literally brought the sacred down to earth. The thesis presented here in countering sacred violence, especially in its humanist manifestations, is to rethink the politics of love and its poetics. We understand the humanist tradition as emerging through the crises of God and reason, and the subsequent crises of that sacred and sacrificial order. But what was truly at stake, ranging from the celestial to the depths of human suffering, was made explicit by Dante's love and reworked as such in light of these crises. Dante's poem is undoubtedly an epic tale, which at its heart is concerned with foundational sacrifice.[41] Indeed, when invoking the terms "love" and "poetics," any critic armed with sacred reasoning might point to Dante as an example of why these constructs need to be understood within a sacrificial frame.

But our task is not simply about making a savage break with sacrifice. We have no need for Perseus in this drama. Instead, we must rethink what love and poetics might actually mean as political categories, which, still rejoicing in the art of the possible, recognizes the sacred as nothing more than a violation that binds us to violence, and that the sacred sacrifice ultimately gives us over in a perpetual fall to a violent love. In this regard, while Dante is important—especially in allowing us critique sacred violence and its mimetic reciprocity—even his most avid supporters note his willingness to assume the role of the martyr, and his ultimate unwillingness to "leap into the void."[42] Hence, as it shall be argued in the final chapter, it is for this reason Dante needs to be seen from a different vantage point, and actually taken back into the wilderness of life.

Dante has been pivotal in how we learned to morally witness and, in the process, underwrite sacred violence in the modern world at the point of humanism's arrival.[43] Indeed, while Kant later inaugurates the modern image of thought through his Copernican adaptations and reworkings of the Fall in secularized theological ways,[44] we must not overlook the role Dante plays by giving rise to a new literary imagination[45] in which mortal suffering was given its most potent and explicit treatment. While Dante personalizes the violence and its sacred claims, he also gives us a language that fuses the theological with the act of killing for earthly notions of justice—a living holocaust, in which we would all be forced witness and accomplices to the torment and the shame brought upon the damned of history.

Part of Dante's genius is that he includes Virgil as his poetic guide and learned sage, allowing Dante to traverse both the classical and the Christian world, even if the poet himself is ultimately unable to pass over into heavenly salvation and the paradise that awaits. As Giambattista Vico once wrote: "For all his erudition and esoteric knowledge, Dante in his Comedy portrayed real persons and represented real events in the lives of the dead. And he titled his poem the Comedy because the Old Comedy of the Greeks portrayed real persons on the stage."[46] Such human misery and pain is evidenced in William Bouguereau's 1850 masterpiece *Dante and Virgil* (fig. 2.1). Indeed, more than merely inventing

Fig. 2.1 William Bouguereau, *Dante and Virgil*. 1850. Oil on canvas. Public domain.

Hell, as is often claimed, the *Divine Comedy* stresses the importance of situating condemned figures within specific scenes of damnation, where their sins are directly punished by a sacred violence of unquestionable justice, where every act of violence inflicted has both a transcendental and an earthly meaning, and where the terrestrial nature of the violence is made explicit by its extreme ecological framings.

Dante brings together the figurative, the scenic, and the ecological with such command that the lasting sacred effects of his work can still be appreciated today. Hell, he maintained, was no longer ephemeral or outer-worldly, as if belonging to some unlocatable and inaccessible milieu of human existence. It was a place one entered, clearly marked by its borders of entry and exit—an infernal cartography of infliction and suffering, which could be defined, mapped out, chartered, and physically experienced by a sensual appreciation of space and time, wherein all the damned of the earth could be found.[47] In the worldly drama of suffering, as Dante narrates, everything endures. Nothing disappears. For even the greatest sinners—the traitors whose torn flesh is to be perpetually gorged upon by Satan himself—still have the presentness of mind to feel their torment, to be anguished by the screams of the Devil, and to act as witness to the suffering of others for all eternity.

According to the work of Antonio Manetti—the fifteenth-century Florentine architect and mathematician who diligently sought to give specific form and measurement to Hell—Limbo itself was apparently 87.5 miles across. Dante managed to bring the cartography of suffering alive by directly connecting legitimate forms of torture and punishment, along with notions of redemption and salvation with the earthly elements as they become an active part of the witnessed scenes of torment. Dante thus inaugurated a profound moral economy of political aesthetics, which not only inspired artists, writers, and theologians, but also would become integral to ensuing political understandings and representations of what we might call the natural history of violence.

That nature was capable of adding to the torment through the weaponization of the elements is a recurring theme throughout the *Inferno*. Dante begins his journey alone in the dark woods, full of self-doubt. The landscape thus becomes a metaphor for his uncertainties and the wounds he harbors. Dante then moves from darkness to light, and back again, before meeting the poet Virgil and beginning their descent into the circles of Hell. As Dante famously writes: "I found myself, in truth, on the brink of the valley of the sad abyss that gathers the thunder of an infinite howling. It was so dark and deep and clouded, that I could see nothing by staring into its depths."

But Dante soon becomes witness to an entire ecology of suffering. In Canto III, for example, Dante's crossing of the river Acheron, guided by the mythological ferryman Charon, forces him into a trance from the sheer terror and unspeakable violence of his surroundings. In Canto V, the very air is a violent force that sweeps up those who have been condemned to eternal damnation for the sin of lust. The souls who in life had succumbed to their carnal urges are caught in a whirlwind of despair, or what Dante calls "the infernal hurricane that never rests," which he describes using violent, sexualized language as "hurtl[ing] the spirits onward in its rapine; whirling them around, and smiting, it molests them." Here we encounter Francesca di Rimini and her lover Paolo, with whom Dante empathizes and wishes for an end to their torment: "O Poet, willingly, speak would I to those two, who go together, and seem upon the wind to be so light."

While the fifth circle of Hell and the River Styx capture the imagination, as the toxic and polluted waters separate the different tiers of the damned from one another, the seventh circle offers still more vivid descriptions of extreme ecologies of suffering. Policed by the Minotaur, it contains those who have committed violence upon other humans and are forced as punishment to wade through a river of boiling blood and fire. Dante and his guide move on to witness those who have committed violence against God and therefore have to live on the burning sands of a desert expanse drenched by a fiery rain. Dante thus depicts a cycle of revenge by connecting the violence of humans with the extremities of worldly elements, which are so brutal they are afforded the willful capacity to become active elements and an integral part of this horrifying regime of terror. This is further exemplified in the forest of suicides where the limits of our free will are made explicitly clear as the body which has chosen through its own volition to renounce itself and commit to a non-existence is not simply bestialized, but anthropomorphized into a truly vegetative state of ecological suffering and damnation. The body that commits violence against itself is not only rendered less than human, it is preyed upon by obscure beasts or Harpies (part bird and part woman) who, feasting on their leaves, at least make their suffering known.

As we reach the lower depths of Hell, the cruelty and literal coldness of divine retribution appear in their most naked of guises. Gustav Doré's *Dante and Virgil in the Ninth Circle of Hell* (fig. 2.2) offers a remarkable visual testimony on both the

Fig. 2.2 Gustav Doré, *Dante and Virgil in the Ninth Circle of Hell*. 1861. Oil on canvas. Public domain.

ecological brutality and the symbolism of this setting. Surrounded by despairing bodies eating one another's flesh, Virgil and Dante stand on the icy surface populated by these barely human forms. Virgil is cloaked in red in a way that is symbolically reminiscent of El Greco's *The Disrobing of Christ*, a work that proved integral in disseminating Christianity to native populations in the Americas (fig. 2.3), thereby suggesting the importance of the poet as one who has already sacrificed and is therefore able to direct and impart knowledge. Virgil is determined. And the path he sets for Dante is preordained. Dante in contrast is wearing blue and looks more youthful, with an air of confidence and surety, as he has seen the worst of the human condition and ventured into these most desolate of landscapes. He wears a laurel wreath—an allusion to Apollo, the god of poetry—signifying that Dante is a supreme poet armed with divine wisdom. Dante has suffered into the truth of a poetic being whose legacy will outlive that of his master, though he will remain forever indebted to him. While Virgil must continue to sacrifice without personal reward, forever denied redemption, as he was born

Fig. 2.3 El Greco, *El Expolio (The Disrobing of Christ)*. 1577–1579. Oil on canvas. Public domain.

prior to the arrival of Christ. Therefore, he suffers the same fate as all nonbelievers, on account of a system of absolute justice that is chronologically skewed in favor of those born more recently.

At the Earth's core, Dante encounters the three-headed Satan encased in ice, appearing as both the tormentor and tormented par excellence. A parody of the beauty of God and the tranquility of Heaven, Satan is disfigured and bestial, like the true embodiment of the dark event at the heart of all myths, unable to contain his own rage as he screams out to give Hell itself the most violent of compositions. It should be noted that in marked departure from such imagery, Milton's *Paradise Lost* moved away from this spatial conditioning, and instead sees Satan proudly boasting of his freedom beyond the confines of his incarceration: "The mind is its own place, and in it self/Can make a Heav'n of Hell, a Hell of Heav'n."[48] Not only then was the Devil part of the territory of the mind; as Milton explained, the capacity for violence was unbounded and yet subject to infiltration and demonic possession. What was Hell? In short, it belonged to the realm of the imagination, and hence was open to subjectivization. By that token, we might gesture, so too were the ecological conditions of suffering and torment in Dante's Hell.

Critics of this position have stressed the dangers of these subjective and internalizing claims as effectively denying the realities of a designated place that might be so defined as wretched.[49] It might also be argued there is a need to insist upon the raw realities of suffering and the ways in which space can be "objectively" determined as either being peaceful or witness to bodies which appear full of mortal pain. Such debates between the imagined as "subjective" and the experiential as "realism" have in fact been apparent in many of the debates, which have shaped crude distinctions between continental and analytical traditions. But to say the imaginative and the subjective belong to a world of pure abstraction is to miss the most fundamental point stressed by Dante. Namely, if we are to understand violence, first we must be accompanied by the poets of history, for they have learned to stare into the abyss, confronting the worst of humanity and walking for all eternity with the unbearable. They have thereby moved beyond the act of merely bearing witness to the violence in order to recognize and carry the intimate burden of pain and suffering.

Dante is the guide who led us into our modern conceptions of humanism. It is violent, and it is sacred. While his poem was explicitly bound to religious themes, it factored in earthly desires, transgressions, punishments, and sacrifices. Guided by Virgil, Dante offered a literal figuration of the world, depicting the passions of the earth and drawing upon the imagination to communicate with poetic revelry the importance of the arts in overcoming humanity's fall from grace. What Dante didn't imagine, however, was the wretchedness and cruelty that would hold sway once God abandoned the earth and left its inhabitants to their own devices. Dante's Hell would be unleashed on earth, leaving the humanists to try to recover something of the human out of the topos of the meaningless encounter. Earth would become as infernal as the world Dante imagined—not by connecting to the old gods, whose suffering was so visible on the cross, but by appealing to a new order of sacrifice, whose sacred object would also be quite literally pulled down to earth. Christ would no longer be the suffering or the resurrection, and God no longer the final arbitrator of justice. Man would learn to set himself up in the image of God, and the poets of history would move from Hell into the trenches. Those who suffered and those who bore witness to suffering would all be carried forward on the unstoppable winds of change, which would sacrifice all that stood before them. The sacred order of politics would thus fall to earth with the mightiest of bangs.

DISASTERS OF WAR

Bodies again appear before us, violently torn. Their flesh hangs from natural wooden structures, denying it any metaphysical claim except for the weaponization of gravitational force. But the suspension only adds to the suffering. Men are brutally castrated, women savagely raped and violated in the most graphic ways. Heads are cut from their dismembered bodies, decapitated depictions, with the consequences of war shown in unflinching detail. All the while children appear as witnesses to the suffering of those who they once went to for protection. Animals gorge upon the dismembered flesh. Famine consumes all.

Such desperate scenes are necessarily confrontational. They stab at morality. They unapologetically violate the senses and ask no forgiveness. Who could grant it anyway? Scene upon scene appear before us, like a series of sadistic montages, where the victims are helpless against their ruthless torturers. There is no salvation or redemption here, except down the barrel of a gun. The cross is now an unforgiving tree, and the victims now all too human in their desecration. The only thing that remains is the materiality of destruction. Still there is a pleasure to be had, for those who take solace in the pain of others. These unbearable torments bring laughter to those who find savage joy—brutally erotic and full of nihilistic glory—in inflicting punishment. Bodies are mutilated, lives cut short, just because—or so we say, because the violence is just. All color is abandoned in these arbitrary and bleak landscapes. Thus, we are forced to witness the suffering of such inhumane actions as the violence is inscribed on the naked bodies of the condemned. We watch as they are torn from limb to limb. But what is it that so perturbs us? And do we really feel or empathize with the pain of others?

If the modern condition intellectually begins with the Kantian injunction to place the human at the center of its mortal universe which, building on the foundations of Dante's sacred earth, renders life already guilty of its own potential (un)making; the aesthetic secularization of life begins with the raw realities of degradation, torture, and human suffering—an image of life reduced to its abstract nakedness. Francisco de Goya's *Disasters of War* series depicted the brutalities of war in their most nakedly ambitious and unforsaken forms.[50] Printed thirty-five years after the artist's death, Goya's meticulously carved prints denounce war through their depiction of an immense aesthetic violence. He engraves the unspeakable. He forces us to face the intolerable, over and over, offering a visual anthology of the worst episodes in the history of the human condition. Transcending any particular conflict, these images show our capacity to deny fellow humans any claim to a shared humanity.

Engaging in acts of violence as refined as Goya's testimonies, every figure in this series of prints has a role to play. And for this, Goya makes no apology, nor does he leave anything to a slumbering reason. As the British artist Jake Chapman (whose work we shall return to later) has observed:

> Take *Great Deeds Against the Dead*, [fig. 2.4] for example, from the Disasters of War series. This is image is particularly heretic because it denies the idea that this sagging Newtonian flesh can be redeemed from the physics that will see it eventually melt into soil. The systemic murder of these three figures utilizes violence for the purpose of a warning to others, but the divine violence exhibits the heresy of gravity, acting upon their bodies indifferently, without purpose.[51]

So in Goya begins, as Bernard Berenson once wrote, "the beginning of our modern anarchy."[52]

Fig. 2.4 Francisco de Goya, Plate 39 of *Great Deeds Against the Dead*. 1810s. Copper etching. Public domain.

Goya draws the death of God. In doing so, he portrays the crises inherent to a particular model of sacrifice, a unified and transcendent morality, as once represented by the image of crucifixion. The ultimate tragedy would no longer appear before us like some original sin, giving rise to its own Manichean claims of purity and daemonic possession, but instead it would be soaked in the blood we bring upon ourselves; our productive capacities would orchestrate our own devastation. Humans were now the monstrous creators of the worlds of ruination. The Fall, in the end, proved itself more potent as a secular tale of man's potential to bring about his own destruction.

Nobody understood this better than Nietzsche. What did it truly mean for him to declare the death of God? Sure, Nietzsche was very critical of Christianity and the indoctrination of the Christian church, especially its allegiance and pious devotion to suffering. But we might also say that the death of God terrified him, and this proves to be his most powerful and prophetic legacy. As he recalled in the important fullness of the parables explanation,

> God is dead. God remains dead. And we have killed him. How shall we comfort ourselves, the murderers of all murderers? What was holiest and mightiest of all that the world has yet owned has bled to death under our knives: who will wipe this blood off us? What water is there for us to clean ourselves? What festivals of atonement, what sacred games shall we have to invent? Is not the greatness of this deed too great for us? Must we ourselves not become gods simply to appear worthy of it? There has never been a greater deed; and whoever is born after us—for the sake of this deed he will belong to a higher history than all history hitherto.[53]

Indeed, as Nietzsche further qualified elsewhere, "If something sacred is to be set up, something sacred has to be destroyed."[54]

While we shall return to the worthiness of the sacred below, it is worth asking what becomes of this place called hell with the advent of modernity and secular reasoning? Carl Schmitt provided a healthy reminder that all our modern concepts are secularized theological concepts, and as such, forced us to recognize the delusions of secularity as the pure abandonment of theological ascription.[55] As the myth of God was displaced by the myth of Nations, not only would the theological find its points of reentry into the political fabric of modernity, but the myth of Nations would breathe new and arguably more potent life into figurative and ecological narratives of earthly suffering. Goya's testimony was merely the start.

And yet, as notions of Heaven and Hell have been reimagined through utopian and dystopian belief systems, bringing both Heaven and Hell firmly down to earth (it is worth noting that Heaven always remained for Dante beyond space and time), there was a new adversary that appeared, which both drew the focus of—and yet tormented it to the point of outright denial—the modern mind. If life truly was all we had to hold onto and value, then nihilism—meaning the will to nothing and the denial of absolute valuation—was the true enemy,[56] one which nobody wished to confront, as to do so would mean destroying modernity itself. If Heaven required the existence of Hell in order for salvation to have any meaning, the modern condition needed its potential absence to give sacred meaning to its material form. Nobody understood this better than Nietzsche, who in a sentence that chimes with Dante read out in a somber tone, "And if you gaze long enough into an abyss, the abyss will gaze back into you."[57]

Goya produced his *Disasters of War* series as engravings precisely because they could be reprinted, over and over, to warn of the raw realities of war across generations.[58] Sadly, the memories of warfare often fade across time, with suffering becoming spectacle and violence pushed into the realm of passive and unreflective voyeurism. And still the violence continues. Nobody depicts the mutilated body in all its intimacy better than Goya. Nor has anyone managed to capture raw terror with such devastating realism. Goya mastered the capacity to show impending loss at the point of its forced denial. The madness of civilization is projected in the disoriented stares of his subjects, as bodies interact and engage the viewer without obvious direction. Violence occurs before the eyes of the damned, who have already suffered and witnessed too much. This violence consumes all, even the painter's own state of mind. We can all witness too much suffering. The poets of history who have stared long enough into the depths of void, especially those who have entered in solitude, know this all too well. Or maybe the insanity is in the revealing of the truth. Maybe it is found in being conscious of the way the body can be so ruthlessly discarded, the way that ultimately bodies do not matter except for their mere physicality, and that the only certainty is a mutated history, violently severed from its own nihilistic path to glory.

Goya's reproductions disturb the viewer as the capacity for love is mutated by the liberation of perverted desires, which appear all too normal in a state of war. But Goya's etchings—the photographs of his times—should not be seen as static or final depictions of harrowing scenes. The reproductions are reproductive. Violated bodies produce violated offspring. And there is an enduring madness, presented after the fact, just as children are born in torment, having been conceived from the most savage acts of violation, the male sexual organ wielded as a weapon to cause infliction. Once everything is reduced to such materiality, the only decision that remains is whether to reproduce or be discarded upon the scrapheap of history. Goya's etchings thus might be interpreted as the eighty-two commandments of modernity, spanning from a life's beginning to its meaningless end.

But Goya also understood and documented something just as important in his work, as the sacred found a way to mark its reentry, coursing deep into secular wounds. As humans openly celebrate the death of God through violence of their own making, themselves becoming something far more terrifying and judgmental in the process, so religious mythology would need to be replaced by

Fig. 2.5 Francisco de Goya, *El Tres de Mayo (The Third of May)*. 1814. Oil on canvas. Public domain.

a more powerful myth capable of mobilizing entire populations for the purpose of slaughter. Such a myth would speak in the name of Nations, and the body of Christ now displaced by that of the military hero or revolutionary. We see this compellingly portrayed in Goya's masterpiece *El Tres de Mayo* (fig. 2.5), whose central figure "wears white, a colour of purity and surrender, and flings his arms and hands out in a beseeching pose, reminiscent of Christ in the cross."[59] Bodies can be destroyed, but ideas—including the idea that some things are worth killing for, worth dying for—linger on. So while the nation gave consolidated meaning to such violence—something to symbolically uphold and identify with—it was the birth of ideology and the progressive onslaught of modernity which gave rise to the biopolitical authorization and sanctioning of the massacre of millions. Each of these victims of wholesale slaughter would be individually forgotten, but collectively they would be redeemed through the body of the hero, the individual who performed the ultimate sacrifice by dying for our all our sakes and freedoms. As Zygmunt Bauman reminds us:

> God meant, first and foremost, a limit to human potential: a constraint, imposed by what man may do over what man could do and dare do. The assured omnipotence of God drew a borderline over what man was allowed to do and to dare . . . Modern science, which displaced and replaced God, removed that obstacle . . . God was dethroned, but the throne was still in one place. The emptiness of the throne was throughout the modern era a standing and tempting invitation to visionaries and adventurers. The dream of an all-embracing order and harmony remained as vivid as ever, and it seemed no closer than ever, more than ever within human reach. It was now up to mortal earthlings to bring it about and secure its ascendency. The world turned into man's garden but only the vigilance of the gardener may prevent it from descending into the chaos of the wilderness[60].

WORTHY OF THE SACRIFICE

The first "great" political event of the twentieth century was undoubtedly the Mexican Revolution. Aside from the way it connected to and profoundly reshaped the ideological currents of the time, what was striking about its violence was the aesthetic importance given to the revolutionary hero. No artist captured this better or had greater impact in terms of fostering a national identity through the consecration of myth than Diego Rivera, the most famous of the Mexican muralists.[61] Octavio Paz once observed: "People contemplate their painting the way devout believers contemplate sacred images. Their walls have become not painted surfaces that we may view but fetishes that we must venerate."[62] A critical eye on Rivera's work in particular sees how it was easily put to use in the service and consolidation of power through national culture. Whether it is art or simply propaganda is certainly open to interpretation.

Alongside Rivera, however, were more compelling and less romantic visionaries such as Jose Clemente Orozco, another (though certainly less deterministic) artist in the muralist tradition. While Orozco's *Epic of American Civilization* at Dartmouth College in New Hampshire offers a truly powerful history of sacrifice across twenty-four frescos, from Ancient Sacrifice, to Cortés and the Cross, on

Fig. 2.6 Jose Clemente Orozco, *Man on Fire*. 1939. Fresco. Photograph by McQueen Parker. Creative Commons Licence. https://www.flickr.com/photos/133850233@N02/19901012171/.

to the modern soldier and the industrial man, it is his truly exceptional *Man of Fire* (fig. 2.6) at the Hospicio Cabañas in Guadalajara, that commands our attention. Situated above representations of artistic forms of creativity, here we have a modern-day Icarus who has taken hold of the Promethean gift; having replaced God and dared to fly, he is surrounded by the elements of his making. But the man of fire is burning, and he is willing to watch the whole world burn, to sacrifice it on the altar of progress if it doesn't fit with his sacred vision. A man naked in his bestiality, elevated by the coming storm of techno-scientific rationality, and truly capable of exterminating the world before him. Benjamin also recognized this theme in Paul Klee's *Angelus Novus*, which the author owned and retuned to continually as he tried to "understand a humanity that proves itself by destruction."[63]

While Emiliano Zapata was still leading his revolutionary forces, shots were fired in Belgrade that would open a wound in the flesh of European soil that still bleeds today. And what Goya did for the Peninsula War with his emphatic *Los Caprichos*, Otto Dix reworked in his *Der Krieg* (War) series, which depict the indiscriminate horrors of World War I in the wake of Archduke Franz Ferdinand's death.[64] Drawing upon his firsthand account of the harrowing realities of warfare in the trenches, Dix confronts the barbarity and sheer madness of the slaughter, but in a more haunting and environmentally framed way than Goya. Unlike Goya, where the landscape is ambivalent and peaceful, even as its materials are actively recruited to become an intimate partner in suffering, Dix consciously attends to the devastation of entire ecosystems, populating them with figures that are visibly traumatized from witnessing such violence.

And yet, Dix remained committed in terms of his desire to experience and depict suffering as a living aesthetic memory, rather than resigning it to obscurity. As he once responded, "I had to experience how someone beside me suddenly falls over and is dead and the bullet has hit him squarely. I had to experience that quite directly. I wanted it. I'm therefore not a pacifist at all—or am I? Perhaps I was an inquisitive person. I had to see all that myself. I'm such a realist, you know, that I have to see everything with my own eyes in order to confirm that it's like that. I have to experience all the ghastly, bottomless depths of life for myself."[65] Such ghastly depths were made possible by tales of heroism, which not only romanticized war, but turned it into a form of sacred freedom that justified the act of killing as bringing about glorious death for lives well lived. As Susan Sontag later wrote in her brilliant essay "Looking at War" that appeared in the *New Yorker*:

> Photographs of mutilated bodies certainly can be used . . . to vivify the condemnation of war, and may bring home, for a spell, a portion of its reality to those who have no experience of war at all. But someone who accepts that in the world as currently divided war can become inevitable, and even just, might reply that the photographs supply no evidence, none at all, for renouncing war—except to those for whom the notions of valour and of sacrifice have been emptied of meaning and credibility. The destructiveness of war—short of total destruction, which is not war but suicide—is not in itself an argument against waging war, unless one thinks (as few people actually do) that violence is always unjustifiable, that force is always and in all circumstances wrong: wrong because, as Simone Weil affirms in her sublime essay on war, "The Iliad, or, The Poem of Force," violence turns anybody subjected to it into a thing. But to those who in a given situation see no alternative to armed struggle, violence can exalt someone subjected to it into a martyr or a hero . . . Photographer-witnesses may try to make the spectacular *not* spectacular. But their efforts can never cancel the tradition in which suffering has been understood throughout most of Western history. To feel the pulse

of Christian iconography in certain wartime or disaster-time photographs is not a sentimental projection. It would be hard not to discern the lineaments of the Pietà in W. Eugene Smith's picture of a woman in Minamata cradling her deformed, blind, and deaf daughter, or the template of the Descent from the Cross in several of Don McCullin's pictures of dying American soldiers in Vietnam.[66]

There is no sacrifice without myth. And the greater the myth, the greater the sacrifice demanded. Earlier eschatological pronouncements stemmed from the imposition of a formidable regime of truth, which demanded allegiance and weighed salvation against eternal damnation in the life to come. The modern state turned the demands for sacrifice into an earthly quest for material enrichment and worldly salvation in the name of security and prosperity.

As orthodox religions had their own unique spectacles of violence, the lasting power of the modern state was partly located in its ability to fully uphold the myth of belonging. Truth was foundational, and as certain as the ground you walked upon. Subjects were robbed of the right to disbelieve the myth, as its gravitational pull consumed every aspect of existence. That one belonged to some mythical unity, from cradle to grave, was a de facto given. And the sacrifice it demanded, as such, would be bounded to the unquestionable given of its terrestrial space.

But what makes a myth endure is precisely its ability to remain beyond comprehension. The power of the Christian God ultimately lay in its unprovability; after all, by definition you could never disprove an infinite potentiality. And since the universe was beyond all comprehension, there had to be something greater than the souls of men. The mystery is the excess which binds the mythical project. This, however, demanded a new configuration with the advent of the state and its claims of ontological and epistemological certainty regarding the identity and value of all things. What becomes of the binding principle here then is something we might call, borrowing from Goya, the "emphatic truth," the magisterial force of worldly reckoning which sweeps up the fallen of history and carries them forward on the winds of change. The emphatic retains something of the mystery in the form of the ungraspable, even as it preaches of the virtues of certain knowledge and truth. But in order to carry this out and reach deep into the souls of nonbelievers, spatial realities needed to add vitality to the sacrificial demands, which in turn depended upon a reworking of the order of time. As it was, time existed as a fragmented memory of the past and the promise of the future, also fragmented, and open to the possibility of continued renewal and transformation.

It is no coincidence that the advent of modernity coincides with the logics of progress. Progress is the insertion of temporality—the advance and the retreat—into an emphatic truth, which required rearticulating the sacrificial motif for the purposes of lasting allegiance. While the memory of the past was sacralized in the name of those who had fallen for our freedoms, that same past was invoked as a warning against a return to a more primitive state of affairs. It was the excessive uncertainty of the future, both a threat to the preserved order and a condition of possibility for a technologically driven vision of progress, which demanded continuous sacrifice. Both the winner and the losers in this game found themselves drawn into a condition of perpetual enmity. And there was no greater emphatic symbol for such regimes than the fallen military hero.

None of this was lost on Sontag. As she noted, from the Spanish Civil War onwards, the problem of violence has always been associated with various truth-telling exercises—not least the attempts to authenticate "truths of war." Robert Capa's famous photograph *The Falling Soldier* was important in this regard. Critically, for Sontag, what was striking about Capa's image was the way its 1937 publication in *Life* magazine turns the violent moment into something which resembles a beautiful death, while affirming familiar masculine and militarized qualities.[67] The violence here is both domesticated and commodified, as it would be published alongside an advertisement for Vitalis, a men's hair cream product, which seemingly added a certain glamor to the portrait. What is also striking about Capa's image is the way in which the subject is captured in a pose that blurs the line between death and dance.

This reminds us of the American artist Robert Longo's monochromatic *Men in Cities* series. Sontag knew that war was seductive. And there was no greater seducer than the idea of the hero whose sacrifice in the theatre of battle has been valorized as a "death well served." There are a number of compelling Hollywood representations of this. Perhaps the more famous is the onscreen killing of Sgt. Elias in Oliver Stone's *Platoon*, who as he is killed holds his arms out in a gesture of redemption. This was a cinematic reworking of Art Greenspoon's photograph of a wounded soldier being shot in South Vietnam 1968. Perhaps this image also marked a point of realization that the hero was just as vulnerable and ephemeral as everything else.

Such symbolic gesturing to the heavens as the essence of the military hero was more recently replicated with the death of King Leonidas in the deeply Orientalizing movie *300: Rise of an Empire*. Sacrifice here is a performative act that overpowers forces that far outnumber the individual facing mortal finitude. The death of the hero thereby stakes out a profound metaphysical claim in the drama of its witnessing in the theatres of war. The movie begins with the death of Leonidas at the hands of the mortal-turned-god Xerxes, whose transformation from grieving son to brutal monster occurred after a stint of wandering in the desert, even unto madness. Leonidas's severed head is then projected as a triumphant symbol, symbolic of a return and symbolic insomuch as it might be thrown away, as though his humanity was but a fleeting claim.

The symbol of his head is then superseded by the ritualistic displays of vengeance perpetrated by Artemisia, who has mastered the art of decapitation, having defected to Persia after seeing her family raped and murdered by Greek soldiers. Artemisia takes the desire for spectacular violence to such a level that it becomes erotic (most notably in a scene where she is shown kissing a decapitated head). Here the performative act of beheading (along with suicide) signifies certain acts of violence as revealing broader cultural tendencies. Very much along the lines of the racial stereotyping on display here, the Spartans, in contrast, are portrayed as achieving "beautiful death." It is less a question of defeating the enemy than dedicating one's life to heroism, such that one's finest moment is realized in glorious death on the battlefield.

The hero would for a prolonged period have their time and place in the glorious light. However, as the twentieth century came to a close and the world moved out of the Cold War, there would be the need to fully underwrite the new interventionist impulse. The groundwork had already been done for this, as international political architectures had bound the idea of humanity to some of the worst episodes in its history. Nevertheless, it would take some time before the conditions were right, and before the self-confidence of a globally ambitious liberalism replaced the dominance of the military hero with the sacred object of the victim.

That didn't mean the hero left the political and sacrificial stage. They would be recast, no as longer defenders of the realm, but as protectors of humanity. This, in the process of mobilizing them for wars in the name of humanitarian principles and causes, resulted in a humanization of the soldier as a subject who was just as vulnerable as the victims whose precarious image they now served. Just as global liberalism would be defined by the biopolitical attempt to secure all life on the planet, so the sacred object of its power became the global victim. Seen as part of some natural and enlightened unfolding of history, this allowed for retrospective judgment on the entirety of the human condition. No historical crime should go unpunished. And no victim from history should be denied. That, at least, was the theory. In practice, the concept of the victim would prove to be just as contingent and prejudiced as all other sacred claims to truth and recourses to violence.

CHAPTER 3

The Shame of Being Human

TRIALS FOR HUMANITY

Humanity is not a self-evident truth. It is a concept developed in response to the most abhorrent crimes against those who have been denied a place in that imagined collective by their fellow humans. In terms of how we have come to philosophically and politically understand this concept, we cannot overlook the importance of Hannah Arendt. As Judith Butler writes, "By writing about Eichmann, Arendt was trying to understand what was unprecedented in the Nazi genocide . . . Just as the failure to think was a failure to take into account the necessity and value that makes thinking possible, so the destruction and displacement of whole populations was an attack not only on those specific groups, but on humanity itself."[1] As a result, Butler maintains, "Arendt objected to a specific nation-state conducting a trial of Eichmann exclusively in the name of its own population."

Leaving aside the evident Eurocentric historicism at work with regard to connecting "humanity" to an atrocity against European Jewish populations, it is important to stress the legacy of Arendt's thinking in terms of how humanity has come to be a juridical problem. And in turn, how this has given rise to a certain conception of rights and legal protections. Arendt's insight works on two levels. Butler emphasizes that in terms of addressing individual responsibility, Arendt's well-established thesis explained the Holocaust as a profound failure in thinking. "Thought itself," she maintained, "arises out of the actuality of incidents, and incidents of living experience must remain its guideposts by which thinking soars, or into the depths to which it descends."[2] But her lived experience of the Holocaust, including her own status as a refugee, pointed her more broadly to reasons why entire peoples, like herself, were being denied what ought to be inalienable—their right to partake in the world. What was "unprecedented," she explained, was the "impossibility of finding" a new home in a world that ought to provide refuge.[3] With places that people once called "home" now populated by ghettos, with grassy meadows now featuring gas chambers, there was a need to recognize the importance of rights even as they were being denied.

What becomes important here is how this powerful call for a recognition of inalienable protections ultimately bound the concept of humanity to the structures of liberal democratic societies and the recourse to international law. Indeed, while the trials in Jerusalem proved to be a failure of humanitarian possibility, for Arendt the International Military Tribunal that sat earlier in 1945 offered something more considered in terms of legally defining crimes against humanity. As Michael Shapiro argued, "the primary discursive condition of possibility for the Nuremburg war crimes trials was not simply a new framework for international justice, but the birth of a new collective and vulnerable subject, humanity."[4] As Shapiro acknowledges, in order to raise the possibility that a crime against humanity existed as both an evidential fact and theoretical possibility, there was a need to develop juridical discourse armed with a new anthropological object—namely, the human as a collective entity—which could be consciously endangered.

In the epilogue to *Eichmann in Jerusalem*, Arendt describes the Holocaust precisely in these terms, recognizing it to be "new crime, the crime against humanity—in the sense of a crime 'against the human status,' or against the very nature of mankind."[5] This phrase "crimes against the human status" draws directly upon the words from the French prosecutor at Nuremberg, François de Menthon, to offer an account of genocide as being "an attack upon human diversity as such, that is, upon a characteristic of the 'human status' without which the very words 'mankind' or 'humanity' would be devoid of meaning."[6] What starts to appear, then, is a direct correlation between the victims of atrocity, the crimes they experienced, along with the most pressing of considerations—namely, the realization that the human condition in its fullness may in the end, as a result of our own failures to consider its very humaneness, ultimately lead to the absence of all meaning. What was therefore required was a protective mandate, which could ensure political belonging for all, thus saving humanity from itself, from its own inhumane excessiveness.

While we will later deal with the problem of directly attributing dehumanization in the original scene to an absence of law (see chapter 7), at this stage we need to critically question the true depths of such dehumanization. In particular, how are we to understand what crisis has emerged from this horrifying chapter in history, especially in terms of how those in positions of authority avoided genuine self-reflection, which resulted in the changing sacralization of power? Leaving aside Bauman's compelling claim that modernity itself should have been put on trial, Agamben has pointed out how the true horrors of the Holocaust have still evaded serious political and philosophical attention.[7] The figure of the Muselmann being here most instructive as the tormented soul nobody wanted to look upon and dwell with any considered length. The holocaust would bring forth a notable crisis in the representation of the figurative as a sacred form. Drawing upon Primo Levi's testimony, for Agamben the Muselmann was a figure who had been exhausted, malnourished, and physically tortured to the point of lacking the will to live and even being incapable of thought. Even among other inmates, they were no longer seen as alive or even human. They had been thrown into the horrifying depths of the void, and there was nothing to be reclaimed or rescued. It is, Agamben noted, easier to look upon masses of dead bodies than upon a single wretched soul who has been killed yet remains alive. Hence, for Agamben, it wasn't mass violence or the willful destruction of entire populations that marked a new departure. It was their presence that truly represented an "absolutely new phenomenon."[8] Showing us the full depravity of the Nazi experiment, they took us over the threshold for all ethical and humanitarian concerns. What, after all, could politics, psychoanalysis, or philosophy possibly have to say about humankind, when there was nothing left of it worth saving? If Agamben was correct, that this figure of the Muselmann revealed the true depths for our inhumanity, it also revealed the crisis of the sacred. For, while the specter of the Holocaust would be integral to the moralization of liberalism as a global force, the figure we should have been forced to confront was ultimately too intolerable and, in all its physical lightness, too difficult to bear.

Perhaps this is what is meant by the "unrepresentability" of the Holocaust. This is not to say that we can't point to terrible images or write about the violence that occurred, but rather that the Holocaust denied, through the presence of its most wretched forms, any sacred claim by which humanity might be redeemed. And yet, for Agamben, this is precisely where ethics should begin, for "no ethics can claim to exclude part of humanity, no matter how unpleasant or difficult that humanity is to see."[9] Not only does this require moving beyond our limited conceptions of what it means to be "human," as Levi explained with remarkable courage and dignity, it also demands bearing witness, through whatever grammatical expressions we choose, to the sacrificial fire. Even if our words and expressions fail us that doesn't mean to say that, unlike the event we are attempting to describe, they are completely incomprehensible. On the contrary, the real meaning is for us to come to terms with the ordinariness of the violence, or what we might see as the normalization of the sacrificial.

"One of the lessons of Auschwitz," Agamben adds, "is that it is infinitely harder to grasp the mind of an ordinary person than to understand the mind of a Spinoza or Dante."[10] While we shall turn to the question of aesthetics and representation in the face of annihilation later (chapter 7), it is worth turning our attentions briefly to the work of Marc Chagall and the way he redeployed the image of the crucified Jesus as a tragic messenger, whose purpose was to highlight the suffering of the Jews and bring it to the attention of the world. In a number of his works, the most striking being *White Crucifixion* (1938), which featured refugees fleeing from a burning village, Chagall appropriated the tortured and vulnerable figure of Christ the man to convey the plight shared by oppressed peoples across different times and places.[11] He would explore this idea in various interpretations of the crucifixion, reworking Christian iconography to make it much more than an expression of a particular theology. Chagall would even depict himself as the one being crucified in a number of the scenes. This certainly offered a provocative twist, given the fact that throughout history Jewish people were often scapegoated for causing the death of Christ. But maybe the image of the crucifix needed to be subverted in that way to make explicit a shared sense of empathy? Or maybe Chagall's reworking of the crucifixion scene shows that even in suffering we can never seem to leave the scenes of the sacred and their retributive calls for justice?

The trials at Nuremburg set the scene some fifty years later for the establishment of the International Criminal Court (ICC), which responded to the violence of the New Wars, including the massacres in Yugoslavia and Rwanda.[12] The ICC, in fact, appeared in 2002 at the moment when global liberal power was at its most self-righteous and where the sacralization of the victim was well established. Leaving aside the arguments of Western imperialism, in terms of developing a critique of "crime against humanity" as a legal construct, Shapiro puts forward a case for what he terms "literary justice."[13] Bypassing the legalistic account of rights which by now have ritualistically tied ethics and humanitarian concerns to juridical frameworks, Shapiro draws attention to a particular moment from Mathias Enard's remarkable novel *Zone*, where the key protagonist,

Francis Servain Mirkovic, sees his former Serbian commander Blaskic on trial in The Hague. As Enard narrates:

> In his box at The Hague among the lawyers the interpreters the prosecutors the witnesses the journalists the onlookers the soldiers of the UNPROFOR who analysed the maps for the judges commented on the possible provenance of bombs according to the size of the crater which gave rise to so many counter-arguments all of it translated into three languages . . . everything had to be explained from the beginning, historians testified to the past of Bosnia, Croatia, and Serbia since the Neolithic era by showing how Yugoslavia was formed, the geographers commented on demographic statistics, censuses, land surveys, political scientists explained the differential political forces present in the 1990's.[14]

Evoking memories of Eichmann, who appears in his opaque glass cage as if on exhibit, Blaskic is also inserted into a conceptual landscape, which reinforces the idea of justice as a network of relations wholly dependent upon regimes of visibility. And, like the transparent structure in which he is inserted to be analyzed and dissected, this setting also reveals processes of subjectivation that concentrate the reader's focus. Enard's masterful prose also reveals something powerful concerning the historical relationship between the body of the perpetrator and that of the victim, which, like a broken mirror image of Hobbes's Leviathan, violently cracks its own shattered form.

The self-consciously exhibiting Mirkovic further laments his imagined performance,

> I thought about what I would have said if they questioned me, how would I have explained the inexplicable, probably I too would have had to go back to the dawn to time, to the frightened prehistoric man painting in his cave to reassure himself, to Paris making off with Helen, to the death of Hector, the sack of Troy, to Aeneas reaching the shores of Latium, to the Romans carrying off the Sabine women . . . Blaskic in his box is one single man and has to answer for all our crimes, according to the principle of individual criminal responsibility which links him to history, he's a body in a chair wearing a headset, he's on trial in place of all those who held a weapon.[15]

This narrative certainly echoes Schmitt's earlier criticism of the formidable power possessed by those able to declare a person to be an "enemy of humanity," and the incommensurable historical weight put on those who are on trial in its name. But there is another qualification to add here to this narrative, which Enard addresses. Despite the fact that the idea of the enemy of humanity would be presented as a positive development in the age of liberal reason—and was especially internationalized in the post-Cold War period, as evinced by the NATO intervention in Kosovo—the recourse to international justice has nevertheless proved to be wholly contingent. As Enard narrates of "characters in the Great Trial," it is all about inserting some order into the law of murder, charged with knowing at what instant a bullet in the head was legitimate de jure and at what instant it constituted a grave breach of the law and customs of war, referring endlessly to the rulings of Nuremburg, Jerusalem, Rwanda, historical precedents recognized as such by the status of the court, retracting customary international law in the interpretation of the Geneva conventions.[16] Such is the force of law.

While these legalistic developments raise notable points of contention, it is important to stress that liberalism has never been primarily driven by juridical or constituted forms of power. From the outset, liberalism has been defined more by biopolitical attempts to promote the life of the species for its own productive betterment.[17] And with Dante having brought the politics of sacrifice firmly down to earth, philosophers from Kant onward have attempted to master the biopolitical contours of human life, which is said to be potentially guilty of its own degeneration, and have imagined a mastery over life across the widest possible terrain. Liberalism, in the end, would mean nothing at all without its commitment to govern all planetary life. It would, however, take the crisis of the sacred object for power as being tied to the telluric world of nations, and in doing so open a fissure in the order of time and make this ambition a real possibility. Constituted power thus becomes important for liberalism as a statement of verification and point of recognition. Indeed, it offers a means for consolidating the idea that there is such a thing as planetary life to be protected, and that all the impediments to such protections could be rightfully bypassed as a matter of right and obligation. Now the term "humanity" can be monopolized, not because this is the first time it was imagined, but because there has been a takeover in what passes for the constituted conditions of truth.

Invariably, it would take some time before this possibility mobilized sufficiently to translate the idea into political practice. And it should not be overlooked that as the century progressed, humanitarian policy was less about its juridical deliberations than the complex interplay between development strategies and intervening military forces, which promised to secure and progress the human condition as part of a global, biospherically determined collective. This in fact only adds further weight to a reading of liberalism as a regime of biopolitical power. It also means that while Arendt would become an integral part of the drama by setting out the legal and philosophical coordinates for what would become a more articulate and committed liberal conception of humanity, we mustn't lose sight of the fact that this globalist ambition was already there in the colonialist minds of liberal thinkers, who imagined a world that could be defined by its internal civil wars, allowing its ambitions to cut across the planet and destroy any semblance of bounded space.

Law here acts as something always at the service of a much wider economy of power. In this regard, whatever its protective claims, the law has always been a violent force for intervention, which has, as Kafka imagined, literally inscribed the body with markers of guilt before crimes have occurred. But it cannot be divorced from the realm of power-politics and the way its coding is inscribed through battles won. Seen this way, the much-vaunted laws of war, which have often been cited by liberal advocates of the ICC as protecting humanity against war crimes, properly appear as the wars of law, notably manifesting themselves in appropriations of suffering, complicity, and shame for the purpose of furthering of political agendas and moral claims. Indeed, if some liberal nations (notably the United States) have been reluctant to give themselves over fully to the statutes of the ICC, this is due to a) their wish to remain immune to a set of international laws and b) their desire to be able to continuously wage war in the name of peace to come. Law, as the continued outcome of the new battles which connect the national to the international, thus proceeds by recognizing how juridical proclamations are not the final arbitrator for power but merely part of the complex global jigsaw puzzle.

International law appears as a multilayered system of governance, forceful codifying normative behaviors, not merely reducing "humanity" to law but connecting it to a much wider biopolitical account of life incapable of being defined by some juridical claim. What is then at stake is how the juridical language of rights can also be incorporated and indeed subordinated to the uncodified laws of the market and its violent segregations.[18] That doesn't mean to say that shame had a limited purpose. On the contrary, the politics of shame has been integral to the development of architectures of global liberal power, notably the political and the economic as a moralizing force for worldly transformation. In the process of absorbing the weight of history, this force has colonized the political imaginary, inscribed particular narratives of redemption, and repackaged the burdens of historical guilt to inspire the politics and cultures of everyday behaviors as well as fully transform illiberal societies. In doing so, the very order of political subjectivity has been put on trial and has needed to continually prove itself against the secular adaptation of the Fall while reaffirming the fallibility of an endangered, insecure, and ontologically vulnerable life.

THE POLITICS OF SHAME

In his powerful and sensitive reading of the testimonies of Levi, Deleuze forced us to confront what he termed the "shame of being man." Such shame derived from the realization that humans were both capable of and complicit in the most inhumane atrocities. Yes—we were able to rationally send millions into oblivion, all in the name of precious or sacred space. This reality was a collective burden we were all forced to inherit. For Deleuze, however, this burden should not simply force us to confront the ways in which historic fascism has forced many to shamefully compromise with power. Wilhelm Reich has already set out those details with enough conviction.[19] Rather, Deleuze maintains, this burden demands a more complex and sophisticated grasp of the question of human survival—or, to be more precise, it requires us to ask what happened in the order of biopolitical conditioning such that all human life should bear this guilt at the heart of its very existence, and yet we are still able to return something of the human with critical meaning and purpose?

As Deleuze explained:

> It does not mean we are all assassins, that we are all guilty . . . of Nazism. Levi says it admirably: It doesn't mean the executioners and the victims are all the same . . . There are a lot of people who maintain, "Oh yes, we are all guilty" . . . No, nothing of the sort. We cannot confuse the executioners with the victim. So, the "shame of being a man" does not mean we are all the same . . .

The "shame of being a man" means at once "how could men do that"—some men, that is, other than me—how could they do that? And second, how have I myself nonetheless taken sides? I didn't become an executioner, but I still took sides to have survived, and there is a certain shame in having survived.[20]

Levi more than anyone tragically embodied this shame for having survived the unimaginable. He showed that "surviving survival" was sometimes a weight that was too difficult to carry, especially when faced with such continuous, abhorrent denial of the human and its place in this world. Or, as Theodor Adorno put it more pessimistically in his philosophical lament *Minima Moralia*, "There is no exit from the entanglement. The only responsible option is to deny oneself the ideological misuse of one's own existence, and as for the rest, to behave in private as modestly, inconspicuously and unpretentiously as required, not for reasons of good upbringing, but because of the shame that when one is in hell, there is still air to breathe."[21]

There is a tragic duality to survival at work here which needs to be accounted for in the context of shame. As Deleuze maintained, what made a holocaust possible was less the appeal to the old sovereign right to protect, and more the "survival of a population that believes itself to be better than its enemy, which it now treats not as the juridical enemy of the old sovereign but as a toxic or infectious agent, a sort of biological danger."[22] And yet, as Levi showed, to be a survivor meant that one hadn't reached the true depths of despair or touched the bottom of the abyss. The witness may have certainly stared into the void, but without falling fully into its dehumanizing pit. In his essay on survival, which takes its cue from Levi's burden, Gil Anidjar writes, "The survivor is dead and alive, witness and *muselmann*, spared and petrified. More importantly, survival is the inherently collective and political significance of one individual figure . . . The survivor is dead and alive, killer and victim, perpetrator and survivor, all at once. He is also the one and the many, individual and crowd at the same time."[23] In this setting, Derrida's idea of "survival by deferral" resonates, as it brings us back directly to our sacred compulsions:

Survival in the conventional sense of the term means to continue to live, but also to live after death. Speaking of translation, Walter Benjamin took pains to distinguish between *überleben* on the one hand, to live after death, as a book can survive the death of its author, or a child the death of parents, and

on the other hand, fortleben, living on, to keep on living. All the ideas that
have helped me in my work, notably those regarding the trace or the spectral,
were related to the idea of "survival" as a basic dimension. It does not derive
from either to live or to die. No more than what I call "originary mourning." It
is something that does not wait for so-called "actual" death'. And yet the survivor is continually forced to confront death every time they are called upon
to give sacred voice to the memory of victims—to speak sacred words for the
fallen, in whose haunting image they act to redeem not only themselves but
all of us for having existed.[24]

Humans should feel ashamed when confronted with historical atrocities that
could have been prevented. Indeed, as Deleuze insisted, not only must we continue to address our own shameful compromises with power, we also need to
address injustice and the perpetuation of violence. But shame is not a universal
sentiment. Neither has its liberalization marked a definitive break with history
and sacrificial forms of violence. The conditions of shame, as attested by Levi,
among others, have brought about a complex interplay between acts of violence and their forced witnessing, resulting in the disruption of absolute moral
demarcations.[25]

What is more, as shame has been recast in relation to the global victim, it has
never been objectively determined, but often applied as a posthumous political
inscription in order to justify violent actions for the sake of the protection of
the living. And let us not also forget how the destruction of the human, even
when that human is technically still alive, doesn't necessarily happen only in
"exceptional" conditions. As Zygmunt Bauman reminds us, what are on the surface the most extreme forms of violence are often arbitrary, banal, and normalized in their altogether routine enactments of suffering.[26] Attentions as such
have turned to the perpetuation of oppressive logics, which defy neat or reductive ideological explanations. Griselda Pollock and Max Silverman, for example,
have identified a "concentrationary imaginary,"[27] which demands continuous
vigilance for incidents of everyday human subjugation. This includes the hidden
order of politics, which frames violence as spectacle, a necessary and even righteous part of the human condition.

Shame has never been a value-neutral emotion. It has often been pre-figured
in the collective consciousness. Inextricably bound to the politics of authenticating "the victim," the question of shame has been continuously mediated through

hierarchies of tragedy and suffering, through which the deaths of some have been presented as more valuable than others. How many Western scholars, for instance, begin and end their studies of human atrocities with the Holocaust, without attending to other genocides throughout history—not least the persecution of racial minorities and indigenous populations effected by all modern political projects? Now, of course, the feeling of shame—like remorse and genuine regret—may have been evident in the reflective sensibilities of some of those who have perpetrated acts of violence. The shame of being human, however, points to a more generalizable field in which the forces of history assume certain political qualities by drawing our more intimate attentions to particular memories of human suffering and devastation. The shame of being human thus conceived has worked in many ambiguous, highly contingent, and, at times, deeply conflicting and philosophically contested ways.[28]

This can be partly explained by the lived experience of catastrophe and its "internal presuppositions," notably the shame and guilt felt by survivors, who might have considered themselves heroic and blessed with good fortune were they not laden with the need to come to terms with the lasting memory of atrocity. And yet, this melancholic burden, which refused, as Freud might have noted, to be consumed by the open wound, can also be overcome when the bearers distance themselves from shame by attempting to invoke moral concepts like desperate alibis, or when they assign different degrees of guilt between executioners, accomplices, and victims.[29] History shows how apportioning shame has often been divorced from its wider operations, motives, and sacred claims. Indeed, the potential for historical shame to be appropriated and used in the propagation of violence is evident to any student of the history of warfare. The failure to intervene in Rwanda, for example, was one of the most politicized pretexts used by leaders such as Tony Blair to justify the invasion of Afghanistan and Iraq. The collective shame of genocide has ushered in the potential for even greater violence, underwriting the slaughter of tens of thousands of innocent people in the name of humanitarianism and the desire to save persecuted strangers from themselves.

What we might refer to as the "burden of shame" has therefore frequently been deployed in the guise of a resurrected moral symbol. It has appeared like a specter, either haunting those who have benefited least from the so-called age of enlightenment or, more recently, morally justifying violence to sanction liberal interventionism. In light of this, asking "what is shame?" proves to be futile, as it merely points to prefigured ideological claims—that is, the event of shame occurring is already determined. What matters more is how the concept of shame functions politically, setting out the moral parameters (including the justification for violence) which, emanating from the tragic figures of history, have authored conditions of the new sacred order for politics. Whose shame have we actually been referring to? What were we authoring and what were we denying even by invoking such shame? How has the politics of survival been bound up and further released through this burdensome discourse? And how has the very idea of the victim appeared as a sacred object, only to be set adrift upon the blood-soaked shores of history?

What is at stake here is precisely how we imagine, conceptualize, and politically respond to the victim of history. In a particularly insightful contribution to the discourse on the horrors of the twentieth century, Simona Forti set out the problem of violence in relationship to the victim (importantly in that order) as being presented in morally certain ways.[30] This is what she terms "The Dostoyevsky Paradigm." Alluding to the figure of Nicholas Stavrogin from Dostoyevsky's powerful and prophetic masterpiece *Demons*, Forti points to the predominance of a historically grounded and deeply structured understanding of mass violence, in which absolute power is mobilized against the absolute victim. Focusing on Stavrogin—who, like a fallen angel, is said to be the most magnificent and the most damned character in all of Dostoyevsky's works—Forti recognizes how his body is inscribed with the markings of the violence of a century, in particular its ontologically determined signature of evil, which is largely explained in terms of the "abyss of freedom" or what Bauman would identify as modernity's "abhorration."

An account of political events would be definitive here, as history has often been analyzed in terms of neatly marking out *wicked demons* and *absolute victims*. Forti explains this by recounting Stavrogin's confession to Bishop Tikhon in a crucial chapter following the psychological desecration of the young girl Matryoshka:

> The freedom that makes him capable of destruction goes past the point of
> no return. It does so, without any possibility of redemption, when the wick-
> edness he is capable of has its object the absolute innocence of the victim. It
> is one of the greatest literary moments in the book, but also one of its most
> philosophically eloquent. This relationship of oppression—*with an all-powerful*

perpetrator on one side, faced by the total powerlessness of the victim on the other— expresses what I believe is Dostoyevsky's concept of *evil in its absolute pure form* . . . And if in this case of the radical action of evil is portrayed in the microcosm of a personal relationship between two people, a little later it will be ready to be projected on a large scale and refined, providing his twentieth century heirs with the hermeneutic key to absolute political evil.[31]

As Forti rightly argues, while Dostoyevsky later presents more nuanced dialectical tensions in the widely cited fable of the Grand Inquisitor from *The Brothers Karamazov*, some of the certainties that appear in these literary examples are found wanting when applied to the violent behaviors of the masses. Again, in ways that are all too reminiscent of the warnings provided by Reich in his book *The Mass Psychology of Fascism*, the Grand Inquisitor fable is rightly shown to be limited in its scope. Its message rests upon an understanding of the organization of violence that ultimately draws upon the perceived docility of populations, which ultimately don't really know what they are doing and hence lack positive agency. The story thus falls short when accounting for techniques of domination by which those in power can positively manipulate the masses' desire for violence in life-affirming ways. This can manifest itself in encouraging the masses to passively support policies of an engineered racial and social hierarchy for their own personal benefit, which often reveal deeply held prejudices that already exist within the political system. More troubling still, populations can be pushed to willfully invest in the subjugation of others. Overcoming this, Forti explains, demands a return to the work of Levi:

> Thus, by ideally opposing Levi to Dostoyevsky and what the Russian writer represents, we can conclude that the muselmann—what resulted from the degradation of the camp—was not solely and not predominantly the product of the abyssal freedom of a subject who had taken the place of God; nor was he the object on which the perverse *jouissance* of the death impulse had been discharged. He became what he became through a dense but ordinary weave of intentions, actions, and objectives whose weft proved fatal.[32]

This brings us directly to the question of responsibility—in whose name do we act when we put things on trial?

IN THE NAME OF THE VICTIM

The question of who or what gets to claim the position of the victim would slowly become the most fraught of political quandaries. We can see the legacy of this played out as Europe's collective shame would lead to the pronounced support for the foundation of the state of Israel, which in turn would produce what Edward Said noted were the "victims of the victims."[33] More recently, and with the second coming of identity politics, we have witnessed the proliferation of distinct claims to vulnerability that have moved across lines of race, gender, and sexual orientation, leading to competing and often tokenistic (notably materially enriching) demands, which account for the most authentic victims of history as unrivalled in their experiences of persecution. Central to their claims to persecution are determinable histories and quantifiable assumptions on the definitive character of power, along with statistical measures which could be presented as fundamentally determined by distinct identarian characteristics that often amount to tick-box claims devoid of actual histories or political and socioeconomic context. In short, since the dominant characteristic for power would be white, male, heterosexual, and protected by the history of Anglophone privilege, the further an individual's identity moved away from those categorizations the more they would be victims of entrenched violence. And yet, as the slow catastrophe of the liberal wars started to morph into the global refugee crisis, the unexpected return of class politics exposed the limits of this liberal entitlement model. The claims to victimhood were also now about power and entitlements. And it has been precisely here that forces of contemporary fascism have proved to be most parasitic, as the concept of the white male as a victim of history becomes truly contentious, and unacceptable, for those still wedded to pure liberal dialectics.

Our problem here is not with the mobilization of white rage and the impact it's had on destroying liberalism from within, though it certainly needs to be accounted for when confronting the death of liberalism (see chapter 5). What needs to be recognized at this point is how, as François Laurelle insisted, the victim has become a thoroughly overdetermined figure in contemporary political philosophy.[34] Just as victimology has rendered everybody a possible victim, ontologies of vulnerability have naturalized insecurity and the fragile sediment of existence. Underwriting this would be profound liberal suspicions on the nature of the political subject, which, certainly since the Holocaust, have seen the subject burdened with the guilt of its own political failures. This has grad-ually added with considerable universal force a moral imperative to Foucault's observation that the destiny of the human species was to be wagered against the successes and failures of its own political strategies. Because of the shame that would ensue, the act of killing could not simply be sanctioned for the protection of a nation and the preservation of its heroic past deeds, however righteous. The killing had to be tied to the creation of a humanitarian ethos where the very idea of the human community would be realized through the wars fought in its name. But there proved to be no promise of salvation. Inse-curity had become the new normality. The demand for "resilience" in the face of catastrophe taught us that much. In fact, there no longer even seemed to be any shame left in politics, no subject taboo, and nothing that couldn't be said by those in power. Indeed, we are left today questioning what is actually left with regard to discourses and narratives of historical shame when its mobiliz-ing subject matter—the victim—is no longer bound to the tragedies of a ruin-ous past. Rather, the victim is now tied to a violently devastated—albeit as yet imaginary—future, incapable of mobilizing anything remotely credible for rethinking a shared collective consciousness.

We can date some of this intellectual trend back to the mid-1980s, which saw the twinned intellectual and strategic shifts in discourses on human security and victimology. While the term "human security" would not become a global doctrine until 1994, with the launch of the United Nations Development Pro-gram's annual Human Security Report, the idea that the body could be a site for rethinking national and transnational security concerns was pioneered during the explosion of illegal drug use in many developed countries, notably the United States. Indeed, while the use of crack cocaine presented clear detrimental effects upon users' bodies, which would be further compounded by connections between injected drugs and the AIDS epidemic, it was the presence of these drugs and the violence they brought to middle-class white neighborhoods that ended up being a catalyst for a brutal military "crackdown." The drug-ravaged body of the user would be crucial here in terms of connecting lives in the global North to those in the borderland areas of the world. The process of looking upon a body that was literally wasting away, slowly decomposing before our eyes, forced us to recast the very understanding of insecurity and vulnerability within the tranquility of the metropole.

Securitization theorists have thus provided a rethinking of liberalism as a global commitment tasked with saving the individual human from the violence of abandonment and political neglect.[35] Meanwhile, authors such as Robert Elias have performed studies on the politics of victimization. In their attempts to move beyond reductive liberal/conservative impasses, they have foregrounded the political qualities of the victim in the metropolitan homelands to account for structural forms of violence beyond individual and juridical transgressions.[36] What was really at play here was how the victim was to be named, seen, and solved as a political problem. Indeed, while appreciative of the victim's capacity for being appropriated for political gain, we still observe the need to speak in the victims' name, and to imagine them as a moral and political force for good.[37] Though it must be noted, while critics were already acutely aware of the over-zealousness of some proponents of victimology, especially when it came to touting the victimhood of children, it would still present itself as a radical humanist movement, bringing a distinct humanism to legalistic and scientific inquiry. As such, the victim would be openly embraced by a community of specialists capable of representing their concerns and speaking in their name, even if their interpretations demanded war and the sanctioning of violence to be enacted upon those responsible for these victims' plight.

The emaciated body would appear here as symbolic of a world that was literally being starved of liberal nourishment. Still haunted by recent history, the harrowing sight of a body slowly withering away (see also chapter 7) would sanctify a number of universal icons of suffering, which had been borne of political neglect. From images of famine victims in Africa and prisoners behind barbed-wire fences in the former Yugoslavia, to images of drug addicts who had been locked in their homes, away from all light, the slowly diminishing body would become another way of imagining the annihilation of life from the promise of its liberal appearance. Emaciation as such would literally bring us to the point of death, the exact moment of an unnecessary departure. Visualizations of this would include Kevin Carter's famous photograph of the emaciated Sudanese child which seemed to enact its own unbearable claims, as well as the photograph capturing the final moments captured of AIDS victim David Kirby, which could easily draw comparisons with the *Pietà*, with its subject depicted as Christ-like, lying on the bed and suffering until his very last breath.

And yet, despite the importance of these images in documenting human atrocity, what was more notably at work here was the rearticulating of relations of power. "As appropriations of suffering," David Campbell writes in the context of famine, such photographs are affective rather than simply illustrative. They are designed to appeal emotionally to viewers and connect them with subjects in a particular way. The message is that someone is suffering, and that we should be sympathetic to his or her plight and moved to do something. However, the lack of contextual support means that viewers regard action to alleviate suffering as coming from outside.[38] The subjects of these photographs thus underwent a form of victim transfer, from suffering into redemption, from an isolated figure to a systematic imperative, from the moment of death to the promise of a better tomorrow, from the invisible to the sacred object; all the while, the emaciated body would be purposefully displaced in the arena of presence by the photogenic humanitarian soldier, who may not save the victims' bodies, but could at least dignify their memories through sacred violence that carried the weight of the absent victims, which could now find consolation in some historical context.

As the logics of the New Wars would be later appropriated by the global wars on terror, the very idea of the victim went global, its appeal made to everyone on the earth. We were all, it was said, at risk of becoming a victim to some indiscriminate attack, which might strike without warning, rendering linear notions of space and time meaningless and redundant. Everything was to be thrown into the "zone of indistinction," for nothing was certain. The impact on subjectivity would be striking, as we would all have to learn to exist in a world that was fundamentally insecure by design. And yet, as the speed, frequency, and intensity at which humans were made victims was broadcast instantaneously through the digital platforms, even some of the staunchest liberals started to question whether Susan Sontag was right and there was such a thing as "compassion fatigue."[39] Were we now confronting that "crisis of pity" borne of indifference to suffering?[40]

As Luc Boltanski inquired, "Why is it so difficult nowadays to become indignant and to make accusations or, in another sense, to become emotional and feel sympathy—or at least to believe for any length of time, without falling into uncertainty, in the validity of one's own indignation or one's own sympathy?"[41] While there is certainly some truth that the onslaught of images brought about by the age of digital media has led to desensitization, it cannot fully explain the situation. Unlike former totalitarian regimes that were hallmarked by secrecy, there is no doubt that liberal regimes mediate suffering through a certain informational and sensory overload every second of every day. And this has proved to be exhausting, especially when there seems to be no end or solution in sight. But cultural and entertainment forms of representation aside, overexposure to the raw realities of violence and its effects are not what liberal societies suffered from. What we have become exhausted by is the overdetermination of the victim as framed through normative liberal claims, which have been shown to be illusionary and beyond resolution by strategic design.

To understand this fully, there is a need to recognize how the myth ascribing a sacred quality to the victim has ultimately been exposed and its claim to respect humanity debunked. The more the victim would be foregrounded within the liberal political imaginary, the more we realized the contingency of the commitment and response. While less emphasis was put on the vulnerability of the victim, protection and violence were still administered in wholly selective, inconsistent, and unequal ways. More troubling still, the moves toward ontologizing vulnerability and making it a universal principle actually opened the gates, allowing outraged white males to appeal to exactly the same concerns and demand the same recognition as victims. Actual victims would be increasingly caught in this crossfire, as politicians debated the relationship between the globally vulnerable and the locally precarious. And, in the process, the duplicitous principles upon which the global ambitions of liberalism, as wedded to the identity politics of victims, were based would be fully revealed.

This has become the staging ground for the emergence of new fascisms, which have become parasitic to the plight of victims as framed through the dialectics of division and the resurrection and reworking of older mythical ideas regarding belonging. Furthermore, unscrupulous leaders have coalesced (in an equally duplicitous way) around the notion that the myth of nations has been abandoned, and that this betrayal is the reason why we live in a state of permanent siege from forces beyond the control even of their authors. What could possibly be left to say when in answer to the question of who the victim was, the crowd answered "everyone"? And what possibility was there to reclaim something meaningful for the globally subjugated and dispossessed when the self-identifying liberal, already armed with their authenticating narratives of victimhood, countered "everyone, but you"? Having reached such a situation, we knew the concept was soon to be exhausted, and the name we gave to the victim would need to be rethought.

THE SACRED BODY OF THE VICTIM

It needs to be recognized that the history of the victim has never been a universal story. Neither has the subjugated body always been bound to appropriated liberal articulations. Some of the more radical and self-conscious representations of bodily repression would initially find powerful expression in earlier reworkings of the figure of the martyr. Contemporary understandings of martyrdom are undoubtedly colored by the high-profile actions of suicide bombers. Such violence is marked by sacred claims and its explicit onto-theological remnants.[42] But we should not also lose sight of the contested nature of the martyr as a historical figure, especially when it ruptured conventional notions of both militaristic and revolutionary heroism.

There is something particularly striking about St. Sebastian and the image of his bound body shot through with arrows on the orders of the Emperor Diocletian. Sebastian has always seemed to capture the radical imagination. In exile, for example, Oscar Wilde took the alias name "Sebastian Melmoth," and Thomas Mann would claim in his Nobel Prize speech that Sebastian's real heroism was represented by "grace in suffering." Adaptations of his iconic image (arguably the epitome of martyrdom) have ranged from Frida Kahlo's anthropomorphic *The Wounded Deer*, which is yet another brilliant example as to why her work and her figurative interventions were far more revolutionary and radical than Rivera's ever was; to Yukio Mishima's eroticized portraiture (the actor himself would eventually commit ritual suicide); onto the 1968 cover of *Esquire* magazine featuring the greatest sportsperson of all time shot through with arrows, accompanied by the caption "The Passion of Muhammad Ali." Such artistic adaptations take the martyred St. Sebastian and bring him directly into the present. And, in doing so, they explicitly seek to work against the cult of sacred memory. While bringing the violence of modern regimes into stark relief, they shed a critical light on the nature of sacrifice from the perspective of the victim. Whether this act then elevates the martyr to the level of a sacred or sainted object,[43] like Sebastian or Paul, whose suffering has been seen as a cosmic wounding, is open to question. Or, to put it another way, what matters here in the space between are the types of politicization that follow, which may or may not justify violence in their image.

But in 1972 another image would profoundly shift the terrain in terms of the aesthetics of suffering, and mark a definitive moment in the appearance of the global victim. It is worth emphasizing that the Holocaust stood as the shameful catalyst for Western liberal powers to reassess their history and justify their subsequent military interventions, and it provided the necessary impetus for the International Criminal Court to respond to genocidal actions. However, the general politicization of the Holocaust was not something that happened in the immediate aftermath of World War II, particularly in respect to directly impacting global politics in a way that permitted liberal powers to advance.

While it seems common today to look upon, acknowledge, and write about, while legally and ethically redressing the concerns of victims, they have a relatively short history in terms of being a dominant aspect of the everyday political lexicon. To speak of victims' suffering was often unthinkable in the Christian world, which seamlessly moved from ascribing a certain piety to suffering to the modern notion that victimhood was a sign of weakness. The emergence of a globally ambitious liberal power would change all this and result in a profound rewriting of the history of liberalism itself, to be expressed through its humanitarian ethics and desire to save strangers from unnecessary suffering by means of global peace and security. Indeed, given there was no self-evident truth to the necessity of universal liberal rule, nor was there some collective awakening to its contingent reasoning and rationality, the victim as a global political construct would need to be presented as the sacred truth for an interconnected world brought together through a shared sense of precarity and vulnerability. Thus began the move away from the emphatic truth of the hero to the empathetic truth of the victim. And yet, this shift toward recognizing the vulnerability of all would eventually reveal the tolerance thresholds of liberalism and prove to be the source of its inevitable narcissistic undoing—externally and internally. In order for the victim as a sacred object to hold appeal—without which liberal rule would have remained wedded to the telluric world of nations—there was a need to carry out violence in the victim's name.

The naked child appears before us, screaming in excruciating pain, fleeing with her arms outstretched, carrying her own invisible crucifix. Its unbearable weight burrows deep into her back. Her stigmata are not from the lacerations of the Romans, but inflicted from a distance by the American empire. This photograph, taken by Nick Ut, of the nine-year-old Vietnamese girl Kim Phuc, fleeing her village after a napalm attack, remains one of the most iconic images of warfare ever taken.[44] Critics have often questioned the role of the photograph in reshaping national consciousness or the power of this and similar images in bringing about an end to such indiscriminate violence.[45] However, what's left out of the discussion is whether the image crosses a threshold into a terrain dominated by concerns with the victim as an innocent sacred object. The girl, a living Iphigenia and Christ bound up into one globally recognized figure, ran—both literally and metaphorically—down the road and into the homes of those living in the age of the global media spectacle. In doing so, she provided the age of the victim with a new icon it could connect with, thus rescuing liberalism from the failure of one of its most brutal adventures. For while a leading liberal democratic nation was actually the perpetrator of this violence, the problem lay in its lack of a truly global ethical sensitivity that emanated from its attachment to the old heroic model, which ultimately died when Art Greenspoon captured that jungle war's final breaths.

But for all the pain it depicted, the image of Kim Phuc would be mediated to have the most desired political affects. It would be more tolerable to look upon the image of a naked young girl, who like so many other young girls had been violated and exposed to tremendous suffering by this colonialist war, than to be presented with the visible sight of her burns. Kim Phuc thus marks the start of the bloodless violence of the victim (see chapter 5): her suffering was mediatized and mediated, as was the story of her survival and redemption, her conversion to Christianity, the eventual revealing of her healed scars. So, too, was the violence propagated in her name by humanitarian bombs dropped from those high-velocity crosses in the sky. Now the sacrificial flames she carried would be concealed behind the shield of liberation. Kim Phuc would embody, like the burn marks on her tortured back, the more occluded nature of the sacred in the contested spaces concerning the visibility of the victim. Who, after all, was truly able to recognize the words beneath the silent screams?

Kim Phuc is another example of how the recurring motif of crucifixion, as in the *Pietà*, is able to connect violence against the victim across the oppressive landscapes of time. There are many examples we might draw upon here, which in light of the sacred appropriation of the victim mark out both a distinct yet altogether universal history of suffering. One of the most harrowing examples of this is the scene of the crucifixion of the girls in the 1919 silent movie *Auction of Souls*, based upon the testimony *Ravished Armenia* written by Aurora Mardiganian (who also featured in the production). While the exact details of the portrayal of the crucifixion would later be contested, Mardiganian noted that what really matters is how crucifixion can appear in many different ways as a devastating symbolic form of punishment. She clarified that, during their slaughter of the Armenian populace, instead of using it to put suffering on public display, the Turkish army turned the cross into a weapon of sexual violence: "The Turks didn't make their crosses like that. The Turks made little pointed crosses. They took the clothes off the girls. They made them bend down, and after raping them, they made them sit on the pointed wood, through the vagina. That's the way they killed—the Turks. Americans have made it a more civilized way. They can't show such terrible things."[46] The iconography of the crucifixion, in short, remains bearable to those who witness the suffering if it appears within a familiar and normalized sacred gaze.

In more recent times, we could also point to the Cuban artist Erik Ravelo, whose images of crucified children addresses multiple themes of victimization, from pedophilia within the Catholic Church, sexual abuse and sex tourism of children in Thailand, the ravages of war in Syria, the trafficking of children's organs on the black market, the gun deaths of children in the United States, and child obesity fueled by profit-driven fast food companies.[47] We might also think of how the blood-soaked hoodie belonging to Trayvon Martin, a seventeen-year-old African American boy who was fatally shot, was exhibited in the courtroom trial of his killer, presenting a potent symbol of race relations in the United States and the crucifixion of black youth by other means.[48] The strength of the hoodie as a legal exhibit is evinced by the removal of Trayvon's face from the partially see-through encasement of a certain essentialism. While "seeing through race" has become a hallmark of the post-racial,[49] the exhibit transcends this particular injustice, as the face of any dispossessed black child could appear in the frame. Whether it should subsequently be considered a work of art is still open to debate.

It is here we should return to Agamben, who has undoubtedly pushed forward our thinking on the idea of sacrifice as a fundamental political category in the context of the willful, calculated, and systematic killing of human lives. As already noted, the Holocaust was particularly instructive for him in this regard, as he purposefully articulated throughout his politically and philosophically rich *Homo Sacer* series. The dehumanized subject—what Agamben terms "bare life"—refers in this context to those sacred lives which can be "killed without sacrifice" or without their deaths being considered a crime. Such lives, he claims, provide a key for understanding the organizing principles of sovereignty (albeit in a way that remains for the most part a hidden secret). Hence, unlike Schmitt's well-established idea that the political is all about demarcating who is the friend and who is the enemy, for Agamben the history of sovereignty is all about determining which lives are worthy of political qualification, as opposed to those those which may be destroyed without any attributable blame.

In a strange reversal, the sacred man for Agamben is precisely that desecrated body that is denied categorization as sacrifice. While fully appreciative of Agamben's theological sophistry and brilliant close reading of scriptures and texts, I find his analysis to be unnecessarily obscure in the face of evident acts of sacrificial violence carried out by sacred regimes during contemporary times. This has everything to do with Agamben's ethical sensibilities, which, in wanting to foreground the victim's "original" position in a sacred order of things, ends up revealing his own messianic politics. Of course, the focus on the testimony of the victim is important in our attempts to make sense of history and renew our ethical demands in the face of atrocities. But what if, even in the telluric world of nations, we shifted the referent object from the victim, which was never a dominant standard or concern, to the body of the hero? Might we not then have a better understanding of sacrifice and the ways its violent logics reveal certain continuities, and yet change and adapt over time, so as not to uphold some definitive naming of the victim as bare life or any other hermeneutic reckoning? And, moreover, what happens when the victim becomes a sacred object in its own right, when its embodiment becomes the basis for commanding legions and authoring violence?

My understanding of the sacred is worth clarifying here. If the question of the intolerable designates a political category which provides critical insight regarding the threshold between acceptable and unacceptable forms of violence as a form of public spectacle, while the unbearable refers us to what we are forced to carry as a result of our forced witnessing, the sacrificial overwrites all this by providing the metaphysical pretext and rationale for justifying the act of killing. But the sacred has never been a fixed category, and, despite Agamben's protestations, neither has the victim been devoid of a sacrificial sacred claim. Indeed, in the age of liberal reason, it has been precisely this presentation of the victim as a sacred object which has demanded a certain justice and violence in its name. From this perspective, we are compelled to ask what exactly is being inscribed upon the bodies of the victims? How does the unbearable turn into something more tolerable? And which horrifying qualities can be removed to make us spring us into action for the purpose of confirming the sacred qualities of life?

We can, it seems, carry the weight of the suffering if the suffering means something, and if that meaning can be acted upon. In this regard, while the sacrificial refers to the deaths of the victims, which in a symbolic order of things are intended for public consumption, our concern is to look more intently at the mediation of spectacles of violence. That is, we must account for those deaths that have been recorded and appear to be rightful casualties of systemic oppression, so that we can identify how the sacrificial is mobilized to govern life by retaining something of the mythical and its unequivocal allegiance to violence. Qualities that are said to nevertheless reveal something of the mystery of existence, like a divine revelation that appears in our darkest hours.

Resurrecting the victim in the face of twentieth-century nihilism was no doubt an understandable aim. Without the reappearance of the victim, our philosophical and political coordinates would have seemed meaningless. After all, how could we understand the human as an entity to be valued when confronting the denial that it has any meaning at all? But while nihilism is often presented here as the total eradication of all value and meaning, this is a mistake. There are after all different kinds of nothingness. Or if the impulse for annihilation does result in the triumph of death for all, this only occurs once the nihilistic ambition has been actualized, which consequently also signals the end for nihilism itself. As Samuel Beckett puts it, "Nothing is more real than nothing."

So until such time that all forms of life are totally extinguished from the face of the earth, what we can refer to as nihilism is more about the attempted eradication of all difference—which includes the capacity to imagine difference, to breathe difference, to feel difference, to live with difference—as overlaid with a determinable value and certainty of meaning within a totalizing sacred and sacrificial framework. But since any attempts to eradicate difference end up facing resistance, which in turn exposes the myth behind the attempt and its nihilistic intentions, what comes into focus is the uncompromising violence in the order of this battle. Under such conditions, the nihilist draws upon the power of the sacred, invoking the memory of the past and presenting a vision of a unifying future, while destroying the poetic sensibility. Hence, nihilism itself is prone to adaptation and change, and, in our current times, what carries it forward is the positioning of absolute victimhood in relation to a wounded life. Such nihilism doesn't close the wound; on the contrary, it keeps it alive and at a healthy distance, like some object that has been frozen in time, and is thus beyond all critique. Such wounds never heal. We see this happening time and time again, as the historical memory of atrocity is appropriated for the present moment—a transmission of a pure image of the wound, which becomes the basis for further violence in its name. Such images, loaded with symbolic resonance, tell us less about the actual experiences of the victim than they do about contemporary political aspirations far removed from human sensibility. To confide with the wounded of history implies their wounds are open to transgressive potentiality. It is to listen to the intimate chorus of its screams, to feel its pain, to recognize how the wound itself changes over time and how in the process the ontological conditions concerning what it means to be human—from the memory inscribed upon the earth to the way it projects a certain potentiality for woundedness onto the future—leads to the death of the present human subject in a way that liberates the human to come.

The liberalized victim shows us that a death by sacrifice requires the sacrificial victim to assume certain symbolic importance. The death must appear to be worthy of something. However tragic, there must be value attributed to the singular loss of life. Here, then, we encounter a fundamental difference between the wider phenomenon of human disposability, where the victims rise in number and yet their biographies remain unwritten, in contrast to those who come to embody certain tolerable and intolerable conditions by which we learn to attribute a metaphysical meaning to suffering as manifested by our witnessing a death. Unwittingly or not, sacrifice demands some connection to a "greater good," or an understanding that it is worthwhile because of the sacrifice it incurs. Like the Christian son, there is in fact no meaning without it. At least, this is what we are told by every new generation of prophets marked by a sacred history. So while the sacrificial in these terms may concentrate our attention on unbearable conditions, there is an evident danger to the symbolism, as the complex nature of sacrificial deaths is overlaid with authenticating narratives and definitive truths. Rather than putting systemic forces on trial, this ends up precluding serious critical attention. Once the sacrificial makes its entry into political discourse, complicity is easily written out of the script as the need for new thinking is displaced by the intellectual violence of rehearsed orthodoxy that continues to reveal its theological origins.

BEHOLDING THE PAIN OF OTHERS

Humanity was borne of the collective idea of unnecessary suffering and persecution. It appeared to us through the weight of history, its persecutions and massacres of innocents still so apparent in the world. To understand humanity in such terms has meant recognizing the brutal disposability of life and the needlessness of the sacrifices many have had to make. But it is also to recognize the way value is attributed to the victim after their very humanity has been denied. It is to account for the processes in which the casualties of history have been afforded a certain metaphysical ascription so that, in death, the body that needlessly suffered could become an active memory to steer history in a particular direction. This requires us to recognize and feel the pain of others so that the very order of politics might be transformed and a shared ethical consciousness reawakened. But such a posthumous ethical orientation has not only proved to be deeply flawed in terms of the mobilization of death and the politicization of shame, it often proceeds within very narrowly conceived normative frameworks. These frameworks reaffirm deeply set assumptions on the nature of humanity, while recalibrating existing structures for power along racialized lines. The reappropriation of past victims into present scenarios to inscribe value upon their bodies, and the body of humanity more generally, worked to reinscribe Westernized logics for power, which have been continuously reaffirmed through an allegiance to a sacred order of politics borne of sacrifice.

The sacred order of the victim also gave rise to a universalizing conception of forced witnessing, wherein an individual act of violation, which could not be ignored, connected the sense of intimate loss to the broadest understanding of the human condition. And yet, there remained an important caveat: humanitarianism was not a given; it needed to be proved in the very act of saving strangers from danger. Humanity would be a hollow vessel were it not for the wars fought in its name. As a concept, it demanded both protection and accomplishment. The specter of humanity was thus an affront to particular ideals concerning the human condition. It would underwrite certain ethical virtues ascribed to a sacred or politically qualified life, while through the battles fought in the name of the victim this specter would seek to realize its very potentiality as a figurative unity. Witnessing the pain of others, in this context, registered as both an obligation to recognize suffering and a call to action for the sake of protecting the wretched victims of history.

One was not therefore simply bearing witness to the suffering of humanity; rather, humanity's pain was beholden. The way beholding is conceptualized here is not just in reference to the act of looking upon, or for that matter witnessing, with any due care or consideration a particular event or occurrence. To behold is to take full possession and offer up a new forced unity by means of the appearance of the phenomenon in the eyes of the beholder. It is to internalize and project in the same movement. Beholding is thus an ontological presence in the order of being and a dedicated move toward some imagined togetherness. It joins the verb "to be" with the signified "holding" and alludes to incorporation, care, and attempted mastery of a totalizing field of perceptions. Little wonder the question of beholding (especially in the biblical tradition) is often associated with suffering in the face of some tremendous, earth-shattering violence. It thus gives rise to the aesthetico-theological conditions of sacred possibility, where the act of witnessing immediately connects to a higher purpose.

Those of us who continue to enjoy the privilege of being digitally connected are all bearing witness to acts of violence in one way or another. Such witnessing has never, however, been a neutral and objective process. What we "witness" is often highly policed by aesthetic regimes of mediated suffering, which prioritize the gaze by making us forced witnesses to historical events that appear beyond our control. This has required us to become more astute in attending to the cultured production of violence, addressing the relationships between individual desires, representations of human suffering, along with a wider economy of collectively desired pleasure in which humiliation and death play a part. And yet herein lays a fundamental ethical problem all humanists needed to acknowledge. While we have known what it's like to sanction the slaughter of millions, we have become incapable of feeling the pain of just a handful of deaths. As we confront such large-scale tragedies, the statistical measures through which we understand, document, and record the denial of life are the only true measure by which we are capable of conceiving with any forensic or analytical certainty the horrors of history.

Nevertheless, such measures have proved time and again to be complicit in the removal of any experience of others' humanity from scenes of collective slaughter. With the question of our capacity for extreme inhumanity reduced to our asking "how many were killed?"—our mapping out the where and when—so the task becomes one of producing officious measures for the atrocious, and, by that token, the apprehension of some objectified fact to register the most barbarous acts conceivable. All of this would be bound to preconceived normative registries, which enable discerning between better or worse forms of violence. Pain and loss as such lost all claims to innocence the moment they arrived, for in the very act of imposing hierarchies of suffering, which determined which lives mattered more in death, so did we bring the innocent into an orbit of intense political conflict, sanctioning further violence in their names.

The resurrection of the biblical motif of the "massacre of the innocents" (notably the innocent mother and child) would prove on many occasions to be integral to this drama. It permitted a certain metaphysical ascription, which, returning to a brutal mythical scene in the history of Christianity, connected violence to tales of indiscriminate slaughter while preventing the bodies of the victims from vanishing from our collective memories. This also means that such victims have needed to be resurrected, continuously, so that the memory of the atrocities they suffered might counter the nihilistic impulse to reduce the innocent victim to nothingness. Their existence would therefore be suspended in a liberal purgatory, waiting to be called upon during wartime, deployed on battlefields which were yet to be determined.

This tactic was never geostrategic. It would tear open a wound in the fabric of time, pulling tortured specters from the past in a holy pact with demons and angels from an unforgiving future. Metaphysics then, as properly conceived here, once again appeared to be in the order of the sacrificial with regard to denial and recovery. Metaphysics' constant demands for something "greater than here, better than now" proceeds by injecting violence into all grammatical registers, while naturalizing the power over life by imposing determinable historical claims that had been unquestionable from their highest position of authority. And so, if there has been one notable truth to the evolution of Western conceptions of the metaphysical, from Ancient Greece to the fall of liberalism, it has been the continuous allegiance toward some sacrificial model. This allegiance underwrites everything we know about politics, law, and what it means to live a meaningful life, right up to the very point of death. Moreover, taken to its logical conclusion, it would result in the global liberal will to rule and the fated ontologizing of the victim as a sacred form.

PART II

The Fall of Liberal Humanism

CHAPTER 4

A Higher State of Killing

L iberalism offered a secular reworking of the biblical idea of the Fall. Just as life was considered to be ever potentially guilty of its own (un) making, so the very idea of human progress was tied to its potential ruination. This proved to be the condition of possibility for liberal rule. Indeed, the farther humanity fell, the more liberalism was able to soar into the metaphysical stars. But the tragedy of liberalism was already scripted. If the myth of universality was the mask of mastery for the liberal will to rule over a fallible and precarious planet, so the desire of the liberal order to incorporate other powers into itself invariably met with resistance and violent encounters. What therefore became paramount was being able to justify killing for some "higher purpose" as a moral right and humanitarian claim. Thus, in the process of waging war to create a planetary peace, liberal powers fully revealed their theological inscriptions. Violence has always been the most cutting diagnostic of any political project. And it is toward conducting an autopsy on the body of liberalism to which we shall now turn our sacred attentions.

CRITIQUE OF VIOLENCE

What exactly does it mean to violently end a life? And how does this connect to a sacred claim to truth which states that the act of killing, the denying a particular life its right to exist, makes other forms of life more worthy of living? Every mass killing needs to come off as preordained—as though it was written beforehand in the stars—so that the violence might be considered part of the cosmic order of things. For any form of violence to register beyond the singular act of its occurrence, it needs to connect to a higher state of killing, to something that is greater in meaning and potential than the mere act of severing a life from existence. While this commitment to the sacrificial has remained a constant throughout Western history, like the shifting sacred objects for power, its rationale and justification have nevertheless changed over time. With the advent of liberal modernity, we would move from the mythical model for sacrifice, and its demands of allegiance in accordance with foundational claims to sovereign truth, to the more liberated, yet no less violent or ontotheologically pronounced, divine forms of articulation. These, in a promissory way, pointed toward a metaphysics of planetary becoming tasked with seeing that humanity achieves completeness.

Such a system would, however, have fateful consequences. In order to produce this vision of humanity, the very principles upon which liberalism was said to depend—universality, peace, rights, and justice—were exposed, their mythical qualities shown to be illusionary and their humanism a deception. Moreover, as liberalism would be undone by forces from within (see chapter 5), its regimes would also have to contend with the reappearance of sacrificial killing—the monstrous doubling of the sacred violence espoused by liberal powers, which, moving beyond the spectacular, put on trial and publicly executed the human in its most vulnerable and ecologically exposed state of helplessness. This would see the literal return of blood to the scene of the crime. Thus, despite liberal ideology presenting itself as a sacred way of life, as emphasized through its commitment to victims, it would end up confronting its own mimetic double. This double, hyper-humanizing the logics of slaughter, would shadow the concept of a more exalted killing and the liberal myth for humanity as violently demanded in its unifying forms.

To make sense of this, we need to return to the work of Walter Benjamin, whose writings on violence have captured the attention of many great scholars.[1] Benjamin's contributions are rich and complex in terms of their philosophical layering, which has proved to be the source of admiration and frustration alike for students of his work. His classic *Critique of Violence*,[2] for instance, forces us to question how violence has been integral to the formation of all modern political systems. What's more, as his work triangulates politics, religion, and violence to ask difficult questions regarding the theological nature of modern secularism, it situates the problematic of violence in much broader and more challenging frames. It is also undoubtedly an obscure provocation that remains open to interpretation and continues to be fiercely contested. Its principal message we can take here, however, is clear: since all violence takes us into moral relations, bringing the past into the present in fragmented ways, any critique of violence must address fundamental questions of political theology and its conceptual heritage concerning the sacred. As Benjamin writes:

> However sacred man is (or that life in him that is identically present in earthly life, death, and afterlife), there is no sacredness in his condition, in his bodily life vulnerable to injury by his fellow men. What, then, distinguishes it essentially from the life of animals and plants? And even if these were sacred, they could not be so by virtue only of being alive, of being in life. It might be well worth while to track down the origin of the dogma of the sacredness of life. Perhaps, indeed probably, it is relatively recent, the last mistaken attempt of the weakened Western tradition to seek the saint it has lost in cosmological impenetrability.[3]

Our trajectory in this search for the lost saints of modernity, as indicated in the previous chapter, will take us from the hero to the victim as the dominant object for sacred power in the world.

Let's begin here by situating the *Critique* in the time of its arrival, so to speak. Given the revolutionary spirit and personal tragedy associated with Benjamin's life, it is easy to see why his analysis is often interpreted as a way to link violence to pedagogies for the oppressed. Those confronting systems of illegitimate power have aligned themselves with key Benjaminian conceptual distinctions, in particular as a means for theorizing why people continue to resist that which they find intolerable. This literal reading wagers the revolutionary spirit of what Benjamin termed "divine violence" against the "mythical violence" of established order. While these distinctions remain worthy of our attention, it is not sufficient to simply comport Benjamin into the twenty-first century as though contemporary structures of power and logics of violence have remained consistent since his time. We are living through a different political moment. So, while there is still much to be gleaned from Benjamin's text, there is also a need to rethink and extend the narrative if it is to have any bearing on our current era, allowing us to critique more recent history.

While it can be argued that orthodox readings of Benjamin's work allow for neat explanations of violence within the spatial framework of sovereign states, armed with their "protective" mandates tied to the myth of nations and the sacredness of the hero, the global ambitions, adventures, and changing fortunes of liberal power in the past few decades demand a new angle of vision. As liberal forms of violence would increasingly take place without formal declarations of war, it would no longer be satisfactory to start our analysis with some foundational myth as defining of the political landscape (that is, the myth of nationhood) or to equate divine violence simply with the "violence of critique," as often deployed by critical advocates. Our task then is to ask what became of violence when the promissory nature of humanity was fully reconciled with the lethality of liberal freedoms, whose violence in the name of the sacred victim would cast aside any pretence for sovereign integrity, and in the process would reorient the mythical model toward a conception of humanity-in-the-making?

Returning to the specifics of the text, what Benjamin terms "mythical violence" relates to an original use of force that is necessary in the very constitution and unification of political order. The famous cover that adorns Thomas Hobbes's *Leviathan* provides the most obvious representation of this. Law is understood here as a manifestation of that mythic power, which translates the will to collectivize into a distinct and notably organic persona founded upon a certain forced ordering. It would be the figurative embodiment for the Leviathan that allows for a reimagining of the body-politic itself—the body of the political— as a living form.[4] Such symbolic violence, Benjamin showed, is contradictory, as it takes the state of nature as its point of departure, and yet forces the human to remain imprisoned within a state of "natural life." There is no alternative, as the guilt of existence is continually reaffirmed by the specter of violence law permits. And yet, it is precisely the specter of this violence, and its ability to kill while it embraces, which makes the mythical appear real, and the violent force of its law as foundational and eternal demonstrated. This is something Franz Kafka understood all too well.[5]

In contrast, "divine violence," Benjamin notes, constitutes a form of violence that is law-breaking. If the mythical sets boundaries as determinable markers of belonging—or what we might refer to as the limit conditions of the mythical bind—then divine violence boundlessly destroys. If mythical violence brings at once guilt and retribution, divine violence transgresses to bring about conditions of the new. While mythical violence therefore demands some concept of original guilt so that all must stand in obedience before the law—offering a potent rearticulation of the Christian doctrine of original sin—divine violence challenges the power of sovereign authority by virtue of the sanctity of the living: "Mythical violence is bloody power over mere life for its own sake, divine violence pure power over all life for the sake of the living. The first demands sacrifice, the second accepts it."[6] But what is the order of this acceptance? And does it now need to be rethought in light of more recent history?

Divine violence appears here as a form of violence that takes place without being sanctioned by an authority. It moves beyond any Schmittean notion of sovereign privilege, especially the sovereign's claim to hold a territorialized monopoly over what can rightfully be killed in its name. In doing so, divine violence represents a categorical denial of sovereign claims to authenticity and its brutalizing mythical hold over the idea of a political community at the moment of insurrection. As Benjamin explains, it "strikes them without warning, without threat, and also does not stop short of annihilation. But in annihilating it also expiates, and a deep connection between the lack of bloodshed and the expiatory character of this violence is unmistakable."[7] This evidently influenced Derrida's thesis on the "Force of Law." As he writes, while there is something mythical about forms of violence that can be traced back to the Apollonian Greek model, the genealogy of the divine is more in tune with anti-idolatrous Jewish scripture:

> There are two violences, two competing *Gewalten*: on the one side, decision (just, historical, political, and so on), justice beyond *droit* and the state, but without decidable knowledge [this is, the "Jewish" divine violence]; on the other, decidable knowledge and certainty in a realm that structurally remains that of the undecidable, of the mythic *droit* of the state [Greek, mythic]. On the one side [Jewish] the decision without undecidable certainty, on the other [Greek] the certainty of the undecidable without decision.[8]

Agamben in particular has provided a novel interpretation of these typologies.[9] Foregrounding the originality of the mythical as constituting the bounded realm of sovereign order, he highlighted the paradigmatic importance of the spatial figuration of the camp and its relationship to those lives that are denied all political standing. This provided the setting for rethinking divine violence as a pure form of resistance, which by definition is radically distinct from law. Importantly, for Agamben, divine violence would be the very order of the political as it revealed a "bloodless potentiality" (that is, the capacity to bring about new conditions on earth in a way that takes us beyond literal sacrifice), which is unmediated and without end: "Here appears the theme—which shines only for an instant, and yet long enough to illuminate the text in its entirety—of violence as 'pure means,' which is to say, as the figure of a paradoxical 'mediality without end': i.e., a means that, while remaining such, is considered independently of the ends it pursues."[10] This focus on the pure means would allow for a nonviolent interpretation of the divine. Thus, bloodless violence became the expression of an open-ended critique and is deemed to be pure insomuch as it operates free from structural constraints. Divine violence would put itself on the side of life against the exceptionalism of sovereign power, which could only enact violence in order to politically authenticate the true meaning of subjectivity *contra* the most violent forms of disqualification from the realms of civility. In the process, mythical violence would be exposed as the hidden foundation to political sovereignty. It would be understood as a normalizing force, whose very "order of being" waged continuous violence upon the internal order in the name of security, protection, and identity formation.

This different sacralization of the mythical referent in Agamben's interpretation has demanded a radical rethinking of law in respect to its claims over life. In particular, it is only by exposing the necessity of the divine as a pure form of critique that Benjamin allows us to bring the violence of law and order into critical question. Moreover, since the mythical in this context has always been confronted with the possibility of insurrection, due to the capacities for critique that exist in any given political system, Benjamin's framework also points more affirmatively toward the formation of alternative subjectivities whose forms-of-life are pure potentiality (*potenza*). As Agamben writes elsewhere, this formulation "defines a life—human life—in which the single ways, acts, processes of living are never simply *facts* but always and above all *possibilities of life*, always and above all power."[11] Importantly, for Agamben, this *potenza* begins in the imaginary: "I call *thought* the nexus that constitutes the forms of life in an inseparable context as a form of life . . . only if, in other words, there is thought—only then can a form of life become, in its own factness and thingness, form-of-life, in which it is never possible to isolate something like naked life."[12]

Critical thinking thus appears in this guise to be conterminous with the divine, as it constitutes a direct challenge to the possibilities of reducing life to the biological act of being—life in a naturalized form—or what Agamben (in) famously terms "bare life." Judith Butler would be in some agreement, and she followed this nonviolent reading of divine violence to develop her earlier concerns with the (dis)qualification of lives through the powers of mourning. This allowed her to conceive of an alternative "nonviolent violence" which could be "invoked and waged against the coercive force of law."[13] Highlighting Benjamin's messianic-Judaic heritage, Butler "unleashed" divine violence "against the *coercive force* of that legal framework, against the accountability that binds a subject to a specific legal system and stops that very subject from developing a critical, if not revolutionary point of view on that legal system."

Central to Butler's interpretation is the claim that a critical demand explicates forms of violence that depend on establishing the foundational nature of guilt, as identified by Benjamin's earlier provocation. The divine thus appears here as a strategic form of ethical and political intervention, which, waged over the right to critique, manifests itself as an intellectual conflict with all-too-real forms of violence, moral entrapments, and forceful unifications justified by juridical systems. Butler writes: "The desire to release life from a guilt secured through legal contract with the state—this would be a desire that gives rise to a violence against violence, one that seeks to release life from a death contract with the law, a death of the living soul by the hardening force of guilt."[14] Though also intrigued by the potential for the divine to bring about political change, Slavoj Žižek is less convinced by this nonviolent reading, demanding instead an account of the divine that engages seriously with the Benjamin's examples and remains grounded in the reality that history's revolutionary moments have been far from "bloodless."[15]

Despite their differences here in terms of conceptualizing violence (notably between the figurative or literal interpretation of the divine), each of these authors nevertheless started their analysis with the dominance of a mythical paradigm as related to the sovereignty of states. Everything, in short, begins with a mediation on preexisting sovereignty as it is connected in some fashion to debates on the sovereign ban and the violence of its exclusions. Moreover, each of these theorists also accepted that what makes the divine politically appealing is how it offers a pure means for challenging the violence of the established order and dismantling the forces of tyranny, thereby extricating itself from of the monopoly of violence in the name of the living. The mythical as such would be collectively read here as the forced embodiment of a foundational unity, whereas the divine appears to be an unmediated revolutionary potential, capable of bringing about the conditions of the new. If the mythic used its sovereign integrity for the preservation of order, the divine disrupted internal oppression and brought into critical question the various systems of ordering integral to sovereign authority and its mythical demands—hopefully without actual violence.

Here was the problem. In order to sustain these positions, the *Critique's* structural and juridical frames needed to be presented as the dominant paradigm for political power and oppression in the world. The state, in other words, along with its constituted forms of juridical power, remained the principal referent object for political analysis. Such a reductionist approach, however, was no longer satisfactory, especially in an era defined by the end of the Cold War and the emergence of a truly ambitious global liberalism. Not only would the sanctity of the modern nation-state (the principal source of authority) be undermined by forces beyond conventional territorialities, liberal regimes would begin to openly operate in the global space of flows, detaching themselves from traditional sovereign moorings and claims to geospatial integrities. Liberal violence, in fact, would be overwhelmingly driven by biopolitical concerns. This would not simply be a question of contingency in respect to the political environment and an interest in intervening to save endangered peoples. It would take us to the heart of what actually constitutes liberalism in terms of its ambitions for biopolitical control and waging global violence in the name of a sacred victim that's never foundationally determined, but always catastrophically in the making.

Liberal theorists and practitioners would often validate their actions by pointing to universal commitments and shared "values" of freedom, of upholding the rule of law, justice, and inalienable rights. And yet, even the most orthodox of theorists have appreciated how each of these terms remained deeply contested, masking the most contingent abuses of political power. Indeed, there is an alternative, and no less real, history of the liberal rise to power, which has been continually marked by violence, racial subjugation, military intervention, and the persecution of those deemed to be of a different kind.[16] Crucially, for our purposes here, if we insist that the defining characteristic of liberalism is to subject the entire world to their biopolitical rule, then there is a need to engage more critically with its historical effects at the level of power, and not abstract idealisms. From this perspective, we can define liberalism by its biopolitical imperative of "making life live," regardless of the fact that the lives being made to live are violently disqualified from life in the process.

Operating within a global imaginary of possibility and endangerment, liberalism has posited the life of the political subject as central to its strategies and ambitions. Such a reading has allowed us to acknowledge its forced compromises with the structural limitations imposed by the world of nations, while appreciating how liberal ambitions sought to create one global system that incorporated all life into its domain. Liberalism as such appeared promissory in that it was predicated upon a political system yet to be fulfilled, as well as providential in that every subject was assumed to be in need of freedom from whatever unnatural shackles kept it from revealing itself. But since the idea of making life live was never compelling enough to bring about a self-evident revolution in political consciousness—a true global liberal awakening—liberal powers had to justify their ambitions by connecting the promissory "myth of humanity" to the crisis of the human as an ontologically vulnerable, insecure, and fallible form. Without liberalism, the entire world would be plagued with widespread suffering, which would potentially have catastrophic global consequences, 9/11 being a case in point. Hence, narratives of suffering opened up global possibilities for the liberal powers, illustrating for them the value of the victim. What the crisis of the sacred in the aftermath of World War II truly came to represent was the possibility for global rule.

Foucault's biopolitical intervention thus appeared to be much more than an attempt to provide new conceptual tools for critiquing power and revealing the racial stakes.[17] It took us into the heart of the political rationalities of liberalism by foregrounding the crucial questions: what happens when power takes all life to be its object? And what then happens when the destiny of the species as a whole is hinged on the successes or failures of its own political strategies? These questions demand approaching violence outside of a sovereign/mythical frame. What's more, they force us to rethink the Benjaminian divine as being capable of describing real forms of violence (albeit with its aesthetically mediated spectacles of rivers of blood), which have taken place in more recent times. The divine is thus devoid of any need to adhere to sovereign claims of territorial integrity and promises of noninterventionism as enshrined in the Peace of Westphalia. The divine, in other words, allows us to gain a real tangible purchase on the theological nature of liberal power and its sacred forms of violence. This is a power which takes all life to be its object and acts without consideration for any authority but its own, employing violence that doesn't call upon some preexisting myth, but rather unleashes its own mythical potentiality.

HUMANITARIAN WAR AS DIVINE VIOLENCE

Benjamin argued that "a cause, however effective, becomes violent, in the precise sense of the word, only when it enters into moral relations."[18] What is always at stake when it comes to political violence are the intimate relations between morality, violence, and political theology. It is now well established that the idea of sovereignty reveals powerful theological traces akin to the mythological contours put forward by Benjamin. As Schmitt asserted, "All significant concepts of the modern theory of the state are secularised theological concepts."[19] This has led James Martel to observe that "Schmitt articulates exactly how this notion of a break itself disguises the crucial (and theological) continuities with medieval and Christian notions of sovereignty . . . In this way, modernity has a new 'political theology,' one that serves to disguise both the more traditional Christian inheritance of the modern state as well as the fact that the modern sovereign, like the Christian God, continues to decide upon the exception."[20] But if "modern politics is a chapter in the history of religion,"[21] as John Gray maintains, how should we grapple with the complexity and meaning of the term "political theology" without referring to something that is altogether beyond comprehension in any verifiable sense of the term? And how can we further link this to our concern with the sacred dimensions of liberal violence and the past few decades of global wars waged while appealing directly to humanitarian concerns?

Critically engaging with John Pocock's much celebrated book, *The Machiavellian Moment*,[22] Michael Dillon developed the concept of "factical freedom," that is, a "condition of possibility" which operates though a "radically contingent time without warrant."[23] This account of freedom, as Dillon suggests, not only makes the decisionism of sovereignty (central to theorizations of its mythical qualities, as per Schmitt) possible, it forms the basis, as Machiavelli understood, of a lethal violence by "constantly re-writing the signs of the times via a continuous calculus of necessary killing." While the question of the "sign," as it appears in time, is paramount to the sacred, such calculative violence would also, as Dillon understood, be locked into a strategic predicament devoid of any sort of clear, universal ethical coordinates.

As Dillon writes, Factical freedom as semiotic battle space is continuously required to signify how much killing is enough. But it can never resolve this strategic predicament because the very contingency of evental time upon which its freedom relies denies it the possibility of ever securely computing the strategic calculus of necessary killing which ultimately defines its moment. When asked to say how much killing is enough, whatever it replies, factical freedom is equipped to give only one answer: more. However, since "more" is never enough of a reason, in its strategic decisions of the lethality that are inseparable from modern conceptions of freedom, especially the liberal, still there is the need to draw upon something of the order of the sacred:

> If it cannot secure a strategic calculus of necessary killing, the Machiavellian moment becomes guilty of mere murder. It must therefore also deliver without being guilty of homicide; failing to establish the necessity of its killing. Its violence must therefore somehow expiate as it prevails. In want, however, of a strategic calculus of necessary killing which would do precisely that, by determining how much killing is enough, the only violence capable of meeting its requirement of "cruelty well-used" is one so great that it will prevail without application; since any and every application, in practice, is subject to the fallibility of any and every strategic calculus in force. Such violence is the messianic violence which Walter Benjamin called "divine violence."

Freedom as presented here appears as both a violent and a productive condition of possibility. And cruelty well used can become strategically virtuous if aligned with a sacred justification. This is exactly how liberal violence (as justified in the name of the freedoms of the oppressed) has operated in practice. Foucault had already explained how the liberal concept of freedom does not refer to a state of affairs where the subject is simply allowed to be free. Fearing the autonomy of their subjects, liberal powers have designated the production of particular conceptions of freedom within a broader milieu of contested and conflicting circulations. Liberal freedom, in other words, is presented as virtuous insomuch as it claims to be the most enlightened and progressive discourse for total human emancipation. Simultaneously, it is presented as strategic insomuch as its all-inclusive understanding of freedom is dependent upon the necessity of forceful interventionism to save the human condition, along with a continuous recourse to lethal calculations in everyday policing.

Like its account of freedom, however, the liberal problematic of security reveals itself to be no mere static or foundational affair. It continually proposes a humanized account of security that was globalized during the 1990s. This joined matters of (under)development, catastrophe, and everyday states of unending emergency into a consolidating nexus in order to promote forms of political governance that take direct aim at the productive life of globally endangered/endangering subjects.[24] Freedom well served thus points directly to a deeply moralized terrain of regulated circulations. It manages to reconcile, without contradiction, universally endowed moral claims to security, justice, and rights with the contingent deployment of violence, forceful social transformation, and a continuous recourse to policing in the name of life necessity. Complementing the strategic calculus of necessary killing, these violent contours of liberal rule also point to a distinctly moralized biopolitical heritage, which, as noted previously, are properly articulated in the economizing thought of Kant.

Despite their claims to endorse peaceful cohabitation, liberal regimes would be compelled to make war upon whatever threatened them.[25] The liberal account of freedom depended upon a principle of lethality, which, discursively wrapped in the humanitarian language of rights, security, and justice, inaugurated a global state of siege and warfare. It promoted freedom from unnecessary suffering, which, in the process of overseeing the lives of its political subjects, linked human potentiality to the possibility of the species' very ruination. If liberal violence had therefore produced a necessary lethal corollary in its mission to foster peace and prosperity among the species in order to eradicate unnecessary suffering from the world, it also needed to stake its righteous claims to that suffering, and to foster a belief in the necessity of violence in the name of it. The suffering needed to be presented as real, the global consequences made self-evident in order to necessitate the liberal solution. This revealed a number of important points, which ultimately proved defining.[26] In addition to relying upon technological supremacy and universal claims to truth, liberal wars would be overwhelmingly driven by a biopolitical imperative, which displaced concerns with sovereign integrities with forms of violence carried out in the name of an endangered humanity.

In this regard, having destroyed the pretense to noninterventionism enshrined in the Peace of Westphalia, liberal powers embraced the politics of endemic catastrophe, and the violence suffered by the victims of such events, which became the condition enabling the liberal will to rule. As they proceeded on the basis that all life should necessarily be included within their strategic orbit, the evisceration of any sense of "the outside" (as conceived in terms of the political imaginary) led to the blurring of all conventional demarcations between friends/enemies, citizens/soldiers, wartime/peacetime. What is more, as the biopolitical contours so central to the promotion of life became increasingly central to questions of security, broadly conceived issues of development would no longer be regarded as peripheral to the war effort. They would become a central motif as articulated in such strategic mantras as "War by Other Means" and "War for Hearts and Minds."

This would point to new forms of depoliticization, which would have less to do with Schmittean exceptionalism than they were explicable in terms of the political and social transformation of societies. It would also lead to the production of violent subjects, as the recourse to violence became sure testament to a conception of humanity realized through the wars fought in its name. Liberal violence, in other words, proved to be unbounded, unlimited, and without conventional sovereign warrant—namely revealing the fundamental principles of what Benjamin once termed "the divine" in all its transgressive permutations. Indeed, if the violence of political realism, at least in theory, appreciated the value of limits and boundaries, the lethality of liberal freedom would be defined by a commitment to war without boundaries—for an idea that was truly limitless. As Dillon and Julian Reid acutely observed:

> [L]iberal peace-making is lethal. Its violence a necessary corollary of the aporetic character of its mission to foster the peace and prosperity of the species . . . There is, then, a martial face to liberal peace. The liberal way of rule is contoured by the liberal way of war . . . Liberalism is therefore obliged to exercise a strategic calculus of necessary killing, in the course of which calculus ought to be able to say how much killing is enough . . . [However] it has no better way of saying how much killing is enough, once it starts killing to make life live, than does the geopolitical strategic calculus of necessary killing.[27]

THE BLOODLESS VIOLENCE OF THE VICTIM

In order for global liberalism to distinguish itself from liberalism of a more realist and self-contained kind, there would be a need to sever the bonds which tied it to distinct ethno-national concerns. For liberal internationalism, in fact, the very idea of "blood and soil" would be the surest impediment to its ambitions for global rule. It was the mythical foundation that drew unnecessary lines in the sand and curtailed liberal thought. While the notion of blood had always had a metaphorical appeal, the historically astute liberal could nevertheless point to the rivers of blood flowing from the battlefields of the twentieth century, which ultimately connected to the rivalry between nations and their attempts to overcome the politics of the exception. It wasn't that Schmitt was wrong in his deliberations, they held, he just needed to be vanquished! But as the blood continued to flow, in order for liberal powers to justify their actions they would need to provide evidence of the success of their methods, while still allowing themselves the room to fall back on the claim that if there was violence, then the world simply wasn't being liberal enough. This could be the vehicle to justify further interventions, as the cache of victims of history was being constantly replenished, both physically and conceptually, through the general ontologizing of insecurity as it could be applied to most (though not all) planetary life. But the liberal always feared the return to blood as a marker of identity, and as a force to mobilize internal resistance against liberal forms of intervention that asked nothing of local approval. Indeed, while the advent of a globally ambitious liberalism would result in a proliferation of victims, permitting intervention and lasting influence into the depths of all social bodies, there would be a notable absence of that element which truly defined human existence. Liberal aesthetics would in fact largely depend upon bloodless violence enacted upon the victim.

This brings us to Steven Pinker's *Better Angels of Our Nature*.[28] Blinded like John Rawls before him to any considered understanding of structural violence, while reworking the well-rehearsed liberal peace thesis, Pinker viewed the world as less warlike because of our shared liberal togetherness that had brought about global political and moral maturity. Leaving aside the evident theological undertones to Pinker's work, along with the numerous empirical flaws in his thesis, his work at least accredited its Eurocentric sources of inspiration to matters of civility: The reason so many violent institutions succumbed within so short a span of time was that the arguments that slew them belong to a coherent philosophy that emerged during the Age of Reason and the Enlightenment. The ideas of thinkers like Hobbes, Spinoza, Descartes, Locke, David Hume, Mary Astell, Kant, Beccaria, Smith, Mary Wollstonecraft, Madison, Jefferson, Hamilton and John Stuart Mill coalesced into a worldview that we can call Enlightenment humanism.[29] Pinker's entire thesis is a mammoth testimony that is blinded to the violence we know yet do not see: a violence that is all too easily concealed beneath the crudity of statistical measure, and which believes that our sacred order has somehow pushed violence to its margins. John Gray would be rightly suspicious, noting:

> Along with liberal humanists everywhere, he [Pinker] regards the core of the Enlightenment as a commitment to rationality. The fact that prominent

Enlightenment figures have favoured violence as an instrument of social trans-formation is—to put it mildly—inconvenient . . . No doubt we have become less violent in some ways. But it is easy for liberal humanists to pass over the respects in which civilization has retreated. Pinker is no exception. Just as he writes off mass killing in developing countries as evidence of backwardness without enquiring whether it might be linked in some way to peace in the developed world, he celebrates "re-civilization" . . . without much concern for those who pay the price of the re-civilizing process.[30]

Gray, evidently concerned with the promissory nature of liberal violence, viewed the religious violence of the liberal missionary intent on saving the world from itself as illustrating Nietzsche's claim that God is dead, and man has killed him, with a more devastating humanistic application and critique.[31]

It is now well documented how throughout the wars on terror liberal regimes went to considerable lengths to mediate the excesses of the violence they perpe-trated, including the wounds inflicted on their own soldiers.[32] The vulnerability of the injured soldier would in fact become a powerful motif in the further shift toward ontologizing the insecurity of the political subject, reinforcing an authentic basis for subjectivity invested in the notion of the resilience of life. However, this symbol of the wounded soldier would only fully appear after the wounds had properly healed. But the flow of blood never left the scene of the crime. It was witnessed only by those in whose name the violence was being delivered. Literal sacrificial violence started to reappear in crisis zones, matched elsewhere by a new populism which appealed directly to people's insecurity and vulnerability by calling for an ethnonationalist return to greatness based on blood and soil.

In April 2004, one particular image of a bloodless victim exemplified what the author Tom McCarthy suggested to be the "poetic truth" to the liberal way of war.[33] This image became part of the collective consciousness when CBS News published a series of photographs depicting the torture and abuse by American soldiers of prisoners at the Abu Ghraib detention facility in Iraq. What made the images all the more devastating was the fact that the prison had previously been the interrogation and torture headquarters for Saddam Hussein's regime, and the exact same violence was now taking place in the name of democracy and political liberation.[34] Many of the photographs are striking depictions of deprav-ity and dehumanization, it was the image of Abdou Hussain Saad Faleh (fig. 4.1),

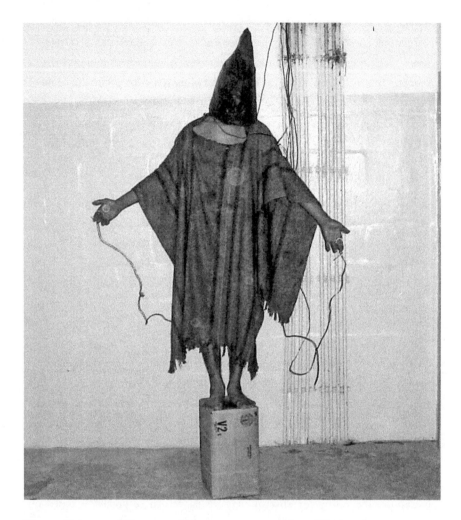

Fig. 4.1 Unknown, *Gilligan*. 2004. U.S. government copyright, public domain.

nicknamed "Gilligan" by U.S. soldiers, which has proved an iconic representation of the death of liberalism.

The victim appears standing on a wooden box, his arms outstretched in a Christ-like manner. In lieu of a cross, he is fitted with electric wires—the terror of the pain they will potentially cause him is part of the torture. Even the robe he wears, and the hood that covers his head, looks biblical, and might easily evoke memories of the Shroud of Turin. Abdou was a victim of the victim's war. There is no blood depicted in the photograph, though the violence is stark. It is consciously theatrical, and it even mocks its own sacredness. Abdou represents the writing on the wall for a political project that would be undone by its own narcissism. Precariously elevated and photographed for all the world to see, Abdou would become the icon that would reveal the divine violence inherent to liberal interventionism. This icon would undo the myths that bound the claim of sacredness to the victim, as well as the liberal pretense to having any commitment to rights, justice, and peaceful cohabitation. Soon however, the image of Abdou was replaced by that of the bloodied and sodomized body of Colonel Gaddafi, displaced by liberal powers who had washed their hands of any consequences of their retreat. The liberal powers, their hold over the region broken, were reduced to fighting wars at a distance while the broken communities they left in their wake tore apart liberalism from within.

IN THE BEGINNING . . .

The order of politics is dependent upon the creation of myth; that is central here to our critique. What matters is how some historical event is transformed into something of profound meaning through the experience of violence. Leaving aside here the well-rehearsed debates concerning ritual and myth (notably the order of their appearance),[35] we can clearly see that the sacrificial act is absolutely necessary for the consolidation and perpetuation of mythical power. We can also say with confidence that the greatest myths reach for the ultimate violence. Their sacrifice is like no other, the power they bestow unrivaled in history. Indeed, the most formidable regimes have all demanded total allegiance to their myth. For, in the absence of the myth, we will understand the horror of existence in a world in which there is no longer any mythical power to be in awe of.

The claim to ultimate violence, then, as Girard expresses with certain affection, is the regulatory function that allows the social order to peacefully continue under the shadow of its annihilations—the threat of nuclear holocaust being the most obvious contemporary example. But to give over to such a mythical state is ultimately to surrender to its power. It is to bow down in awe of its sublime presence, to compromise with its reality, to recognize the excess yet find ourselves incapable of imagining beyond. Concurrently, we must accept the idea that humans were ultimately born of violence, and we must find meaning through the mythical expressions of that violence. In this regard, we can find some agreement with Simon Critchley's distinction between myth and tragedy. As he explains:

> Tragedy is not simply mythic, as many people assume; it is the *problematization* of myth. Tragedy is born at the moment when myth starts to be seen from the viewpoint of the citizen and in relation to law and the city ... Tragedy places a distance between itself and the myths of the heroes at the centre of the drama. Tragedy arises at the point when a gap opens up between the new legal and political thought of the democratic city on the one hand, and mythic and heroic traditions of the archaic past on the other. But this gap must still be narrow enough for the conflict to be a painful one. We may no longer believe in our myths, but we have to pay a price for not believing in them. The tragic hero is not a reality in which we are somehow meant to believe.[36]

Let us now turn to the third verse of Genesis from the King James Bible, which concerns creation and time. "In the Beginning," it explains, "the earth was without form, and void; and darkness was upon the face of the deep." Leaving aside the void for the moment, what concerns us here is the actual phrase "in the Beginning." This is crucial to the mythical narrative, for it suggests the listener is already included, already within the scene. Should it have been written differently–for instance, "at the beginning"–we could demand more empirical verification on this point of origin and the exact moment of its occurrence. But we know that, in order for a myth to be (re)established, it depends upon a certain unintelligibility. The sacred needs to retain something of the mystery–the mythical excess, which demands allegiance precisely because it is greater than any individual soul.

This creates an important schism between the mythical and the ancestral. Our contention here is that all politics is a fiction and dependent upon their own myths and fables. But that doesn't necessarily mean that the fiction needs to constantly fall back upon the sacred. This is not just a question of one's place in the contemporary order of things. It is all about time; the mythical forces us to surrender to its conception of time. Time is dictated. What defines the ancestral, however, is a different notion of temporality and its untimeliness. Integral to the logic of hierarchicalization, the grammars of the mythical come down from on high, whereas the grammars of the ghosts of the ancestral speak across time. And while the ancestral speaks to tragedy, it nevertheless seeks to find reasons to believe in human progress and to break away from the violence which have defined the ages of humanity. None of this is divorced from alternative conceptions of the political. We might think here, for example, of the indigenous peoples of Latin America and the writings of "Subcomandante Marcos," who deploy fables to create a distinct worldview, and which giving priority to difference also work to an entirely different temporality (see chapter 8).

Time is never static. And if we therefore find meaning in the search for origins, it might also mean there is purpose in searching for what was lost once the sacred imagination killed ancestral differences. Why do we continue to teach that the history of the human condition is a history of violence? Is it in order to affirm the need for the sacred and to stress the importance of the sacrificial to that history? Despite his messianism, which ultimately doubles down on the ambivalence of the sacred, Agamben still presents a way to conceive of a poetic counter in *The Fire and the Tale*. Concerned with origins and where we have arrived today, he sees in literature an attempt to recover "a memory of the loss of fire."[37] The symbolic importance of fire should not evade us here, nor its importance to human survival since the very dawn of man. This allows for a rethinking of the idea of the mystical that requires the storyteller to "throw oneself wholeheartedly into the obscurity" so that they might learn "how to discern at the end of this oblivion the fragments of black light that come from the lost mystery."

This is synonymous with throwing oneself back into the void and the darkness of nonexistence. "The writer proceeds," Agamben writes, "in darkness and dimness, on a path suspended between infernal and celestial gods, between oblivion and remembrance."[38] But what form does such a poetic remembrance take? Still influenced by the conceptual work of Benjamin, Agamben turns to the vortex as "the image of the origin."[39] We have already made the case for seeing the void as a vortex—dynamic and in flux, far from empty, static, or meaningless. Agamben would agree with our take, noting that "in the course of our life, the vortex of the origin remains present until the end and silently accompanies our existence at every moment."[40] In fact, it is the very presence of the "black sun" that can appear or disappear at any given moment, like life itself, which marks out the poets of history: "There are beings that desire only to be sucked into the vortex of the origin. Others rather maintain with it a reticent and cautious relation, endeavouring as far as possible not to be swallowed up by the maelstrom. Finally, others again, more fearful or unaware, have not even dared to cast a glance at it." While remaining wary of painting the poets here in a heroic light (see chapter 8), we can further add to this assay by accounting for those who have been thrown into the void—not by choice, but as victims of the violence that has traversed time—those who have involuntarily been swept up by the winds of change and who have since the beginning been thrown into a catastrophically fated existence. As such, this image of the vortex allows us to more accurately imagine and make sense of the movements of the void. It is an account of origins, which, as Benjamin noted in *The Origin of German Tragic Drama*,[41] tells the story of an intense transformation, in which past elements underwent a complex metamorphosis. Deep in the heart of this maelstrom, there lies the question of what it means to disappear. Here we might recall the words from Benjamin's final posthumously published essay "On the Concept of History," in which he returns to Klee's *Angelus Novus*:[42]

His face is turned toward the past. Where we perceive a chain of events, he sees one single catastrophe which keeps piling wreckage upon wreckage and hurls it in front of his feet. The angel would like to stay, awaken the dead, and make whole what has been smashed. But a storm is blowing from Paradise; it has got caught in his wings with such violence that the angel can no longer close them. The storm irresistibly propels him into the future to which his back his turned, while the pile of debris before him grows skyward. The storm is what we call progress.[43]

CHAPTER 5

The Death of the Victim

DEAD IN THE WATERS

On Wednesday, September 2, 2015, the body of a young and helpless refugee washed up on the shores of the Mediterranean. His name was Alyan Kurdi—a three-year child, whose family was fleeing the conflict and violence tearing apart the place he once called home. The devastating image of his body on the sand went viral across social media and also appeared in mainstream publications in western Europe. The caption "Flotsam of Humanity" accompanied the painful photograph of this singular child lying face down at the water's edge. Alyan soon became a potent symbol around which various humanitarian claims coalesced, shining a light on the unnecessary suffering endured by all those who suffered a similar fate. In death, Alyan seemed to speak, to the sacrificial weight of recent history. And yet, the unbearable lightness of his body also pointed to a definitive moment in the history of the victim, in that the over-representation of the victim in liberal tropes had led to its rapid exhaustion as a sacred form. The failure of the image was now apparent in its inability to mobilize with any credible force political change. This has consequently required us to fundamentally rethink the meaning behind humanity, or whether it is being defeated by the resurrection of the old mythical gods?

The image of Alyan's body, facedown and lifeless on the beach, offered another way of seeing the intolerable as its temporality disrupted our aesthetic perceptions by revealing the raw realities of human suffering. It captured a truly intolerable moment, depicting something too difficult to bear yet impossible to ignore. But what would have happened to Alyan's body had this image, like so many others, eluded public attention? What if it hadn't captured the attention of editors at that particular moment in time? What if Alyan's body, like so many others, had been lost at sea instead of washed up on the shore? What if another story had grabbed our attention? The death of this innocent child would have registered as simply another statistic in the ongoing tally of nameless and face-less victims. Could we then use the term sacrifice to describe the violence of Alyan's death if there was no deliberate human action attributed to causing it? What is more, what became of his body when the mythical claim that "all life is sacred" was exposed as a deception? While the photograph of Alyan's body undoubtedly sparked more somber political reflections in terms of the crisis, in the end it had little impact on policy or on the willingness of liberal societies to act on their professed global code of ethics beyond satisfying their immediate material concerns.

But global liberalism, as we have suggested, was already largely defeated and in retreat; open borders have never been on their agenda. And there was another fundamental question which needed to be addressed when coming to terms with the aesthetics of suffering at work here: why did the image of this particular boy, out of all the others, have such an immediate emotional effect? It certainly seemed to break new ground in terms of the media's approach to representations of victims. As Hugh Pinney, Vice President at Getty Images, noted: "The reason we're talking about this photograph is not because it's been taken or not because it's been circulated but because it's been published by mainstream media."[1] He added, "The reason we're talking about it after it's been published is because it breaks a social taboo that has been in place in the press for decades: a picture of a dead child is one of the golden rules of what you never published." Pinney's com-ments invoke memories of Nick Ut's image of Kim Phuc, although in this case the violence of water replaces the violence of fire.

But the media event surrounding Alyan's death could not be explained by sim-ply pointing to some shared empathy, as if the pictures, which exposed us to the horrifying realities of this particular tragedy, perfectly resonated with the sensibilities of both media platforms and the public alike. No other image had attained such universal renown. Just a few days prior, for example, the artist Khaled Barakeh published images of dead Syrian and Palestinian refugee chil-dren whose boat had sunk off the coast of Libya, in a mournful and devastating series titled *Multicultural Graveyard*. His images quickly spread across the internet and social media, but Facebook and other social media platforms censored them, claiming they contravened rules on the publishing of "graphic content."

So, what was it about the image of Alyan that took us over the tipping point? Was this a case where an image of a victim was truly iconic and impossible to ignore? Did it genuinely expose the limits of censorship and the mediation of aesthetic regimes of suffering? Or was there something more at work connected to the sacred order of politics? If this indeed was the case, had it resonated and been tolerated precisely because it could be explained within the sacred discourses that liberalism had consecrated? As Peter Bouckaert, a director at the nongovernmental organization Human Rights Watch, reflected, "What struck me the most were his little sneakers, certainly lovingly put on by his parents that morning as they dressed him for their dangerous journey. . . . Staring at the image, I couldn't help imagining that it was one of my own sons lying there drowned on the beach." He further added, "This is a child that looks a lot like a European child . . . The week before, dozens of African kids washed up on the beaches of Libya and were photographed and it didn't have the same impact. There is some ethnocentrism [in the] reaction to this image, certainly."[2]

Such relationality is often seen as an explanation for empathy. It is also worth suggesting that Alyan's image resonated so powerfully because it focused on a single subject. The other eleven who died when the boat capsized don't feature in the frame. So how are we to make sense of this? In a particularly insightful commentary, Nicholas Mirzoeff directs our attention to the preferred mainstream media image depicting the young child cradled in the arms of a Turkish policeman. Why this composition was so impactful, Mirzoeff suggests, might be explained in terms of Christian iconography: "We can open our eyes to this photograph because it reminds us of images we know well. Such iconic images carry the power of the sacred. The posture of the policeman, Sergeant Metmet Ciplak, who carries Aylan's body, unconsciously echoes one of the key icons of Western art. Known as the Pietà, meaning "pity," this frequently explored motif depicts the Virgin Mary holding the body of Jesus, after he was taken down from the Cross."[3] And yet, despite this evident appeal to the sacred qualities of this violent image, it is important to recognize that the figure of the victim was already losing its hold. As Mirzoeff would explain, "A few months later, however, Britain voted to leave the European Union, largely because of intense resentment of all immigrants, including refugees. Here, then, is the dilemma. Certain images have the capacity to break through the defenses of our optical unconscious, but precisely because that unconscious is a way of dealing with the intense violence of modern life, it seals over quickly."[4]

The question being illustrated here was whether humanity as a concept had any meaning whatsoever in the twenty-first century. As Ian Jack observed, "News editors thought to moderate our distress by omitting an earlier picture in the sequence that shows the dead child lying face down on the sand with his head in the sea . . . Among national newspapers, only the Guardian and the Independent published this image unaltered. The websites of the Mirror, the Express and the Mail used versions that pixelated the body or (in the Daily Star's case) obscured the head. The Telegraph and the Financial Times made the same decision as the BBC and omitted the image from their selection."[5] For Jack, this is explainable, as it suits a "finer idea of humanity," for the alternative "represents the less comfortable proposition that death reduces even the liveliest child to a heap of flesh and bone."

Alongside the image of Alyan, there emerged a number of complementary aesthetic themes, which were no less theological in their composition and narrative. Take, for example, the image of Antonis Deligiorgis, a Greek army sergeant who in April 2015 was captured saving a twenty-four-year-old Eritrean refugee, Wegasi Nebiat. This particular image went viral and featured on the front pages of many news outlets, including the *New York Times*. The topless Deligiorgis, photographed in the process of rescuing some twenty refugees (who have since often been omitted from the media spotlight), was subsequently awarded the Cross of Excellency. And yet, the photograph itself exemplified a particular racial and gendered narrative. It spoke directly to an idealized militaristic heroism, and, as many commentaries observed, both of the figures in the heroic scene are young and beautiful.

This return to the trope of the military hero is somewhat revealing of the political tides. Following the publication of the Deligiorgis photograph, *Time* magazine in turn put out a special edition on the refugee crisis, accompanied by the headline "Exodus" to draw an explicit parallel with the book of the Bible.[6] Biblical stories are bound up with tales of humans fleeing persecution, and are often used by political regimes, leaders, and campaigners to galvanize support for particular causes. Take, for example, Martin Luther King Jr.'s "I've Been to the Mountaintop" speech, which he delivered in Memphis, Tennessee, on April 3, 1968, just the day before his death. By alluding to the book of Exodus, he connected the story of Moses to the civil rights struggle in the United States. However, given the failure of images of suffering to ever have truly global effects in terms of immediate transformations, it is worth highlighting Laruelle's poignant words:

The victim's overrepresentation is the forgetting of its origin, its necessity, and its contingency. Like any term that sees its media moment arrive, the victim passes through a stage of expansion and then of nausea, of ascendance, and of decline. By the time we grasp it, it is already perhaps too late; it is theoretically dubious, eroded by the media and buoyed by the securitarian and juridical rise of crime. As though it were miming and fabricating an artificial unconscious, media corruption has made the victim a new ethical value, a point of condensation and effervescence, of the exacerbation of ideological conflicts.[7]

Somewhat predictably, the sacred did find some form of reentry into the popular consciousness, as Alyan's body was appropriated by numerous politicians and spokespersons to further calls for the mobilization of war in Syria. (Never mind that it was decades of Western policies destabilizing the Middle East that culminated in this singular and now iconic image appearing before us in the first place.) But something had changed in the order of politics. As Alyan's body washed up on European shores, the very idea of global liberal rule was entering a period of lasting crisis. With liberal powers ethically and strategically defeated, they no longer had the political will to engage with borderland populations for the sake of ideological conversion. And they certainly didn't have the political appetite to transform the cartographies of power, which, confronted by the global refugee crisis, favored the building of walls and deepening divisions.

Alyan's death coincided with the death of understanding the victim as an unquestionable sacred object, and it was this shift which showed how it was incapable of mobilizing a true political awakening. In fact, the use of images of innocent children, predictably accompanied by an image of Picasso's *Guernica*, now prove to have very little hold on populations who are both exhausted by the reality of suffering and by their inability to change it in any way. But how did we arrive at this point? And what does this mean for the ethical need to bear witness to the pain of others in order to account for the failures of liberal humanism?

LIBERALISM: THE FINAL CHAPTER

It is now possible to present a brutally honest reading of the history of the liberal encounter by diagnosing its violence. From its inception, liberalism was integral to the onset of the global slave trade, while its mission to spread civilization tied to a more enlightened vision of colonization,[8] thereby introducing the very problem of race as a political category. However, liberalism has gone through a number of effective revivals, which, in the process of reconstructing its own past through the violence of organized forgetting (most often covered by the cloak of idealism),[9] successfully bound itself to universal claims of human rights, peace, and justice. Undoubtedly, World War II was a watershed moment in this history, as liberal regimes positioned themselves as the victors in defeating ideological fascism, often erasing in the process the brutal sacrifices made by communism to achieve the same ends.[10] We cannot underestimate the importance of the Holocaust here in allowing for a recasting of a sacred universality in the face of a particularly traumatic and no less inexplicable event.

As Geoffrey Hartman wrote, "The scholars most deeply involved often admit an 'excess' that remains dark and frightful."[11] In order for humankind to get some sort of redemption from the Holocaust, we must learn to understand it as a progressive narrative, whose underlying trauma could become the catalyst for a new moral universalism whose dramatic sensitivities mean it is *timeless*. The Holocaust would become a sacred wound that would never heal, existing beyond time and place. It would thus force us to confront a tragedy whose depths could never be truly explained, and yet whose tragic memory shadows all history that follows. This is not to question the horrors of the violence, or their unique qualities. It is, however, to recognize how the Holocaust became a liberal condition of sacred possibility in the years that followed. But this would take some time. As Jeffrey Alexander reminds us, on this attempt to turn the Holocaust into a universal symbol:

> This separateness of sacred evil demanded that the trauma be renamed, for the concept of "mass murder" and even the notion of "genocide" now appeared unacceptably to normalise the trauma, to place it to close in proximity to the banal and mundane. In contrast, despite the fact that the word holocaust did not have a formally established English meaning. . . . It no longer performed this sign function in everyday speech. Rather the term entered into ordinary English usage in the early 1960's . . . This new linguistic identity allowed the mass killings of the Jews to become what might be called a bridge metaphor: it provided the symbolic extension so necessary if the trauma of the Jewish people were to become the trauma for all humankind.[12]

As black rain fell over Japanese skies (see chapter 7), burning down through the atmosphere from a fiery Promethean cloud, so the Cold War began, and the first great phase of liberal revivalism in the twentieth century would take hold. While there were a few misguided interventions during this period, liberal regimes largely contracted out their violence to various proxy actors. Their aim was to control popular uprisings in their former overseas colonies at an effective distance, allowing them to serve as testing grounds for upholding "democratic principles."

But it would take the fall of the Berlin Wall to provide liberalism with the unmediated possibility to reenter the global South. Proceeding on the basis that "underdeveloped was dangerous,"[13] they would make moral claims to justify political interventions in developing regions by means of various coercive instruments, from the denial of aid and the slow starvation of recalcitrant populations to their outright obliteration by military force. We can bookend this final chapter in the liberal will to rule planetary life with the crossing of the Mogadishu line in Somalia in 1992,[14] which made explicit their willingness to go to war in order to save strangers and secure their vision of peace. This chapter—what we might call liberalism's "Twenty-Year War"—ended with the violent assault on Libya in 2011,[15]a decade after the fateful 9/11 attacks in New York. During these two decades, liberal powers went from a tacit declaration of a global state of war to a veritable retreat from the world. But as the refugee crises engulfing Europe showed (notably stemming from the repercussions of liberal wars in Iraq and Libya), the populations displaced by liberal wars would no longer accept containment, as they reasserted their long-denied political right to flee.

One of the claims liberals maintained throughout this period was their ability to free the world from conflict. This would result in some rather peculiar intellectual revivalism, from the ideas of Immanuel Kant on the virtues of a perpetual peace (notably disassociated from his racial anthropological concerns and profound religiosity) to the resurrection of the just war theory with its all too theological ascriptions concerning the righteousness of its means and the unquestionable faith in its ends. Some still argued this had been its principal success story, for despite our continued exposure to violent events, we, that is the "liberal we" it was indulgently claimed, had never lived in more secure and less violent times.[16]

With war largely banished to the margins of the liberal purview, liberalism, it was argued, paved the way for peace and prosperity. Their proof for this was that deaths were fewer in number, depending on which Pinker equation was presented. These tallies, however, were always ethically compromised. The more liberalism proclaimed planetary peace, the more it perpetuated war abroad while masking structural violence within its own regimes. And the more liberalism played out this global state of war, the more it publicized its own state of vulnerability, both externally and internally, and the risk that that weakness could be appropriated and accelerated by its political nemeses.

Such has been the lived nightmare for the last remnants of liberal subjectivity today. With all its achievements and material gains being rapidly undone by new forms of political regression, we are seemingly taken back to the dangerously myopic landscape of twentieth-century politics. The world is in thrall of the worst excesses of populist nationalism, where racial prejudice and division are reset as if the tolerance predicate were cast aside, and where the demands for sacrifice in the name of some telluric project bound to geo-strategic divisions can rise again from the ashes to reign supreme. But we cannot turn back time so easily.[17] Nor can we neatly explain the breakup of the liberal world order as a retreat into a space of neat sovereign divisions. What needs explaining is the changing nature of violence in and through the crisis of liberalism, where the multiplicity of crises of its own making proved to be the surest condition of possibility for its intervention and eventual undoing.

What is being played out in the world today has little to do with people's sovereign rights than with a realignment of global power, wherein the global North is moving away from looking to claim the world in favor of preserving what is already in its possession. In this context, it is the once-entitled classes of wealth accumulators and middle-class advocates who are left to tear themselves apart, unsure about their futures, both plagued by the realization that the world is shrinking and becoming increasingly uninhabitable. This is matched by resentment from its own internal, impoverished white colonies, which offer a sobering reminder that the "underclass" never really went away due to the neglect and material forms of discrimination inherent to the liberal order.

During its Twenty-Year War, liberal regimes openly waged war on populations in the global South. Armed with their humanitarian vocation of doing what was necessary to spread their brand of democracy, the violence enacted by liberal powers was transgressive to the sovereign order of things—at least according to the Peace of Westphalia (which was never a truism). Biopolitically authored, the very nature of liberal war went from a mere Cold War ambition to the surest evidence of humanitarianism in practice through the willingness to fight to save the lives and establish the rights of distant peoples. However, the problem with this reasoning was that such people were never distant as far as colonial memory was concerned, and neither were they passive agents acquiescing to the imposition of freedom through violence in their names. Humanitarian warfare would in fact backfire in multiple ways, resulting in terror attacks on the streets of metropolitan capitals, the emergence of more fundamentalist groups far more brutal in their willingness to employ sacrifice and public attacks, as well as the forced displacement of millions of civilians caught up in the conflict, which would physically and philosophically overwhelm the borders (imagined and real) of continental Europe, turning the Mediterranean into a modern-day killing field for victims who had committed no crimes.[18]

This is not to say there were no tensions within liberal ideology. In the final decade of this war, there emerged two distinct yet overlapping schools of thought with regards to how warfare should be carried out. The first was premised on the supreme logic of liberal technology, assuming that high-tech sophistry and digital advancement could replace the need for human casualties (at least on the part of interventionist forces).[19] The idea here was that violence could be carried out at a distance by soldiers working in the post-industrial shadowlands.

The second school of thought was premised upon a more humanitarian ethos, which demanded local knowledge and engagement with dangerous populations. For a brief period in the 1990s, for example, the UN attempted to use the humanitarian plight of war-affected populations to foster peace between state and non-state aggressors by utilizing local mediators who had cultural expertise.[20] The violence of the global war on terror would put this secondary vision into lasting crisis as the violence of liberal encounters fatefully exposed the double standard behind any universal commitment to rights and justice. Not only did liberal regimes appear to be the principal authors of violence in the borderlands of the world, thereby challenging the notion that underdevelopment or poverty was the true cause of planetary endangerment, populations within liberal consumer societies themselves would become increasingly critical of the war efforts, regardless of the moral sentiments that were allegedly fueling them.

The wars would in fact lead liberal societies nearly to economic and moral ruin. Indeed, post-Iraq, if there has been one notable casualty of the wars on terror, it has been precisely the belief we might engage and transform the world and its peoples for the better. The reluctance to put any ground forces into combat in Libya and Syria was indicative of this. Metaphysical hubris had been displaced by phased withdrawal from international intervention as liberalism came to terms with the failure of its ideology and the limits of its territorial will to rule. What would take its place would be an unrivaled technocratic vision for the world (see chapter 6).

With Libya at the mercy of the new mercenaries who profited from its ruin and devastation, the nature of liberal warfare would increasingly become distanced from the public imaginary. As the vocabulary of the New Wars became subsumed within narratives of insurgency, popular uprising, and criminality,[21] the global war on terror would discursively evaporate into the political ether, devoid of political currency and yet normalized to its veritable occlusion. Iraq and Afghanistan would reemerge in the public consciousness on their respective anniversaries to remind us that the violence was, in the end, simply unending. And the vexed political legacy of Guantanamo Bay would now be handed over to the lawyers, who in a world beyond Netflix, captured very little public interest except for the purpose of academic study. At the same time, conscript armies had given way to professional soldiers of fortune,[22] which arguably resulted in the decline of recorded battlefield deaths.

The very location of war had disappeared into the background; this disappearing act rendered landscapes unreadable, as if all meaning and certainty had now collapsed into the complexity void. As a result, domestic constituencies in the global North no longer fully understood the nature of the warfare being conducted, much less could they question with any authority the legitimacy, objectives, or legality of the violent acts carried out in their names. Indeed, it seemed the more information that was leaked about the events taking place in the atmospheric shadows—the more it was instantaneously broadcasted to mobile devices—the more populations became desensitized to witnessing the atrocities being broadcast before our eyes and digitally inserted into the palms of our hands.

Physically separated from a world it could no longer understand or control with any political and ethical surety, liberal regimes increasingly compensated for their distance by carrying out targeted assassination, surveillance, and containment through digital means. Just as liberal agents in the dangerous borderland areas increasingly found themselves operating from the safety of fortified protectorates[23] (which in hindsight revealed their great separation from the world), this was matched—albeit in ways that initially seemed disconnected—by new forms of violence and orchestration that also took place at a distance.[24]

The political and philosophical significance of this should not be underestimated. The strategic confluence between the remote management of populations and new modes of violence-at-a-distance proved to be indicative of the narcissism of a liberal project that exemplified the worst excesses of technological determinism and its full abandonment of any serious claim to humanism. How could you ever possibly claim to be humanist if the prevailing mantra proceeds from the assumption that humans are fallible and can no longer be trusted? However, instead of looking with confidence toward a postliberal society in which we commit ourselves to transforming the living conditions of the world of peoples, we find ourselves facing an intellectually barren landscape, which offers us no alternative other than to live out our catastrophically fated existence with ever greater speed and intensities.

Instead, we are seeing new forms of fascism beginning to raise their heads as populist demagogues pave their rise to power by pitting the lower classes and the impoverished of their own nations against vulnerable immigrants and refugees. This should be instructive regarding how we envisage the end of liberal times as marked out and defined by this incommensurable sense of planetary siege. It also demands new thinking about the human subject and what it means to live affirmatively beyond the catastrophism of liberal rule (see chapter 9).

Populations in more prosperous metropolitan districts have not been exempt from this drama, from the imminent collapse of this sacred order of things. Citizens and professionals have been expected to demonstrate their innocence by living openly before the electronic gaze. To be digitally connected has meant having access to the only rights that seemingly matter—the smart rights of digital passage born of technological advantage and the right to exercise one's consumer spending privileges. Disconnection, on the other hand, would be considered pathologically inexplicable, a form of political and social nihilism and self-harm. Hence, while violence can be continually repackaged for Western media consumption, we have reached the point where the line between the civic and the militaristic has been so blurred that the interconnected subject would be one who actively embraced a technological mindset that privatized everything—violence included. The call to violence but a "like click" away from the composition of a digitalized frame that would be less about contents than the immediacy and potency of affective registers which defy more considered deliberation. Drone violence would be particularly diagnostic here, also revealing of a shift in the liberal worldview that increasingly took place in the atmospheric shadows.

Drone technologies were not simply a new tool of warfare that allowed for strategic reassessment. They would prove to be paradigmatic to late liberal rule. They also further radicalised the very idea of the territorial frontline to the extent that any Schmittean notion of inside/outside became an arcane remnant of an outdated past. By definition, there was no existential enemy to be vanquished, as the outside had all but vanished. There were no fixed lines to be drawn in the sand, no sovereign integrities to claim and protect. Geopolitics would be firmly displaced by complex and dynamic atmospheric geographies whose forms of hostility we have yet to fully comprehend. Drone violence would therefore usher in a post-territorial phase in the liberal wars. While masquerading as a form of civilised advancement that confirmed the oft-touted modernist mantra that technological supremacy automatically bestowed ethical providence, the liberal powers proceeded with their warmongering on the basis that everybody and everything was a source of perpetual endangerment. Thus, it was only a matter of time before they called their drones into action over metropolitan skies. Such is the nature of the colonial boomerang. And human presence only made things worse. Displacing the primacy of human agency from the act of killing represented more than the realization of the military's dream of zero casualties. PSTD, after all, remained an affliction, even for those who enacted violence from a safe distance. What the use of drone strikes actually revealed was the lack of confidence permeating the entire liberal system—they saw their own military as just as fragile and untrustworthy as anyone else. Helping heroes was then to become a broken-hearted cry to help the vulnerable, helping the victims who were once the heroic images of ground strength and territorial ambition. All soldiers required forms of training that authenticated ontological vulnerabilities, thereby paving the way for a truly post-human sensibility wherein the task of policing the global borderlands could no longer be left to the fallibility of human agents.

THE MONSTROUS SHADOW

But we know that real history is not so easily bracketed and shelved. Sacred violence often spawns children who are able to continue the sacrificial rites in a radical inversion of Goya's Saturn; the violence of the liberal wars would unleash harrowing repercussions which still plague the earth today. If the bloodless victim became symbolic of the liberal way of war, its monstrous shadow would return in the form of literal human sacrifice and the macabre spectacle of livestreamed public beheadings. As James Vernini wrote about the momentous battle for Mosul in 2017, "The realest thing in this phone world may have been the execution videos, uploaded and shared not just by jihadist and civilians, but soldiers too—they were as prurient as everyone else watching this war."[25]

Such displays of violence have been termed "intolerable" insomuch as they have exposed the limits of liberal tolerance in terms of acceptable versus unacceptable forms of violence.[26] They have also foregrounded the victim as a hyper-humanized subject whose very identity—the aid worker, the homosexual, the media reporter—would be publicly destroyed, their right to exist eradicated. This amounts to what Adriana Cavarero terms "ontological crime," as it strikes precisely at the uniqueness of the self: "The severed head centres attention and condenses the meanings of the symbol . . . it alludes to a violence that, tearing furiously at the body, works not only to take away a life but to undo its figural unity, to wound and dismember it . . . concentrating itself at the most expressive point of its own flesh, exposes itself intensely."[27] It is important to stress here that the act of decapitation has not in any way been unique to orthodox religions or, for that matter, to fundamentalist branches of political Islam. We might just as well talk about the role beheading played in bringing about the Enlightenment and the strategic use of the guillotine as the effective democratization of violence in the name of such ideas. We might also point to the more recent history of colonization and the use of such symbolic violence in Algeria, the Congo, Vietnam, and elsewhere in order to communicate the terror of bodily dismemberment.

Also striking was how the language of the New Wars of the 1990s and the liberal response that followed would make a direct appeal to Greek mythology. This would be most apparent in the resurrection of both the goddess Athena, whose wisdom was considered integral to any strategic victory, as well as Medusa, who would often be deployed as a metaphor for understanding the nature of the new threats confronting the world. The more you cut into the head of the Gorgon, so the networked theory explained, the more snakes would appear to further the terror. This understanding would be embraced by the RAND Corporation, notably its lead thinkers John Arquilla and David Ronfeldt, who sought to approach the order of sacrifice in a new way:

Athena is the only member of the Pantheon typically depicted with both sword and shield, symbols of her capabilities for both offense and defense. She could be wrathful, but unlike Ares, she took no pleasure in war and preferred to see conflicts settled peacefully, according to laws and with a sense of mercy. She was careful about bearing arms in times of peace, but when needed, she had ready access to Zeus's aegis (a unique, impenetrable body shielding) and to his devastating thunderbolt. While the owl and the olive tree were her chief symbols, she also attached to her hand-held shield the frightening head of the Gorgon Medusa, whose live gaze could turn a viewer to stone. Athena had previously instructed man in the art of confronting such terrors as the Gorgon, showing Perseus how to decapitate Medusa by using his shield as a mirror so that he could approach and combat her without making direct eye contact.[28]

But the threat of Medusa would return, not from Perseus, who enacted Zeus command and whose shield might have protected us, but from the radicalized victims of the liberal wars. Their displays of bloodletting against such diverse backgrounds ranging from deserts to metropolitan cultural centers embodied Girard's theory on the monstrous double appearing from the shadows with renewed force: "In such cases, in its perfection and paroxism mimesis becomes a chain reaction of vengeance, in which human beings are constrained to the monstrous repetition of homicide. Vengeance turns them into *doubles*."[29] Laws are transgressed not to emphasize difference or even to break free from the sacred nature of politics, but instead to reveal what is logically consistent between both protagonist and antagonist in the order of sacrificial crisis. Violence once again becomes the lifeblood for surrogate victimhood. Beheading and other ghastly spectacles of public sacrifice penetrate the myth and tear open a wound at the heart of the metaphysical desire for world modeling and the structure of transcendental pain. As Vernini writes about his witnessing the burning of Mosul:

> Looking onto this hellish cityscape, Bosch's *Last Judgement* with its fiery twilight tortures, came to mind. Then the mind leapt to the images that had led to this war, the art of this surpassingly artistic enemy, its own scenes of torture so minutely and stylishly documented and instantaneously broadcast to the world, videos much worse than viral, of firing squads and beheadings and dismemberments and forced drownings and burnings-alive, of sex slaves,

of triumphant city-taking columns, black banners fluttering across the landscape, images that outraged the world almost as much as they titillated and petrified it.[30]

The severed head has always carried a symbolic meaning in the Western political imaginary. It is, as Julia Kristeva has written in a remarkable short book on the subject, the "terror that confronts us with that revolting abjection," which nevertheless reveals the crisis of the times.[31] As she further explains, it is not surprising to see beheadings appear in the midst of schisms and discord . . . Dante had already expressed this when he placed his decapitation victims in the ninth bolgia in the eighth circle of hell. "Who could describe, even in words set free/of metric and rhyme a thousand times retold,/ the blood and wounds that were now shown to me[32]." To understand the aesthetics at work here, we might return to the beginning of the humanist tradition to recognize how the symbolic motif of beheading would be foundational to its images of the human world and its suffering.

One of the most compelling classical painters who dealt with this method of sacrifice was Michelangelo Merisi da Caravaggio, whose Baroque style remains the source of great admiration. Caravaggio is important for a number of reasons. While a significant number of his masterpieces deal directly with sacrificial violence, it is the artist's assumed role as witness in his works that stands out in terms of his specific ethical contribution, enabling him to transcend the violence and upheaval of his times. As Catherine Puglish writes, in "representing himself repeatedly as a witness," Caravaggio may have "wished to affirm the artist's responsibility to bear witness to the past."[33] Puglish is particularly drawn to the *Betrayal of Christ*, in which Caravaggio paints himself holding a lantern as if to illuminate the role of the witness. The artist's proclivity for inserting himself into his own paintings takes a number of different and compelling forms throughout his work, from signing his name (the only known one of his career) in the blood of St. John (compare to *Beheading of St John the Baptist*), as if to acknowledge that the artist was there at the scene of the crime, to his self-portrait as the severed head of Goliath, held aloft by a contemplative and remorseful David (compare to *David and Goliath*), thereby placing the artist himself in the position of the decapitated victim.

On each of these occasions, important questions are raised concerning the political function of art and how to witness it we must confront sacrificial forms of violence. It is, however, Caravaggio's *The Head of Medusa* that is arguably the most compelling of all. Having been turned into a monstrous form by the vengeful goddess Athena, Medusa's fate at the hands of Perseus (literally translated as "he who cuts") is well documented. However, rather than focusing on the terror of Medusa, Caravaggio undertakes a masterful double movement in his painting, which suggests he is trying to recover her human qualities. Caravaggio redirects her violent gaze (which famously turns people to stone) so that Medusa seems to be looking away from the viewer, and her appearance takes on a different and less vengeful meaning. Caravaggio not only creates another masterly self-portrait, as he appears in the form of Medusa's decapitated head, he also consciously disarms her violence, as the severed gaze looks downward so we can still witness her savagely brutalized form. As Mieke Bal writes, "What could possible frighten her who cannot see the frightened snakes on her head? . . . Medusa looks away in order to get you to look away with her, to escape the myth that binds her into an evasion from that frightening role."[34]

This image of an ancient legend is mirrored by the contemporary photograph of the last moments of Michael Haines, a British aid worker captured by ISIS, whose helplessness and terror was evident as he was about to suffer the same fate as others before him.[35] In one well-publicized image, Haines is depicted in a kneeling position, his eyes closed as if he is resigned to his fate. The intimate touch of the killer's hand on his shoulder creates a chilling effect, as it illustrates that the violence is not an act of spontaneous rage, but a controlled, reasoned, and calculated act that has been well rehearsed. We cannot even begin to imagine the terror he felt and what must have been going through Haines's mind at this particular moment. Empathy is fully denied to us, as the idea that we might be able to somehow relate to this extreme condition is impossible to comprehend.

And yet it might be this simplest of gestures—Haines closing his eyes—that spoke more loudly than anything else in the image. Might it not serve to remind us that, when faced with the opportunity to acknowledge the horror of such a spectacle, many of us naturally look away, rather than force ourselves to recognize that what these victims suffered was truly abhorrent? That our presence only amplifies the intolerability of an unbearable situation too painful to witness? The concept of the intolerable has been used as a way to draw attention to the ways in which groups such as ISIS have mimicked the nihilistic logic of the times by utilizing intolerable imagery to draw attention on an international scale, to devastating political effect.[36] Indeed, the violence of the twentieth century has

normalized forms of dehumanization to bring about the slaughter of millions in
the name of sacred space. As such, the foregrounding of "the human" as a sacrificial category in the globally disseminated performance of beheading has forced
us to reflect more purposefully on the relationship between intolerability, the
performance of killing, the ethicality of sacrifice, and the burden we all inherit as
forced witnesses to such horrors inflicted on victims by victims.

Oscar Wilde's *Salome* can be read here as a provocation for rethinking this
type of sacrificial violence.[37] A human tragedy that forces us to confront the inevitability of killing, this bloody tale of King Herod's stepdaughter is loaded with
symbolic, political, and philosophical resonance. Retelling the story of Jokanaan
(John the Baptist) who refuses the advances of Salome, the performance brings
together the sensual with the savage, the desiring with the destructive, and the
arousing with the violently anticipative, resulting in a sacrifice gifted with brutalizing relevance. Of course, it is all too easy to read the narrative of Salome as
being a mediation and critique of violent extremes. The audience enters, knowing the tale in advance, gazing upon the enchanting seductiveness of Salome as
she performs her Dance of the Seven Veils, only to recoil in horror as the play
climaxes with the most fatal of kisses delivered bestowed upon the severed head,
which concentrates our attentions in the most intimate ways.

Salome begins with the question of desire and its relationship to power and
revenge. It connects the anticipative with the logic of excitement, the arousal
of its foreboding, wherein bodies, their movements and masochistic behaviors,
render human contact problematic. It certainly provokes memories of Bataille's
more tearful Eros. But beyond its eroticism and decadent aesthetic, might we
not ask more searching questions about this performance, specifically disrupting
conventional notions concerning the human desire for violence-to-come? What
does the anticipative tell us about the human condition and its sacred demands?
Who actually desires the promise of sacred violence, and who demands its deliv-
erance? Might we turn the question of symbolic violence around to ask more critically of its witnessing and our continued fascination with the sacrificial? If the
desire to exercise power over a life is borne of a certain physical arousal, can we
better differentiate between the logics of excitement, especially how it feels its
way into existence in a manner that appears prophetic of a violently predestined
future? What does inserting the spectacle of excitement into scenes of fantasy
tell us about humanity's approach to the infliction of violence? How does the
fantasy connect with the mythical and its metaphysical claims for togetherness

and human belonging? How might we interrogate such inflictions as a mediation onto forms of (dis)empowerment and what it means to be complicit or critical to its enactment? And if the future is always anticipative, how might we steer it in a different, non-sacred direction?

A RETURN TO THE MYTHICAL STATE?

It is tempting to view the subsequent arrival of new populist leaders, for whom the term "fascist" seems particularly apt, as being a quintessential example of what Zygmunt Bauman explored in his final work, *Retrotopia*.[38] In their attempts to, leverage a population's nostalgia for a rose-tinted past, populist leaders would exploit a nation's retrospective imagination, which considered the present, in all too biblical ways, as fallen into some ruinous state. Rallying against the very idea of globalization and misguided foreign adventures, these leaders appealed to a collective yearning to return to the grand ideas of the past—a time when the world was neatly divided and identities were neatly categorized by means of protective walls and enclosures.

Critics, however, would be equally retrotopic. For many, such nostalgia represented a regression to a time when the world was truly dangerous, especially for the most entitled and educated metropolitan subjects who were part of the enlightened liberal intelligentsia. And so, once again, we would encounter many shadowy figures we thought had been consigned to history: Schmitt, Hobbes, Oedipus, and other mythical entities who now appealed in landscapes where risk, complexity, uncertainty, and vulnerability had once reigned supreme. Girard was right when he pointed out how the desire to reclaim some notion of a lost paradise would be essential to the consecration of myths, which could in turn sanction the most brutal forms of violence for the sake of reclamation. Benjamin was also astute in developing the idea of mythical violence and inserting its logic into the heart of the modern nation-state, which exercised its own myth-making in order to command allegiance and justify the violent sacrifice of millions in its name.

However, the new fascism of today is not about some return to the past, even if it invokes the past to create a certain mythical imaginary regarding belonging in the present. Nor is it about reclamation, even if the calls for material enrichment point to better days. It is about accelerating the forces of history, pushing them to the point of exhaustion, running with the pure materiality of a nihilism that destroys in order to contain, seeking to preserve a world that's shrinking on every possible register, its problems in such close proximity they become impossible to handle. This tendency would reveal further disturbing developments with the onset of the global COVID-19 pandemic (see chapter 6).

This invariably brings us to the more recent rise of democratic authoritarianism driven by the alt-right and its neofascist supporters, which have openly rejoiced in the fall of liberalism. From the United States to Brazil, its leaders would mobilize the spectacle and the language of hatred. But these movements did more in terms of their pedagogical acumen. By appealing to a bygone sense of greatness, not only did they make a claim upon the politics of time, romanticizing the past for the purpose of steering history in a particular direction, they would also mobilize ontological vulnerability to devastating effect. Positioning themselves as embodying the resistive force against a world of inevitable catastrophe and crisis was not simply about securitarian speak. It served as an ontological and epistemological move, a counter to the perceived death of the white Promethean man, offering the ability for followers to be secure about themselves and their place in the world.

It's perhaps no coincidence that the advent of such leaders would also result in a resurgence in criticism of theorists such as Foucault. The shift toward a state of post-truth would be neatly conflated with a certain post-enlightenment collective disposition, devoid of the virtues of reason, rationality, and calm deliberation.[39] The betrayed liberal needed someone to intellectually blame for the demise of their ideology, and this search for a scapegoat would later be pushed onto other living philosophers, notably Giorgio Agamben (see chapter 6). We shall leave aside the nonsensical notion that Foucault, among others, disavowed all notions of truth (though clearly what had previously perturbed many liberals were their concerns with the brutalizing violence of the enlightenment and its deeply racialized images of thought). What became apparent were the ways orthodox liberal thinkers also recognized the rise of the alt-right as offering the possibility for marking their own authentic positions. Forgetting even the recent history of liberal wars, they retreated into a sort of liberal puritanicalism. Once again, the world appeared for them in neat sovereign territories and clear dialectical markers of political (in)distinction.

Like an unwitting student of history, leaders of the alt-right had also mastered the art of distraction by inducing what Marxists would no doubt sum up as "false consciousness." Their false consciousness was consciously dialectical. The nature of the faux retreat demanded it. Calling for the revival of an era of greatness—times that for the vast majority were anything but great—was illusionary in this regard. Leaders of the alt-right would consciously invoke the term "fake" to create a consciousness of suspicion around all traditional sovereign markers (the state, the media, political elites—liberal or otherwise) which had once been familiar, comforting, and secure in their monopolies over knowledge production.

This is where these new fascistic movements were different. The apparatus of the state was both a friend and an enemy. It was duplicitous. It was to be trusted and distrusted, resisted and supported. It was to be drained and yet its walls built higher. Such a contrarian campaign was made possible only through a mastery of the most advanced digital and social media platforms, which functioned beyond the purview of the state. Platforms, we might add, that would show how even the most authoritarian of leaders was ultimately expendable when the time came. And all the while the power of the free-market economy would be unmediated, its forces accelerated and given power over every single aspect of human existence. This was never about sovereignty. It was about training the masses to desire their own containment and separation from one another. These were conditions, we might argue, that were fully in alignment with the demands of global capitalism and the end of a particular phase of liberal globalization, which had already produced so many landscapes of disposability and now demanded total control over the mobility and containment of life. But the sacred object here still remained unclear—or at least it would until an invisible planetary killer of a non-human kind brought clarity to the postliberal setting.

THE EXHAUSTED FACE OF THE VICTIM

Liberalism withstood the violent attacks on September 11, 2001, despite the collective trauma and sudden sense of vulnerability they caused. Liberalism also dealt with the violence and internal conflicts which raged for many decades in parts of the global South. And when communities of racial minorities were caught in the catastrophic crossfires of a world tearing itself apart, such as the humanitarian disaster in New Orleans in the wake of Hurricane Katrina, liberal powers could still draw upon the necessary architectures of containment and militarized policing to stanch the flood of human misery. In fact, such violence and catastrophe proved time and again to be essential to liberalism's globalist ambitions, and each crisis provided a renewed moral mandate to accelerate the liberal interventionist aims to incorporate all planetary life.

What liberalism couldn't abide and contain, however, was the recalcitrance of its own domestic white colonies which felt socially abandoned and politically neglected. It was with these populations that the limits of liberal tolerance would be truly exposed and its duplicitous ontological claims on the vulnerability of the human subject revealed. Another of the great liberal fabulations concerned the triumph of capitalism over Soviet-style communism. This was presented as an external victory, brought about as an oppressed people inspired by the enlightenment of liberal democracy and the free market. But Communism was never defeated by the external forces of liberalism. It imploded due to the desires of a people who were starved of creativity and imagination, as life under the Soviet Union was reduced to the level of a pure economic variable, its citizens deprived of all the things that made them human. Communism wasn't overthrown by the forces of liberal peace; it was cast aside by a human revolution, which quite literally took a hammer to materiality.

Like all great empires, the collapse of liberalism wasn't ultimately brought about by some external force. The death of liberalism would be brought about through revealing the illusion of its myths, the fragility of its claims, the contingency of its eternal glory, and the exhaustion of its modes of subjectification. While the myth of universality would be fatally wounded during its military adventures, which in the name of peace and security sanctioned war and torture, the final blows landed when its interconnected myths of democracy and entitlement were debunked, consequently exposing the inherent violence and prejudices of liberalism.

Liberal societies always had a suspect relationship with any viable notion of democracy. They have shown an active willingness to destabilize and overthrow any regime—especially ones which were popularly elected—that had the temerity to offer illiberal alternatives. From socialism in Latin America through the 1960s and 1970s to the more recent elections in the occupied territories and Egypt, liberal powers always had a reason to claim the victory was misguided and of dubious legitimacy. The problem, however, was that such denial of the electoral process would unravel as underprivileged white communities voiced their resentment and anger through the ballot. The liberal subject would then look on in a state of disbelief, unable to accept the collapse of their entitlement model. It simply couldn't be right that the liberals in the United Kingdom could be stripped of their European citizenship because of the selfishness of the underclasses who had nothing to lose if the world went up in flames. And what injustice! Wasn't it time the United States had a female president, regardless of the fact that she would be part of a family dynasty, had openly called for war against the indigenous of Mexico, and would embody the perpetuation of the liberal war machine?

The word "entitlement" would gain popular international currency in the 1980s with Amartya Sen's pioneering study into the ravages of conflict and famine.[40] It immediately resonated with liberals and could easily be worked into their understanding of multicultural tolerance. It also provided a meaningful replacement of the concept of "class," which liberals have never liked to consider in depth. Entitlement never meant equality, but rather that an individual deserved the wealth they were able to amass, so long as the bare necessities for survival were covered for everyone else and the individual subject with all its normative reasoning reigned supreme. Some could quite rightly be more entitled than others to material possessions on account of their cultural acumen, appreciation of the rules and codes of the liberal game, and correct pedagogical practices. These signifiers marked out in marketized ways the progressive from the regressive, the metropolitan from the borderland. But Brexit took a hammer to liberal entitlements, which were of very little benefit to disenfranchised working-class communities throughout the United Kingdom. Similarly, the defeat suffered by Hillary Clinton was surely everything to do with her sense of entitlement, to assume her privileged position, which was rightfully hers after so many years of dealing with a misogynistic husband, patriarchal oppression, and other forms of discrimination faced by the already materially entitled, but still entitled to more and more as a given right.

By exercising their right to vote, underdeveloped communities in the United Kingdom and United States revealed most fully the illusion of liberal democracy, which viewed any alternative model of government as unjust and fraudulent. The figure of the impostor would appear here as a form of liberal Judas, the untrustworthy person who shouldn't even be on the stage of this worldly theater. It is the syndrome which has always plagued the working class. But the most important and revealing predicate here would be the question of tolerance. Liberalism had always accepted difference, provided it could be absorbed, domesticated, and governed. Difference in itself would be intolerable, especially if its claims to autonomy challenged the liberal will to rule. But the idea of tolerance, which went to the heart of liberal multiculturalism, was never about creating a reciprocal ethical understanding and solidarity amongst the world of people. Tolerance was a limit condition by which difference was inclusively segregated, with cultured rules and social practices, but stripping back the surface of politeness would reveal pervasive violence and exclusions.

And yet, while liberalism was able to tolerate racial differences by continually drawing upon the colonial memory of taming the savages of the world, the limits of that tolerance would be fully exposed when the liberal subject stared into the broken mirror and looked upon a cracked vision of whiteness. For what was being exposed in this doubling of white psychosis was the true nature of liberalism, like a retelling of "The Emperor's New Clothes," but on this occasion it was the people who were naked. This liberalism was all about its own material enrichment, and sought refuge in commodification. Its only salvation was ultimately to be found in the divine power of the market economy, which promised to rid the world of all its deadly sins.

The figure of the victim would again be central to this drama, even as those who believed in the system the most would be indiscriminately and publicly swallowed up and spat out. In the post-9/11 setting, the entitled liberal subject was already under attack from forces it could no longer contain. They would thus embark upon a last desperate attempt at holding onto the liberal ideal in the deluded hope that to bounce back from personal tragedy would at least result in a return to some entitled landscape, with their material benefits reinstated or compensated for by insurance premiums. The outcome of this attempt at resilience was the proliferation of anxiety syndromes resulting from the liberal subject's dependence on private insurance premiums and self-help guides. However, in order for this doctrine to be sustained in a future that was catastrophically scripted, there was a need to ontologize vulnerability. Everybody could potentially be a victim, just as everybody could potentially be a source of endangerment. This flattening of victimhood would again come up against the resentment of broken white communities in liberal nations. It was unacceptable that the underprivileged white male subject could present himself as a victim of history, let alone exercise political agency in a way that, according to conventional democratic mandates, must be respected.

This is precisely where new forms of fascism would appear with such ferocity and dizzying speed. Repackaging these concerns in light of the new order of insecurity, new fascist demagogues would be able to stoke greater divisions and author new forms of violence and exclusion. As further evidenced with the Capitol Hill attacks of January 2021, the advent of white terror proved to be very real, very dangerous, and its fascistic face increasingly normalized as part of the mainstream. New fascism would feed off of white resentment and prove successful in appealing directly to intolerance. It also harnessed the crises of subjectivity and fully exposed the poverty of the liberal political imagination, while continuing to accelerate all divisions to devastating political and social effect. While the truly vulnerable of the world were pitted against neglected white communities, more explicit and openly prejudiced forms of violence and discrimination were being constantly affirmed in the violent space vacated by liberalism. With the new fascists having mobilized ontological vulnerability, they repeated the promise to make those who had never had any entitlement—who had never felt part of the liberal bourgeois project—feel great again.

It would be a grave mistake, however, to see this as a return to twentieth-century ideological fascism. Fascism has always been a mutable beast, capable of transforming and recreating the conditions of oppression without the need for ideological moorings. It has been painful to watch the last remaining liberals trying to fall back without any safety nets on an age of liberal purity, deploying their own retrotopic idealism of an entitled world—the liberal paradise—which was guided by the invisible hand of peace, truth, and justice. We are instead in dire need of a more honest and sobering reflection on the death of liberalism, its sacrificial violence, its duplicity, its tolerance thresholds, and its abandonment of the underprivileged. And this needed to be matched by the continued need to fight fascism in all its forms, its sacrificial violence, its duplicity, its tolerance thresholds, and its abandonment of the underprivileged. This is more urgent than ever in our lockdown age.

HUMANITY IN THE WILDERNESS

There is an evident danger here of associating the death of liberalism with the death of humanity. While the former has effectively monopolized the latter term, and deployed it to justify violence in the name of sacred victims, it is open to us to rethink what humanity might mean in a postliberal world. Indeed, despite the failures of liberalism, the world still faces a considerable ethical challenge, which makes a discussion on the future of our shared human existence both urgent and necessary—especially in light of the global coronavirus pandemic. The overdetermination of the victim, the advent of white rage in broken internal colonies in metropolitan homelands, along with the orchestrated lock-down of the planet, have stripped away any effective capacity to mobilize in a collective and ethically considered way. Rather, we are led to further fragmentation and division, and we still suffer from the daily realities of oppression and violence in a world which is now geopolitically full and yet overwhelmed on all registers. Before dealing with the pandemic, which we might see as the first crisis of the postliberal world, we should return to a problem that in many ways the pandemic brought into focus— that of unregulated global circulation as witnessed in the global refugee crisis that came shortly after the liberal wars. The figure of the refugee is particularly instructive here, notably in terms of the failure of humanism and the death of the victim, in accelerating those logics which demand a separation and surveillance of life on account of the dangers posed by its planetary movements.

By the later part of the 1990s, there were no unclaimed territories left on the planet, and so expansion was a matter of merely changing the guard and redrawing the borderlines. Meanwhile, those who had been cast out and lacked any claim to citizenship were being driven to the ends of the earth. To exist in such a fugitive state, literally stateless, was a nomadism of a truly terrifying kind. Looking upon these precarious and disposable lives, one might think back to Deleuze's insistence that oppression was less about the denial of rights than the restriction of movement.

Indeed, as the refugee fled from unbearable conditions, seeking refuge from their obliterated life-world systems, so Arendt's notion of "worldlessness" returned with renewed poignancy for these globally disenfranchised. As Bauman observed, in such a world, those people who are forced to flee intolerable conditions are not considered to be "bearers of rights," even those supposedly considered inalienable to humanity. Forced to depend for their survival on the people on whose doors they knock, refugees are in a way thrown outside the realm of "humanity," as far as it is meant to confer the rights they aren't afforded. And there are millions upon millions of such people inhabiting our shared planet.[41] So, what could be learned when the only destinations left were the desolate, uninhabitable spaces that nobody wanted to claim? And what terms could we draw upon to make sense of those conditions? In the history of theological reckoning, the name given to this unforgiving space was "the wilderness."

If the history of the sacred is all about questioning the altars it produces, there is also a need, as Dante maintained, to account for the eco-theological scenes of its sacrifices and the spaces where its myth was brought into question. The young Oedipus managed to survive being left for dead in the wilderness. This would result in a sacrificial doubling, not only of son and father, but also between the desert and the city—both of which have their distinct yet reinforcing logics of violence and desolation. Another reworked narrative is that of the original biblical sacrifice, the story of Cain and Abel, where the former was forced to become a wanderer with his descendants inheriting the city of men, built upon bloodstained soil. Cain's treachery against his brother would require further sacrifice for humanity's atonement. Indeed, there are numerous tales from the monotheistic traditions, from Moses to Christ to Muhammad, which look upon the wilderness as symbolizing the surest test of faith in the most punishing crucibles of doubt. The Renaissance would immortalize these earthly ascriptions through the words of Dante: "At one point midway on our path in life, I came around and found myself now searching through a dark wood, the right way blurred and lost. How hard it is to say what that wood was, a wilderness, savage, brute, harsh and wild."

It is now well established that one of the defining hallmarks of modernity has been the attempt to domesticate the wilderness, for that was the dwelling place of the most savage elements of our own political animality.[42] What separated humankind as a species was our mastery of our environment and our ability to tame its more uncivilized lifeforms. This included the ecological. And yet the wilderness, the call of the wild and its bestial states, always threatened to return at any given moment. Max Ernst masterfully captured this drama in his surrealist paintings, from his scene of *Napoleon in the Wilderness* to the harrowing depictions of the violence of World War II as presented in the unsettling *The Eye of Silence* and the ecologically disfigured landscapes of *Europe After the Rain II*.

Where Christ's faith was tested and ultimately strengthened by his overcoming temptation in the wilderness, modernity—like Christianity itself—was never able to wrap itself fully in the triumphant cloak made from its mythical claims. The sacrifice was never quite enough. The cult of the hero was undone by the unforgiving jungles of Vietnam and the inhospitable desert terrains of Afghanistan and Iraq, landscapes which still remain scarred by the sacred memory of those who tried to uphold the nation. But if there was any particular setting which truly tested the liberal conception of humanity and its sacred claims, it would be the seas, which had become the backdrop for so much misery.

While the modern political imagination was colonized by its material foundationalism, invariably giving rise to grounded imaginations, there was also a rich history to the phenomenology of bodies of water. The Roman Empire, for instance, always understood the political importance of water as an element. This was witnessed through their identification and imperial reworking of earlier Greek deities, which were invoked in order to emphasize their relevance to social order, human mobilization, and population control. The oceans in particular had a special meaning and were essential to Rome's vision of the world, as can be seen in the Punic Wars and the importance of naval warfare. Whereas if we return to Hobbes's *Leviathan* (the leviathan itself was a biblical sea monster), the motif of the waters represents the sovereign king, who also embodies the body politic. And we owe it to Schmitt for showing how the embodiment of space and the eventual cartographical and phenomenological separation of the oceans from the land were pivotal in the development of those key ordering principles that have come to define worldly affairs.[43] Indeed, just as we may write a violent history of the earth, applying biological terms such as dissection with equal force to populated spaces, so too do global bodies of water tell their own stories of violence and oppression. However, whereas suffering often leaves permanent scars on geographical landscapes which are integral to the memory of loss, tragedy, separation, and ruin, the sea, like the desert, retains its terrifying capacity for making individuals and entire populations disappear.

Contemporary stories about human suffering on the open ocean resurrect the wretched ghosts of the transatlantic slave trade, a mass commodification of human life which resulted in the genocide of millions of Africans. Far from standing in opposition to the slave trade, as many liberal revisionists like to claim, early humanism, in fact, marched hand in hand with it;[44] the ocean is a veritable graveyard of human disposability and denial. Its victims thus speak to the untraceable histories of those who were violently uprooted from their homes, whether as slaves or as contemporary migrants putting themselves in a perilous situation because it was better than what they were leaving behind.

The ocean points to a spatial genealogy of violence, though tracing the heritage and origins of its victims is far more difficult. We need to keep hold of the idea that space—including ocean space—is always embodied as far as politics is concerned. Geographical demarcations would be completely insignificant were they not underwritten by political and philosophical claims of habitus. It is life that bestows particular meaning upon the otherwise empty signifiers of spatial integrities and habitual residency. Space in this regard has always been occupied and overlaid with meanings and attributes, which point directly to assumptions made about its inhabitants. But such meanings are never static, just as the ground itself upon which they are inscribed is always in the process of ecological and subjective transformation.

Oceans and deserts would become the final frontiers in a world which was assumed to be full.[45] There was no longer any outside to run to. This demanded a logical inversion of spatial politics—not in ways that would continue to prioritize geographical demarcations, thereby concealing preexisting biopolitical assumptions about the human condition, but rather in ways that would look at the body itself as providing critical insight into these violent geographies, which had long since abandoned centuries of topographical awareness. Such inversion required a foregrounding of the life of the subject in ways that could be attendant to those forces, which overwhelmed the logics of containment. Or as Herman Melville would write, "It is not down on any map; true places never are."

The refocus on these violent geographies added new drama and insight to the logics of space purposefully theorized by Gilles Deleuze and Félix Guattari.[46] Drawing upon a range of sources, they explained how the history of the modern human condition was marked by the tension between nomadic and sedentary ways of living, which invoked particular understandings of space in terms of its smooth versus striated qualities. Modernity, they argued, represented a mammoth exercise in the mass sedentarization of populations for the purpose of productive needs and appropriations. We might again recall Schmitt's influential analysis in the *Nomos of the Earth*, which showed how the ordering principles for world incorporation were originally conceived by attempts to map the world's oceans. In fact, if Dominic Lorsurdo was right, what made the inception of liberalism possible was its involvement in the slave trade, which financed its global ambitions and provided the necessary routes for exporting its "enlightened" claims.[47] Hence, we went, quite literally, full circle. And perhaps then it was no coincidence that the body of Osama bin Laden was dropped into the ocean instead of being laid to rest in an unmarked grave, which used to be the burial style for monsters.

Liberalism never abandoned containment and division. In fact, it made these tactics all the more biopolitically entrenched, policing them in the most sophisticated ways. For some time, it has been common to write of "Fortress Europe,"[48] which might be seen as a subsidiary to a broader "Wall Around the West." Liberal powers had routinely contained populations by appealing to the logics of underdevelopment in order to better manage the life-chance divide separating the global North and South. Such divides were never geographically fixed, but rather were determined on a subjective basis which could vary from person to person, depending on who was requesting passage. Borders in this regard were always embodied and biopolitically authored. While there was a broader genealogy to consider that went back to the Palestinian crisis of 1947, it was important to situate more contemporary mass displacements in that global liberal context.

Nobody understood the plight of refugees better than Bauman. As he has explained, what defined the refugee was a "frozen transience," where the preferred bureaucratic method of processing refugees by placing them in camps meant they were "catapulted into a nowhere."[49] Such enclosures should not however simply be interrogated on the basis of both security and human-rights violations. They demand an ethical critique, which, appreciative of the history of the violence common among the camps, looks directly into the way they distance inhabitants from the larger population, reducing them to a problem population stripped of agency. As Bauman further reminds us:

> Contemporary menaces, and particularly the most horrifying among them, are as a rule distantly located, concealed and surreptitious, seldom close enough to be directly witnessed and very rarely accessible to individual scrutiny—for all practical purposes invisible. Most of us would never have learned of their existence were it not thanks to the panics inspired and boosted by the mass media and their alarming prognoses composed by experts and swiftly picked up, endorsed and reinforced by cabinet members and trade companies—hurrying as they do to turn all that excitement into political and commercial profit.[50]

The planetary refugee reveals the crisis of containment, which once provided for a managed or durable form of disorder at the heart of global liberal power. This is the case whether we recognize the desire to flee war-torn situations instead of waiting for some international response, which in the end sought a local solution in order to maintain the integrity of borders, or to acknowledge those who resisted the policies of encampment which was evidently deployed by many who understood the meaning of these spatial confines. That many preferred to make the treacherous journey across the Mediterranean, instead of seeking refuge in the camps of a neighboring Middle Eastern state, speaks volumes in this regard. As the poet Warsan Shire writes in her devastating poem "Home," "No one would put their children in a boat unless the sea is safer than the land."

Indeed, while some policy makers and theorists wrote of these conditions in terms of economic opportunism, as narratives from mainland Europe showed, refugees were fully aware of the political function of the camp, and how its humanitarian ascriptions were illusionary. Containment therefore went into crisis mode, as the camps were being overwhelmed physically, politically, and ethically by those whose humanitarian appeals were no longer being recognized. In the radically interconnected world of liberal power, defined and shaped by imaginary global threats, the camps were already subsumed within broader logics of power.[51] This added further depth to Peter Sloterdijk's idea of living in a world interior.[52] And yet, there was always something that managed to over-spill even the most violently policed containments. As Brian Massumi forcefully stated:

> The complexity of the interlocking systems we live in, on the social, cultural, economic and natural levels, is now felt in all its complexity, because we're reaching certain tipping points, for example, in relation to climate change and refugee flows. There is a sense that we're in a far from equilibrium situation where each of the systems we have depended upon for stability is perpetually on the verge of tipping over into crises, with the danger that there will be a sort of cascade of effects . . . And there's no vantage point from which to understand it from the outside. We're immersed in it.[53]

This notion of immersion into the all-consuming forces of history also brings us directly to the climate crisis. Human life has always been affected and its politics transformed by the environment. Or to put it another way, from Aeschylus's *Oresteia* onward, the environment has always been of metaphorical and phenomenological significance to the political order of things.[54] However, avoiding the reductionist tendency to directly correlate climate change with the causes of war and violence in underdeveloped regions, such that once again a self-validating moral imperative serves to demonize illiberal ways of living, following Sloterdijk, it can be seen as more meaningful to understand the conscious manipulation of climatic conditions within a military diagram for power.[55]

In this regard, it wasn't that climate change led to social and political collapse. A more astute understanding assesses how climate change, brought about by forms of environmental militarism, allows for the bypassing of racially coded determinism while still segregating and killing vulnerable populations. Such theorizations concerning ecologically determined violence are after all seldom applied to the way peoples in metropolitan areas might respond to changes in their environment. Thus understood, the environment hasn't simply related to biospherical conditions; it is *bios*-spherical, pointing to an always and already politicized notion of active living space, necessary to the sustenance of life and whose catastrophes are the result of a failure of the political and ethical imagination to frame itself in planetary terms. This was a logic set well before the coronavirus appeared.

Bauman's claim that the refugee was to become one of the defining political problems of the twenty-first century was partly convincing. What he didn't fully appreciate perhaps was how the problems they embodied would be accelerated and inverted for the sake of controlling all life on the planet. The global refugee has overwhelmed the physical, political, and ethical registers in ways that are still demanding a rethink on the relationship between humans and the world. How could humanism have any meaning if it so openly managed to "inclusively abandon" so many to such a terrifying fate? This would become all the more pressing with the realization that changing environmental and health conditions—whether understood through the immediate catastrophe of hard militarism and the pandemic or the slower catastrophe of environmental degradation—would in all likelihood result in further population displacements.

To reiterate, it is not being suggested that changes in local environmental conditions necessarily produce the conditions that give rise to wars and violence. Such violence is more likely to be borne of the response, including the containment of those who have every right to flee from devastation, and through the denial of the most basic of human freedoms—namely the right to live with dignity and in the hope their families can find more peaceful habitation. If humanity cannot deal with this, then "humanity" means nothing at all.

Part of the challenge here is to rethink this problem in more affirmative ways. Much has already been made of the distinction between the migrant and the refugee in terms of their political framing and significance. The migrant is not seen as problematic, for we are all, ultimately, the result of human migrations. The designated term "refugee," however, has proved divisive, as it presupposes a "refuge," that is, a form of protection. Etymologically, it is also supplemented by the "refusal" as a political act of denial by those who may ultimately become complicit in the oppression. The word "refusal" also draws us to the tensions presented by the word "refuse," which oscillated between negation—that is, to refuse somebody something—and the production of something worthless that can be thrown away—as in refuse as trash or rubbish. Despite its more overt political connotations, over the past two decades international organizations and governments have actively used the term "refugee" as the favored nomenclature when containing populations in sites that soon became permanent residences in the way that Bauman called "permanent temporality."[56] Refugees, in short, were a problem to be solved, not people in need, to be welcomed and shown hospitality on account of their shared humanity. More important were the ethics informing the discursive labeling of victims, whom we preferred to keep at a safe distance.

Let us conclude here by returning to the image of Alyan and how it compared to another devastating photograph, more recent but with clear similarities. The picture of the El Salvadorian migrants Óscar Alberto Martínez Ramírez and his young daughter Valeria, drowned in the Rio Grande in June 2019, immediately invoked comparisons with the image of Alyan.[57] Both could be seen lying face down in the water which had claimed their lives. And, strikingly, both were wearing red clothing, as if to emphasize how the bloodless nature of their deaths still found its way to haunt us. There continue to be striking comparisons between the conditions faced by refugees fleeing to Europe across the ocean and those experienced by migrants crossing into the violent space at the border between Mexico and the United States. Both populations are casualties of the changing cartographies of global liberal power, which continues to build walls around the West while presenting the violence endured by some vulnerable peoples as an outright political assault, while other incidents of migration are considered a personal family choice—often motivated by economic reasons—completely devoid of the history of colonization, the subtle everyday realities of racial politics, and the continued appropriations of resources and displacements of peoples.

The violence endured by those who entered this uninhabitable wilderness was all too apparent. Those who perished on the journey were still denied any considered and sustained attention as to their political significance—other than to further militarize and weaponize the borders. What remained were the faintest traces of existence, often a torn piece of garment or discarded children's soft toy, which removed the body of the victims and their life stories from the scene of the crime. The disposability with which the victims' lives were treated was most apparent, in both wildernesses, in that they were buried in unmarked mass graves, which hearkens back to the most brutal of totalitarian regimes. It is worth stressing that more people would die illegally crossing the southwestern border of the United States in the last decade and half than were killed in the 9/11 terrorist attacks and Hurricane Katrina combined.[58]

But what was truly devastating about the image of Óscar and Valeria was the tenderness shown in their last moments, with Valeria holding onto her father's shoulder for dear life, unbearable in its intimacy. There was no notable iconography here, just two bodies intertwined, face-down and abandoned to the unforgiving waters. And yet, what was the most evident narrative was unconditional love; this was a love without sacrifice, defiant in the face of a violence which should have stopped everything in its tracks. A love that asked nothing sacrificial in return, until the very end. There was no higher purpose at work, despite the evident intensity and depths of that love. Such love was not of any hierarchical order—it completely resisted any imposition of command.

Of course, we have become resigned to the fact that images like this do not have the impact they should on the collective political consciousness. And we know that, despite our moving into a postliberal world, more bodies will appear, and whatever claim is made upon their status as victims, the once-liberal attempt to turn them into sacred objects has been completely undone. Those lives, those bodies, were human—all too human—and that should have been more than enough. So if there was something to remember, it was that love could outlive the sacrificial, if we could only find the philosophical courage to imagine it freed from its violent embrace. This might just allow us to recover the concept of humanity, which, finding itself lost in the wilderness, could only end up returning by falling back upon the sacred terrain.

CHAPTER 6

A Sickness of Reason

SICKNESS OUT THERE

There was a sickness out there. And it struck us down with silence. Even when people were in close proximity, their voices were noticeably quieter. It was like the world had become a solemn cathedral in which we collectively mourned, where we all whispered and seemingly had greater respect for, yet also greater fear of, the very air we breathed. That's perhaps what Dante didn't fully appreciate. Purgatory was not always full of howling screams; it could also be deadly silent. And yet, many noted how the beauty remained. Nature had never looked so majestic, its sounds so delicate, its innocence more pronounced. It felt like the animal world had found a new freedom, which forced us to take note in our humbled and vulnerable state. We were all thrown into a humanitarian crisis, borderland conditions of anxiety now thriving within every single metropolis, while the ecological conditions of life managed to replenish themselves. But there was a sickness out there, that much couldn't be denied. And the lockdown only added to the silence, the alienation, the remoteness. Maybe the sickness was already within us, coursing through our systems. And yet we continued, haunted by the other pandemics we had chosen to ignore, plagued by our own inhumanity and failure to take seriously the biospherical conditions that constituted planetary life.

What we would come to appreciate more fully was how humanity had been sacrificed at the altar of its own failed realization. As the COVID-19 pandemic spread across the world, there was a glimmer of hope that something called humanity might just emerge from the shadows of isolation. That dream ended quickly, as the eruption of racial violence provided a stark reminder that liberalism had never resolved the problem of race that was its own creation. As early narratives of war that appeared at the start of the outbreak ensured that the sacrificial was already being discursively reset, the true accelerationists and technocratic visionaries were already prepared to take advantage of the emerging postliberal disorder. The governing logics were already in the making and the technologies for control already in production. Tracking and surveillance systems were developed by a technological army, faceless and nameless, with no national allegiance to speak of, nor a doctrine to advance. They were not only part of the fight against the virus, key to how we might emerge into the "new normality," they were the principal architects of this postliberal world. For quite some time, those who had been operating in the atmospheric shadows, watching over us like some science fiction fantasy waiting to strike, now appeared as real as the virus that sought to also inhabit every organ we possessed. What they needed was a crisis devastating enough to provide the necessary conditions of possibility. The sacred order of liberalism had passed. And the victim, as we had seen, was defined only by its literal absence. They too had become as invisible as the virus that had killed them.

Giorgio Agamben would be open to ethical question on a number of points (see below). But his autopsy of the present has led us to one distinguishable truth. As the providential machine of liberalism gasped its final breath, the new age, the new normal that had already arrived, was profoundly theological. While Agamben turned his attention to the religion of medicine, which he saw as an unrivaled continuation of the biopolitical, the new dominant paradigm of the sacred has to my estimation unequivocally become a *global techno-theodicy*. This represents the inauguration of a new age where humanity itself has now become the sacrificial object, where the victim is now imagined in the absence of its very denials, where we all come face to face with the terrifying void, where the transcendental is virtual, where the future is already present, where technology is the only thing that might save us, and where the poetic is only of use if it can be appropriated.

Such a condition is necessarily bound up with a post-political imagination, micromanaging every breath we take, turning the intimate into a dangerous reckoning, augmenting a simulated reality in which the forces of militarism thrive, while enforcing the most micro-specific segregations and prejudicial assumptions that venture deep into the souls of all planetary life in the name of sheer survival. The technology revolution had no doubt already broken down many barriers. It was also seen as enabling. And it had connected humans in the simulacrum of its infinite vortexes, which truly collapsed space and time. But when the technology becomes the rule, when the invisible programmers become the principal architects for the new structures of power, when they govern all aspects of life while the systems they create appear like a new mythical force—which, reaching down from the ephemeral clouds, promises to be our only salvation—so it is pertinent to write of a new chapter in the sacred order of politics. And, like every sacred order, it is already demanding its sacrifices, learning to seduce and enslave its followers as it masters the new art of killing through intimacy. The condition catalyzed by the pandemic, which gave rise to such technological supremacy, was not just a lockdown. Nor was it some fantastical conspiracy; it was a catastrophe. It was an opportunity. And it proved to be the first truly global experiment of the postliberal age, testing what humans were willing to tolerate and what rights they were willing to give over to preserve their lives.

In his astute reading of the global pandemic, the artist Jake Chapman observed how the human had collapsed fully back into the species.[1] That we were a singular organism was no longer in question, no longer in doubt. But if this collective species had a body in its vulnerable and interconnected state, it was not one that could be allowed to reach out and touch. We were connected in our veritable contagion. Every movement, therefore, needed to be controlled, every choice anticipated, every droplet and secretion monitored, every congregation denied, every alternative medicated. The parallels with the aftermath of 9/11 were striking. We had already come to terms with the idea of some invisible enemy who could indiscriminately strike at us in terrifying ways. Such violence was also ecological, inducing its own climates of fear. Although we were unable to identify those invisible enemies with any degree of certainty due to the nature of our complex and ever-changing systems, we cast wide nets over anyone seen as potentially dangerous. But this position was always questionable. The idea that everyone was potentially dangerous was difficult to sustain. That was no longer the case. The enemy was now truly an "invisible killer," but the enemy was also within us. The species was therefore truly at war with itself. What this required therefore was to summon an isolated retreat as we had come to learn to fear everyone, even those we loved the most.

Some would argue that in the immediate aftermath of the pandemic too much had already been said about the birth of biopolitics and what it meant to the history of modern government. Yet it is worth reiterating that, despite modern states' formidable biopower, among the most guarded of all our rights have been the records both of our political allegiances and of our voting habits, along with the confidentiality agreements concerning our physical and psychological health. While the former had long since been overridden by those who commanded the information amassed across digital media platforms, the final frontier in the battle over our privacy of information was in the health sector—a frontier that's now been crossed.

Critics might question who speaks about rights anymore anyway—except the far right, who have turned the discourse on its head. The brilliance of Donald Trump would be to make us believe there was still something called politics, something to be debated, contested, fought over. Trump created a dialectic he knew he could win. As I argued in the previous chapter, he pitched an illusionary battle—as outrageous as it was false—against a liberal enemy which was already dead. As outrage spread across the echo chambers of social media (where else now?), so the masses disbelievingly warned people not to drink or inject bleach, while trying with desperation to say something they hoped could at least become as viral as the virus. Trump placed nostalgia at the heart of every political claim. So, while many were looking over their shoulders to the ghosts of politics past, lamenting the time that had been lost, the techno-theodicy drove onwards at ever greater speed and intensity. And Trump himself would pay the ultimate price when the strategic moment arrived, subjected in public to the original sovereign decision: the right to enforce a ban.

They say reality is stranger than fiction. But we have now entered the age of science fact—where the debate is over the truth of the modeling, the medicated demands, the battle of the competing algorithms, the tensions of the technocrats—all the while the writers, critics, artists, and poets slowly fade into the virtual ether, merely tasked like a medicated ointment with pathological soothing. There was no more tragic vision for art in the age of this techno-theocracy than a geriatric member of The Rolling Stones, sitting socially distant in his mansion and beating a nonexistent drum to "You Can't Always Get What You Want." While on the subject of music, how ironic that a band called The Police had us singing about every breath, while not standing so close to them. Yet as the drones started to fly through metropolitan skies, promising to keep us safely distanced from our neighbors, the real policing ultimately proved to be internal.

During the pandemic, guilt and shame reemerged with their familiar sacred potency. Deployed by shameless leaders who absolved themselves of any guilt, knowing we would be less forgiving of the same transgressions when it came to ourselves, the question of shame proved inseparable to our forced witnessing to a global tragedy from safe distances. It would be further deployed and weaponized against those protesting a far more familiar killing in the aftermath of the death of George Floyd, a Black man who had been killed by a police officer. And who didn't feel ashamed about the conditions of life on earth? Ashamed that we didn't do more to help—that we couldn't do more to help, apart from isolate? Ashamed as we continued to watch the numbers of daily fatalities in horrified submission? And who wasn't slightly relieved it wasn't them being reported upon, thankful to have survived another day? Who wasn't ashamed that we hadn't been killed by the invisible enemy? Might we have even been among the contagious? Unwitting carriers of the virus, bringing premature death to others? And what of our role in society, which appeared so underprepared and ill-equipped? Should we have been ashamed that our societies are so incapable of slowing things down? That we were so caught up in our own frenzied lives that our only encounter with death was when we learned about the passing away of an elderly neighbor, who had been slowly dying for years? Were we not ashamed of supporting governments whose investments in guns and bombs and other high-tech weaponry for destruction proved so worthless against this new onslaught upon life? Or were we even ashamed for buying a plant or walking a little too far from home? And what of our leaders, who proved themselves to be shamefully compromised, dancing with death in their primary insistence upon business as usual, neglectful in their actions, while woefully out of their depth when it came to showing the humanity required?

Guilt, as we have come to understand, sets the limits of prohibitions, the cultural norms which dictate behaviors, cultural codes, technological solutions, and legal pronouncements. None of this is new. War and plagues have always marched together, as we have learned to suffer our way to truth.[2] The plague that first struck Athens in 430 BC had a notable impact on many of its thinkers, beginning with Homer and then later Sophocles and his Oedipal mediations.[3] Moreover, the Black Death, which arrived into Florence almost immediately after Dante's death, influenced his student Giovanni Boccaccio, whose *Decameron* has become a classical text set during the epidemic.

In Homer's *Iliad*, the relationship between the sacred and the markers of an invisible killer are already established. Apollo is presented as both a healer and a bringer of violence whose divine arrows can inflict pestilence and death. He had the power to kill, teaching humanity a brutal lesson, and in the process of destroying life he revealed his true sacred power. This idea would later be taken up by Christianity, whose God could also inflict the most devastating violence upon humanity, turning sin into a deadly plague.[4] It is here we recognize again the importance of Sebastian in the iconography of the Renaissance and his veneration as a plague saint, who, as Louise Marshall noted, offered his body in sacrifice to reveal the sacred majesty of the very God which sent the very plagues of human misery to begin with:

> Sebastian's cult as a protector against the plague must be sought in the confluence of arrow imagery with the Christian concept of martyrdom as the most perfect imitation of Christ. As indicated in the Passio, Sebastian's trial by arrows was understood as a real martyrdom from which he was resurrected by divine power. Thus, archbishop Antoninus's observation that Sebastian "through two deaths, possesses two crowns of martyrdom". It is in this context that the Passion-like drama of suffering, death, and resurrection that Sebastian undergoes takes on a salvific charge. In direct analogy with Christ's redemptive death, Sebastian's martyrdom by the arrows of the plague becomes a vicarious sacrifice offered up to God. Christ-like, he takes the sins of humanity upon himself and makes restitution for these sins with his own sufferings. His resurrection demonstrates the acceptability of his sacrifice before the divine judgment.[5]

The arrows that pierced the flesh of Sebastian were replaced by the volleys of bullets fired across the battlefields of the world and into the bodies of expendable millions. Though as the Spanish flu of 1918 showed, in terms of war, a pandemic was never far away.[6] While the myth of liberal modernity subsequently claimed to have finally pushed violence to the margins of societies (which would be further exposed as racial tensions flared up cities across the United States), it also claimed for a while to have tamed the ravages of infectious disease through a mastery of scientific reason. Whatever remained of the world's illnesses could at least be neatly contained in the remote borderland areas of the world.

However, if pushing violence to the margins had concealed the normalization of civil war throughout the body politic, wherein the language of sacrifice became integral to the fabric of everyday life, the healthy liberal subject would always be plagued by the potential for its infection, medicalising the world for the sake of its own vitality and productive energies. Narratives of health have never, in fact, been apolitical. They take us into the heart of modern politics to see how governments regulate and deny the flows of human life. Indeed, any exposition of history shows that populations can be mobilized and pitted against each other far more effectively if individuals feel themselves to be under threat from some infectious agent, human or otherwise, than by appealing to any abstract notion of sovereignty.

Turning to a familiar example, as the bubonic plague spread throughout Europe, there was a well-documented need to partition societies into infected versus uninfected, healthy versus unhealthy, populations. For Foucault, this particular plague was what gave rise to the apparatus of governmentality through which the biopolitical marks its appearance upon the bodies of the living.[7] The plagues left governments armed with the ability to intervene in human activities, to monitor and segregate the species for the sake of their own social and political well-being. The plagues also consecrated the power of the "human sciences," whose assay of life coincided with the permanent appearance of the "dangerous individual." Such persons would no longer be marked out retrospectively on the basis of crimes already committed, but based on what they might do in the future. "Dangerousness" meant that the individual "must be considered by society at the level of his potentialities (*ses virtualites*) and not at the level of his acts."[8]

The twentieth century witnessed the worst effects of the biopoliticization of health and its narratives of endangerment. New propaganda took its inspiration from the practice of political animalization, the strategy of correlating humans with vermin (the carriers of disease), which has been apparent in nearly every modern genocide, from the Holocaust to Rwanda. After all, it is far easier to exterminate human life when the life in question is equated with that of a rodent or cockroach. Deleuze recognized how the biopolitical made it possible to justify political violence in all our names and for all our sakes:

> When a diagram of power abandons the model of sovereignty in favour of a disciplinary model, when it becomes the "bio-power" or "bio-politics" of populations, controlling and administering life, it is indeed life that emerges as the new object of power. At that point law increasingly renounces that symbol of sovereign privilege, the right to put someone to death, but allows itself to produce all the more hecatombs and genocides: not by returning to the old law of killing, but on the contrary in the name of race, precious space, conditions of life and the survival of a population that believes itself to be

better than its enemy, which it now treats not as the juridical enemy of the old sovereign but as a toxic or infectious agent, a sort of "biological danger."[9]

Or, as Foucault would now explain, "One might say that the ancient right to take life or let live, was replaced by a power to foster life and disallow it to the point of death"—a "Right of Death and Power over Life."[10] But, as we have shown, biopolitics alone was never sufficient. There always needed to be an idea behind the necessity for slaughter. And that idea remained sacred. But how are we to understand the political stakes of what's taking place in the postliberal moment? Or, to be more specific, what does the first crisis of the postliberal order tell us about the world we inhabit and the sacred order of politics into which we have been thrown?

THE PLAGUE OF PHILOSOPHY

Albert Camus's haunting novel *The Plague*[11] tells of the small town of Oran, whose population is wiped out by an invisible killer. Once thriving and wealthy, Oran is thrown into a state of terror and suspicion as its citizens start infecting one another. Believing their advanced society had rid itself of such evils, the citizens of Oran now have to confront the absurdity of their myths and a past that was never really buried. As one character in the storyline exclaims, "It's impossible it should be the plague, everyone knows it has vanished from the West." To which the protagonist replies, "Yes, everyone knew that, except the dead."[12]

But Camus was never concerned with allegory simply for the sake of it. His eponymous plague is already present—within our societies, within our reasoning, within us. Indeed, while Camus narrates a tale that questions the meaning of humanity in the postwar era, while also going to great lengths to challenge both our attachment to the sacred (notably in his depiction of the priest Paneloux) and the heroism of those who become accidental saviors, he also forces us to ask ourselves the question: how do we live in perilous times? And, in the process, he asks what types of critical intervention does the world need when invisible forces, sacred or otherwise, reveal themselves in all their brutal arbitrariness? As he writes:

> Pestilence is so common, there have been as many plagues in the world as there have been wars, yet plagues and wars always find people equally

unprepared. When war breaks out people say: "It won't last, it's too stupid." And war is certainly too stupid, but that doesn't prevent it from lasting. The citizens of Oran were like the rest of the world, they were humanists: they did not believe in pestilence. A pestilence does not have human dimensions, so people tell themselves that it is unreal, that it is a bad dream which will end. The people of our town were no more guilty than anyone else, they merely forgot to be modest and thought that everything was still possible for them, which implied that pestilence was impossible. They continued with business, with making arrangements for travel and holding opinions. Why should they have thought about the plague, which negates the future, negates journeys and debate?[13]

Mindful of Camus's prophetic warnings, we could do no better in addressing these important concerns than by turning to political theology's most renowned student of contemporary times. Agamben's initial remarks on the coronavirus and its philosophical meaning and implications have certainly proved contentious. For some, his statements during the immediate aftermath of the outbreak in Italy were ill-timed and suggestive of flagrant self-aggrandizement and theoretical posturing. Even the arch-provocateur of theory, Slavoj Žižek, was critical of Agamben's extreme views, claiming it represented a "social constructivist reduction," which through an excessive allegiance to dogmatic theory presented the problem as too much in the abstract and overly removed from the devastating reality.[14] Others derided him for collapsing theory into a form of paranoia that was both deluded and conspiratorial.[15]

However, while a number of the criticisms leveled at Agamben at least tried to deal with the substance of what he said, others brushed him off as behaving in a predictably philosophical way. Here was another elderly white sage, they said, too close to a problem to let it breathe, and simultaneously too intellectually distant and abstracted from its devastating consequences. They quickly vilified Agamben, stating that what the world really needed right now were the voices of the virologists and epidemiologists, along with others tasked with saving lives. Who really cared what a philosopher had to say, except for those with the luxury to think unworldly thoughts? Who gets to speak, and when is the right time to do so in a time of great upheaval that appeared central to our concerns?

But perhaps there was something deeper being revealed here. Maybe the question was not simply about what many found so perturbing about Agamben's thoughts on the subject of the epidemic, but about what critical thought itself can bring in the immediacy of such violence, and in the transpiring of one sacred order into another? Were the critics right that writing while a crisis was taking place was an act of complete insensitivity—or, worse still, an attempt to put one-self at the center of a debate that wasn't really happening? Might the intervention not appear to be a form of intellectual violence, provoking anger just for the sake of proving that your thoughts on the world and its future had been right all along? And what happened to the idea that philosophy itself required consideration and distanced reflection?

Agamben would make a number of interventions during the pandemic, which although written in the immediacy of the crisis are actually most revealing when thinking about the relationship between critical thinking and the crisis of the sacred. For our purposes here, we should focus on three notable interventions: "The Invention of an Epidemic," "Clarifications," and "A Question."[16] With each mediation, Agamben seemed to triple down on his stance without offering any apology for his initial remarks, and his detractors became more and more aghast.[17] Ironically, then, as Agamben perturbed and incited many counter-provocations, this also raised interesting questions about when is the right time to critique a critique? The question of timing is one which cannot be ignored. Politics, in fact, as Agamben has consistently argued, is all about time: the time that has passed, the time in which we live, the time that remains. Given the meticulous nature of Agamben's work, maybe some were surprised by the speed with which he published his thoughts on the coronavirus pandemic.

And yet, as his article "On Security and Terror"[18] showed when published shortly after the 9/11 attacks, he does have a tendency to respond quickly during a crisis—especially when it is an "exceptional" one. This is important. For as Agamben maintains, the exceptional moment is important. Whatever our reservations, Agamben's interventions are fully in keeping with his character. They remain consistent with his intellectual concerns when confronting the dangers inherent to states of exception, notably when they might lead to the reduction of politics to the question of pure survival—the very basis for his understanding of bare life, which despite running against the moral grain, doesn't appear to be parasitic and certainly not allegiant to the conditions into which we have been immersed. Such critiques about the timing of interventions do, however, raise a fundamental problem, which cannot be divorced from the world that we are now immersed in. Paul Virilio has already shown how speed was the defining element of human interaction.[19] Indeed, the crisis showed us that our societies were designed to never allow things to slow down, let alone come to a grinding halt—except for the benefit of the few.

With our societies overwhelmed by the prospect of inertia, what was really at stake was the order of competing temporalities in the organization of power. If the systems in which we live were to be defined by the logics of speed in the flows of life, what we understand to be philosophy would have no time for any mediation taking place at the speed of thought. But philosophy doesn't and shouldn't exist in some isolated metaphysical capsule, where the learned enter for solitary awakening when the time suits. Philosophy places immanent demands upon us in the immediacy of thought and action, and in that sense it cannot be divorced from the political. Unless, that is, we buy into the idea of a marked separation between thought and action. Here, then, is the crux of our problem. In the aftermath of a crisis, especially a crisis in which the very sacred order of things is unraveling, it is expected—even demanded—that politicians, scientists, and the new technocrats provide immediate solutions. Political philosophers, however, must learn to wait until the dust has finally settled. And yet, advocates still wonder why the technocratic is always one step ahead of the poetic. Critics might counter by saying what we need is the slowing down of all things. This is agreeable. But that doesn't mean to say that immanent thought is necessarily bad or dangerous. Moreover, if any author could speak with authority on the links between states of emergency, the bio-political, and technology then surely it was Agamben?

The idea that critical thought must learn to wait literally turns philosophy into a joke. This is something Simon Critchley has spoken of approvingly. Take, for example, the comedian who knows that timing is everything—a joke about a suicide bomber in the immediate aftermath of 9/11 ends up falling flat on account of its being in bad taste, yet a few years later it can have audiences in hysterics; the philosopher merely adds a depth of meaning by bringing death to the forefront of our concerns. Philosophy is all about, it is said, learning to die. Not so much a divine comedy, but more a tragic one, a point Critchley made in the aftermath of the pandemic.[20]

While mindful of the important political role comedy can play in speaking truth to power, there is a danger that the waiting game simply abstracts thought from power. This in turn runs the risk of collapsing ethics back into some self-important study and concerns with a learned self who is properly reflective with hindsight. Indeed, what is really being challenged if the critical intervention only occurs once the curtain has come down, after the audience has left, and one's performance no longer runs the risk of saying something untimely? Moreover, when can we be sure that the dead are truly dead and a problem has had enough time to breathe in the afterlife of its awakening? If the lockdown has showed us anything, surely it was how containment led to a proliferation of the technologies that have redesigned all forms of social interaction. This is not a question of death, though the unseen dead are sacrificial objects. It is a fundamental question about what happens to the lives that remain.

In his "The Invention of an Epidemic," Agamben certainty sparked some outrage by lamenting "the frenetic, irrational and entirely unfounded emergency measures adopted against an alleged epidemic of coronavirus." For Agamben, what was taking place was a hijacking of a medical problem and turning it into an "authentic state of exception," which could potentially become (as 9/11 had) the normal paradigm for political rule. Hence, the limits to freedom of movement revealed a much broader and lasting militarization of society. According to Agamben, this represented a new chapter in the history of the politics of fear: "It is almost as if with terrorism exhausted as a cause for exceptional measures, the invention of an epidemic offered the ideal pretext for scaling them up beyond any limitation." All of this was written before the death count really started to rise in devastating numbers across northern Italy. Had Agamben been too quick in applying his already prepared theoretical take on this particular exceptional situation? Where was the nuance and attention to detail? Was he not guilty of flattening all events in the immediacy of the moment, so that everything from 9/11 to the pandemic becomes part of the same oppressive story of will to rule by exploiting the conditions of emergency and its biopolitical matrices of control? And were we right to have been so skeptical of Agamben's insistence that the bio-political was enslaving us? Was that not the paranoid delusion of a madman who had taken all theoretical leave of his senses? Who, after all, didn't want to survive this pandemic in good health? Which among us was not truly thankful for the healthcare workers who had been tirelessly putting their bodies on the line? Or maybe, as Camus suggested, it wasn't just about living, nor about offering a critique of the past, but about questioning the type of life will we come to live in the aftermath?

Critics immediately personalized Agamben's provocative comments by drawing attention to Jean-Luc Nancy's response,[21] which alerted people that

Agamben had once advised him not to go through with a heart surgery. "I would have probably died," Nancy stated, adding further critical fuel to the arguments of those who wanted to condemn Agamben as belonging to some anti-bios death cult.[22] Considering Agamben's commitment to his anti-biopolitical position (which he had affirmed when explaining his refusal to travel to the United States on account of its introduction of biometric surveillance),[23] one could now read him as either a nihilistic philosopher who was putting himself on the side of the virus, or as simply engaging in inhumane theoretical semantics, which he couldn't possibly believe in. Here one might remember Mahatma Gandhi's response when his wife was stricken with pneumonia. When British doctors offered a shot of penicillin that would have saved her life, Gandhi refused to allow alien medicine to be injected into her body. Kasturba Gandhi died. Shortly after, Gandhi himself caught malaria and, relenting from his previous moral standard, allowed doctors to save his life with quinine. The politics of health is often filled with such contradictions. What was lost here, however, in the criticisms of Agamben's anti-bio-political stance were Nancy's more sensitive words, which noted the kindness and humility of his friend. Recognizing then the humanity of Agamben while still demanding more in terms of the immediacy of critique, which still mustn't be denied. "We must be careful," Nancy added, "not to hit the wrong target: an entire civilization is in question, there is no doubt about it. There is a sort of viral exception—biological, computer-scientific, cultural—which is pandemic. Governments are nothing more than grim executioners, and taking it out on them seems more like a diversionary manoeuvre than a political reflection."

The biopolitical raises fundamental questions of who can live and what must die in the name of life necessity. But what happens when the order is inverted, and death comes to us? What then with our concerns about the power over life? What many found concerning about Agamben's commitment to his original schematic is that he was now seen to be assuming the role of the sovereign. Like the masses in the United States calling for their bodies to be liberated from the lockdown state, Agamben holds that it is better to die with freedom than live on a precarious life support. Now, while we can bring Agamben to task for what his position means in terms of social responsibility, we do nevertheless need to consider the trade-off he puts before us. Or, to put it another way, why had we arrived at such a situation where the survival of the species was now being wagered upon our ability to adhere to lockdown regulations, which would provide the state an opportunity to accelerate the necessity for technology, thus fundamentally redesigning the logic and governance of our societies? Was Agamben not simply being blamed for being the soothsayer in all this? Was he explaining the new Faustian pact our societies had been forced to sign with whatever digital signature?

While it was painfully evident that the most capitalistic systems were the ones least able to cope (in human, not militaristic terms) with the lockdown, there was a need to ask whether the trade-off was as inevitable as Agamben claimed. Were we now simply condemning ourselves to biopolitical enslavement? There were undoubtedly some early remarkable displays of human solidarity shown the world over. And these events should be remembered when conducting an inquiry into the meaning of humanity in the twenty-first century. What is more, Agamben had previously showed remarkable empathy with the victims of 9/11, while still managing to forewarn us of the dangers of collapsing terror into the body politic. Indeed, despite my own theoretical reservations with the state of the exception, I find it possible to recognize the terrible conditions created by a crisis, while also criticizing those parasitic forces which use the crisis as a means of authoring new forms of political rule.

As Marco D'Eramo explained:

> By the end of this crisis, then, the surveillance powers of governments will have increased tenfold. But, *contra* Agamben, the contagion remains real, deadly and destructive despite this fact. That security services are likely to benefit from the pandemic does not justify a leap to paranoid conspiricism: the Bush Administration did not need to destroy the Twin Towers itself in order to pass the Patriot Act; Cheney and Rumsfeld could legitimize kidnapping and torture simply by seizing the opportunities that 9/11 presented.[24]

Furthermore, while Agamben could be brought to task in terms of the need to distance from one another as a temporary measure, his point on the militarization of societies should not be overlooked (something that was again made painfully evident with the later militarized response to the riots resulting from Black Lives Matter protests). Nearly every leader has consciously adopted the war metaphor in describing our fight against an "invisible enemy." More than political expedience, this is a proven way to improve popularity ratings. It is a means of curtailing thought and paving the way for the outright denial of resistance, except in the comforting and isolated confines of the digitally simulated desert of the real. In our critique of Agamben, we must therefore be mindful of our allegiance with the policing and lockdown of thought. This is something that "progressive" liberals have never had problems with observing and carrying out with all their due moral diligence.

And yet, the question still remains about who gets to speak truth to power during a period of upheaval? Was Agamben not revealing in himself, through what he embodied, a sense of entitlement to a certain theoretical privilege, which is also revealing as to why the humanities themselves have failed? Privilege is a difficult issue to deal with in this context. Is it not a privilege—indeed, a luxury— to say, "let's take the time to reflect"? Who really has the time for such reflecting, given the insecurities many face as the speed at which events transpire has thrown millions into a state of self-perpetuating anxiety? What good will reflection be five years on from the crisis, except for returning some intellectual parlance to the discourse after the sacred order for politics has been renewed? And does it not also reveal a certain privilege to say we can't really say anything at present, because what we are facing is too "new" to comprehend? New for whom exactly? Moreover, was there not an inherent contradiction to the immanent criticisms of Agamben made by the mortally affected digital hordes, many of whom had evidently read very little of his work? Such offended voices ask for no such time when it comes to their own righteous declarations.

The point here is not about denying the scale of the atrocity. However, while the crisis produced an entirely new structure of feeling throughout the world,[25] leaving nobody untouched except middle-class Europe and the United States, some of the characteristics of the crisis did nevertheless look eerily familiar. We should be reminded here of Saidiya Hartman's powerful comments as she tried to come to terms with this new state of crisis in her essay "The Death Toll":

> How does one navigate across the scales of death? Reckon with the distinc-
> tions between the hundreds of thousands of children who died in Iraq as the
> result of the US embargo and the hundreds of thousands who will die from the
> coronavirus? Many of us live the uneventful catastrophe, the everyday state
> of emergency, the social distribution of death that targets the ones deemed
> fungible, disposable, remaindered, and surplus. For those usually privileged
> and protected, the terror of COVID-19 is its violation of and indifference to
> the usual distributions of death. Yet, even in this case the apportionment of

risk and the burden of exposure maintains a fidelity to the given distributions of value. It appears that even a pathogen discriminates and the vulnerable are more vulnerable . . . Who lives and who dies? I fear the answer to such a question. I think I know what it is.[26]

Crises have a way of revealing what's already broken. Indeed, as Hartman reminds us, what can appear exceptional to some often proves run of the mill to others. This is not to downplay the severity of the crisis or engage in ethically remiss statistical comparisons, which we might expect from the likes of Steven Pinker. It is to demand equality in our understanding of suffering and to pay more vigilance to those lives which are continually rendered disposable by our societies.

This does invariably force us to confront the problem of race, along with other markers. The idea that we were "all in this together" has proved to be an elitist smokescreen. We have all experienced the pandemic in profoundly different ways, depending upon our race as well as class, gender, ability, and age. But it is also important to recognize that for many the virus is not the greatest perceived threat to their security and welfare at the level of everyday survival. As those who live in precarious conditions in the informal economies of the world have shown, the idea of locking-down was a luxury they could not afford. For them, it was not a matter of choice, but literally of life and death. Indeed, under lockdown the forces of structural violence became even more pronounced and the afflictions that already existed even more brutal. As Arundhati Roy observed in her essay that turns an eye to the human consequences of the coronavirus pandemic in India:

India revealed herself in all her shame—her brutal, structural, social and economic inequality, her callous indifference to suffering. The lockdown worked like a chemical experiment that suddenly illuminated hidden things. As shops, restaurants, factories and the construction industry shut down, as the wealthy and the middle classes enclosed themselves in gated colonies, our towns and megacities began to extrude their working-class citizens—their migrant workers—like so much unwanted accrual . . . As they walked, some were beaten brutally and humiliated by the police, who were charged with strictly enforcing the curfew. Young men were made to crouch and frog jump down the highway. Outside the town of Bareilly, one group was herded together and hosed down with chemical spray.[27]

AN ABSENT DEATH

In his essay "Clarifications," Agamben responded to the initial controversy sparked by his previous remarks, moving away from the need to take the virus seriously onto a request that we have more "respect for the dead." Might this have been the time for an apology or admission of having misunderstood the gravity of the situation? For Agamben, the opposite was true as the pandemic had revealed more fully the normalization—and our obedience to this new trend—of reducing life to bare survival. "The first thing the wave of panic that's paralysed the country has clearly shown," Agamben responded, "is that our society no longer believes in anything but naked life. It is evident that Italians are prepared to sacrifice practically everything—normal living conditions, social relations, work, even friendships and religious or political beliefs—to avoid the danger of falling ill." This fear of losing one's life to an invisible invader was, for Agamben, by definition dividing. Even the rites once so sacrosanct, he argued, had been overcome, and the familiar pillars of sacred power, notably the priest and the jurists, remained all but silent. "The dead—our dead—have no right to a funeral and it's not clear what happens to the corpses of our loved ones," Agamben explained.

The lockdown then was not only an assault on the freedom of movement, it was assault upon the political and emotional field of human togetherness. The implications were two-fold. First, for Agamben, we were entering a new chapter in the history of battle with no life now excluded. "It's not surprising," he wrote, "that we talk about the virus in terms of a war. The emergency provisions effectively force us to live under a curfew. But a war against an invisible enemy that can nestle in any other human being is the most absurd of wars. It is, to be truthful, a civil war. The enemy isn't somewhere outside, it's inside us." And second, with all the old sacred models for societies being equally overwhelmed, what was emerging was a truly post-political theology: "May an end be put once and for all to meetings and gatherings to talk about political and cultural questions, may we only exchange digital messages and may wherever possible machines replace any contact—any contagion—between human beings."

Following these discussions, Agamben eventually connected his concerns with the governance of the virus directly back to the question of "humanity" and its complete evisceration. Agamben began his mediation with a single question: "How could it happen that an entire country has, without noticing it, politically and ethically collapsed in the face of an illness?"[28] Invoking with careful consideration the term "abdication," Agamben took to task the way so many had been willing to renounce their ethical and political principles in response to a collective state of fear. For Agamben, this was not simply about the collapse of an old order (which he had consistently critiqued). Rather, we were at risk of losing those very qualities that distinguish humanity from barbarism. Here, Agamben returns to the deathly figure of the corpse to ask, "How could we have accepted, solely in the name of a *risk* that it was not possible to specify, that persons who are dear to us and human beings in general should not only die alone, but—something that had never happened before in history, from Antigone to today—that their cadavers should be burned without a funeral?" Agamben's concern with the funereal would strike at the very heart of our conceptions of love, compassion, and friendship. And, in doing so, it would force us to confront the true abstraction of splitting the human from the spiritual realm—a contradiction which we believe only a turn to medical science can save, but it won't because life is ultimately mortal and finite. So, how then might death function differently?

In the last interview given before his passing, "Learning to Live Finally," Derrida reiterated his claim that in order to know what it truly means to live in the world, it is necessary to learn how to die. Writing with the knowledge of his imminent death, he raised the question of finitude by engaging with the issue of survival by deferral: "Survival in the conventional sense of the term means to continue to live, but also to live after death." Crucially, for Derrida, this idea of survival brought him directly to the idea of an "originary mourning," something that "does not wait for so-called 'actual' death." Like Barthes, Althusser, and Foucault before him, Derrida understood the ways in which death appeared to be an untimely rupture, which forced a doubling of the author's persona. While the body literally dies, something of the specter or trace remains:

The trace I leave to me means at once my death, to come or already come, and the hope that it will survive me. It is not an ambition of immortality; it is fundamental. I leave here a bit of paper, I leave, I die; it is impossible to exit this structure; it is the unchanging form of my life. Every time I let something go, I live my death in writing. An extreme process; we exert ourselves without knowing whom exactly the thing we leave behind is confided to. Who is going to inherit, and how? It is a question that one can pose oneself today more than ever. It constantly preoccupies me.

Deleuze also appreciated this double meaning to one's encounter with death and the question of what remains. As he wrote in relation to Maurice Blanchot's mediation on the subject, "Any death is double, by the cancellation of the great difference that it represents in extension, by the swarming and the liberation of small differences that it implies in intensities."[29] While there is then a very personal experience with death that affirms the finitude of our fleeting existence, something of us lives on in the realm of the infinitely possible and yet to be anticipated trajectories of memory and thought, which allows for a rethinking and reimagining of the political. But in order for this to happen, the trauma we feel when confronting death needs to be exhausted. And for that to occur it needs to be faced, not medicated or kept at a distance.

We also owe it to Deleuze for explaining how exhaustion, as a prelude to death, is different from merely feeling low in vitality or having spent oneself sexually. Referencing characters from the work of Samuel Beckett, Deleuze argues that it implies the exhaustion of all possibilities and potentials. It is to be done with the current state of affairs. This is not, however, a cause for lament. Exhaustion is fundamental to the creation of new subjects. But what remains of this idea when liberalism itself has already presented the notion of the post-political subject, a subject that was already dead, but which lived on through the inevitable crisis of its sacred order? A subject whose final words added to the realization that the only alternative is fascism? A subject who could either deny what was happening or resign themselves to another suffocating embrace?

The tragedy of liberalism was not its death, but its being forced to endure, endure, and endure! This brutal form of nihilism thus bound the world to its catastrophic fate. It also raised many questions of what it meant to live in such a soulless state, evacuated of all meaning. What would it imply, in other words, to be deprived of the ineffable and unable to find enough reasons to believe in this world? And yet, our concern today should not be about disappointment with the death of liberalism, but with whether the disappointment now leads to a more insufferable existence. Political life is meaningless without the prospect of death, as it is denied the very possibility of individual and collective transvaluation and transformation. Indeed, while the technical world continues to kill in the millions while remaining incapable of feeling the pain of its unfortunate victims, it comes up against its limits when faced with the question of death. Death, in fact, as Agamben suggested, has also been abandoned. And yet, death renders the technical imagination arbitrary and redundant, even as its searches

for immortality while forgetting the human. Reason can only reason more violence when confronted with the insecure sediment of existence; it takes a more
poetic imaginary to think the world anew.

FROM LIBERALISM TO A TECHNO-THEOCRACY

Despite our antipathy to Agamben's initial provoking remarks, there is much to
agree with him on his approach to the question of death, the extension of the
military paradigm, the implications of the potentially permanent clearing of the
streets, the emergence of a brave new world in the form of a new theology, and
what this means for any viable understanding of humanity that thrives on love
and connection. Thus, instead of dwelling on what Agamben badly misjudged,
we must consider the conditions he forewarned us about and what this might
mean for the widespread eruption of violence and protest that followed the initial lockdowns. As D'Eramo suggested,

> Agamben is both wrong and right; or rather, drastically wrong and somewhat
> right. He is wrong because the basic facts contradict him. Even great thinkers
> can die of contagion—Hegel perished from cholera in 1831—and philosophers
> have a duty to revise their views when circumstances call for it: if coronavirus
> denialism was faintly possible in February, it is no longer reasonable in late
> March. However, Agamben is right that our rulers will use every opportunity
> to consolidate their power, especially in times of crisis. That coronavirus is
> being exploited to strengthen mass-surveillance infrastructure is no secret.[30]

Among the most haunting images of the global pandemic was the aerial photograph of a mass burial on Harts Island in New York, backdropped by ruined
buildings. This particular site is a symbol of human disposability in the capitalist
system. Having gone through a number of uses, from a historical mass burial
site for those dead of infectious diseases like tuberculosis, to a sanatorium for
women, a military base, a prison, a homeless sanctuary, it now has over one million unknown bodies buried there. Most of the bodies were initially buried in
the north of island, but this changed in the early 1980s when victims of the AIDS
pandemic were buried in the southern part. The rationale there was the fear
that the dead could infect the other dead! As Agamben has suggested, there is

something significant about the dead being buried without any loved ones present. What Harts Island shows is how conditions of disposability in the denial of life to a dignified ending had become normalized. Here we see burials without any congregation, except for other dead people. Funerals can be a place for intimate mourning, but they are also profoundly political events. We only need to remind ourselves of what happens when revolutionary figures die. Funerals can also give us a more intimate relationship to death—and hence a more vital connection to life—in deeply political ways. What the mass graves of Harts Island perhaps truly represent is another chapter in the history of human disappearance: no mourning, no affect, no love, no political. And in the lives that follow, nothing lives on. So, perhaps here we can, as Agamben insisted we do, have a new conversation on what the term "humanity" actually means. Security means nothing without a prior conception of love. And the abandoned buildings in the background of the Harts Island burial grounds are not just a metaphor for abandoned lives, but for a system whose humanism was already in ruins.

Let's now turn to the civil war that Agamben suggested was being reworked through a return to domestic militarism in far-reaching and more intimate ways. It was certainly the case that the wars on terror had evaporated into the discursive ether. Indeed, we had in many ways already entered into a period that was beyond war—which is not to say that the violence had abated, but simply that war no longer even needed to be declared. Furthermore, there was no denying the parallels between the coronavirus lockdowns and the aftermath of 9/11. As Massumi explained,

> Following 9/11, the language used around the threat of terrorism had a viral
> ring to it. Direct comparisons between the terrorist and the virus were not
> infrequent. Both had a way of hitting unexpectedly, suddenly irrupting from
> below the threshold of perception, attacking with inhuman implacability and
> scattershot lethality, if not killer precision. The threshold of perception was
> often taken to coincide with the national border. The terrorist was the "face-
> less" enemy, as "other" as a rogue strand of RNA hiding in a swine, waiting to
> detonate in human flesh.[31]

Viruses like COVID-19 were said to be indiscriminatory. This is a myth, but it's one that's now integral to the new order of things. It is true that anybody can be infected. But it is no coincidence that those who die are often the most vulnerable, the most disposable, those who are least protected and have no security, no insurance. Moreover, catastrophes and pandemics reveal not only the hidden order of politics, but also the prejudices upon which our entire societies are based.

Take, for example, the well-documented assumption that certain ethnic groups bring disease and infection with them. The first outbreak of the Black Death in Europe saw a sharp rise in anti-Semitism (some believe this was the first incidence of it occurring systematically) with Christians massacring Jewish communities, who they blamed for bringing the disease into Europe (from the Far East along the silk routes through northern Italy). As these massacres were taking place, in Strasbourg on February 14, 1349 some two thousand Jewish people were burned alive.

We might also return here to Hobbes's *Leviathan*, which states that there are no politics without security and no security without the state. This has remained foundational to modern politics, and yet, despite the work's association with sovereignty, its theories only make sense by appealing to life itself. Hobbes would refer to sovereignty in terms of an "artificial lung," whereas the very frontispiece to the book, showed how sovereignty was always embodied with rulers and citizens. The importance of Abraham Bosse's frontispiece has also been central to Agamben's earlier mediations on civil war. It also strikes the reader today as remarkably prescient. As Agamben explains, "The city, with the exception of some armed guards and two very special figures situated close to the cathedral with whom we will soon be concerned, is completely devoid of inhabitants. The streets are perfectly empty, the city is uninhabited: no one lives there."[32] Agamben points out that the two "very special figures" he mentioned are in fact plague doctors, and he goes on to explain, "While perfectly illustrating the paradoxical status of the Hobbesian multitude, the emblem of the frontispiece is also a courier that announces the biopolitical turn that sovereign power was preparing to make."[33] Thus, in the name of the health of a society, through taking life itself to be the object for power, a permanent civil war is effectively inaugurated, with pandemics and warfare being powerful tools in the management of populations.

In the first few weeks of the pandemic, an internet meme went viral showing the *Leviathan* frontispiece with the boxes beneath its body made up of a virtual cast of online participants on the Zoom platform. Joyfully presented, like all the other viral memes that were in vogue at the time, promising we would pull through thanks to our virtual togetherness, the *Leviathan* meme actually embodied a dystopic post-human landscape, which cast a long, digitally enhanced shadow and exacerbated beyond measure Manuel Castells's concept of myopic social morphology.

This brings us to Mark Duffield's insightful work on the digital poor or "workhouse."[34] Mapping out the changing nature of frontier conditions within the framework of civil war as previously presented by Agamben, Duffield draws particular attention to the realms of invisibility. As he writes, "There is a dialectical relationship between visibility and invisibility. The one requires the other; they cannot exist alone. Capitalism is visible because its old extra-economic means of supranational legal encasement have broken down. Since the world has changed, however, rather than a repair exercise something new is required. Increasing authoritarianism is important." Crucially, for Duffield, what's at stake here is a reworking in the logics of production that is completely "*indifferent* to the human condition." This would be one in which the vast majority will lead lives defined by isolation and insecurity, and where the only way to travel and experience the world will be through virtual reality, while the elite will have the luxury of walking down the cleared streets of Venice, gazing upon the dolphins in its crystal-clear canals, before heading over to Paris to visit the largely empty Louvre and look at the Mona Lisa with a perfectly uninterrupted view.

The pandemic was a form of humanitarian blowback. As Gareth Owen, the director of humanitarian affairs and a lead organizer during the ebola crisis response of 2014 observed, "It is definitely a case of humanitarianism coming home. The sight of Londoners from all walks of life nervously queuing together outside the supermarket door, spread two meters apart by social distancing as they wait to pick over half-empty grocery shelves, is a desperately familiar one. I have organized such food queues the world over, but I have never stood in one myself. It is a humbling new experience."[35] While these conditions offered another tragic inversion of politics, Virilio had already anticipated them for quite some time. As he noted after 9/11, "To create an event is thus to reject whatever is now nothing more than a 'thirdworlding of human societies', representing a shift from the EXOCOLONISATION of erstwhile empires to the ENDOCOLONISATION of the terminal empire."[36] This, Virilio understood, was less about space, than it was about the mastery of time. At a personal level, time under lockdown might have felt like it slowed down to almost a standstill, but this was an illusion. The mechanisms of power had been speeding up in ways that would have been unimaginable only a few years prior to the pandemic. This was not a rupture or lockdown, but an acceleration.

Virilio captured the importance of this in one of his later books, *The Futurism of the Instant*, noting,

> Just like the elementary particle at the heart of Geneva's Great Accelerator—the large Haidron Collider—we will then not only be "filed", but tracked, making knowing where we permanently reside completely pointless . . . The pathological sequelae of this are unknown. The myth of some happy, beneficial neo-nomadism wont long survive the experience of being locked down in a closed circuit, within the now relative non-expanse of this life-bearing star of ours.

Crucially for Virilio, such endocolonization was not about the world catching up; it was in fact accelerating regression, driving us toward a world where technological advance was synonymous with borderland conditions:

> So, let's not be under any illusions! What is happening in Africa and Asia, with the 50 million people qualified by the Office of the United Nations High Commission for Refugees as "victims of forced displacement," is no more than a clinical symptom of the domiciliary emancipation, the freeing up of settled living currently underway that will in turn hit Europe and the Americas and the rest of the developed world.

Virilio forced us to confront contradictions to see that beneath the surface they were not contradictory at all. It was possible to accelerate while regressing, support life while destroying it.

Throughout history, pandemics and war tend to go hand in hand with the creation of new political orders, new visions of the world, and new sacred claims. Moreover, they produce potent humanitarian crises, which in turn have drastic and lasting effects on the operations of power. But the pandemic's humanitarian blowback into the metropolitan areas of the world would be compounded by the realization that the global liberal order, which had mandated borderland interventions for the past three decades, was falling. We only needed to look upon the elected political opposition leaders in the UK and United States to recognize how liberalism had effectively become a parasitic movement, which would rather suck the life out of what remained of the radical left than bring about a true revolution in human affairs.

Those who took to the streets and started tearing down the statues understood this better than anyone. Indeed, while the viral image of Trump supporters demanding the reopening of stores in Columbus, Ohio drew tongue-in-cheek comparisons to the movie *Dawn of the Dead*,[37] there was far greater vitality in that frame than in any bourgeois liberal Zoom call. As for the blowback, only now are we starting to appreciate what a humanitarian crisis in postliberal times looks like, for it has included all of us, without exception. This is a crisis in which the right has triumphed, where capitalism has thrived under lockdown, and where technology is presented as the only thing that could possibly save us from ourselves. In this regard, while the Black Lives Matter protests that punctured the lockdown with a rapturous return to a violent reality could also be seen as a potent expression of a new political awakening, not only was its resurrection of the sacred motif of the victim misplaced, but those who mastered the technology openly welcomed the symbolic focus on the past. This focus has actually enhanced the power of those digital platforms which have led to a fundamental reorganization of the sacred object for power in the world. Every great empire knows how to divide and rule; the sacred demands it. The danger, however, is not simply in the multiplication of difference, but in the advent of a new digital inquisition.

So, where does this leave us with regard to radical politics in this postliberal age? Were many not already calling for such a disruption to the system—albeit without the soaring death count from a widespread contagion? How many had been calling for us to slow things down, to be more mindful in our consumption patterns, for the privileged among us to have better appreciation for our food and health security, to spend more of our time reflecting upon the fallen conditions of our shared demise, to enact (impossible, they said) a major shift in our lifestyles for the purpose of slowing climate change, to learn to respect others' personal space, to consider implemental a universal living wage through unprecedented state intervention, and to take full advantage of the power of technology, which meant nearly all office jobs could be done remotely? So, there we were, then.

And yet, something didn't quite sound right, look right, feel right. The lockdown certainly didn't resemble the vision for a postliberal emancipatory society so many radicals had been dreaming about. Its design in reality was far more suffocating, debilitating, and divisive than we ever could have imagined. But this was not unexpected. Nietzsche understood long ago that if you have something important to say you won't be dismissed. Truly radical thought is always appropriated and turned back upon itself. It is all about ensuring that when everything changes, everything remains the same. Indeed, this is what Agamben shows to be the defining measure of a civil war: stasis. That's progress.

Utopia is dead and rotting in the violent and barbarous ruins of twentieth-century thought. We have entered the atopian age. The concept of the atopia once referred to an inhospitable place without borders or dwellings. Now we are all inhabiting the inhospitable—we keep all strangers at a distance, with every home turned into a sanctuary, prison, medical quarantine, and asylum. But the language of the atopic also takes us to its use as a medical term—the word "atopy" refers to an individual's heightened response to a common allergen. We have learned that the one thing we all have in common is the contagion. And it is for this reason, more than the evident presence of the military state, that the atopian vision is truly terrifying. As Agamben reminds us:

> Epidemic, as the etymology of the term suggests (*demos* is in Greek the people as a political body and *polemos epidemios* is in Homer the name for civil war) is above all a political concept, which is preparing to become the new terrain of world politics—or non-politics. It is possible, however, that the epidemic that we are living will be the actualization of the global civil war that, according to the most attentive political theorists, has taken the place of traditional world wars. All nations and all peoples are now in an enduring war with themselves, because the invisible and elusive enemy with which they are struggling is within us. As has happened many times in the course of history, philosophers must again enter into conflict with religion, which is no longer Christianity, but science or that part of it that has assumed the form of a religion. I do not know if bonfires will return and books will be put on the Index, but clearly the thought of those who continue to seek the truth and reject the dominant lie will be, as is already happening before our eyes, excluded and accused of spreading fake news (news, not ideas, because news is more important than reality!). As in all moments of emergency, real or simulated, we see once again the ignorant slander philosophers and scoundrels seeking to profit from the disasters that they themselves have provoked. All this has already happened and will continue to happen, but those who testify to the truth will not stop doing so, because no one can bear witness for the witness.[38]

Every political system produces its own unique sacred objects. It also produces its scapegoats. No author understood this better than Girard, who recognized the need for a certain sacrifice in order to dispense with the old and bring about the new.[39] While the sacrificial thus becomes integral to how we attribute new meaning to the system, the scapegoat is vilified, cast out as the excess we no longer need. As societies continue to operate within sacred paradigms, Agamben warns us that it is precisely in exceptional times—during a crisis of a sacred order—that the transgressive life can be stripped bare. This is not just a physical act (although a symbolic physical act often occurs); to be stripped bare means the removal of all ethical and political agency, notably including the right to critique.

My interest here, when dealing with thought in a time of sacred crisis, is not in defending Agamben, nor is it to defend any of the other theorists, who are too often put on their own sacred plinths. The world is too full of academics who bestow their truths from the higher reaches of the intelligentsia. Ultimately, my concern is what the coronavirus crisis has revealed to us about the crisis in thought. In the backlash against Agamben, the cries of "too soon," the transposition of the old theory by an old theorist into the conditions of the new, was critical thought itself not in danger of becoming another casualty of the pandemic? As we enter a new, postliberal age defined by the rise of a global techo-theocracy, we can see how humanity itself has now become the sacrificial object, and the critical thinker become one of its most immediate scapegoats.

Just look at universities today to see in sharp focus what's valued and what's expendable in this future order that is rapidly becoming the present. It is obvious how the crisis has strengthened science and technology studies (notably supported by military research and development), while very few (except in the most elite institutions) who work in the arts and humanities, languages, and the social sciences feel any sense of security in their jobs. And yet, these latter subjects encourage a better appreciation of compassion and dignity. They inherently bring people closer to together, while insisting that a central purpose of the university is to speak truth to power and hold those in positions of authority to account. Those who survive will have to adapt to a virtually augmented pedagogy for an educated post-political workforce who are unlikely to ever meet in person. And, in the end, this will be presented as "progress" for humanity and the human condition.

A few months before the coronavirus outbreak, I noticed a pair of black ravens nesting in the woodland opposite my apartment. I watched them every day, circling in the skies, attacking any rivals in their less polluted airspace, occasionally swooping down for the kill. Not only have these particular birds been associated with prophecy and insight, they have also been recognized as the forebearers of death and messengers for lost souls. The raven's prominent black beak is eerily reminiscent of the mask of medieval plague doctor, which can be faintly made out on the barren and desolate streets of the Leviathan's frontispiece.

Two days after Agamben finished typing his third essay on the pandemic, I stood on my balcony and noticed a strange dark object in the garden below. Upon investigation, I found it to be a largely devoured carcass of a very young fox cub. I proceeded to bury the dead animal in the nearby undergrowth. That evening, the raven appeared in the garden, looking for something it had evidently lost. The following morning, the corpse had returned, a little rottener and more consumed. The following day and night, the same process of burying the corpse and its subsequent reappearance repeated itself. One of the birds kept returning, keeping watch, in silence. So, I decided to leave the corpse where they left it. Humans are fond of projecting meaning onto symbols of death. What this returning corpse represents, however, is open to interpretation.

THE GHOSTS OF HISTORY

On September 26, 1940, in the picturesque Spanish port town of Portbou, Walter Benjamin tragically decided to take his own life.[40] Having made the perilous journey across the Pyrenees, this intellectual and political refugee became another casualty as Europe continued to colonize itself, becoming a graveyard of human disposability. Benjamin's only meaningful possession at the time of his suicide was a briefcase which contained a manuscript he was writing. Its importance to Benjamin was paramount: "Whatever happens, the manuscript must be saved. It is more important than my own person."[41] But the manuscript disappeared without a trace, and its contents remain unknown to this day.[42] Likewise, its author was buried in an unmarked grave, his body never properly recovered.

Most likely buried in a communal grave, Benjamin shows there is no solidarity in the collective burials of those denied their place in the archive of humanity. But what can we say of this text that was swallowed by the maelstrom of history, and how might it enable us to rethink the importance of origins in a way that's consistent with Benjamin's poetics? Could something be revealed about the life of an author whom the Nazis failed to consign to oblivion, even if the search for the manuscript was ultimately in vain? Indeed, might we not think about the disappeared text as revealing the possibility for language—that it is not absent but in fact appears in the unread fragments and untraceable letters that reveal the potential for critical language as such? That its appearance is pre- and post-discursive, something that doesn't require inscription and which points to the writing-to-come? What, after all, is the message of the text—what is it that must be saved—if not to direct our attention to the yet-to-be-written, which like the author's public memorialization walks us through life's narrow and suffocating corridors, only to open onto the most beautiful shores?

Benjamin's lost text reminds us of the importance of language. Its absence is a devastating loss to critical thinking and what it might have become. There is a real tragedy at work in the story of a man who personified the intellectual refugee in more ways than his individual flight from danger. Benjamin continually asks us to consider what time we are actually living in. And yet, his fragmentary life was ultimately ended by the violence of time. With the Nazis advancing and his movements curtailed, Benjamin sensed that time had finally caught up with him, and he ended his life on his own terms. Had he waited just another day, the passage of time would have given him the freedom he desired, and which he had physically suffered in order to obtain.

That Benjamin was buried in an unmarked grave only adds to the indignity of his death and subjects him to a double disappearance. With both his body and his text vanished without a trace, violence has consequently been inflicted upon both the memory of his existence and the future of his thought. The romantic among us may like to think the briefcase is somewhere on this planet, and that the manuscript will eventually be read, though only when the world is ready for the power of its mediations. Then again, perhaps the greatest gift Benjamin gave us is the possibility of the text, something that retains a sense of mystery and wonder, and whose principal message, in defiance of those who seek to destroy a life and erase its memory, remains an ancestral opening to the potentiality for thinking anew. It's unknown words, never to be read, speak to a future for language. It is the book every critical theorist aspires to do justice to, the unseen, ghostly words of an author who helps us better understand Deleuze's claim that there's no better reason to write than the shame of being human.

The ghosts of our failures haunt our conception of humanity, that much is clear. But part of our challenge, as Benjamin's life demands, is to learn how to make sense of this haunting. History is a battlefield littered with apparitions, whose very specters are imprinted upon the present. The very air we breathe is full of silent screams, which have faded with the passage of time. Politics, philosophy, and poetics are all concerned with the order of this battle, for the enduring fascination with existence is what compels us to excavate the past in the present moment. Phantoms of history are always at play, waging an endless confrontation over the meaning of time and the temporality of meaning, orchestrating in a violent symphony those disharmonious visions that come to define our images of thought. We are, it is fair to say, always walking among ruinous landscapes of memorialized and forgotten times, populated by the ghosts who still accompany us until the end.

Maybe this is what Derrida had in mind when he said "we owe ourselves to death."[43] Death is the always and already present haunting the living unto its death. And "ghost" is the name we give to apparitions that take the shape of those who were once here. Such ghosts occupy the present as a traumatic reminder, collapsing all linear notions of space and time. Such trauma acts like a psychic wounding, a visual reminder of the unknown, and a form of condemned subjectivity that is not only dead by a defining void. An apparition of denial, whose meaning is only made possible by accounting for the voiding of existence, and which aims to defeat any sense of history, negating whatever boundary exists between past and present. In this regard, as Derrida suggested, the figure of the ghost is not just a memory of something that has died. Its indeterminable traces and projections ensure it is neither present nor absent, neither dead nor alive.[44]

Ghosts, then, are more than historical figures; they continue to haunt the body politic in ways that fracture the lines between life and death. The literary significance of this is apparent. As Maurice Blanchot noted in respect to death, it is "the eternal torment of our language," which produces a "longing" that "turns back towards what it always misses, through the necessity under which it labours of being a lack of what it would say." The ghost of Benjamin—the disappeared refugee whose final words remain a mystery—belabors us in precisely this way. And, in doing so, in the face of potential destruction, he asks not only what is the time in which we live, or whether we can develop a critique of violence adequate to our times, but whether we have the fortitude to go on writing and creating in the face of the promise of annihilation.

From Plato onward, it has been argued that to philosophize is to learn how to die. Philosophy is all about learning to live through the tragedy of existence and come to terms with the finitude of existence. Ultimately, letting go of the past might at least allow us to make sense of life and find some form of comfort at its end. But, detached from its sacred moorings, this claim to be about learning how to die is still overly fatalistic. How can we possibly glean something meaningful from life if we accept that it is hurtling, seemingly with accelerating speed as we grow older, into the void? Indeed, what does it mean for critical engagement when the very movement of the dialectic—the negation of its negation—seems irrelevant once positioned at the very end of its reasoning?

There is nothing to negate once negation confronts, in the end, the eventual will to nothingness and the disappearance of every trace of a meaningful life. Is not the act of negating the void simply an attempt to mirror its absence, falling further into its depths with only oneself for company, dying alone? Clearly, we cannot retreat and behave as if the void hasn't colonized the progressive imaginary and come to dominate the shadows of thought and the very practice of what it means to be human. Countering the void requires entering its depths and becoming intimately acquainted with the violence of its embrace, while also understanding it as a space for creative potentiality. Thus, as Paul Celan understood, we must go a stage further than the philosophical commandment of learning how to die and re-enter into the void at the moment it appears in the final scene. We must turn this around with the most defiantly loving of faces in the search for a new conception of justice, which might become the new starting point for our critical mediations.[45] We must look upon life from the always and already perspective of death. We must offer a post-existent resistance—a resistance that defies the violence of time and the depths of nihilistic abandonment and its sacred annihilations. There is nothing to be negated, only affirmed, for life literally is all we have. This requires a rethinking of what we actually mean by the term "humanity." It does not signify something that reduces the human species to the question of pure survival, so that it ultimately submits to the nihilistic impulse of total disappearance/extinction. Rather, we must ask what a more poetic understanding of humanity might mean at the level of collective thoughts, words, actions, and being in the world.

Derrida ventriloquized the position of the ghost asking what a living person thought about their earthly meaning. "Here, the ghost is me," he quipped. But if we are living embodiments of ghosts already in the making, might we not also be the ones who are doing the haunting? We are carriers of past suffering, preventing with our sacred resurrections the dead from resting in peace. There is no perpetual peace, we have learned, even in death. The memory of suffering and the loss of innocent life are continuously resurrected to appease the sacrificial needs of the new metaphysical order and the logics of violence perpetrated in its name. The promise of future violence takes us into the depths of the nihilistic void—the inescapable abyss of total annihilation. Here we are haunted by the mirroring of the images of the void, which create a spectral proto-reflection of ourselves, already working in preparation for those earthly disasters yet to be come, always writing in advance of ourselves, anticipating the insecure futures we will be forced to inhabit, shamed into thinking that the only world possible is the one into which we have been fatefully thrown.

But if this is our fate then why do anything? If we are all hurtling into a mean-ingless absence, facing the omnipresence of death, incapable of escaping from the tragedy of the human condition, why act at all? Simon Critchley and Jamieson Webster pick up this question as they mediate on the most famous haunting in all of English literature—Shakespeare's *Hamlet*.[46] In their reading, Hamlet is not a man of prophecy who is destined to bring about worldly change; haunted into submission, he embodies the incapable and the inactive. Hamlet is stripped of all capacity for meaningful action, for he has stared too long into the violent abyss. But to ask "why at all?" is not what we need to address. Such a question falls back upon the comforts of some sacred ground. More purposefully still, we must ask why we continue to refuse death in the time that remains. The answer to this question can only be arrived at through a more poetic and affirmative concep-tion of resistance, which breaks out of the nihilistic cage in which the world has imprisoned us. Or as Derrida wrote in his final interview, "This surviving is life beyond life, life more than life, and my discourse is not a discourse of death, but, on the contrary, the affirmation of a living being who prefers not simply that which remains but the most intense life possible."[47] That is, we must strive for an existence that looks at life from the perspective of death and still finds reasons to resist those who would, through willful abandonment and sacred deed, send it into oblivion.

PART III

Into the Void

CHAPTER 7

Annihilation

OBLITERATING THE HUMAN

In order to break free from the realm of the sacred, one must confront the terror of the void. This requires facing the intolerable and looking deeper into the crisis of ethics where humanity appears in its most naked forms. This brings us back to the question of extreme violence and its sacred demands, which post-War liberalism also took as its point of departure. Violence is an assault upon a person's dignity and sense of selfhood. It seeks to strip the human of their very humanity and right to beingness in this world. Sometimes this assault is carried out to ensure obedience and force compliance. Other times, it is driven by the need to eradicate entire peoples, entire cultures, entire memories, entire futures. Such violence is properly described as annihilation. Etymologically derived from the medieval Latin *annihilatus*, the word denotes a "reduction to nothingness" and shares an evident relationship to nihilism—stemming from the Latin *nihil*, the discursive realm of absolutely nothing.

But what is the order of this nothingness with regard to its conscious destruction? What is actually being vanquished when the aim of violence is to ultimately leave no trace? And how does this further expose the terrifying immensity of the void, which, in the process of carrying out the dream of total annihilation, reveals fully the brutalities of the technocratic mind? What we can say is that in order to dream of nothing, we must be capable of dreaming of everything, to liberate the violence of movement so that there are no limits to what humanity can achieve in its push for collective suicide and its ability to reason itself back into the dust of the earth. The infinite possibility that everything under wounded skies can be destroyed, where matter and antimatter collide in full homicidal glory, where the tears of every violated body bleed from life all the colors of existence, to produce not just the death of material things but a total extinction event that forces time itself to crack and be swallowed by the vortex—where the sacred will be resolved, and all will be revealed as if nothing has ever happened.

It is here we should return to Arendt, who still remains one of the most astute thinkers on this terrifying process. Arendt rightly connected the history of total-itarianism back to its colonial heritage and the willingness to stake its claim to the world.[1] She also understood that violence was qualitatively different to power, though the lines between the two are often more blurred than her definitions might suggest. Her analytics of violence, however, are what still command our attention, notably the stages of violence she identifies, which map out how violence is fully compatible with our ideas of civility, progress, and the betterment of lives.

Agamben has been right to suggest that any analysis of biopolitics is incomplete without paying proper attention to the theoretical debt owed to both Arendt and Benjamin. Might we even be talking about the biopolitical at all were it not for the critical insight Arendt offered in *The Human Condition*, especially her notion of the animal laborans and the modes of active experimentation (violent or otherwise) this permits in the name of order and progress? As she wrote, in a style that evidently later inspired Bauman and his work on the violent production of expendable lives, "One of the obvious danger signs that we may be on our way to bring into existence the ideal of the animal laborans is the extent to which our whole economy has become a waste economy, in which things must be almost as quickly devoured and discarded as they have appeared in the world, if the process itself is not to come to a sudden catastrophic end."

Arendt was writing from a deeply personal perspective, which gives her insight even more credibility. She became stateless and was forced to flee following internment. If we follow her logics through, it is tempting to begin our analysis of dehumanization with the stripping away of fundamental rights and legal protections. While this has a material component, it is fundamentally the denial of a person the right to exist and have a place they call "home" that is the true first step in the process.[2] As she wrote, "The fundamental depravation of human rights is manifested first and above all in the depravation of a place in the world which makes opinions significant and actions effective."[3] What is at stake here, as Richard Bernstein reminds us, is "the right to have rights," which "means the right to belong to some kind of organized community where rights are guaranteed and protected."[4]

Bernstein pays particular attention here to Arendt's idea put forward in the *Origins of Totalitarianism*, which states, "Only the loss of a polity itself expels him from humanity." The promise of annihilation appears in this schematic when someone is denied the political. While there is some agreement to be had with the idea that violence begins with the stripping away of political agency, we must avoid falling into the liberal trap of seeing violence as a failure of liberal democracy and its vision of modernity. Indeed, given Arendt's focus on rights, it's evident why her thought has appealed to liberals who invest so much energy in the promise of international law. Bernstein affirms this point when he argues that "the first stage in the process of total domination is to kill the juridical person in man."[5]

More important is the ontology and phenomenology of domination, where spatial forms of enclosure created human laboratories, which in the name of protecting sacred space, meant that everything became possible. From his juridical perspective, Bernstein situates the violence done to individuals at the end of the line. The ends of annihilation are, according to Arendt, to "destroy individuality," for this means to "destroy spontaneity, man's power to begin something new out of his own resources, something that cannot be explained on the basis of reactions to environment and events."[6] The outcome of this is ultimately to turn the camp into a corpse factory, populated by barely living forms, condemned to oblivion. But what if we reverse the order of annihilation, to see the organization of violence as precisely the attempt to destroy, from the inception, alternative claims to the future? Let's consider this following quote from *Origins*, which Bernstein also recalls:

> Total domination, which strives to organize the infinite plurality and differentiation of human beings as if all humanity were just one individual, is possible only if each and every person can be reduced to a never-changing identity of reactions, so that each of these bundles of reactions can be exchanged at random for any other.... The camps are meant not only to exterminate people and degrade human beings, but to also serve the ghastly experiment of eliminating under scientifically controlled conditions, *spontaneity itself* [emphasis added] as an expression of human behavior and of transforming the human personality into a mere thing, into something that even animals are not.[7]

What is the ontological condition of this spontaneity if not something we might refer to as the poetic? And what is the poetic if it's not something original?

That which remains irreducible to didactic reasoning yet is all too real to the human condition. We might recall Arendt's insistence here that "nothing we hear or touch can be expressed in words that equal what is given by the senses." Some things are beyond representation, beyond words, but it is through art and language that we are able to glimpse their immensity. Hence, to witness is not rendered inviolable; on the contrary, it is to affirm what actually makes us human and the limits we impose upon ourselves. This is true for the act of creation as much as it is for infinite depths of despair. To kill the spontaneous is an attempt to destroy the poetic in life, to vanquish an affirmative mind. It is, as such, to kill someone while leaving them nominally alive, to turn a human being into a phantom whose singular purpose is to live out their fated existence.

The ends of which are not simply about breaking the body down, but bringing about the effective disappearance of the human and the negation of its very claim to existence. In the process of annihilation, there are therefore two stages that also need to be considered. But these stages are not the ends of the process; they are literally prefigured into the violence before the body appears on soon-to-be-violated ground. Annihilation seeks to bring about the disappearance of life. From the Atlantic Ocean to the concentration camps to the woodlands of Europe, the Rio de la Plata in Argentina, to the dense jungles in Guatemala, to Palmyra and the open desert expanse in Iraq today, this world is populated by unmarked mass graves for the bodies of the disposable of history. And what are these pits if not further testimony to the terrifying idea that the greatest act of violence is to take a life and make it so that it never existed? To weaponize the void and turn the absence into the sum of all fears?

But if disappearance is the ontological purpose of annihilation—to render beingness absent from itself—there is a final original stage, what we might see as a violence over violence, the final burial of the already subsumed, where even the witnessing of history is denied and its memory destroyed. Acts of genocide have become public events marked by memorialization and the often-hollow calls to learn from the past to ensure such violence never happens again. But while this memory is often used to sanction further violence in the name of what's absent, more often the very intention to disappear is denied. Such denial amounts to the disappearance of disappearance—what Henry A. Giroux has called the violence of organized forgetting, where violence is wielded against history itself and the lived memory of atrocities committed against entire peoples and cultures is presented as a mere mishap, an accident of history, or even an exaggeration. What's at stake here is not simply the politics of truth, justice, and reconciliation, though there is no doubt that confronting disappearance quite literally presents us with the gravest of responsibilities. If we fail to grasp the violence of annihilation by dealing with the phenomenology of disappearance and the will to obliterate life and void existence, then we end up simply falling back upon the comforts of juridical solutions. Barring that, we end up looking inside ourselves for a better understanding of the sacredness of life, and we fail to ask more searching political and philosophical questions that deal with how we imagine and ethically encounter the world.

THE DEPTHS OF INHUMANITY

Those who have been thrown into the terror of the void know the real depths of our shared inhumanity. Writing on the sacrificial fires of the Holocaust, Giorgio Agamben draws our attention to the figure of the muselmann, which, he argues, was the one unique aspect of the Holocaust. It wasn't the violence that was original, nor the Third Reich's willingness to slaughter millions in the name of sacred space; for Agamben, the muselmann marked a new departure in the history of human suffering, the likes of which had not been seen before. While the terrible sight of naked bodies stacked on top of one another is a spectacle that reaches back to ancient times, "the sight of the muselmänner is an absolutely new phenomenon, unbearable to human eyes."[8]

The term "muselmann" referred to inmates of concentration camps who had reached such a state of emaciation they were seen by others as the "walking dead." They were the victims of a slow annihilation, drawing out the final act of killing, such that their claim to belong to any race—especially the human race—was categorically denied to the point that even their testimony was muted. Their physical and psychological suffering had become so extreme that it had killed them in both mind and spirit, even while their bodies were still, barely, alive. A system of punishment worse than death weaponized the vulnerable body against itself to the extent that the presence of death permanently hovered over it. A muselmann's existence served only as a reminder of how ghastly the human experiment truly was.

As Primo Levi explained in his harrowing recollections, "One hesitates to call them living, one hesitates to call their death death."[9] These "living corpses" whose bodies and minds had been consumed by starvation and exhaustion, had not only lost the capacity for living, but they were seen as irredeemable—what Levi referred to as "the drowned," that is, beyond all psychological, political, and physical rescue. All they could do was react, just barely. As Arendt explained, "The old spontaneous bestiality gave way to an absolutely cold and systematic destruction of human bodies, calculated to destroy human dignity, death was avoided or postponed indefinitely . . . [and the camps populated by] ghastly marionettes with human faces, which all behave like the dog in Pavlov's experiments, which all react with perfect reliability even when going to their own death, and which do nothing but react."[10] Little wonder society (including even the most critical of theorists) preferred to turn away from thinking about these wretched and irredeemable souls. Not only were they beyond the reach of any rescue or redemption, they offered no solution to the question of human depravity.

And yet, for Agamben, it is only by looking directly at these figures that we might rethink ethics beyond the moral entrapments of sacred forms of judgment, which became all too pronounced in the wake of liberalism's apparent triumph. As he writes, "In Auschwitz, ethics begins precisely at the point where the *muselmänn*, the complete witness makes it forever impossible to distinguish between man and non-man."[11] Leaving aside those who are concerned by Agamben's privileging of this figure and the challenges it means for dealing with the question of witnessing the unspeakable (something that is also connected to Levi's testimony, and his shame for having survived Auschwitz, for which he ultimately took his own life),[12] it is nevertheless surprising Agamben, after his analysis of the muselmann, doesn't seek to take us directly into the void but instead turns more attentively to spatial figuration of the camp.

The spatial violence endured by those imprisoned within the concentration camp are not in doubt. Like Dante's Hell, Auschwitz was a place one entered and did not emerge from. The site was clearly marked on a map, with its cartographies of suffering now determinable for all to see. And yet, as Levi suggests, there was much more at stake here than any geopolitical placement:

On their entry into the camp, through basic incapacity, or by misfortune, or through some banal incident, they are overcome before they can adapt themselves; *they are beaten by* time [emphasis added], they do not begin to learn German, to disentangle the infernal knot of laws and prohibitions until their body is already in decay, and nothing can save them from selections and death by exhaustion. Their life is short but their number is endless; they the muselmänner, the drowned, form the backbone of the camp, an anonymous mass, continually renewed and always identical, of non-men, who march and labour in silence, the divine spark dead within them, already too empty to suffer.[13]

It is the phrase "beaten by time" that provides us with a new point of entry to understanding the violence suffered by those who had endured the worst and ended up becoming witness to the total collapse of their own humanity, even to the extent of their capacity to recognize a fellow human. As Levi further explained in a passage that has been pivotal to Agamben's thinking:

> I must repeat—we, the survivors, are not the true witnesses. This is an uncomfortable notion, of which I have become conscious little by little. . . . We survivors are not only an exiguous but also an anomalous minority: we are those who by their prevarications or abilities or good luck did not touch bottom. Those who did so, those who saw the Gorgon, have not returned to tell about it or have returned mute, but they are the "Muslims," the submerged, the complete witnesses, the ones whose deposition would have a general significance. They are the rule, we are the exception . . . We who were favoured by fate tried, with more or less wisdom, to recount not only our fate, but also that of others, the submerged; but this was a discourse on "behalf of third parties," the story of things seen from close by, not experienced personally. When the destruction was terminated, the work accomplished was not told by anyone, just as no one ever returned to recount his own death. Even if they had paper and pen, the submerged would not have testified because their death had begun before their body. Weeks and months before being snuffed out, they had already lost the ability to observe, to remember, compare and express themselves.[14]

There is no doubt Levi suffered from a certain shame from having survived. But it would be a gross mistake to see his point here about the nature of witnessing as somehow a resignation or even a claim that the indescribable has totally defeated us. He is suggesting no such thing. On the contrary, we must try to draw upon whatever grammatical tools are at our disposal to counter the violence of such annihilating tendencies. Alongside Levi's words, our understanding of the existence of the drowned also owes a great deal to the power of visual testimonies and their importance in witnessing the unrepresentable in the destruction of the human as a dignified and free political form.

Our attention could invariably turn here to the haunting works of Aldo Carpi.[15] A professor and dean of the faculty of painting at the Brera Academy in Milan, Carpi was deported and interned at Gusen, which was a satellite camp of Mauthausen in Austria where only 2 percent of the prisoners survived. Carpi managed it by using his artistic abilities, by painting his captors and their children in tranquil landscapes and homey environments. And yet, alongside these, his clandestinely produced sketches and subsequent paintings of the harrowing conditions of life in the extermination camps offer the most devastating testimony on the worst of the human condition. His works, like the harrowing *Il Deportato* (1951), are populated with ghostly figures who appear naked and totally vulnerable, blurring the lines between the living and the dead, flanked by guards who represent the juxtaposition between the powerful and the damned. While we shall return to the figure of the ghost later, here we must stress how Carpi's depictions further evidence the importance of art. His depictions of the muselmänner serve as one of the few visual testimonies to their existence, rendering intelligible the barely living and the already dead of the camps in their abstract nakedness.[16]

Like many of the inmates of the camp, the muselmann was painfully emaciated, but also completely stripped bare (to echo Agamben's terms) of all mental aptitudes to the point that they had lost all concern or awareness of their place within this zone of indistinction. They had lost all sense of belonging, become almost totally abandoned by this world, had been left alone to the unforgiving elements, had been fully consumed by the terror of a space that no longer made any sense. Their extreme emaciation—the last stage in a ghastly experiment before the sacrifice by fire—was but a further sign of the violence inflicted: the violence of starvation, the violence of hunger, the violence of neglect, the violence of decay, the violence of slow catastrophe, witnessed by all who were interned in the same environment, unimaginable to those beyond the wire. But if we think about this emaciation phenomenologically, might we not see it as more than just a warning to the other inmates, who preferred not to look upon what might be their potential future selves? Might the emaciation in fact be revealing of the violence of disappearance, which Nazism systematically embraced and modernized, happening right before our very eyes? Is not the slow withering of the body, mind, and soul as it is fully consumed by nothingness, nihilism complete?

To talk about such depths of inhumanity means that we need to move beyond spatial cartographies of suffering. Or, to put it another way, we need to have a better understanding of the differences between notions of place and space, and how they relate to the terror and creativity of the void. Violence upon bodies always takes place within the bounds of time and space. There is the moment of its occurrence and there is a discernible location in which the violence is committed. This is self-evident. But we also know that before and after the event, there is a much deeper psychic life to violence—that is to say, while ideas of placement are important to give context and quality to specific crimes, our concerns with the phenomenology of violence (especially its sacred motifs) demand a more intimate analysis that is willing to confront the terror of the void. Our conception of politics is dominated by narratives of place. Place is defined by placement. It is marked by the ability to establish points of location and fixed coordinates, to draw lines in the earth and map out borders and irrefutable limits, while consecrating memories of belonging and abandonment to further sanctify the natural order of one's place in time.

Space, in contrast, is the milieu of existence that is open to the infinitely possible. While a space can be claimed and turned into a habitable place, it always has greater potential when it remains riven with contradictions and contesting boundaries. But what becomes of a body or a territory once it is swallowed by the void? The body is also a place, for it too is marked by many borders that seek to fix into place lines of identity. The body is inhabited. And it may also become uninhabitable. Indeed, to violate a body is always to violate a place, to maim or destroy an idea of how a place may be inhabited, its future character expressed by its most defining element: life itself. Those who are consumed by the void find, as Dante knew, their body becomes a prison and their sense of place is completely destroyed. But, unlike Dante's vision of Hell, this condition of violence is a non-place, without clearly defined points of entry and exit. To become a prisoner of one's own body and mind means that resistance—let alone escape—is a challenge which the liberators of a physical place can never fully understand.

The void is a non-place. It is a swirling vortex where the forces of history and the irreducible qualities of human existence collide. And, while we define the void by its depths, especially the depths of inhumanity, these are not literal, physical depths—rather, they are marked by an intensity of experience. And such intensities work to different rhythms, from the chaotic to the slow and painful, such that time itself is weaponized and turned back upon survivors so that they cannot escape their position as victims of history.

The void belongs to the territory of the mind. It is consciously—in its supra and sub variants—neuropolitical. It is the infinite promise and the unknown terror. It is the unscalable height and the bottomless depths. The void is the infernal hurricane and the embracing winds of wonderment. It is pure potential. The space is of such immensity that its violence needs to be measured by the intensity of its depths and the power of its creative flight. And given that the life of the mind is inseparable from the body it occupies, however much it is able to separate itself from within itself, what belongs to the void is shaped and transfigured by the supra-sensible world. It responds to every glorious sunset, every feeling of bitter coldness, every emotional state, every scream of broken time. The void is affective and affecting, spilling over into silence, turning the banal into the sublime and the sublime into the atrocious.

That is why the mindset for thinking about the void always begins with the body. But the body is only the mind's casing, for it is the mind, immersed in its own world, which becomes the ultimate arbitrator between the imagined paradise or the reality of Hell. It is a mistake, therefore, to see the void as either a place that we can neatly draw with scientific precision or as some autonomous, detached anatomical form separated from the world. It is inhabited. After all, the supra-sensible is an entire ecology of meaning, immersing the body into its aesthetic, atmospheric, and affective registries that shape what we know to be the human condition. It exposes the mind to the wonder and the violence of existence.

Since World War II, images of emaciated bodies have become far more commonplace. We have ready access to historical photographs of prisoners of war— among the most striking being John Florea's 1945 portrait of Joe Demler, an American prisoner of war—and to contemporary images of child victims of war and famine in sub-Saharan Africa and the Middle East. In these examples, the subjects' emaciation invariably speaks to something in the order of the sacred, pushing us to imagine the possibility for redemption. Perhaps they remind us of the crucified Christ, whose body appeared not only emaciated, but violated and exhausted by the violence it endured. Two notable examples of this emaciation can be seen in Matthias Grünewald's *Christ in Majesty*, which appears in the center of the Isenheim altarpiece (1515) at Colimar in France, along with Bartolomé Bermejo's sorrowful *Christ at the Tomb Supported by Two Angels* (1474). We can also think of the starved and broken body of Christ after his death in Michelangelo's

Pietà, which, as we have already noted, has become iconic in liberal representations of victimhood.

But there is always a fundamental difference between depictions of Christ and contemporary examples of emaciation in victims of war and famine. It's all in the eyes, said to be the window to the soul. Christ's eyes may appear closed, sorrowful, questioning, and even purposeful, but there is no doubt that his gaze communicates a universe of meaning. The damned of history, however, offer no such reflection. Theirs is an absent gaze. It is literally devoid of meaning. It communicates only absence. Sometimes this absence looks intensely focused, like the madman in Goya's *Yard With Lunatics* (1794) or the grief-stricken father in *Ivan the Terrible and His Son Ivan*, Ilya Repin's harrowing and controversial masterpiece (1885) where the delirium of violence has an almost hypnotic quality. But other times their gaze looks totally helpless, defining the face as a face truly on the precipice of death, even to the very thought that something, anything, may once again be worth looking upon. An absence—they are lost in a cavernous vortex, consumed by a nihilistic darkness and drained of all color and vitality. All that's left is a blackness that is not the sum of all color, but devoid of all meaning—something so unreadable there is nothing to say, every spark of life extinguished as the will to live has fully vacated.

The exhaustion of such a sight is beyond our reach, beyond testimony. And we too can only look back upon this gaze for a brief intolerable moment in the uncomfortable silence of an unbearable confrontation in the optical presence of those who have touched the void and returned seemingly blind to the world. What, after all, can be read by pupils so dilated by the blackness that all has been consumed and we can see the memory of a person fading in our very presence? We can recall here Simone Weil's notion of appearing under erasure:

> It will surely kill, or it will possibly kill, or perhaps it merely hangs over the being it can kill at any and every moment ∴ . . . it turns man into stone. From the power of transforming a man into a thing precedes another power, otherwise prodigious, the power of turning a man into a thing while he is still alive. He is alive, he has a soul; and yet, he is a thing . . . Still breathing, he is nothing but matter, still thinking he can think nothing.[17]

In Canto XXIV of *The Divine Comedy*, Dante encounters from the forbidden woods a group of emaciated bodies, which he describes in the following way:

"And shadows, that appeared things doubly dead. From out of the sepulchres of their eyes betrayed. Wonder at me, aware I was living." What does it mean to recognize those in purgatory—between life and death—as being "doubly dead"? And what does it mean to make a sacred tomb of the eye or consider more its deathly gaze? Unlike Dante's emaciated souls, who wanted to be seen and could be looked upon with pity, according to Agamben those existing at the threshold between life and death are unbearable to human eyes. In the concentration camps, those who were at the point of death did not instill pity but terror. Others feared looking upon them lest they may see a promise that they will suffer the same fate.

But what is the order of this terror, not only for those in the concentration camp, but for those of us who turn away from this intolerable image? Is the sight of such wretched figures unbearable precisely because in the act of recognition we realize there is nothing to recognize in their absent stare? That their lost gaze offers no testimony, gives nothing except a reflection of a mind that is now also reduced to nothingness? A window into a destroyed soul, which in such a catatonic state makes the idea of purgatory seem terrifyingly apt. Vilo Jurokovic wrote that the muselmann with "fallen in or bulging eyes, was a picture of misery, of weakness, hopelessness, and horror."[18] Whereas Levi remembered their "faceless presence; I could use this familiar image to sum up the entire suffering of our age: a broken man, chin down, whose faces and eyes showed no traces of thinking." Citing a study carried out among Auschwitz survivors by Stanisław Kłodziński (who also survived the camp), Zdzisław Jan Ryn writes:

> The dominant features of the *muselmänn*'s face were his eyes, "heralds of death in the camp," as Stanisław Pigoń put it. The look in those eyes was devastating: "The eyes of a concentration camp prisoner would have betrayed him even if he could have managed to escape, wash, and be fed and properly dressed, and at first glance seem normal. Those eyes were restless, staring in all directions and constantly on the lookout for fear of impending danger, or a chance to obtain things he needed; those eyes seemed to be popping out, glowing with a strange phosphorescence like the eyes of a wolf, glowing with hunger. Yet at the same time the look in those eyes was alert, lively, taking in everything around. The *muselmänn*'s eyes were restless, but they stirred only for one thing: where to obtain food. The look in those eyes was apathetic, sunken under the eyelids, shining green, they seemed dead already, showing not a will to live, but a blind and vacuous hunger."[19]

So, what are we to make of this gaze in relation to the concept of humanity? Levinas once argued that "the eye does not shine, it speaks." It speaks to the face of the other, the face of the stranger, the destitute, the living presence of something that is more than I, the face of humanity that is able to weep and recognize the pain of others. Herein this abject vision—a gaze hollowed out by absence, symbolic of nothing, total abandonment—appears before us like the very collapse of humanity. We stare into eyes that no longer even cry at their fate. This gaze has seen so much suffering it is now colonized by cruelty and coldness, denying understanding, forcing us to flee in terror from what the reflection may reveal about ourselves.

When explaining the meaning of those emaciated subjects in Purgatory (notably between the two cantos dedicated to poetry and love), Virgil alludes to the Ovidian myth of Meleager, whose mother kills him by burning a log that is connected to his life. Furthermore, Virgil tells Dante that the sight of those he referred to as "doubly dead" is nothing more than a mirror. "If you recall how Meleager was consumed," Virgil says, "just when the firebrand was spent, this won't be hard to understand; and if you think how, though your body's swift, your image in the mirror captures it, then what perplexed will seem to you transparent." But what confronts us in this glass if not the intolerability of our shared inhumanity? The void is a mirror, and the gateway into its territory is through the absent gaze. But, like Rodin's gates, these mirrors do not open upon request, nor can they be ventured through to access the abyss. There is no clear opening or path into objective witnessing that allows us to proceed with certainty along suffering's journey once we have been thrown into the depths of the void. It demands a different intuition, whether we have gone willingly or under duress. And yet, we are able to glimpse from time to time the immensity of its presence. The eye is the gate. The mind is the territory. The body is the prison. The world is the milieu. The experiential is the tragedy. And life is the damnation.

THE DREAM OF TOTAL ANNIHILATION

Once humankind achieved its full possession of the world, it put into practice the idea that the planet could be destroyed. This dream of total annihilation doesn't come from the artists or poets of history; it is exclusively the property of the scientific and technocratic mind. As Deleuze wrote, "The technocrat is the natural friend of the dictator—computers and dictatorship; but the revolutionary lives in the gap which separates technical progress from social totality, and inscribed there his dream of permanent revolution. This dream, therefore, is itself action, reality, and an effective menace to all established order; it renders possible what it dreams about."[20] But there is always the threat of appropriation, the technocratic desire to mobilize the poetic.

Indeed, the driving goal for regimes of annihilation has always been the appropriation of the force of creative production: *the destruction we create is greater than the creativity we destroy*. To bring about the conditions of the new, something needs to be replaced. But the difference here is that while the poetic continues to speak to the ancestral, the technocratic seeks to fully obliterate the past in all its irreducible forms. And yet, while the poetic seeks to transgress the sacred, the technocratic needs to maintain the appearance of the sacred in order to give meaning to an otherwise empty existence. If the hidden secret of the sacred is the way it inspires people to kill in its name, the hidden secret of technology is not simply the wish to control life through the automation of human existence, nor even the inventor's desire to appease their immortality complex. Technology's secret is its attempt, by controlling the speed and intensity of human interaction, to master the creation of the void: to tame and manage its appearance with controlled precision, to speak the language of liberation to ghosts already in the making, while opening with engineering precision devastating ruptures in the fabric of time, of such immensity they can consume all life in their vicinity.

There is to be nothing beyond the technocratic vision and its sacred pursuit of happiness. Let us recall then that all violence, especially modern violence, is a violence of movement. There is no greater freedom than to deliver violence without mediation. This is the foundational principle of every colonial project and the defining characteristic of the United States today. The nation itself is a globally ambitious project whose entire history has been defined by migration, flight, and the nomadism of its killing machines. As the homeland of such inventors as Gatlin, the Wright brothers, Ford, Oppenheimer and his team who worked on the Manhattan project, and more recently the DARPA scientists tasked with creating the World Wide Web and data-fueled systems of algorithmic violence, the United States is the embodiment of the notion that if war is the motor of history, technology is the motor of war. And what is the purpose of war if not to master the forces of annihilation?

There is little doubt that post-World War II, the West faced a tremendous ethical and intellectual crisis. Adorno was certainly not alone in feeling that all was
lost and the best we could do was to live doing as little damage as possible. How
could humanity possibly rescue itself following the horrors of the death camps?
How, in other words, was it possible to bring the humane back from the brink
of its potential obliteration, having realized that humans were capable of committing atrocities upon their fellows in the name of the advancement of the species and the creation and protection of sacred space? While the label of ideology
was important in separating fascistic from liberating forms of extreme violence,
the answer would actually be found in the mastery of scientific prowess and the
acceleration of the power of technical thinking. Modernity itself was never to
be put on trial,[21] even though its insistence on promoting the technical over the
poetic was the key determinant in accelerating society's capacity for violence in
the name of its sacred claims.

An evident outcome of this acceleration was the reduction of the logics of
genocide to a particularly abhorrent moment in history—something unique
to a distinct ideology, which therefore appears to be an aberration, or a devia-
tion from the otherwise emancipatory road of human progress. But, as we have
learned, the term "genocide" has been fraught in the extreme, often deployed
in order to sanctify certain groups of victims while withholding such a status
from others. At stake here is not just the capacity to authenticate the true victims
of history, but to allow claims of victimhood to translate into sacred forms of
violence. The deployment of this sacred violence is consequently both righteous
and just, as it is always a response to the threat of total annihilation, even if it
is driven by the imperative for annihilation, haunted by and yet allied with the
presence of the void. In the pursuit of everything, nothing prevails.

Leaving aside the overtly politicized debates on genocide that end up being
truly subjective (that is, less about actual numbers killed and more about which
group was the victim), our concern should be with how we might further critique
the forces of annihilation in light of their technical attributes. Invariably, here
we could ethically insist on focusing on intent: (was the destruction intentional?)
or scale (Holocaust? or holocaust?). Alibis and unintended consequences aside,
we must ask the question from the perspective of the victim: does the intention really matter? Can it absolve the perpetrator from their crimes? Berthold
Brecht's "Interrogation of the Good" still echoes across the ages here.

And while we could say the Holocaust was clearly genocidal in intent, does that make its atrocities any worse than the annihilation of indigenous populations throughout the Americas as a result of violent conquest, slavery, and infectious disease? Today Hernán Cortés might have called these "collateral damage." And what about the crudity of statistical measures, which are often used in highly contingent ways, so that they actually reaffirm the positivism of the technocratic mind? Might a thousand deaths register as a genocidal act but nine hundred ninety-nine count merely as a mass killing? What's painfully needed in these deliberations is something that looks behind the act of annihilation to address the weaponization of nihilism, individuals being openly recruited to the terror of the void, and the nightmarish disappearances that ensue. To annihilate is to disappear a life—in body, spirit, memory, and thought. At its extreme, it is in fact about the annihilation of annihilation, the disappearance of disappearance, the absence of absence, the sacred completion of time and the reduction of everything to nothing, even while it is all still alive.

If the concentration camps have shown us the real depths of our inhumanity in the most intolerable ways, we should be no less concerned with our sending entire cities into oblivion, collectively and in the same moment, by delivering violence from wounded skies. While there are many examples we can draw upon here, there are two cities that expose most clearly the obliteration of life made possible by advanced technology: Guernica and Hiroshima.[22] When we remember the Spanish civil war, we invariably think about Pablo Picasso's most famous painting, *Guernica*, a copy of which hangs outside the United Nations Security Council in New York. How many times has war been justified by the leaders and politicians who walk past this visual testimony of human suffering? And yet, in testament to the importance of art, how many of us would remember this atrocity at all were it not for Picasso's intervention?

The bombing of Guernica forced us to confront the devastating and indiscriminate violence we visit on one another from the skies. Picasso's famous painting commemorates the day when Guernica, a town largely populated by women and children, was bombed into oblivion. This was another experiment. And as the correspondent George Steer wrote in the immediate aftermath, "When I visited the town the whole of it was a horrible sight, flaming from end to end. The reflection of the flames could be seen in the clouds of smoke above the mountains from 10 miles away." Such conscious destruction would become a favored strategic policy thereafter, with many of Europe's great cities targeted in aerial assaults during

World War II. We might recall here Alan Resnais and Robert Hessen's powerful short film *Guernica* (1950), which features the artwork of Picasso and words of the poet Paul Éluard. Edited together using a cutting technique, the film presents us with a cacophony of fractured images which act as a requiem for the dead. In doing so, it captures the brutality of the assault, made all the more harrowing by the appearance of men, women, and children who appear momentarily in the chaos to remind us of what no longer exists. Their memory owes everything to the power of artistic testimony. As Éluard narrates: "Friendly faces faced with nothing. Poor faces, sacrificed. Your death will be a warning to all ... Monuments of distress. Beautiful ruins ... Death interrupted the comfort of time."

World War II brought into focus the real horror and devastation of warfare. In terms of urban devastation, the siege of Stalingrad also stands out as one of the most atrocious in human history. As the Nazis laid siege to this major Russian city, it is estimated that up to two million people were killed, disappeared, or suffered a prolonged death due to starvation. And while the Allies' firebombing of nonstrategic cities such as Dresden remains an ethical challenge for many today, the bombing of the cities of Hiroshima and Nagasaki remains indefensible. On Monday, August 6, 1945, the United States dropped an atomic bomb on Hiroshima, killing 70,000 people instantly and another 70,000 within five years. They unleashed the same violence on Nagasaki three days later. Splitting the atom had resulted in, to use the words of Harry Truman, a "harnessing of the basic power of the universe. The force from which the sun draws its power."[23]

If Hiroshima was exceptional, the subsequent bombing of Nagasaki normalized it. In both cases, the victims were vaporized, ghostly shadows on the ground all that remained of their bodies; an entire ecology was annihilated, its people sent into oblivion, erased by the promise of peace. As Miyuki Broadwater, a child survivor of Nagasaki, recalled, "For people underneath an A-bomb to have become shadows on the wall, and charcoals, before they could fall to the ground, no one wanted to believe it. But it happened."[24] They had become victims to the invisible fire and the black rain that fell from Japanese skies. In the *New Yorker* shortly after the bombings, John Hersey wrote a devastating description of the atrocity and its effects, which are now so often removed by the unpopulated representations of the cloud:

On his way back with the water, [Father Kleinsorge] got lost on a detour around a fallen tree, and as he looked for his way through the woods, he heard a voice ask from the underbrush, "Have you anything to drink?" He saw a uniform. Thinking there was just one soldier, he approached with the water. When he had penetrated the bushes, he saw there were about twenty men, they were all in exactly the same nightmarish state: their faces were wholly burned, their eye sockets were hollow, the fluid from their melted eyes had run down their cheeks. Their mouths were mere swollen, pus-covered wounds, which they could not bear to stretch enough to admit the spout of the teapot.[25]

Thousands who survived were blinded, debilitated by radiation sickness, and emotionally traumatized. In the immediate aftermath, the carnage visited upon civilians was buried under official government pronouncements celebrating Victory over Japan Day. U.S. censors in Japan forbade any public mention whatsoever of the atrocity until 1952. Official military photographs of the mushroom clouds were similarly censored; they were released on August 11 and would only feature in the back pages of national newspapers.[26] Extraordinarily, not a single national newspaper in the United States featured the iconic photographs on their front pages. *Time* and *Life* magazines did eventually use the images in their August editions. In the *Time* magazine section, the two photographs were reduced in size and accompanied by a picture of Prometheus with the caption "Progress has its price."

The atomic bomb was widely celebrated by those who argued its use was responsible for concluding the war with Japan. They applauded the power of the bomb and the wonder of science for creating it, and hailed the atmosphere of technological fanaticism in which scientists had been prevailed upon to create the most powerful weapon of destruction then known to the world. Conventional justification for dropping the atomic bombs held that it was the most expedient measure to securing Japan's surrender and that the bomb was used to bypass a long, drawn-out of war, thus saving American lives.[27] This argument was wielded against growing objections to the use of atomic weaponry put forth by a number of top military leaders and politicians, including General Dwight D. Eisenhower, who was then the Supreme Allied Commander in Europe, former U.S. president Herbert Hoover, and General Douglas MacArthur, all of whom argued it was not necessary to end the war.

The mass killings proved to be another ghastly experiment in human disappearance and annihilation on an epic scale. Not only did they demonstrate the unimaginable force of scientific efficiency and effectiveness, they effectively proofed the unbounding of annihilation from any ethical compass.[28] Hiroshima and Nagasaki also showed how the erasure of the human from the scene of the crime, both physically and through the media's focus on the image of the mushroom cloud rather than the human devastation it caused, permitted the most banal and horrifying displays of public celebration of this new technology. This ranged from Miss Atomic Bomb beauty pageants to photographs like the one in *Life* magazine in 1946 that featured U.S. Navy Vice Admiral William H. P. Blandy and his wife cutting a cake made in the shape of a mushroom cloud. The real challenge, therefore, was to try to bring the human back into any discussion of this atrocity, something that Alain Resnais achieved in his masterful and deeply moving film *Hiroshima Mon Amour*, which connects the atrocity to the complexities of human relations and our often misguided conceptions on the violence of artificial love. To echo the lines of the film's heroine, played by Emmanuelle Riva:

> Listen to me. I know something else. It will begin again. 200,000 dead and 80,000 wounded in nine seconds. Those are the official figures. It will begin again. It will be 10,000 degrees on the earth. Ten thousand suns, people will say. The asphalt will burn. Chaos will prevail. An entire city will be lifted off the ground, and fall back to earth in ashes . . . I meet you. I remember you. Who are you? You're destroying me. You're good for me. How could I know this city was tailor-made for love? How could I know you fit my body like a glove? I like you. How unlikely. I like you. How slow all of a sudden. How sweet. You cannot know. You're destroying me. You're good for me. You're destroying me. You're good for me. I have time. Please, devour me. Deform me to the point of ugliness. Why not you?

Photographs of Hiroshima and Nagasaki have been refined and normalized over time. The bombings appeared like some ultimate cosmic force, inevitably unleashed—for they were too powerful to contain indefinitely—yet scientifically controlled, somehow ordered and reasoned, as if adhering to unquestionable laws. The bombings were presented as both awe-inspiring and beautiful, their soft-hued composition domesticating the terror and brutality within. The atomic cloud has in fact become so iconic that it is difficult to think about modern disaster movies featuring end-of-the-world narratives that don't make use of its imagery. It has become embedded in our culture, part of the fabric of a normalized imagining of annihilation.[29]

Peter Sloterdijk remarks on the importance of this particular image:

> Terminator 2 is a landmark in media history; not because it uses film as a medium in particularly advanced ways, but because the medium of God, the missionary, the man on a mission, appears here in a new aggregate state—like an angelic machine an archangel who has exchanged his sword for an updated weapons system. Arnold is the modern St. Christopher who carriers the saviour of humankind across the world as if it were a battlefield.[30]

Let's put aside the fact that the only nation to ever use such weaponry has positioned itself as the moral voice of reason so as to act as its own custodian over such devastating scientific potential. What remains particularly abhorrent, and yet instructive for future wars, was the attempt on the part of those who defended using the atomic bomb to construct a redemptive narrative through a perversion of humanistic commitment, in which mass slaughter is justified in the name of saving lives and winning the war.[31] The ends, quite simply, justified the means.

There is another more contradictory and yet now well-established logic of modern warfare which emerges from this atrocious event. Supporters of the attacks used Hiroshima and Nagasaki to perversely rescue the concept of humanity, so challenged by the Holocaust, by turning the event into a humanitarian act made possible only through advanced technology. If war would only be made more terrifying still, we might hear Gatlin exclaim. Indeed, the more advanced a nation's technology and capacity to wilfully invest in intelligent forms of annihilation, the more likely that nation is to reveal its civilized credentials in the face of annihilative potentiality. Hiroshima and Nagasaki did not bring about the end of war, as those who sanctioned its use initially predicted. The scientific beast of destruction showed a remarkable capacity to reinvent itself. Rather than marking the end of a war to end all wars with the use of a technology so devastating it could bring about total annihilation, it actually marked the beginning of another chapter increasingly marked by proxy violence, which spread across the world at lightning speeds. At the level of the imaginary, what this violence forced us to recognize was that, in the final act, there might be nobody left to witness the devastation, nothing left to be seen.

TO DISAPPEAR A LIFE

Nazism showed how an entire society could be mobilized for the purpose of wide-spread slaughter. The Holocaust in particular, and the subsequent discovery of extermination camps in places such as Auschwitz and Bergen Belsen, made the concept of humanity both necessary and yet redundant at the same time. Humans were, after all, capable of the most inhumane acts upon their earthly fellows. Such violence, as Arendt insisted when writing about the trial of Adolf Eichmann, truly was a crime against humanity. But what crime was Hitler really guilty of commit-ting? What was it that truly transgressed the acceptable or justifiable violence that otherwise takes place in wartime? It is tempting, of course, as is often argued by the victors today, to explain Nazism as a perverse failure of modernity—a brief, inexplicable episode in human evolution. This narrative presents the Holocaust as an exceptional event, something that happened to a specific group of people in a unique time and place in modern history. This would be the mask of mastery for liberalism. Everything could be reduced to an extreme perversion of ideology, not the commitment to order and progress that liberalism embodied.

But the silent voices of innumerable ghosts haunt this narrative. The Nazis' real crime was to turn Europe itself into a colony, utilizing methods of warfare and dehumanization which had already been tested in overseas colonies upon native populations whose humanity had always been questioned. Evidently draw-ing upon Arendt's notion of the "boomerang effect," as Michel Foucault would explain that what was perhaps at stake here was using the most dehumanizing forms of violence to make visible the order of power which is concealed within the machinations of political rule:

> While colonization, with its techniques and its political and juridical weap-ons, obviously transported European models to other continents, it also had a considerable boomerang effect on the mechanisms of power in the West, and on the apparatuses, institutions, and techniques of power. A whole series of colonial models was brought back to the West, and the result was that the West could practice something resembling colonization, or an internal colo-nialism, on itself.[32]

When the British soldiers liberated Bergen Belsen in 1945, they found piles of corpses. Slowly walking among thousands of sick and starving prisoners, they soon discovered mass graves in which thousands of bodies had been buried. BBC television footage captured the moment and brought home the horrors of the camps which Levi and others later described in deeply moving testimonies. But it's important to remember that the Nazis didn't invent concentration camps. Internment first appeared in Cuba in the late nineteenth century, with Spain's reconcentration policy during the Ten Years' War that resulted in close to a quarter of a million casualties.[33] Concentration camps would subsequently to be used in a more systematic way by the British, targeting an entire population during the Second Boer War. Initially set up, it was argued, to contain and manage the local "refugees," their numbers grew following the implementation of Kitchener's scorched-earth policy—which included the systematic destruction of crops and livestock, the burning down of homesteads and farms, the poisoning of wells, and the salting of fields. But both outside and inside the camps the local people faced death from starvation and disease. In the colonial setting, warfare thus became ecological and biological in the most concentrated and systematic of ways. A temporary Hell could be created on earth, its borders drawn, its inhabitants selected, its punishments ritualized, and its forms of justice enacted in the eternal and sacred name of nations. And in this setting, the violence of disappearance could be enacted.

Moreover, it is also important to remember that forced disappearance and the creation of mass graves were not a Nazi invention. The Nazis simply mastered these tactics with engineering precision. The logic of abduction was in fact a hallmark of the transatlantic slave trade. As Achille Mbembe noted, "Any account of the rise of modern terror needs to address slavery, which could be considered one of the first instances of biopolitical experimentation."[34] Between 1526 and 1867, some 12.5 million slaves were shipped from Africa. Humans, including children, were abducted from their homes and packed into the hulls of ships; they underwent the most indescribable of journeys, before being sold on the market like cattle. They wound up working in brutal conditions on plantations for the enrichment of their wealthy owners.

Many of the enslaved would never complete the journey across the Atlantic, and their fevered bodies would often be thrown overboard when there was a financial incentive to do so (Let us not forget here that the slave-owning merchant classes developed many of the early economic ideas concerning trade, its legal regulations, and its benefits.) This was depicted in J. M. W. Turner's painting *The Slave Ship*, which offers a devastating commentary on a true event in history.

In 1781, the slave ship *Zong* was caught in a ferocious storm. Assessing the situation, the captain of the vessel ordered the slaves thrown overboard so he could collect insurance for property that had been lost at sea. When Turner exhibited his painting in 1840, it was accompanied with an extract from his then-unpublished poem "Fallacies of Hope":

> Aloft all hands, strike the top-masts and belay;
> Yon angry setting sun and fierce-edged clouds
> Declare the Typhoon's coming.
> Before it sweeps your decks, throw overboard
> The dead and dying—ne'er heed their chains
> Hope, Hope, fallacious Hope!
> Where is thy market now?

The Atlantic Ocean is a vast graveyard, full of absent bodies whose names and human dignity will never be recovered. Disappearance takes many different forms, though the voiding of existence is always its endgame. Its aim is ultimately to leave no trace. What is also clear is that the violence of disappearance takes a great deal of organization, planning, and administering if it is to be truly effective and have the desired political effects. It is reasoned, rationalized, and calculated, with its psychological effects delivered with scientific precision. Disappearance communicates through the absence of bodies. It feeds off the negation of presence, tormenting the realm of the visible and the order of appearance. And the terror it induces lingers in the minds of those who live with the unknown consequences.

As Edelberto Torres Rivas has noted, disappearance is even crueler than assassination, for it creates an "imaginary world" of a death that is "prolonged over time."[35] Families living with a loved one's disappearance know what it is like to be thrown into the terror of the void, to fall into the abyss, where all familiarity is unsettled, where one's eyes deceive as one searches frantically for the one precious thing which has snatched away, where time itself has been torn and one's sense of place has been broken apart with furious abandonment. Disappearance is the greatest violence of all. It is truly intimate and yet earth-shattering. It not only denies the body, it brings violence into every thought, even against the ghosts of those who have been denied a dignified burial and peaceful ending. Disappearance furthers the violence by allowing for the denial of the violence occurring in the first place, the disappearance of disappearance as if the victims were somehow complicit in their own assault. What's being denied here is not simply the right to life, but the right to ever have been—it is violence committed against the memory of what once was and against a future yet to be lived, now erased from the world. Allen Feldman explains:

> Enforced disappearance attacks the right of its victims to appear on the earth and classifies persons and populations as improper for cohabitation on the terrestrial surface of the planet. A nomos of the earth is advanced through enactments that void the diversity of cohabitation. In removing the disappeared from the terrestrial surface the executive power expansively virtualizes itself through the programmed immateriality of an absence—the deletion of the somatic materiality and biographical gravity of the vanished. Here the executive power delimits its dominion—not over the amassed corporeality of a body politic, nor even over the disfigured backs of the subjugated, but over the ephemeral historical dust, and faded footprint of the absentee and deportee.[36]

Disappearance would become the hallmark of totalitarian regimes across the world in the postwar moment, notably favored by military juntas in Latin America during the late 1970s and 1980s, as well as in Bosnia, Cambodia, Nepal, Iraq, and elsewhere. Perhaps not incidentally, since it took in many Nazi exiles (including Eichmann), Argentina was instructive in terms of this practice.

In her harrowing book on the history of violence in Latin America, Jean Franco forces us to recognize how systematic disappearance goes hand in hand with an order in which the very existence of the victim has already been negated. In a chapter titled "The Ghostly Arts," Franco addresses both the violence inherent to disappearance as well as possible strategies for resistance. With regard to the mothers of the disappeared in Argentina, she writes: "Disappearance was a form of cruelty that affected families for whom there could be no closure and whose agony turned into public scandal . . . "[37] What remains, she explains, are mere snapshots of an existence, which "in their very normality they defied the ferocity of an end that could only be surmised." This act of openly displaying the intolerable reveals fully the disappearance of disappearance, and in so doing opens up more searching questions on complicity and culpability: "The silence of the demonstrating mothers and the silence of the disappeared were met by the silence of the authorities, all of which converged on the silence of the photograph." This brings into focus the extreme pathos of absence, which points to a "foregone conclusion" even though relatives are still desperate to "restore their humanity" in the face of a future that's also violently scripted.[38] A profound yearning in the presence of a horror that denies the body its place in space, while cutting with torturous intent the image of a life as it may have or could have been in the present and into the future.

Modern liberal societies created an internal peace by exporting their violence to the global South. Sometimes these lands were landlocked. Other times they were bordering on the liberal nation in question. Mexico has been most instructive in this regard. As a nation that was at the forefront of the war on drugs (which in many ways was a precursor to the wars on terror), it has seen its very social fabric shaped by explicit and structurally entrenched forms of violence that can be only explained by accounting for external forces .[39] And even as Mexico revealed its liberal democratic credentials with the fall of its one-party rule, the violence and corruption proved wholly compatible with its free market dictates.

We also know that every significant technological advance has transformed the nature of war and violence. The digital and communications revolutions have been no different. Just as modern technology has exponentially increased our capacity to annihilate, counter to those who believed in the potential for new liberal forms of communication to bring about lasting peace, one of the apparent ironies of this age of radical interconnectivity has been the increasing ease with which bodies can simply vanish. We could turn our attention here to Ciudad Juárez, which emerged as an explosive and dynamic borderland city following the signing of NAFTA in 1994, fully integrated into global liberal architectures for production, power, and the political will to rule exploited life. While the world was coming to terms with the new access to political power created by the internet and the very first digital revolution in the southern state of Chiapas in direct response to the North American Free Trade Agreement, in Juárez stories started circulating about an alarming rise in the disappearance of young women and girls. Over time, it became clear that the city had become the site of the systematic abduction, abuse, mutilation, killing, and desecration of over a thousand women—some of which bore sacrificial scars.[40] A painted black cross acting as a sacred memorial to disposable bodies who were brutally discarded.

Systematic disappearance in Mexico can be traced back at least to the tumultuous global political events of 1968. That date would resonate again in 2014, following an attack on students at Rául Isidro Burgos Rural College in Iguala, in the state of Guerrero. Following a coordinated assault by unidentified gunmen on five buses, the violence left six dead, forty wounded, and forty-three forcibly disappeared.[41] Their whereabouts remain unknown, though mass graves continue to be discovered in the region, and most have come to fear the worst. All that remains of the victims are the memories their families preserve. One symbolic victim was found the morning after the attacks—Julio César Mondragón, whose discarded body was the evidence of a harrowing fate. His facial skin and muscles had been torn from his fractured skull and his internal organs severely ruptured.

Courageous journalists concerned with the plight of the so-called Forty-Three focused on state corruption, the influence of narco-trafficking in one of Mexico's poorest states, and how local elected leaders operated more like mafia organizations, controlling their fiefdoms through violence and intimidation in coordination with the state apparatus. This resulted in violent retributions, making this "liberal democracy" the most dangerous place in the world to be an investigative reporter. Liberal peace certainly had no purchase in a land where structural forms of liberal violence had been imported and normalized for decades. Hence, we need here to ask more searching questions about this particular disappearance and its place within a broader history of denial. As already argued, disappearance is the most potent and devastating example of the violence to being, as it denies survivors access to the truth. And yet, politics is all about the battle for memory, to the extent that we often see in the political arena open contestation of truths about the violence of the past. These memories do not exist in time capsules, neatly placed in some historical archive. The way we narrate the past is integral to how we imagine the present and how we will perceive the future. But how do we memorialize the tragic loss of those lives which are now absent? How can we resurrect the memory of a life whose actual existence has vanished without a trace?

Memorialization takes many different forms. It is as complex as life itself and open to various interpretations. Indeed, unlike the memorialization of military generals and political elites, who are immortalized in cast iron form across many cities of the world, the memorialization of the expendable, the downtrodden, the forgotten of history necessarily takes a more human form. Loved ones bring their memories back to life through candlelit vigils and intimate stories about their lives, idiosyncrasies, hopes, and brutally shattered dreams. There is a human dimension to this type of memorialization, which speaks to the human in all of us. And so, the human in all of us should be compelled to listen.

Absent any public recognition of the importance of the disappeared lives, it is common for their loved ones and those calling for justice to mobilize around alternative symbols. Often, we see this take the form of numbers—as in the Forty-Three—as if to both emphasize the scale of the atrocity and serve as a potent symbolic reminder. But this tactic also has its limitations. Not only can it lead to remiss comparisons (as in the work of Pinker) between different atrocities as the number of victims becomes more important than the uniqueness of the act. It is all too easy to lose sight of the fact we are dealing with forty-three individual victims with their own life stories. What happened in Iguala was the destruction of a life full of promise and ambition, forty-three times over.

Another question we need to ask concerns global media interest, or lack thereof, when dealing with disappeared lives. This is not incidental. While the impact of media events has a significant political bearing in terms of influencing the demands for justice and political response, it is also fully revealing of the politics of disposability and the ways some lives through their absence are seen as more valuable—hence more worthy of living—than others. This is not meant to be a commentary on the evident levels of compassion and empathy many feel when hearing about such atrocities. It is, however, meant to acknowledge much broader questions of power when it comes to the politics of mourning and what Judith Butler calls a grievable life.[42]

For Butler, to ask the question of what life is publicly grieved is to also ask about the importance and value attributed to one life over another. Grief or its denial is therefore a political act, which opens up various hierarchies of suffering. Furthermore, it is a point of entry into the logics of power, as it exposes more fully what a society is willing to protect against those elements of society, which can vanish without any consequence. The Iguala students were already lower down in the hierarchy of importance in a country that should have been nurturing their potential. Within global power structures, built on the colonial architectures to which Mexico has historically been integral and further exacerbated by the global drugs trade, the relative value of the Forty-Three in relation to the white Anglo-Saxon descent is painfully evident.

Defenders of the corporate media might argue that the reason such violence doesn't register on the global scene is because of its frequent occurrence. As Eduardo Galeano once pointed out, Latin America is so soaked in the blood of history its opened veins even look like an ailing and weeping heart on a map. The media certainly has a fixation on what is deemed exceptional. And what passes for the exceptional often shares certain fetishized aesthetics with the spectacular. Images of exploding towers capture attention. Disappeared bodies are less compatible with the preferences of "image conscious" societies. It seems we would rather confront the realism of the spectacle, which removes the actual body from depictions of violence, than dwell on the horrors of a problem that demands more sustained and searching reflection. But there are a number of points that we do need to address here. What passes for an "exceptional" event is viewed through racialized filters. Some events are so spectacular they cannot possibly be ignored. Nevertheless, the media will often take two events that are comparable in terms of aesthetic qualities and the scale of devastation (often of a lesser scale in terms of "our" relatable suffering) and mediate their importance. Furthermore, this fixation with the politics of the exception is dubious. From the perspective of the victims, Iguala was a truly exceptional and unique event, regardless of the fact that it took place in a state in which violence has become normalized. Hence, the reduction of this event to the vocabulary of the normal is also part of the politics of memorialization and its hierarchies of grief. After all, it is far more difficult to critique something that appears normal than something that appears exceptional.

History teaches us time and time again that political violence is not carried out by irrational monsters; it is rationalized, reasoned, and calculated. It is also purely subjective. This is not simply a reference to the fact that some forms of violence are seen as necessary and even tolerable, while others are considered abhorrent, intolerable, the personification of evil. Violence is all about inscribing upon the desecrated body markers of identity. The perpetrator of violence in the act of violation cuts away at the existing qualities of a life in order to undermine and negate its very existence. It's never arbitrary. Violence finds us. Sometimes it arrives at night, other times in broad daylight. It seeks us out and executes its plans.

Now, of course, it is tempting to make comparisons between different forms of violence in order to try and identify their consistent and unique qualities. While it is important to focus the uniqueness of each atrocity committed so that we don't fall into the ethical quagmire of ranking acts of violence in a hierarchy of severity (that is, each act should be condemned on its own terms), there is nevertheless the need to situate all violence against a broader historical and systemic context. Very little violence is randomly carried out. It is part of a longer historical process, which reaches into the depths of systematic oppression and persecution. All political violence has a historical temporality that also needs to be acknowledged, but such temporalities are politically fraught and subject to interpretation. How far back in history, for instance, do we begin to date the assault? Do we go back to recent history or should we demand a broader, even colonial, assessment? Often what stands out here are important historical events, which are fully loaded with their own symbolic memory and resonance.

Nevertheless, it is wrong to see the act of disappearance as some anti-spectacle event, or even as a form of violence devoid of communication. The spectacle of potential absence is projected onto the bodies of the living, those who now fear for their lives, just as the message speaks in a haunting language through its victims' silent screams, which can be deafening to those who hear them. That anybody could disappear at any given moment just for holding certain principles, for reading troublesome books, or even for having a friendly relationship with somebody who happens to be politically active points to an ecology of violence—a true climate of fear—which is both physically real and has a life independent of its actual occurrence. The act of disappearance takes us into the realm of the unknown: a mental space of anguish, torment, and imagined possibilities. It is part of the psychic life of violence, which turns imagination into an enemy of the self. This is why disappearance is much more than simply the denial of a person's right to be on the earth. The memory of those who disappeared serves as a warning to others, that they might suffer a similar fate and be forgotten entirely. It is therefore not only the denial of life, but also an assault on the very idea that a meaningful life eventually finds dignity in death. Disappearance then is a form of violence against the future. It immobilizes. Through the negation of life, it openly recruits the haunting memory of ghosts in order to impose a tyranny over the will of the living. And, in doing so, it resurfaces the bodies of the disappeared through the very act of denial, miscommunication, injustice, and the long, drawn-out nightmare of uncertainty over whether the deceased might eventually be located, and their bodies and minds laid to rest.

THE AESTHETICS OF DISAPPEARANCE

Disappearance takes us into the realm of the unknowable. It blinds all judgment by exposing us to the scattered dust of history. It belongs to the unintelligible. Striking with such a bloodthirsty pursuit against a life, and in doing so denying that life the right to ever have existed, it eviscerates what might be presented as meaningful. To disappear a life means to render it absent, to remove it from the realm of visibility and the certainty that comes with a presentness of mind as life appears before us as an embodied and recognizable form. With this in mind, we could be forgiven for seeing disappearance as rendering the aesthetic altogether meaningless. And what can art possibly say when the "here and now" is replaced by the "nowhere and never"? It certainly takes us beyond the limits of philosophical and aesthetic understanding.

Yet, while there is a devastating silence that accompanies the photographs of those who will never be recovered, we have seen that the ghosts of history refuse to be condemned to a death that doubles itself as it tries to kill memory and annihilate the past. There is always something that remains through the traces of history, the wounds that cut so deep their lines show through, the torments so excruciating even the monstrous believe their victory was total and nothing could survive. But to cede victory to nihilism is to fail to understand the memory of the void. It is also to deny the power of the ancestral and the fight for dignity against the savage ecologies of the world. As Jean-Luc Nancy reminds us:

> The word imago designated the effigy of the absent, the dead, and, more precisely, the ancestors: the dead from whom we come, the links of the lineage in which each of us is a stitch. The imago hooks into the cloth. It does not repair the rip of their death: it does less and more than that. It weaves. It images absence. It does not represent this absence, it does not evoke it, it does not symbolize it, even though all this is there too. But, essentially, it presents absence. The absent are not there, are not "in images." But they are imaged: their absence is woven into our presence. The empty place of the absent as a place that is not empty, that is the image. A place that is not empty does not mean a place that has been filled: it means the place of the image, that is, in the end, the image as place, and a singular place for what has no place here . . . [43]

The vanishing body that leaves its trace was an integral element of the work of the Cuban-American artist Ana Mendieta. While her work made evident connections to the ancestral in order to open up critical discussion on the questions of absence and presence, might we not also use it in a more political context to account for the forced disappearance of bodies from the terrestrial plane? As she wrote in 1981, "Covered by the earth whose prisoner I am, I feel death palpitating underneath the earth."[44] Some have suggested that her work was tragically fated, as it prophesized her own violent death. It has also been noted how her work has a dimension of conscious decolonization, as it connects to indigenous ideas regarding the life/world relationship outside of the triumph of reason.[45] But what might her work tell us about the violence of femicide, which often occurs as a hidden spectacle that is subsequently repackaged for public consumption, while on other occasions connecting to the hidden order of violence and the denial of one's right to live in any affirmative sense? Mendieta's *siluetas* (silhouettes) stand out in this regard, as a form of self-portraiture and testimony to a body that is now elsewhere, and which, like in her *Untitled* (1976), reveal to us an open wound in time. What remains here is precisely the image of absence, whose ghostly social presence actually makes the figurative more apparent. To look upon the works of Mendieta is to confront the intense vertigo one feels as the myth is presented fully.

A further compelling example of this vertiginous displacement can be seen in *Silueta en Fuego* (1975), where the body is seen to be violently taken by the original fire of the earth. And yet, there is something in this composition that points to a more critical understanding—the poetic fire within, where the abyss opens up and presents itself to the world. Memory thus becomes as ephemeral as the wind, its testimony written in the moving depths of the fragile earth. In the words of Mendieta, who speaks of her art emerging "out of rage and displacement": "My works are the irrigation veins of the universal fluid. Through them ascend the ancestral sap, the original beliefs, the primordial accumulations, the unconscious thoughts that animate the world. There is no original past to redeem; there is the void, the orphan-hood, the unbaptised earth of the beginning, that time from within the earth looks upon us."[46]

The violence of disappearance forces us to account for the violence of sacred time. This is articulated in the work of Bracha Ettinger, who has consciously positioned her work as an aesthetic memory against atrocity that seeks to break away from the sacred order of politics.[47] We can see this most clearly with her *Eurydice* series, in which the memory of the Holocaust is re-membered and returns in a more ghostly and challenging way (fig. 7.1). These works reconcentrate our attention on the harrowing scene of naked Jewish women and children being led to their deaths from the Mizocz Ghetto in Ukraine in 1942.[48] As a second-generation Shoah survivor, Ettinger sees in Eurydice a figure who was emblematic of her generation and whose message resonates with the disappeared of history.[49]

As the myth relates, fleeing from the advancing Aristaeus (who was son of the huntress Cyrene), Eurydice, upon stepping over a viper, is bitten and killed. Her lover Orpheus is left wandering in the wilderness until the gods instruct him to recover her body from the underworld. Once in the depths of the underworld,

Fig. 7.1 Bracha Ettinger, *Eurydice* series. Copyright Bracha Ettinger. Permission granted by artist.

Orpheus's sorrowful lament is enough to convince Hades and Persephone to allow Eurydice to return to the land of the living. There was, however, one condition. Orpheus must lead the way out of the underworld and not turn back to look at Eurydice until they reach the summit. The dutiful Orpheus obeys the command until he reaches the light of the living world, at which point he casts a glance back to see if Eurydice had followed. But she had not yet crossed the threshold from the world of ghosts and so is immediately thrust back into the depths of the abyss.

Eurydice is thus subjected to a second death because Orpheus succumbed to his doubts.[50] She is, in fact, caught between the realm of two disappearances, between presence and absence, between death and annihilation, between memory of loss and total forgetting. As Maurice Blanchot writes, "There is a void within [Eurydice] that constitutes her."[51] Her disappearance points us toward a psychic wounding in which the layers of history, as with Ettinger's artistic method, are revealed to be an accomplice in the brutal destruction not only of a life, but of its memory as well. It is to confront the disappearance of disappearance, which brings violence to trauma and the denial of the gaze within the community of the annihilated. As Ettinger explains:

> We join in sorrow so that silenced violence will find its echo in our spirit, not by imagination but by artistic vision. After an earth-shattering catastrophe,

must I not allow the traces of the horrifying to interfere with my artwork? Why should this be any different to psychoanalytical and critical interventions? . . . Art proceeds by trusting in the human capacity to contain and convey its rage and its pain, and to transform residuals of violence into ethical relations via new forms of mediation that give birth to their own beauty and define them. It is to trust that we will be able to bear in compassion the unbearable, the horrible and the inhuman in the human . . . When the witnesses disappear and only witnesses to those first-generation witnesses can speak, art's role is to create a humanizing space. While art evokes memory, it invents a memory *for* the future.[52]

Disappearance concerns memory. It concerns the past. It concerns the future. It concerns bodies. It concerns absence. It concerns wounds in time. And it concerns the terror of the void. The political function of art is therefore called upon in response to these challenges. Art navigates through the paradox of simultaneous forgetting and remembrance to convey the imminent catastrophe that sets out to destroy a life. It moreover gives us a perspective into unimaginable suffering by presenting historical violence as being all too real. This is more than representing simplistic and easily appropriated notions of victimhood. Art short-circuits this aspiration by demanding a more considered and intimate reflection.

It's at this point we can turn to the work of the Mexican abstract painter Chantal Meza.[53] Her *State of Disappearance* series asks us to consider the thresholds between life and death, appearance and absence, time and space, bodies and their place in the world. From images of ecologies of devastation in her *Fragments of a Catastrophe*, to ghostly figures in the *Apparitions* series, to the brutal and savage images of *Obscure Beasts*, her work critically questions the very idea of what disappearance means. It shows that the state of disappearance is a state of mind—a realm that only makes sense if one interrogates in the most searching ways the psychosis of violence (fig. 7.2).

And yet, there is a larger story here; the same darkened and solitary spaces into which life has been thrown also appear like expanding vortexes, pulling everything into their nightmare depths. The bloodstained canvases, populated by demons, monsters, and wretched souls, testify to the worst of the human condition—our capacity to inflict the most inhumane acts upon our fellow humans. Meza's work also utilizes an original aesthetic vocabulary and visual testimony, where terror bleeds into memory, forgetting into public recognition, and, most importantly,

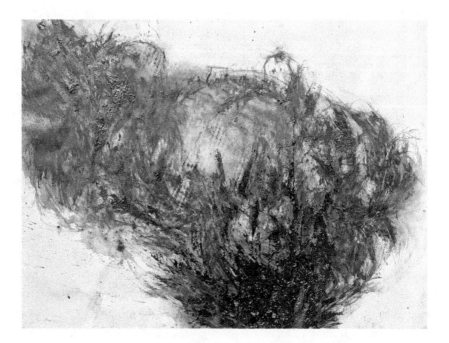

Fig. 7.2 Chantal Meza, *Obscure Beasts*, no. 1. 2019. Oil and ink on paper. Copyright Chantal Meza. Permission granted by artist.

the nightmare into the dream of an alternative future. This state is not some place that objectively appears on a map; it is imagined, and yet it is all too real. And, like the violence it confronts, its real depth is that of emotion, feeling, sensation, and desperation. Meza's work opens wounds that have existed before us, to ask how we might outlive their unique repetitions. This has nothing to do with confession. There is nothing to confess. The destruction of a life, which simply demands to exist with freedom, integrity, and dignity, is not a crime. What's imagined instead is a forceful opening into the innumerable wounds inflicted upon the bodies of innocent victims. It is a silent visual cry, which demanding immersion and reflection speaks louder than those who try to rationally justify why such abhorrent acts occur.

The challenge presented here is no doubt formidable. What, after all, is left to paint when the body is absent? How can we possibly portray something of the human when its very presence is denied? And how can we develop aesthetic testimonies of suffering without glossing over the complexities of human loss, while accounting for the ways the lines between perpetrator and victim are often blurred beyond all certainty? This brings me directly to Meza's *Obscure Beasts*, in which dark images emerge through the violent traces torn into the flesh of the canvas and its mutilated landscapes of historical despair. These abstract figures dance with raw realities of human misery and its unnecessary deaths. Upon closer inspection, the landscape itself is too close and yet still out of reach, confounding any attempt at forensic certainty. It is full of lines of miscommunication, which, subtly revealing tortured bodies and disfigured forms, draw the viewer into the scene like some unwitting accomplice.

Meza's obscure beasts are not confined to a specific time or place. She presents us with a visceral account of the human condition, its contradictions and dispossessions, its flight and horrifying entrapments. The black swallows the red, and yet the blood still flows out of the dark spaces. Bodies appear brutally contorted and disfigured, haunted by forces beyond the reach of any canvas. This has nothing to do with statistics or the silence that accompanies the photograph of a forgotten individual. It reaches beyond the singular and yet down into the most intimate depths of suffering. Meza embraces the abstract to show how pain is beyond explanation. But the shattered skull on display in her work is never anonymous. It belongs to somebody, and that somebody is a casualty of an imperial history which colonized the imagination and left centuries of devastation in its wake. We are reminded here of Fredric Jameson's notion that "History is not something we can know directly; it is available to the scholar only as a combination of traces or wounds. It can be apprehended only through its effects."[54] The artist gives us a sense of a different apprehension—or might we say a different apparition.

Meza's work deals with the brutal repetitions of history, where victims become tyrants, and where the persistence of annihilation results in perverse and monstrous outcomes. Speaking in solidarity with the dispossessed, the refugee, the abducted, the disposable, and the family that lives with the memory of an untouchable loss, Meza traces these wounds to expose us to an absence that shows how even invisibility itself can be weaponized to project violence into the future. Ghostly figures thus appear not simply as a testimony to the massacred of history; her work is not about representing the past. What these ghosts demand is a different conception of justice. And so, as we look on in silence, we too come face to face with the immersive power of a violence that knows no limits and ultimately sees itself as the beginnings, the means, and the ends. So, where does this leave us in terms of our lasting concerns? Recalling once again how I felt gazing into the vortex of Meza's *Mirroring the Void* (fig. 1.3):[55]

Mirrors hang to reveal a landscape of human devastation. But these mirrors are not simply reflective. They have no concern for the passing viewers all too fleeting curiosities. They know they outlive us. Side by side, what they offer is a visual testimony to histories of persecution. Fixed into place, they immobilize us with their dark movements. Yet walking past, it is clear they don't exist for our purpose or aesthetic pleasure. They speak to themselves. Assuming the right to project their truth back to each other, back unto the world. Having already foreseen the extinction of all human life, they never required our narcissistic presence or self-centred validations. And they have no care at all whether humans need art. These mirrors ask whether art ever needed us?

So, it begins, as always, with a misplaced sense of elation—the violating optimism. Once again, the masses are seduced by the promise of power. Flight into the future is presented as the only solution to the curse of the past. History has a way of making such things appear inevitable, certain, foreclosed. Such is the grand sweep of an uncompromising force, which has the capacity to displace all that stands before it. How they learned to desire their own oppression. This is the force of nihilism and the violence of reactive minds. And so, the lines begin to appear, yet already torn. Deeper and deeper, they cut into the canvas, revealing bodies caught in the unstoppable winds of a merciless storm.

Yet still they project their ambition across planes of denial. Cutting into certainty, feeling their way into existence like a liberating force already cloaked in the blood of the innocent. There is no absolving the shameful destitution. This is always their intention, always their desecrating purpose. They carry life with them on their fated journey.

But the majestic lines witnessed on their destructive flight soon turn into the most intimate voids of despair. Everybody is a victim. Everybody is complicit. Our attentions therefore shift onto another frame of reference and suffering. Into the abyss we now descend. The pain appears to us in the hopeless depths of subjugation, taking control over every aspect of human existence. That's why the void is a mirrored sight of anguish and madness. They who stare into the depths and see the Gorgon with his deep black eyes at the bottom of the icy pit look back with a monstrous vision. Inner demons thus return as wretched souls of prejudice and hate. Their intimate violence provides a new chapter in the brutalizing movements and flight of men. But it's a mistake to see them as victims born of the original scene. They were already there, waiting, alongside. This is why mirrors always double. Grandest historical claims are nothing without the intimate depths of passion and outrage.

But there is no tale of redemption or salvation here. The white glare of optimism proved blinding to those who already witnessed too much, and yet still persisted as if nothing had happened. Absolution reigned supreme, until the end. They held their trials. They condemned as guilty many in their midst for the inhumanity they showed to fellow humans. But never did they see the mirrors for what they truly were. Maybe they didn't have the courage to see themselves truly ravaging the beauty of the world? And maybe they didn't want to see how they ultimately destroyed themselves and thus played out the most fateful of all the worldly tragedies? And so, all that remained was for each soul to be captured in its nihilistic fall from grace, visibly caught up in the flight from meaning and forever lost in depths of these mirrors of the void.

CHAPTER 8

The Transgressive Witness

THE TRAGEDY OF ART

What is the role of art in the post-political world? How can we learn from its past in order to develop the critical tools necessary in these less than human times? There is an urgent need today to rethink the art of living and the aesthetics of existence in ways that don't simply fall back upon the comforts of rehearsed orthodoxy and the metaphysical binds sacrificial violence permits. This is not a call to paint over in peaceful or romantic colours the tragedy and pain of existence. Some of the most violent compositions show no explicit violence at all. What's required is a rereading of the political function of art and the forms of aesthetic engagement, so that by confronting the intolerable we can separate the unbearable from the objectification and subjectification of a life that only appears meaningful if it's afforded sacred ascriptions.

In this regard, art should not be seen as an object to be studied. It is a living and breathing form of aesthetic intervention that allows us to develop new ways of seeing and relating to the world. Indeed, just as aesthetics have been central to how we understand the changing sacralization of life, so, as we have already seen, the role of the artist has always been to provide potent witnessing to the horrors of humanity. But this does raise a very important question that we must confront: what is it about some forms of art, and the lifestyles they create, that ultimately proves too unbearable for its producers? Our societies are fascinated by the idea of the "tragic artist"; it's nearly a cliché that great art demands the ultimate sacrifice, as the creative act eventually takes the life of its author.

We might think here of the black finally consuming the spilled red blood of Mark Rothko's paintings, or Paul Celan's final leap into the void. We might also think of the origins of such tragedy, whether it was the young Frida Kahlo being hit by that tram, condemning her body to a life of suffering, or the eight-year-old Jean-Michel Basquiat being hit by a car, which set him on the road to anatomical discovery and his eventual untimely death. Both vehicles in this case served as a poignant metaphor for the artists' lives moving onward, to be constantly hit by the world against which they reacted while desperately wanting to be accepted; to be ferociously knocked to the ground by an unstoppable force, only for their corpse to be picked up and paraded across the rooftops, like the skeletons above Kahlo's bed, so that we might consume their tragedy, profit from their fate, over and over, through every possible appropriation of their image and desecration of their memory. This is why the Chapman brothers' reworkings of Goya are far more ethical, as is the denial of the work as some pure "sacred object," than the fashion trend of reproducing Kahlo's face on garments and accessories for purely aesthetic means.

If we are to challenge the sacralization of politics and the delusional objectification of existence, then part of our task is to break open from within what constitutes the sacred order of things. It is to undo the violence of every sacred embrace, and to creatively tear at the seams of all sacred objects, unstitching their mythical binds, so we might liberate those seemingly inseparable godly daughters who continue to mark their conjoined political presence. This requires us to separate tragedy from the "human," the human from "suffering," suffering from "art," art from the "world," the world from "thought," thought from the "academic," the academic from "discipline," discipline from "life," life from "peace," peace from "order," order from "law," law from "justice," justice from "retribution," retribution from "settlement," settlement from "love," and love from "sacrifice." This in turn requires us to think through and move beyond the tragedy of the poets of history. We must not seek to return to some utopian state where every landscape looks like a Monet—soft-hued dreamscapes where even the storms are robbed of their lightning—but to expose more fully the unbearable weight of history, which, in trying to impose some higher meaning to the wretchedness of human suffering, reasons the suffering away. We must undo every sacred demand, expose the illusions of the highest orders, and bring into question violence in all its forms, especially the sacred claims to violence advanced by every single Caesar who walks the earth.

What marks out the poets of history—those who are able to visually and verbally sculpt with time for a time which remains, effacing all known grammars for a language to come—is precisely their willingness to act as transgressive witnesses. They belong to a movement that breaks open from within the prevailing claims of belonging, that reveals the violence of its myths, rendering intelligible the visceral scars whose wounds allow us to question the irrefutability of all known sacred claims. Authors of their own untimely mediations, their inhospitable dwelling place finds creative renewal in the destruction of the void. They turn the oblivion of utopia and its dystopic twin into an atopia of their own, as time moves beneath their feet and the nihilistic air ignites a poetic and no less revolutionary flame. They renounce claims to sovereign mastery, despite the master's presence, transgressing their own vocabularies and shattering the order that dictates who is meant to speak on the planes of existence. They push up against every limit, not to negate what is possible, but to affirm the line of flight. And they paint upon the daggers stuck into the emperor's back, not to revive the empire but to find reasons to believe without good meaning in this world.

What the poets bring is never biographical, even though they demand the most intimate attention to history every time the slate is said to be wiped clean. They know the *tabula rasa* is equally a deception of the sovereign power. Their demand is to be open to the ineffable, even as they know there is a danger they might all too easily fall back down to earth in another mythical form. Satan was always a very easy-to-imagine creature. This is not about reserving some privileged place for the artist, or to claim that only the poets have the courage to seek out the innermost truth. We don't need yet another sovereign dressed in red. Nor is it to buy into the classical humanist conceit that only art can save us. Humans don't need saving, nor is a life a problem to be solved. We are human (all too human), which is more than enough. Instead, we seek to recognize what the poets open up through their mediations—not to authenticate a particular image of thought, but to see the world through different eyes. We seek to invert and rewrite the journey of Dante, venture into the void and reemerge into the wilderness, having exhausted the sacred and breathing a different concept of love? We seek a strange love—the only love that may liberate us—for it asks no sacrifice in return. We might even find reason to forgive Agamemnon.

THE VIOLENCE THAT REMAINS

Critics of this poetic demand and position might invariably return here to Adorno and his insistence on the barbarism of poetry after Auschwitz. On the one hand, we could say that Adorno was correct: after all, what does it mean to live on or even exist after such an experience, to carry its barbaric memory and come to terms with the shame of being human. Thought, existence, memory, dreams, all seem barbaric in light of the fact that the world survived, even as some of the Holocaust's most important witnesses found survival itself a burden too difficult to carry. Primo Levi is the most obvious case of someone who endured the unimaginable only to be unable to survive survival. We might also agree with Adorno on the failure of culture to prevent the Holocaust: "That it could happen in the midst of all the traditions of philosophy, art and the enlightening sciences, says more than merely that these, the Spirit, was not capable of seizing and changing human beings. . . . Whoever pleads for the preservation of a radically culpable and shabby culture turns into its accomplice, while those who renounce culture altogether immediately promote the barbarism, which culture reveals itself to be."[1] But might we not see the barbaric condition here as precisely upheld by a particular conception of art, the art which claims to speak to a universal history full of sacred qualities, which found its most potent expressions in Eurocentric notions of humanism and its claims to tame the natural world? We do not advocate, then, a full abandonment of the poetic (which Adorno never made), but for a reimagining of the poetic, especially in times when the aporetic conditions of life seem inescapable and its violence insurmountable.

What was nevertheless clear, as Adorno intimated, was that aesthetics would never be the same again. After the mass violence of World War II and Europe's importing of the concentrationary logics of the camp back into Europe from the colonial borderlands, the promise of art faced a notable crisis. What remained of the human to recover? After all, how could any knowledgeable and self-critical society deal with representations of the figurative when the human figure knew only pain and suffering at its own hands? What could be reclaimed for art when art itself had been appropriated for such destructive ends, and when its favored subject—the human form—brought so much devastation in the name of sacred glory for nations and the eternal rule for men on earth?

But art was never simply propaganda, nor was it irrevocably bound to universal history. The signs of its resistive potential were always apparent, even in the darkest chapters of history. Nazi Germany's designation of "degenerate art" is sure enough testament here to the way oppressive power feared free expression and creativity. Held in Munich in 1937, this exhibition ("Degenerate Art") was meant to show how art could lead to cultural and social decay, which, as the Nazis knew all too well, would be an integral element in the war over the mythical and sacred qualities of the nation. The Nazis waged open warfare on artists, including Paul Klee, Otto Dix, Marc Chagall, and Ernst Barlach, whose *Magdeburger Ehrenmal* (fig. 8.1) sculpture, which had been officially commissioned by the German state in 1929, eventually marked him out for particular attacks. The rather prophetic memorial is loaded with biblical significance, depicting a crucifix surrounded by three traumatized figures bearing the marks of horror, pain, and desperation. In the center is a priest-like mythological figure, standing proudly behind the cross, who bears an eerie resemblance to a young Adolf Hitler.

While the degenerate art exhibition would categorize art into various sub-groupings as the Nazis carried out their own creative assay, which mapped onto its biopolitical segregations, so the life of the body and the life of the mind would be brought together for the purpose of collective shaming. Abstract art would be notably set apart and housed in a dedicated space called "the insanity room." The rationale for this was clearly spelled out in the exhibition catalogue:

> This section can only be titled "Complete Lunacy." It takes up the largest part of the exhibition and includes a cross section of the spawn of all the "isms" that Flechtheim, Wollheim, and the "Cohn-sorts" have hatched, promoted, and flogged over the years. In the pictures and drawings of this chamber of horrors it is impossible to tell in most cases what those sick minds were thinking when they picked up the brush or pencil. While one eventually "painted" using only the contents of garbage cans, another made do with three black lines and a piece of wood on a large white background. A third had the bright idea to paint "some circles" onto two square meters of canvas. A fourth consecutively used a good three kilograms of paint for three self-portraits because he could not decide whether his head ought to be green or Sulphur yellow, round or rectangular, and whether his eyes are red or sky blue or whatever. In this group of madness, visitors to the exhibition only shake their heads and laugh. Certainly not without reason. Yet when one considers that all of these "artworks" were taken not from the dusty corners of deserted studios but from the art collections and museums of major German cities, where some of them still hung in the initial years after the National Socialist takeover and were presented to the astonished public, one can laugh no longer: all one can do is grapple with one's anger at the fact that a people as decent as the Germans have been so gravely abused in such a manner to begin with.[2]

Fig. 8.1 Ernst Barlach, *Magdeburger Ehrenmal (Magdeburg cenotaph)*. 1929. Photograph. Creative Commons, https://upload.wikimedia.org/wikipedia/commons/4/42/Barlach _Magdeburger_Ehrenmal.jpg.

We should not forget the courageous works artists, poets, and writers who have continued to produce in the face of annihilation. As the Viennese artist Gottfried Helnwein has explained:

> Nothing scares authoritarian regimes more than art and free creation. Why would Hitler burn mountains of books and paintings and ban all arts? Why would Stalin—the master over life and death of almost 300 million people, a man who commanded the biggest army and secret service that ever existed— be afraid of the poems written by Anna Akhmatova? Why would Mao be so obsessed with destroying China's entire cultural heritage? Why would FBI director J. Edgar Hoover, while denying the existence of organized crime in the United States, put so much effort into harassing and investigating every artist of any significance from Hemingway to John Lennon?[3]

What remained after the slaughter has always found a more poetic expression through the creatively expressive works of those who bore witness. However, after such devasting violence as witnessed during events such as the Holocaust something had to change in the order of aesthetics and the political function of art. While we will deal with the potential of abstract expressionism in the following chapter, it is important to look at the way art has responded to the crisis of the human and how it deals with humanity's more intimate and tortured state. Moreover, as we are entering into the age of our forced witnessing of violent spectacles that appear beyond all control, along with the commodification and proliferation of every type of image, violent or otherwise, what needs to be accounted for is how art acts as a transgressive witness, to narrate in order to bring about the effacement of the image, so the world's aesthetic pain and beauty can be felt and reimagined anew.

If Paul Klee's *Twittering Machine* (fig. 8.2) was one of the first artistic works to properly explore how the triumph of technology has led to the abyss, while teaching us more generally about the importance of art as a truly sensory experience, pushing us to train ourselves so that "one eye sees and the other feels," it is with Francis Bacon that the explosive potential for art to challenge the violence of figurative realism would become truly sensational. According to Deleuze, Bacon's work "distinguishes between two violences, that of the spectacle and that of sensation, and declares that the first must be renounced to reach the second, it is a kind of declaration of faith in life."[4] Bacon's isolated and disruptive figures, as Deleuze maintained, "break with representation, to disrupt narration, to escape

Fig. 8.2 Paul Klee, *Twittering Machine*. 1922. Oil and ink on paper. Public domain.

illustration, to liberate the figure."[5] He goes on to write, "Bacon's Figures seem to be one of the most marvelous responses in the history of painting to the question, how can one make invisible forces visible? This is the primary function of the Figures."[6]

Indeed, for Deleuze, the importance of Bacon is that he breaks away from "figuration" and its penchant for imposing a determinable sacred narrative onto the scene by illustrating the hidden forces of violence at work: "a deformed and deforming movement that at every moment transfers the real image onto the body in order to constitute the Figure."[7] Such a constitution of the body, for Deleuze, points to a different order of violence where movement is defining, "as if invisible forces were striking the head from many different angles."[8] Or, as Bacon would write, "We nearly always live through screens—a screened existence. And I sometimes think, when people say my work looks violent, that perhaps I have from time to time been able to clear away one or two of the veils or screens."[9] In this regard, what once appeared sacred is revealed in its full brutal form in a return to a life now more violently aware that the line separating crucifixion from the slaughterhouse is thinner than it appears.[10] To put it another way, it's simply a banal twist of fate that your body is not on display in a butcher's window and your head mounted on a wall alongside other trophies of wretched screaming beasts.

Bacon's compositions present us with violence—nothing but violence, pure and simple. In making visible the invisible forces that destroy life, he depicts the annihilation around us and the disappearance that emerges from within. He paints bodies that are slowly disappearing through the violence of movement. The body is simultaneously present and absent as Bacon opens the torso up to show there is no soul within, merely a life that can be torn asunder at any moment. But what's also striking about Bacon's work is the voiding of the eyes. The artist was painting at a time when the world had already seen too much violence, and yet remained blinded to countless continuous atrocities. He was also painting at a time when nihilism was fading from public consideration, and hence the void increasingly made its presence felt as the unspeakable truth haunting every thought.

Bacon makes no apology for his brutal honesty in reminding us of this. And yet, he is no longer content to look upon subjects with an absent gaze that negates meaning, for the eyes he paints are already destroyed. He conveys a real terror in their blindness too, as the void is now located in the mouth, throat, lungs, and chest, a new opening which turns violence into an atmosphere of the suffocated breath. This is part of the immensity of Bacon's work, that it confronts the silent and breathless scream, breaking through the black pigment to reveal a horrifying scene of a deluded sacred body vanishing before our very eyes.

Even the two violences that Deleuze identified point to more subtle considerations. Bacon paints the invisible, and in doing so shows that all violence is primarily defined by movement and every act of disappearance cast upon the winds of despair. Bacon's canvas is a theater of violence that exorcizes all its sacred multiplicities and solitary confinements. But the faint lines drawn with their barely visible vanishing points are also significant. If violence is all about movement, it also depends upon the caging of life, the ability to render the victim immobile and trap them within schematics for power which are also barely visible to us.

Jacques Rancière provides a nuanced framing of the history of art in order to wrestle out the invisible forces which destroy life. As Rancière writes, "If there is a visible hidden beneath the invisible, it is not the electric arc that will reveal it, save it from non-being, but the *mise en scène* of words, the moment of dialogue between the voice that makes those words ring out and the silence of images that show the absence of what the words say."[11] If every image contains within its framing subaltern resonances and political traces that can be deconstructed and are open to further interpretation, it is important to recognize the political meaning of art precisely when it de-figures representational schematics. As Rancière explains:

> The German word for the extreme form of that will, as we know, is *Vernichtung*, which means reduction to nothing, annihilation, but also annihilation of that annihilation, the disappearance of its traces, the disappearance of its very name. What is specific to the Nazi extermination of the Jews of Europe was the rigorous planning of both the extermination and its invisibility. It is the challenge of this nothingness that history and art need to take up together so that we reveal the processes by which disappearance is produced, right down to its own disappearance.[12]

Rancière further notes that it is sometimes too easily drawn that the extermination is "unrepresentable" or "unshowable"—notions in which various heterogeneous arguments conveniently merge: "the joint incapacity of real documents and fictional imitations to reflect the horror experienced; the ethical indecency of representing that horror; the modern dignity of art which is beyond representation and the indignity of art as an endeavour after Auschwitz."[13]

Rancière is notably taken here by Larry Rivers's *Erasing the Past II*, which, featuring a partly visible Holocaust survivor (invoking connections with the cover art of the Abacus edition of Levi's *If This Is a Man*), shows why we must approach all representations of historical events with a poetic sensibility—questioning what is memorialized, what is erased, what is being shown, what is being slowly forgotten. This history, he claims, should be rethought by attending to the hidden traces. This leads Rancière to argue that our history has not yet finished turning itself into stories. He cites a range of compelling examples—from Goya to Otto Dix, to Claude Lanzmann, to Zoran Mušič, among others—in order to highlight how the victims of history allow for us to rework the aesthetic field of worldly perception and its distributions of the sensible. This demands a rethinking of the power of aesthetics.

Bacon's work returns here with considerable expressive force. We are drawn to two particular works, which include his *Painting 1946* (fig. 8.3) and *Study for a Portrait 1949* (fig. 8.4). The former masterpiece is arguably Bacon's crowning

Fig. 8.3 Francis Bacon, *Painting*. 1946. Oil on linen. Copyright the Estate of Francis Bacon. All rights reserved. / DACS 2020.

Fig. 8.4 Francis Bacon, *Study for Portrait*. 1949. Oil on canvas. Copyright the Estate of Francis Bacon. All rights reserved. / DACS 2020.

achievement in terms of revealing the violence of the body in ways that unsettle illustrative determinism. The timing of the piece certainly invokes connections to fascism and its theological orientations. And yet, the ambiguities of the main figure offer many diverse readings, such that divisions between human/animal, screaming/laughter, witness/spectacle, and executioner/victim are difficult to establish. The painting also illustrates Bacon's fascination with "the scream," which as Deleuze suggests points to a "coupling of forces, the perceptible force of the scream and the imperceptible force that makes one scream."[14]

The screaming figures points to futurity, as it "captures or detects an invisible force"—the diabolical future, which "contains them potentially."

Deleuze sees this ability to couple the forces—both the perceptible and the imperceptible—which condemn a life to suffering as an integral quality for those armed with a more poetic sensibility. "The finest writers," he argued, "have singular conditions of perception that allow them to draw on or shape aesthetic percepts like veritable visions."[15] T. E. Lawrence in particular expressed "a profound desire, a tendency to project—things, into reality, into the future and even into the sky—an image of himself and others so intense that it *has a life of its own*."[16] Deleuze ascribed the same poetic qualities—what he terms the "fabulatory function"—to the visual arts and their capacity to free themselves from representational schematics. As he writes, "Paul Klee's famous formula—'Not to render the visible, but to render visible,' means nothing else. The task of painting is defined, as he explained, through the attempt to render visible forces that are not themselves visible." But how might we apply this to *1949*, which, depicting a screaming man in a glass cage, shows remarkable similarity to the figure of Adolf Eichmann on trial for his crimes in Israel? What diabolical future might be forcing this most banal of figures to silently scream at its imminent arrival?

Set in postwar Berlin at the height of the Red Army Faction's terror campaign known as the "German Autumn," Luca Guadagnino's remake of Dario Argento's classic 1977 horror film *Suspiria* (made in the same year as the violence) explores this diabolical future with the mastery of simulacrum and mythical power. His retelling seamlessly moves between the themes of witchcraft and delusion, their impact during the previous years of Nazi rule, the mass psychology at work in seducing the masses, and the role of psychoanalysis itself, replete with its own fantasies and violent exclusions. The story tells of an American dancer, Susie Bannion, who arrives at the Tanz Dance Academy, and whose visceral and raw energy quickly transcend the room in which she is performing to attract the attention of the master choreographer, Madam Blanc. Playing upon the ritualistic and daemonic element of dance, the story moves through a number of performative scenes, which become more intense and delirious as they unleash both bodily pleasure and violence among the students.

The most striking scene in the movie is the brutal disfigurement of a dancer who calling out the witches' identity. The scene, like much of the film, plays upon the logics of doubling, the mirroring of performance (this scene takes place in a closed room of mirrors), and the ability to render visible forces that are concealed from sight. While ballet often deals with violent themes, for the most part the violence takes place off stage. The violence becomes a simulacrum which, focusing on the beautiful disfigurements of the trained and contorted dancer, is blinded to its actual effects. This makes the violence tolerable for public consumption—an artform, like opera, full of beautiful deaths and gravity defying killings, which simulates as it slaughters, entertains as it enslaves, triumphs as it tortures. As Susie dances, the scene of the other girl's violent punishment is spliced in, and the duality of invisibility laid bare.

This is an act of monstrous shadowing, as the vibrant movements of the protagonist turn her into an active perpetrator of violence, whose every action makes her complicit in a horrifying assault. Her knowledge of the act is left ambiguous. When later asked how she felt as she performed the dance, Susie responds it was like being "fucked by an animal." Such political animality is telling, as the civility of dance plays out against the rainswept backdrop of postwar Germany, revealing its bestial character and the raw nakedness of its sacrifice. As the film concludes, the double attempted sacrifice of Susie is also inverted, and, in a departure from Argento's original script, moves away from the story of an innocent girl eventually triumphing over evil, to the dancer revealing herself as the Mother of Sighs—the literal mother of all evil. With all the men in the film mocked and reduced to a helpless and vulnerable state of being, she becomes the sacrificial machine—the one who can be ruthless and yet empathetic in her killing, the embodiment of a feminine violence and its order of sacrifice. She represents, perhaps, an imagined future beyond the sacred violence of the victim.

SUBALTERN EXPRESSIONISM

Jean-Michel Basquiat's *Julius Caesar on Gold* (1981) is arguably the most politically subversive of all his works.[17] The artist dealt with many political issues in his tragically short career,[18] most notably police brutality. However, it is his provocative depiction of Julius Caesar as a Black man that invokes a particularly heretical claim on the nature of sovereignty and how its form might be reimagined. The opulence and violence in this image are immediately apparent. Surrounded by a yellow and gold background, the figure strikes a defiant and unapologetic pose. What would it mean to come face to face with legitimate Black violence, he asks? But the dual being proposed here is duality itself. Nation, power, religion, identity—they are all being challenged as the naked Black Caesar confrontationally casts aside the regalia of privilege so apparent in depictions of royalty.

While the usual poetry that adorns Basquiat's works are absent from this piece, it nevertheless reveals his acute appreciation of the history of art and how it connects to dominant political ideas, along with his position as a poetic visionary. Basquiat's Caesar is a stark physical contrast to the world he occupies. He appears before us in a raw and unadulterated form, calm and yet ready to inflict violence at any given moment. It is difficult to tell whether this figure, this Caesar, is a boy or a man. This only adds to the drama. What gives this figure the right to stand before us in such an audacious way? Did colonization not teach us that the surest way to domesticate populations is to reduce adults to children, to infantilize the Other in order to render them as naturally inferior as children are to the patriarchal figure.[19]

This is compounded by the fact that Basquiat's Caesar is far from athletic, his body appearing more emaciated. This adds greater depth and historical resonance by exorcizing the wretched figure away from political idealism. There is no Orientalist seduction for the objectified black body at work here. Neither is there some romantic vision of the chiseled and sculptured warrior, whose muscular and sexualized prowess would ensure a glorious and beautiful death. "To bear witness in his work," as bell hooks wrote, "Basquiat struggled to utter the unspeakable. Prophetically called, he engaged in an extended artistic elaboration of a politics of dehumanization. In his work, colonization of the black body and mind is marked by the anguish of abandonment, estrangement, dismemberment and death."[20] Even—or, we might say, especially—the Black Julius carries these visible marks.

In Caesar's right hand we see a sharpened knife, which looks more like a tribal dagger, whereas in his left hand we see him holding what looks like a scepter. The parallels with Hobbes's *Leviathan* are striking, for God and country, religion and stately violence, protection and punishment, morality and its transgression, the promise of peace and the reality of war are all brought together in sacred union as the sanctity of sacrifice is writ large. But this Leviathan King does not look down from on high; he is grounded, and his feet are visible as he walks on the surface of the earth. Here, then, the golden backdrop takes on a renewed meaning; it represents not the ordered civilized realm that has been cultivated, its forests tamed and cleared,, but the unforgiving desert wilderness where life is in perpetual exile, where banished kings fight to reclaim their thrones, where everything is at stake.

As Thomas McEvilley writes, "In Basquiat's oeuvre, the theme of divine or royal exile was brought down to earth or historicized by the concrete reality of the African diaspora. The king that he once was in another world (and that he would be again when he returned there) could be imaged concretely as a Watusi warrior or Egyptian pharaoh."[21] But who or what is being sacrificed in this scene? Does the appearance of the letter "M" indicate that what's at stake here is not simply the appearance of violence as it is about to be reclaimed by a blackened body, so often portrayed as exhibiting violent tendencies, but to literally mark and memorialize those whom the system has sacrificed and killed off for nothing other than a belief in its own omnipotence—Martin, Malcolm, Mahatma, then later Michel, who was also fated to an untimely death? Was it meant to commemorate those whose commodifiable value skyrocketed upon their death, their revolutionary message domesticated by the liberal logic of entitlement and the desire to attribute value, their life subjected to sacred objectification? That is why this Caesar's journey through the wilderness is so resonant and revealing more fully of his political and philosophical sensibilities. As hooks further writes, "Basquiat journeyed into the heart of whiteness. White territory he named as a savage and brutal place." In doing so, Basquiat exposed "the anguish of sacrifice," which echoes "the sorrow of what has been given over and given up."

Basquiat's Caesar appears on the verge of sacrificing the abstract figure on the table beside him. As we mediate on this, we are invariably drawn to the white lines that overlay the ruler's silhouetted crown, providing a displaced aura to frame the body of this black sovereign. It is tempting at first to see this as representing a halo in a purposeful reworking of Christian iconography. But might we not read this alternatively as a powerful symbolic adaptation of the Fanonian warning—now appearing here as black skin, white crown. A subconscious warning, perhaps, for the artist who would also be king, who is about the take the art world by storm yet knowing how his rebellious aesthetics would be appropriated by everyone, especially the liberal, who would seek to literally make a killing from his work.[22]

Basquiat's anatomical appreciation is all too apparent in this piece. Like the crown, the body is overlaid by white lines. Breaking down the dichotomy between the external and the internal, these lines appear reminiscent of an x-ray, which might symbolize an attempt to reveal more fully the marks of oppression worn by the subjugated. Or, perhaps, it is a nod to the tale of the emperor's new clothes, which always worn-out literally and metaphorically revealed something to those who dare to speak the truth to power. And yet the sacred is still brought into question, its violence revealed before us. We can see traces of crucifixion here, as the Black king has his arms outstretched in that familiar posture. But there is no cross, and this Jesus is armed and willing to fight back to reclaim his rightful position in the world. Borrowing from Gayatri Spivak, we might understand this work as an example of "subaltern expressionism" in the way it rethinks all terms of engagement by exposing its violence in the mirror of history. It is a poignant example of an aesthetic reworking, which takes seriously the violence of the times in order to challenge how the world appears to the dispossessed of the world. This, in the artist's case, meant they were literally living on the streets. Dealing with the harsh realities of being Black in America, Basquiat offers a provocative counter-aesthetic to the sacred violence of the times, reminiscent of what Spivak also terms "affirmative sabotage." As she writes,

> Affirmative sabotage doesn't just ruin; the idea is of entering the discourse that you are criticizing fully, so that you can turn it around from inside. The only real and effective way you can sabotage something this way is when you are working intimately within it. This is particularly the case with the imperial intellectual tools, which have been developed not just upon the shoulders, but upon the backs of people for centuries.[23]

hooks would no doubt be in agreement. To return to her article on the importance of Basquiat's work, she draws parallels with James Baldwin's *The Fire Next Time*, which, she explains, "declared that 'for the horrors' of black life 'there has been almost no language.' He insisted that it was the privacy of black experience that needed 'to be recognized in language.' Basquiat's work gives that private anguish artistic expression."

This resonates with Lewis Gordon's claim on the decolonial nature of art and how its transgressive witnessing relates to historical oppression. Gordon explains:

> Colonialism and other forms of oppression are *human practices* through which *human institutions* of violence are constructed and maintained. What this means is that they could never be complete. They are attempts, as idols and expressions of idolatry, to close human reality through reducing it to one of its elements. In the case of racism, that means the narcissism, as we have seen over the past few hundred years, of white supremacy. The obvious

limitations of all such efforts are that even those who built them eventually find them unliveable and seek alternatives even from those they supposedly "conquered." Colonized people fight, and part of their resistance is in their effort to reclaim their value, often through producing art that transcends the idols imposed on them. Colonial art eventually suffers the fate of all those who imagine they are the end of art, history, and thought.[24]

We are taken back to Foucault's concern with subjugated knowledges and forms of production denied by regulatory powers of the image-thought police. Around the same time as Basquiat was painting his Caesar, Foucault was being interviewed for the French newspaper *Le Monde* under conditions of anonymity. His reasons for concealing his identity were rather straightforward. He wanted readers who encountered his work to judge it based on its content alone. That is to say, if he used his name, the reader would arrive with preconceptions about the author and what he was said to intellectually embody. They cross-reference his works and identify contradictions, or authenticate or disqualify his position that was already set. What troubled Foucault was that his work would not be engaged with in terms of its particular singularity, but situated within a wider and altogether more transcendental body for meaning and truth. He opted to withhold his name, he explained, "out of nostalgia for a time when, being quite unknown, what I said had some chance of being heard." Anonymity was his "way of addressing the potential reader" without framing the work by having them "knowing who I am."

Writing as the "Masked Philosopher" allowed Foucault the luxury of more intense thought—he referenced "the lightning that could strike" in his more poetic and liberated style of engagement:

I can't help but dream about a kind of criticism that would try not to judge but to bring an oeuvre, a book, a sentence, an idea to life; it would light fires, watch the grass grow, listen to the wind, and catch the sea foam in the breeze and scatter it. It would multiply not judgments but signs of existence; it would summon them, drag them from their sleep. Perhaps it would invent them sometimes—all the better. All the better. Criticism that hands down sentences sends me to sleep; I'd like a criticism of scintillating leaps of the imagination. It would not be sovereign or dressed in red. It would bear the lightning of possible storms.[25]

Some four years later, as Mexico was still coming to terms with the devastating aftermath of a brutal earthquake that had ravaged its capital city, and fully revealing the corruption of the regime, a student named Raphael Sebastián Guillén made a trip to Chiapas, Mexico. He would later assume the name "Subcomandante Marcos" as a spokesperson for the Zapatistas, who become the very first organization to openly declare war on an internationally recognized agreement (NAFTA). The Zapatistas' politics broke new ground in terms of the way they connected indigeneity with a politics of difference that, setting aside the colonial dialectic, made nonviolence possible in a land that had only ever known the subjugation, massacre, and genocide of the indigenous. Moreover, Marcos captured the popular imagination with his grammatical interventions, presenting art, aesthetics, and theater as an integral element of the revolutionary struggle. Thus Marcos—another masked philosopher—would emerge as one of the most important critical thinkers of the late twentieth century. And while the local fight for the rights of indigenous peoples has been influential, his critical importance lay in his poetic ability to develop new ways for thinking and writing about politics and the world, which were also defined by their subalternity and creative expressionism. Marcos would show in powerful ways the importance of fabulation and the need to develop a new conceptual vocabulary to break away from the dogmatism of political science. As he explained in one of his many provocative writings:

> Scientists, political scientists, opinion leaders, chiefs of great and small political sects, all have gathered around Newton's fallen apple. All of them analyse, discuss, corroborate. Hours, days, weeks, months, entire years they take up. Finally, they come to the irrefutable conclusion: the apple has fallen because the law of gravity so orders it. It is irremediable, the apple must fall, and, by doing so, it has done nothing other than to subject itself to the law of gravity. The political scientists congratulate each other and then begin great essays in order to show Newton's apple as an example of "real-politik." The chiefs of state talk of erecting a multiple monument in all the palaces of Power . . . But, while the scientists are making complicated calculations concerning velocity, trajectory, much weight, acceleration, wind resistance, impact and similar etcetera's, and while the political scientists are re-writing Machiavelli and discussing prices with the modern princes, the Zapatista approaches the apple, he looks at it, he smells it, he touches it, he listens to it . . . The

Zapatista understands what the apple is whispering in his ear. He understands the challenge demanded by its cry. The apple says that fate does not
order it to fall to the ground, and, since it is a transgressor of the law who
is listening to it, it is about breaking the law of gravity . . . This apple that
Newton has chained to the ground has another destiny. The moon is an apple.
The scales of history need two apples in order to be able to look out at the
morning clearly. The political scientists continue repeating and repeating to
each other the "real-politik," and the etcetera's that already fill the magazines
and newspapers and the radio and television airtime. The Zapatista continues
making calculations. To fall upwards, that is the mystery whose solution has
been proposed.

Having written numerous inventive tales in conversation with fictional or
deceased characters, Marcos would also write a number of original theses on
global power and violence, none more compelling than *The Fourth World War*. In
this treatise, Marcos asks the question, "who is the enemy?" His response: "We
are saying that humanity is now the enemy. *The Fourth World War* is destroying
humanity as globalization is universalizing the market, and everything human
which opposes the logic of the market is an enemy and must be destroyed. In this
sense, we are all the enemy to be vanquished: indigenous, non-indigenous, human
rights observers, teachers, intellectuals, artists."

This war on difference, as Marcos explained, was a war against those who
dared to think and imagine differently. It was a war against humanity in its most
affirmative and freely expressive sense, even though strategists would soon learn
to appropriate those terms of engagement in order to justify violence in humanity's name. And so, what was at stake here was more than just a fight for the
indigenous of Mexico to have autonomy and the right to have rights. It was about
their ability to express themselves and make a claim to be part of a world. Not
for enrichment or to retreat into crude notions of identity—whether they be the
rightful heirs of the nation or the most persecuted people of history (which by
every conceivable measure the indigenous of Chiapas could rightly a claim to
being)—but to poetically affirm their own subjectivity, while acting as a watch-
person to the violence of history. It was not to lament, and certainly not to fall
back into some dialectic of representational purity, but to insist that another
image of the world was possible in creative response to the image of the world
that continued to annihilate.

THE UNSPEAKABLE

Art speaks to the unspeakable. It gives something over to us which cannot always be put into words. But what happens when art is put to the service of the sacred order of things? Can art not be complicit in the policing of thought and the reaffirmation of prevailing sacred tropes? Does it not in this case turn the unspeakable into the unquestionable as the unspeakable truth appears above and beyond all critique as the sacred demand dictates? We might think here about the incomparable suffering endured by Christ, which was spoken in appearance, as it became one of the most formidable regimes of truth inflicted upon a fearful and often illiterate population. It was not through the written word but the silent work of art whose thunderous cries would be internalized to become a source of eternal torment for the sinners of the world. The sacred body of Christ would truly take hold among them, the soul imprisoning the body and rendering it mute in an unproven state of belief.

And we can also write of a time when the glorious dead were also the unspeakable, as the truth of belonging ensured the body would imprison the earlier conception of a religious soul through every single material claim made upon its mortal form. Embodying an untouchable memory, how the victory marches drowned out any criticism as the trumpets heralded a final salute replete with full sacred regalia of states. So, let us reserve a certain caution in our attempts to insist upon the poetic. Like thought, most art is put to the service of the rehearsed orthodoxy. Much of it is mediocre, seduced by the entrapments of power, banal, and blindly following the sacred paths purposefully set by those who promise fame and fortune. That is why we must, as we do for thought and the political, insist upon the exceptionality of art—not to impose some avant-garde hierarchy to mark out the culturally astute, but to recognize that humans are defined by difference, which means differences in abilities and in what makes us human as such, regardless of whatever identities we claim. Basquiat was a terrible musician, but he was an exceptional painter whose works embodied the most explosive subaltern expressionism, as compelling as it was devastating.

But how might we think of the unspeakable in a world dominated by the image? And how can the unspeakable nature of the victim as a sacred form be transgressed? While aesthetics from the 1960s onward would become increasingly dominated by photography and film, the very nature of art would increasingly absorb these mediums and transform their potential. As conceptual art would move away from formalism and toward the incorporation of language, both as literal representations and to provide philosophical justification for its recognition as art as such, so the body would become a site for conceptual expressionism and performative enactment. The conscious positioning of the figure of the artist in positions of torment and subjugation would be striking in terms of exposing the violence and pushing against the limits of the human condition. Marina Abramovich's *Rhythm* series is notable in this regard.

But while the performative brought art to life, the power of photography as it connected with other artistic mediums still resonated powerfully in the ways it pushed us to rethink the importance of the figurative, and in its potential to help us make sense of humanity through the violence we encounter. We see an exemplary example of this with *The Eyes of Guete Emerita* by Alfredo Jaar (fig. 8.5), whose style, as Rancière explains, overturns "the dominant logic that makes the visual the lot of multitudes and the verbal the privilege of the few."[26] In the context of the Rwandan genocide—what is widely seen as a true failure of humanitarianism—Jaar's work confronts the viewer with the gaze of

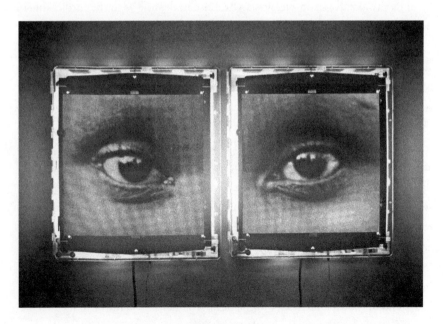

Fig. 8.5 Alfredo Jaar, *Eyes of Gutete Emerita*. 1996. Lightbox installation. Copyright Alfredo Jaar. Permission granted by artist.

a survivor who has witnessed far too much. The viewer is forced to witness the eyes of someone who in turn was forced to witness the most horrendous acts. This demands an appreciation of the way in which the intolerable can be turned into a recognition of humanity. As Rancière further writes, instead of showing images of mutilated bodies, Jaar's work "restores the powers of attention itself."[27] This quality is duly noted by Griselda Pollock, who adds that Jaar's installations asks the question "will you too remember her eyes—eyes that look at you forever but forever *see* murder?"[28] Jolting us "from the kind of consumption of the image that makes images out of atrocity without inducing a political response," *The Eyes of Guete Emerita* "register[s] the experience that others had been obliged to witness. It is this element that marks the singularity of his work in creating encounters for the viewers far away from the event that force them to recognize a gap that has been cut into a living person's life by proximity to atrocity, by the wound that is trauma: an event too shocking to be assimilated." Art then is all about facing the intolerable, As Jaar himself would explain: "We must represent the intolerable in such a way that it can be visible. That is really the big question of our times. And I do not have an answer to that question. Again, that is why I like the concept of exercises in representation. The entire Rwanda project, for example, was an exercise in dealing with the intolerable in one-way or another."

While the subtlety of these figurative engagements has demanded a more considered appreciation of the role of the witness, there remains the temptation to return to the sacred as a dominant theme for art. We have seen some of the most potent expressions of this in the visual theology of Bill Viola. Working within the anatheistic vein, Viola's return to the sacred here is presented as a way to "rehumanize" life, which has lost itself in a world of secular modernity. Such an account sees his artwork as a reimaging of the sacred, "summoning us to a rekindled humanity and a social instinct of empathy with others, what Viola himself described as an 'awareness' that may counter the 'anti-human' tendencies in today's world."[29] What becomes of the sacred in this regard appears through the cracks of the postmodern sublime. For while postmodernity was unable to mobilize any passage into a new politics of a distinct identitarian kind through its faceless transcendence, what becomes of the sacred demands a new presence that "shows up in the sacramentality of the flesh, whether in real life or in its imaginative refiguring by poets, artists and writers."[30] Committed to "restoring" theology to art by addressing grand themes, Viola seeks to "negotiate these sacramental moments in crossing of space and time, breathless moments of eternity in which our being is both slowed and quickened."[31]

What we have here is also an attempt to represent invisible forces, but instead of accepting the ineffable representable, Viola's work seeks a return to the sublime in the form of aesthetic revelation.[32] "The invisible" as Viola argued, is "always much more present than the visible."[33] In order to render the invisible visible, Viola has developed his own methods for manipulating our perception of time through advanced digital film production, so that in the act of slowing things down it becomes possible to reach beyond the limits of experience. What becomes of the sublime in this regard is precisely that which appears beyond reasonable doubt. In a Kantian sense, it reaches for the universal through a sacred encounter, wherein its capacity to transcend the figurative leaves the witness in a state of awe and reverence. Nature here is particularly important in terms of suspending and transforming the human condition in profoundly sacred ways. An example of this can be seen in Viola's *Five Angels for the Millennium* (2001), which, returning to the image of the crucifixion, casts the human body into the "luminous void of the unknown."[34]

It is also worth turning here to Viola's *Martyrs* video installation, permanently on display in the South Quire Aisle of St. Paul's Cathedral, London, which offers a remarkable example of the representational interplay between violence and the sacred, and brings the nature of the victim directly into question. The title of the work—*Martyrs*—immediately invokes political and theological connotations. Depicting four figures on large rectangular plasma screens, visibly overwhelmed as they are submitted to an intense physical trial, the work speaks directly to human suffering. The powerless and immobile bodies in the installation are exposed to the violence of the elements, as placed under intolerable pressure from earth, air, fire, and water. The sequence lasts several minutes.

Aside from the fact that the work follows the familiar historical tradition of prominent religious institutions commissioning artwork, the religiosity at play is apparent. The biblical significance of the four figures would be striking to theologians and students of the New Testament. Viola's work, however, also demands a more secularized and contemporary reading, something which the artist doubtless intended here for his digitalized and humanized performance piece. This is not about the Four Horsemen of the Apocalypse, whose association with violence and genocide signifies the End of Times. Viola's four martyrs, in contrast, are victims (albeit their victimhood is rendered ambiguous as the video's time sequence develops) who are subjected to a slower earthly catastrophe. And yet, the interplay between violence, sacrifice, and redemption through suffering offers less a departure than a contemporary reworking of theological themes, which explicitly emphasizes their political relevance. Viola's *Martyrs* embodies, it might be argued, the foregrounding of a sacred life, whose prerogative is to suffer in full physical gaze. Through a forced witnessing we are finally able to appreciate the physical and temporal predicament of earthly catastrophe and the time of crisis.

Alongside the insertion of life into the violence of his imagery, what makes Viola's work compelling is his ability to concentrate the viewer's imagination by consciously slowing down their experience. This demands a certain reflection borne of one's acute awareness of the passing of time. Agamben has noted this temporal significance, writing, "If one had to define the specific achievement of Viola's videos with a formula, one could say that they insert not the images in time but time in the images. And because the real paradigm of life in the modern era is not movement but time, this means that there is a life of the images that is our task to understand."[35] Agamben's attention here to what we might describe as the psychic life of images, examining it as a means for opening up new critical discussions on the political, places it in direct confrontation with the inscriptions of "spectral destiny."[36] It is not about constructing "the image of the body but the body of the image,"[37] liberating its wider political significance—the life of the image. As Viola explains in a passage cited by Agamben: "the essence of the visual medium is time . . . images live within us. At this moment we each have an extensive visual world inside us. . . . We are living databases of images—collectors of images—and these images do not stop transforming and growing once they get inside us."[38]

But is Agamben's attraction to Viola not revealing of his own messianic ascriptions? What is clear is that Viola's work leaves us in awe, and his martyrs, like much of his work, leave the viewer, as intended, silent. The setting itself demands this, as it once again reminds us of the need to be terrified in a space that speaks to the question of the infinite possibility. This is not just about inner reflection or soul-searching. It is about coming face to face with the power of the sacred and the untouchable silence it commands, where language has gone beyond the bounds of language and has returned mute. The sublime victim thus becomes a subject who is ultimately depoliticized by their own overrepresentation, and whose silent screams deafen us to the intimate subtleties of their poetic verses.

In contrast to the submissive qualities of Viola's sacred catastrophes, Gottfried Helnwein brings into question the purity of the sacred as presented in particular embodiments of the victim, notably within a liberal framing. Growing up in postwar Austria, Helnwein quickly realized the importance of art in terms of confronting the intolerable and challenging dogmatic images of thought. As Gottfried has explained, "I realized art would allow me to communicate something that society didn't want to talk about. To show people something of the horror that perhaps couldn't be put into words. I guess I was searching for a different concept of justice in art."[39]

A central theme in Helnwein's work is the figure of the child. Helnwein explicitly deals with the unspeakable in this context, from his *Epiphany*, which features what appears to be a baby Hitler being shown to an adoring mass of followers in a way that reflects the biblical scene, to his *I Walk Alone*, which shows a blindfolded child walking through a street lined with corpses in an invocation and reworking of the tale of Oedipus in the desert. But it is the artist's *Disasters of War* series which, paying homage to Goya, consciously disrupts the sacrificial motif of the massacre of innocents, as well as the historical narratives that embody it. The series features unsettling mixed-media works that blend portrait photography with painting, and among them we encounter depictions of a blood-soaked young girl whose whiteness is overemphasized like the innocence and purity she is meant to represent.

No. 13 (fig. 8.6) in the series stands out in this regard, as the child is positioned with a lowered head, depicted as sorrowful and yet not easily assimilated into conventional tropes of victimization. Whose blood covers her face and shoulder remains unclear. There is no wound to be seen. But it is certainly not a mediated or bloodless spectacle, which any secular theologian might rejoice at. Might it even be the blood of the girl's victim? The black background only adds to the drama of the composition, recalling the darkness of Caravaggio as it contrasts with the white of the girl, creating a sense of depth in a haunting immersion. It is unclear whether the child is coming into or leaving the scene. Indeed, the scene itself remains unlocatable. It could be anywhere, and yet it retains a dreamlike quality. Is it not, in fact, inviting us into the void? This is not about shocking the spectator into submission through an aura of sacred reverence.

Fig. 8.6 Gottfried Helnwein, *Disasters of War 13*. 2007. Mixed media. Copyright Gottfried Helnwein. Permission granted by artist.

Nor is it simply mirroring experience to bring about empathy or a shallow, sensationalist response. It is to confront the unassimilated, to face the intolerable so that it viscerally registers as such. And, in the process, it is to take the sacredness of the child and ask of her pain, her torment. But it is also to question why a certain image of a child can signify purity and sacredness, and what art can do to unsettle such sacred assumptions as it presents such violence to the world.

THE SACRED UNDONE

There is an evident contradiction which needs to be confronted here when dealing with these aesthetic mediations. While art is able to confront the intolerable and expose the myths upon which all great tyrannies rest, in its attempts to
confront the violence of the real and expose the dangers of sacred claims, it can
all too easily be put to service for sacred ends. In doing so, art turns itself into
an untouchable sacred object far removed from the subject of its concern. Many
contemporary artists have also suffered from this fate, as their brutal depictions
and transgressions against the order of the sacred are repackaged, thus shifting
their value as a means of critique to a monetary investment in accordance with
its approval by the "art world" and the model of mass consumerism. Turning art
into a commodity means that many of its images have become so interwoven
with the cultural fabric of everyday life that any attempt at reworking them is
seen as a moral affront to the purity of art itself. Art literally become the preserve
of the rich and the entitled.

And yet, if we accept that art worthy of the name is that which is committed
to undoing the moral entrapments of all sacred valorizations, even if they may
be appropriated, then, it is surely incumbent upon artists themselves to critically challenge the purification and objectification of cultural output. This is not
about nihilistic destruction for destruction's sake. Nor is it a call to burn to the
ground every Notre Dame or religious temple. It is all about undoing the sacred
so the work carries its critique over into the contemporary.

No greater tragedy befalls the artist than being appropriated by the logics of
power they have spent a lifetime condemning. We could only imagine how Kahlo
would have felt seeing her image being used to sell anything remotely commodifiable, including a deeply Westernized apolitical Barbie figurine. But, as Nietzsche
understood all too well, this is often unavoidable. If you have something important to express, the chances are it will be claimed, domesticated, and turned back
upon itself like Goya's *Saturn Devouring His Son*. Such cultural appropriation
can take many different forms, from turning the art into propaganda extolling
whatever "ism" decides to impose its ideology on it, to forms of mass production
tasked with turning the art into a commodity.

What should also be of concern is the attempted purification and policing
of art by self-appointed justices for all things aesthetically and discursively
authentic. It is here we can turn to the work of Jake and Dinos Chapman.

Fig. 8.7 Jake and Dinos Chapman, *Hell*. Copyright Jake and Dinos Chapman. Permission granted by artists.

There are a number of compelling works in their catalogue, all of which require serious attention and critical acclaim. For our purposes here, we will focus on their extraordinary *Hell* installation, their defacement of Hitler's original artworks, along with their drawings upon the Goya original imprints for both their *Insult to Injury* and *Disasters of the Everyday* series. Let's begin here with *Hell* (fig. 8.7). This gigantic sculpture in nine distinct parts (note it was destroyed in a fire, which raises interesting parallels with the theme of sacrifice), consisted of hundreds of figurines—perpetrators, victims, mutants, Nazis, and beasts—, all positioned within a scorched landscape with rivers of blood and oceans of bodies, an aesthetic of Bruegel meets Goya. This was Dante's underworld literally brought to the terrestrial plane, the abyss opened for all to see. But there no longer seemed to be any reason or rationality to this inferno—every conceivable act of sacrifice is presented in such a way the act of sacrifice itself is consumed, robbed of its excess through sheer repetition. The sacred is exhausted as decapitations, crucifixions, and unholy desecrations, which brought us closer to the cruelty of modern times, are now denied reentry because the killing here never stops. As the original artwork was destroyed in a fire, the artists set about remaking its horrors, not for the sake of wallowing in tragedy, but to show that the violence never ends. When the only recourse for the sacred when confronted with Hell is to—ironically—burn Hell down, the artists' way of denying any sacred return was in their reimagining Hell in even more brutally exposing ways.

A question we are still incapable of answering is what does justice look like in the face of monstrosity? We may wish for the nightmare to disappear, but we also need its memory to serve as a warning against future acts of inhumanity, and to prop up the sacred object for political rule. While some forms of violence are presented as taboo, we also continually encounter the celebration of killing. From the streets of Manhattan, which joyously welcomed Osama bin Laden's demise, to the streets of Sirte where grotesque pictures of the mutilated body of Colonel Muammar Gaddafi reminded us of the horrors which accompanied the man, the death of monstrous figures always appears to be a source for rejoicing in the carnival of misery.

While each of these incidents reaffirms humanity's tendency to counter violence with violence, they also point to a political landscape littered with the secret burials of monsters. Laid to rest in unmarked graves, these most wanted are seemingly provided no meaningful points of reverence, no chance of resurrection, and no meaningful hope of restitution. The killing is easily explained: dangerous beasts need to be slain. This is part of the sacred demand. In spite of the fact that these tyrants are denied any recourse to the rule of law, it would be a mistake to see them as complete "outsiders." Extending Agamben's insight, what defines these characters is a relationship of "inclusive exclusivity." Not only does their presence clarify our strategic commitments, their very existence serves to define our moral, political, cultural, and ethical registers. These monstrous figures mark out the precise threshold between civilization and barbarism, and as such their execution can always be reasoned as having been for the greater good. But an interesting contradiction still appears. While the summary execution is subject to many forms of overexposure to leave the public in no doubt that this particular instrument of terror has been vanquished, the body subsequently vanishes without a trace. This bodily abstraction is not incidental. It cannot, however, be explained by simply stating that we don't want the body's resting place to become a shrine for political extremists. More integral to philosophical rationalities which underwrite contemporary systems of rule, the erasure of the monstrous corpse has everything to do with creating lasting memories which perpetuate the imagined threat.

Secret burials are subject to a horrifying doubling or shadowing of the violence. Tyrants' regimes routinely involve the undignified burials of enemies of
the state in mass graves, where the real terror resides in the threat of one's disappearance. These events create a certain memorialization in which life is physically abstracted from its corporeal state on account of one's ultimate inability to
prove one's existence—for in death, at least, we are eventually able to qualify the
meaning of a life. Thus, the abstraction of tyrants' bodies from permanent sites
that signify their mortal finitude denies lasting closure on account of the unfilled
need to create a lasting memorialization of suffering.

Hitler still provides the untraceable standard. He continues to personify all
that is evil in this world, but it would be a mistake to suggest that keeping the
whereabouts of his remains unknown is simply about preventing a pilgrimage
of neo-Nazis. It is, rather, about creating a lingering specter; the unknown location of his remains affirms the seriousness of his crimes *ad infinitum.* The secret
burial is, after all, only reserved for those who are so infamous that any association with them becomes sure testament to one's place on the wrong side of
moral history. Hence, as the secret burials remove the subject from any locatable
space and time, their mortal abstraction renders them both timeless and universal. Traversing territories and spanning generations, the untraceability to tyrants'
remains serves to echo those crimes which are greater than the perpetrator. So,
while these actions prevent tyrants' gravesites from becoming locatable symbols
of their ideology for dedicated followers, they are underwritten by attempts to
moralize the world in universal terms. This in turn offers a righteous claim to
violence that can appeal directly to the sacred.

The Chapman brothers have adopted a more creative strategy, which brings
a different kind of destruction into play. They have refused to be drawn into
the sacred game for art and politics, especially when it concerns the relationship
between aesthetics and monstrosity. The sacred needs its shadow—which in the
very process of denial also puts it beyond reach, beyond comprehension. This
is apparent in their effacement of Hitler's original artwork, whose memory is
now far from set, exposing the purity of his monstrosity in a different—though
no less accommodating or assimilable—light. By taking Hitler's banal watercol-
ors and painting over them with of multicolored rainbows, floating heart, and
psychedelic skies, the artists imagine "Hitler turning in his grave." They imagine
their reworkings as embodying a poetic justice, defiantly inverting the desecrating spirit of derogatory graffiti scrawled on the walls of Berlin's Degenerate Art

Exhibition back in 1937.[40] If there is such a thing as evil, the artists maintain, it should not be allowed to rest. There is a need, in fact, to emphasize the banality of his work, and, in doing so, reveal more fully the violence of his mediocrity, and how his imagination was far from exceptional.

While the Chapmans' Hitler reworkings offer a far more suggestive way of desecrating the violent memory of the dictator—who, in a form of monstrous sacred doubling, often seems to be beyond reach, as he continues to lie in a state of pure, untouchable evil in an unmarked grave—their *Insult to Injury* series raised a different yet no less powerful question for every humanist to confront. What they violated in this series was more than another body of work. They brought creative destruction to a truly sacred work of art, which had been meant to be preserved for all eternity. This was duly noted by Richard Dorment, who observed,

> in daring to make even a single mark on that pristine impression, the Chapmans have enacted the ultimate artistic transgression. But look again, and you see that the delicacy of their draughtsmanship is anything but disrespectful. Every line is an act of homage to a revered Old Master. What's more, their solemn concentration on the meaning of the images actually enhances the horror of each print, because the perkiness and indifference of the mask-like faces serve to bring out the obscenity beneath the violence.[41]

While these meticulous reworkings invariably attracted the scorn of the purists of the art world who wanted the prints to be preserved in an airtight vault like some brutal final bequest, by puncturing the consecrated memory of Goya's originals, the Chapmans actually stayed true to the artist's memory. Goya had produced the engravings precisely because they could be reprinted over and over, to warn of the realities of war across generations. As Jake Chapman explained, "There's a tug of war between how it is institutionally framed as a humanist work of art that is simply there to depict a moral outrage over man's inhumanity to man—which is the most hackneyed statement always associated with the Disasters."[42] Obliterating Goya's authentic claim to violence, they sought to "gouge them from this moralistic framework and maybe release its libidinal economy to show that these works are much more radically unhinged and unstable, and they don't deserve to be accumulated to some sort of post-Christian redemption."

Yet, sadly, as the Chapmans appreciated, the contingent memories of the suffering of warfare often fade with time, and the violence becomes spectacle as

Fig. 8.8 Jake and Dinos Chapman, *Sad Presentiments of What Must Come to Pass*. 2003. Copyright Jake and Dinos Chapman. Permission granted by artists.

it is pushed into the unreflective realm of passive and sequestered voyeurism. But while their additions to the Goya prints are painfully humorous—for example, the sinister man with the face of a clown emerging from the darkness with his arms stretched out (fig. 8.8)—there is painstaking method to their madness. As Klaus Bisenbach observed, like Goya, the Chapmans "employ labour-intensive processes in their artwork, and the process becomes part of the act of imagining."[43] Far from merely being whimsical vandalism, this speaks of an artistic integrity and spoken honesty to the work. In the Chapmans' theater of cruelty, a different response to the witnessing of horror is required.

While art has always been regulated, in modern times the sacred object of art has given rise to a deeply commodified system in which art and aesthetics are governed by curatorial police whose crude measures of value are all too apparent. And yet, something of the theological still carries over, even as in works, like a shining Jeff Koons balloon dog, which would have far more purchase were it seen with bruised children on the ground, having desperately fallen from its sleek design shouting out "give me my metaphysics." History continues to show that when art becomes part of the sacred order it too exhibits untouchable qualities as its message is transformed into pious objectification. Meanwhile, the political potency of its interventions is reduced to an aesthetic provocation whose means and ends are known in advance, its sensory distributions ferociously guarded.

Though the Cerberus hound guarding the entry to these sacred gates remains a secret, only to appear in the very act of walking beyond its normalized (in)tolerance thresholds, there always remains the capacity for resistance. The Chapmans through their works have undone the sacred object of art itself, the sacralization of its humanism, and its dominant themes of evil, war, and the victim of history. Their work is part of the exceptional in figurative art in the most transgressive sense. They are not content to ask what a body is, or even to rest on Spinoza's aspiration for what a body might become. Their target is the sacred distribution of the sensible, the once insertion of art into a liberal humanist frame, in which violence is tolerated even as it preaches peace, which speaks of pacification as it kills with an enlightened smile. And, in the process, the Chapmans warn us of a future where the poetic is turned into a new sacred game, with its new technically enhanced systems of idolatry, whose knives are already being sharpened.

CHAPTER 9

Wounds of Love

WOUNDS IN TIME

Liberalism is dead. Liberalism remains dead. And we have killed her. How shall we comfort ourselves, the greatest of all murderers? What was holiest and mightiest in all the world has bled to death under our knives: who will wipe this blood off us? What water is there for us to clean ourselves? What festivals of atonement, what sacred games shall we have to invent? While some may lament this passing, there is a politics and a claim to humanity after the death of liberalism. But this requires us to learn the lessons from our sacred past. And it requires us to undo our concept of humanism, so that what arises is not a monstrous adaption of what we have defeated.

We can now see that what Nietzsche called the eternal return is also about the production of gods more terrifying still than those which have been slain. And we are already seeing the emergence of this new god in the guise of a global techno-theodicy. Facing these conditions, now more than ever then we need to rethink love. We need to learn to touch one another again. But if the original gesture of politics is not one of violence but of poetic love, what we need to seek out and narrate is a form of love without sacrifice. That is not to say it doesn't have commitment. Nor does it mean that we deny the ineffable or the mystery to existence and retreat into some secular humanist realm that conceals its theological ascriptions by appealing to the objective truth and scientific facts. The politics of love ought to be exceptional and take us beyond words. But it should also recognize that life is life—and that should be more than enough.

Life is not lacking. Neither does it need to be saved, even if we need to be constantly challenged, our shameful compromises with power openly critiqued and condemned. Still, what of the innocent child who has been tortured, tormented, or even killed, students of Dostoyevsky might counter? Should we not see them as sacred? No child is sacred. Just as no hero or revolutionary figure should be seen as sacred. They are normal, imperfect. Children are children, and that should be more than enough. They are wondrous, full of mystery, and captivated by the inexplicable, so why turn them into sacred objects? Why turn any victim into a sacred object if not to assume a position as gatekeeper of justice in order to call for retributive action from a position of moral certitude? And why give us over to the sacred at all if not to confirm the essential belief that humans are naturally violent, that everything begins with the sacrificial act, and the only way we can save ourselves from ourselves is to bow down before some glorious excess?

When Benjamin rightly insisted that all violence brings us directly into moral relations, he was invoking that now familiar triangulation between perpetrators, victims, and witnesses. Such witnessing has been wrapped up in a moral economy of truth and its deeply politicized modes of subjectification, giving rise in the process to distinct hierarchies of grief and suffering. In addition to this, such witnessing has further been inflected by ecological narratives, wherein the very logics of space and time may or may not be inserted into broader sensorial and analytical frames for the purpose of creating climates and temperaments of affect. While the motif of the massacre of innocents, for example, has repeated itself on local and even national levels, to encounter and be forced witness to a crime against humanity has demanded the existence of a planetary and metaphysical plane wholly dependent upon a shared sense of the universal tragedy. Yet, with the attribution of planetary crimes deployed in wholly contingent and deeply segregating ways, this has led to the weaponization of the ecological in painful and symbolic ways.

To be human is to be part of an endangered humanity, as well as part of a mortal collective, which is tragically fated to walk upon the morally endangered earth. Rather, however, than return to the universal and its claims to the sacred based upon the order of its victims and its regulatory demands, our challenge is to rethink the human as it fully disappears in the abyss—we must reaffirm humanity in the face of its total annihilation—such that we might aesthetically reimagine a concept of life which frees the capacity for love from its sacrificial moorings.

This brings us back directly to the void. How might we see this non-space into which life and all meaning disappears in a way that is about more than just the depths of human despair? Might the wilderness of the void be open to a more affirmative conceptualization? And how might this connect to the poetics of life in a way that doesn't fall back upon sacred ground? Let us first return to the horrors of World War II. While the figurative still remained a dominant standard for representation through 1945, the nihilism of the postwar period brought the very figure of the human as an aesthetic form into question. Humanity had to confront the violence of its own humanism. As Barnett Newman noted, "After the monstrosity of the war, what do we do? What is there to paint? We have to start all over again."

The emergence of abstract expressionism became synonymous with those artists who were so disillusioned by the violence of the human condition, consecrated and mobilized by aesthetic ideas of its perfectibility, they turned away from the figurative to ask still-unanswered questions about what it means to be human. No artist better captured the early power of this aesthetic turn than Mark Rothko, who disavowed formal association with any aesthetic movement in order to authenticate a certain image of thought and the world. His immersive mindscapes are less about the Dante-inspired journey into the flesh of the earth than about opening up wounds in time. As the artist insisted, "You think my paintings are calm, like windows in some cathedral? You should look again. I'm the most violent of all the American painters. Behind those colours there hides the final cataclysm." That cataclysm is the void.

Rothko's life was full of personal tragedy, culminating in his suicide in 1970. It is perhaps no coincidence he took inspiration from the great tragic dramatists, from Aeschylus, after whom Rothko named certain of his paintings, to Shakespeare and Nietzsche[1]. In an essay titled "Whenever one begins to speculate," Rothko specifically draws attention to the importance of Nietzsche's *The Birth of Tragedy*. As he explains, "It left an indelible impression on my mind and has forever coloured the syntax of my own reflections in questions of the art. And if it be asked why an essay which deals with Greek tragedy should play such a large part in a painter's life, I can only say that the basic concerns for life are no different from the artist, for the poet, or the musician." Such concerns for Rothko were the complete opposite of being an academic, studiously painting with technical mastery: "It is a widely accepted notion among painters that it does not matter what one paints as long as it is well painted. This is the essence of academism. There is no such thing as good painting about nothing. We assert that only that subject matter is valid which is tragic and timeless."

During my visit to the Tate Modern, as I recounted in the preface of this book, I encountered a series of nine large murals painted by Rothko, the exhibition atmospherically set in a darkened light. The viewer is immediately reminded by the curatorial instructions that the artist attempted to do what Michelangelo had done at the Laurentian Library in Florence. In Rothko's words, Michelangelo "achieved just the kind of feeling I'm after—he makes the viewers feel that they are trapped in a room where all the doors and windows are bricked up, so that all they can do is butt their heads forever against the wall." One of the lesser-populated rooms at the time (Rothko, in fact, shows the real limits of the modern gallery, horded with tourists passing each exhibit, looking without seeing, having to get through to witness everything with no time to reflect), the dimly lit space that hosts these large yet intimate paintings, creates an immersive experience full of tragedy, terror, violence, and yet optimism. Confronted by these large canvases of red, black, and maroon colors, in the tranquility of this setting, you are unsure whether you are entering the scene or whether the canvases are surrounding you, making you an active witness or accomplice to their drama. The obscurities of Rothko's multiple layers begin to envelop the viewer who is open to this immersive experience, appearing not as paint applied to canvas, but rather as if the colors themselves are emerging from behind the frame. Rothko manages to give depth and perspective while turning these flat and fixed installations into something truly dynamic in all their tensions. Rothko not only takes us on a journey into the intimate depths of the psychic life of power, he allows us to glimpse the void as we enter a different relationship that is lost in the indeterminable places that exists between space and time.

The brilliance of Rothko is that he shows us how the abstract is not "outer-worldly" or "untouchable." On the contrary, it is to take a journey into the intimate depths of human existence. Art was, as he indicated, "an adventure into an unknown world, which can be explored only by those willing to take the risk."[2] This has always been the fundamental mistake made by those who critique the abstract in thought in their crude and reductive assumptions. Of course, to ask questions about the emotional and sensorial qualities of humanity does require alternative conceptual insight and new grammatical interventions. The scientist is fully capable of dissecting a body, telling you how it functions, but never how or why it feels. And we often remember how the feeling of an experience strikes us, much more than some technical procedure which is ultimately irrelevant to our personal lives.

Thus, as Rothko shows, to say the abstract is esoteric displays the greatest ignorance, a critique set in place by reductive regimes of truth. Rothko paints a battlefield of the soul, where the intimate is expelled for all to see, where beauty and pain are revealed as part of all that we are—emotionally, politically and philosophically—and where the task we confront is to face the obscure beasts that dwell within ourselves. As the artist himself explained, "It was not that the figure had been removed . . . but the symbols for the figure. These new shapes say . . . what the figures said."[3]

Rothko asks how the eyes perceive, in the radiating darkness of color, the unknown depths of the void. While from a distance the portraits look like boxes, neatly mapped out in a straight line, upon closer inspection they appear more like indeterminable gates, whose lines are far from limiting or fixed into place. You can imagine their points of entry disappearing at any moment. The lines Rothko paints flow through the composition. He depicts the shadows of emptiness, the temporality of the exhausting gradient that shows everything yet blurs into possible nothingness. The viewer gets the impression that the black may swallow up the red any moment; and yet, nothing is determined, for in the changing depths of the emotional field, filled with unknowable possibility, everything returns.

Rothko paints the passion of the woundedness of humanity. His canvases bear witness to the scar that is never healed, like the future life of a ghost witnessing its own demise, but yet to be destroyed. He knows the layers, the depths of pain, and the blood that seeps out despite the attempt to mask the violence. Rothko paints the history of humanity, its passion and pain, the slow unfolding of time, life broken apart through the continuous movements of its devastating contradictions. He demands intensive reflection, that we take the time to feel every emotion, to short-circuit the immediacy of sensation, to feel beyond the frustrations of representational schematics and the demands for immediate communication and truth. Rothko's paintings are far from static; they are a whirlwind in time, which in their slow re- and de-composition of color intensify everything. Rothko is burning. And his flames reveal a passage into the void for all to enter.

The layering of Rothko's compositions is truly astounding, and as such terrifying. What he achieves is to bring light to the disappeared pigments of existence. Of course, Rothko's work is haunted by a silence. There is no other way to engage with their presence. And what lies beneath their surface threatens to vanish at any moment, as time passes over their almost invisible semblances. though it's sometimes difficult to tell if something is emerging or fading away. It's all a matter of perception. And it is a question of bringing things into the light. Still, what remains is precisely everything. The layers of history appear in faint, yet defiant, specks. There is no nihilistic triumph or victory march as Rothko leads us into the realm of pure denial. Unlike Goya, Rothko doesn't surrender or willingly give over to the violence the power of his colors. The abstract defeats the abstention!

And still there is no lasting comfort, for the terror of Rothko's work, which exists behind the terror of humanity's woundedness, lies in its forcing us to confront the simplicity of disappearance as it occurs in all its visible manifestations. Yet while nothing is certain, such simplicity on the part of the artist should not be confused with mediocrity. It takes a sophisticated mastery to achieve a visual idea that assesses what remains of the possible and confronts the notion that things can simply vanish. That history overlays and makes itself seen, reveals as much as it denies. Such can only be achieved with attention to the historic process.

Rothko shows us the artist is not merely someone who documents history. His work is a form of transgressive witnessing, in which the viewer is accompanied by many other poets from history into the void of humanity. Nietzsche seemed to fear the abyss insomuch as it was a journey one undertook in solitude, and from which one might return severely traumatized. Unlike Dante's Hell, Rothko's gates require you to enter alone. Virgil is not there to hold your hand. The passage into the non-place demands the intensity of solitary reflection. But in the absence of the figurative the solitude quickly evaporates, as this wound in time allows you to both connect with the intimacy of a shared existence and feel the force of Rothko's colors, which paint the imagination. But, again unlike Dante's journey, the return from the reflection of Rothko's work doesn't guarantee paradise. As I left the room, I returned through the adjacent space, which housed Claude Monet's *Water Lilies*. I couldn't help but feel this was the most violent image I had ever seen—and that every image has the potential to be truly violent if we give to it a certain narrative from which everything that was human has been eviscerated.

So, what can we take from Rothko in terms of rethinking the ongoing struggle against the forces of nihilism? The artist asks, as I chose to hear, two very clear questions. First, what does it mean to disappear a body, a memory, or an idea? And, second, why is art so important in affirming our humanity in response to the real force that threatens our existence—the nihilism of the void? Disappearance, as Rothko shows, is the evisceration of the creative act. It is the denial of a life and a surrendering to violence, thus destroying the idea and vision that the world can be different. While it is tempting to see humanity here as a universal subject, united in the realization it is an endangered form, Rothko reminds us that the opposite is true. Humanity lives and breathes through its creative expressions. Humanity is diverse. Humanity multiplies. Humanity undoes the sacred. It is ancestral. It outlives the suffocation of life and its forced disappearances, which can either occur through the forced complicity or outright annihilation of a people.

Rothko thus provides us with an aesthetic opening through which the world's beauty and pain can be rethought. His work is the lightning storm that may just be capable of destroying those sacrificial altars, if only we are able to summon what remains yet to be discovered about the abstract in thought. Rothko's call, if we choose to listen, is for a timeless poetic reverie—a human connection to the ineffable—which in recognizing the violence and confronting the intolerable asks whether a different order for thinking about the meaning of existence is possible. This demands a rethinking of the political imagination and its images of thought. Art, as Rothko shows, has an eternal future in the affirmation of its expression. He reminds us that when you give yourself the task of painting the pain of humanity with whatever grammatical tools, you are tracing invisible wounds. Not that the canvas is yourself as a pure reflection of the world, nor are you the canvas like some authentic representational piece in the human jigsaw. There is no canvas as such, only paint on a surface which reveals the wounds of time.

LOVE WITHOUT SACRIFICE

From the early Greek philosopher to the Christian theologian, from the modern psychoanalyst to the ineffable mediations of the Continental theorist, from the scornful conservative to the sentimental liberal, everyone tells us that there is no love without sacrifice. Love truly is a dangerous affair. And yet even the most brutal of tyrants, those who preach against discord from the pages of Hobbes's *Leviathan*, must at least acknowledge of the existence of love prior to any demands for making life secure in its physical state, along with the security of assumed belonging, truth, and knowledge. Why would any human, after all, seek to protect others if not for some prior conception of love? We know that security is a game played by the ambitious. And we know from history that the surest way to destroy the political imagination is to reduce politics to the question of survival, such that the cliché "everything is possible" means than everything can be annihilated.

But even some of the radical poets of history can understand love as being borne of sacrifice, the violence of which ultimately destroys the love it created.

André Breton's *Nadja* is one of the most devastating examples of this commitment.[4] Love is overcoming, especially as Breton sees it—a power relationship or
takeover, which is only really apparent through the realization of its failure. Love
is severance. Torn asunder, it is the order of vulnerability, already shattered by
the prospect of its eventual loss. Love as such is wounded and wounding. A commitment already devastated by its eventual defeat. And yet, such an account of
love is hard to disprove. In fact, it often becomes prophetic as the mortal finitude
of life gives finite qualities to its relationality, while its inherent free will gives
unto others the capacity to sever the bonds, held so dear and which ultimately
leave us alone in the world. The fragility of love thus ends up confirming what
we imagined all along: that love might be "taken" at any given moment. Sacred
love in its original sense is thus transformed into a modality of a truly epic and
yet quotidian tale of heroic survival. To love is to learn to endure the shared fate
of an uncertain existence, haunted by the prospect of losing something that was
never actually in our possession to begin with. Love, then, is not only loaded with
suspicion—of love itself—it is born of sacrifice and demands allegiance to it on
the part of the lovers who are already in anticipation of a tragic separation that
ultimately awaits. And yet we know that to secure love means it has no meaning.
Like Madame Butterfly in Puccini's masterful opera who, anticipating the sacred
violence that will be visited upon her on account of a contractual obligation, asks
if people kill butterflies and pin them to a board?

Yet it remains the case that the most formidable weapon in the armory of
sacrifice is that of love. Love endures because of the sacrificial order of things.
We need the sacred to protect us, and we need the sacrifice to prove it. It seems
we are incapable of conceiving of its presence in any other way. But how does
sacrifice become the source of our love? For is this not a love that is ultimately
tormented by its own capacities and potentials? A love that needs to verify itself,
over and over, to be exchanged for a love that needs securitizing in the face of its
vulnerability? And a love that still is willing to wager itself against the future for
an even greater claim to truth? Did Agamemnon not love Iphigenia, even as he
was compelled to kill her for some greater good? And was he not then wounded
in return, as a result of wounded love? Or was Iphigenia simply not deceived by
the violence of an artificial love to begin with, the love that demands something
in return? A love that, as we say, merely endures. That stands the test of time, of
its duration and natural unfolding. But what happens if we think of time in a
different way? Not of Chronos and its demands for endurance, but of a concept

of time beyond time—or toward the voiding of time itself, so every second is imbued with meaning and significance. And perhaps it is more radical than we like, to think of the unfolding as a process in reverse. Where the eternal return is not hurtling toward some unimaginable end, into the perishable void and the absence of all meaning, but rather a place we occupy in the already present death of this life. Such a love would be everything in exchange for nothing, for it truly would be all that we had in the moment. And it certainly would not be possessed or haunted by demands for sacrifice in its name.

On the seven hundredth anniversary of his death, Dante may hold the key for us to begin reimagining this reversal in fortunes in the order of love. *The Divine Comedy* is a masterful and brutal depiction of sacrificial love. There is the tale of Paolo and Francesca, whose wretched state reveals the torments they undergo in all their painful glory. Their lust tears their bodies asunder—they remain together, yet helpless at the mercy of the violent storms. But there is a greater tale at work here in the *Commedia*, which overrides this merciless story. Taken literally, it is known that Dante wrote this work as a message of love to Beatrice. And it is she who invites him to take the journey, into the sacrificial depths of Hell and onward to his redemption and salvation. But Beatrice was already dead at the time of writing. And Dante carried the weight of that pain, alone in the woods like a lost soul thrown into the darkness of the unforgiving night. Dante was wounded by love. He felt it as it was torn away with such disregard by a world that teaches us to suffer into truth. Needing to take the fall himself into the icy depths, there was a need as such to witness the wretchedness before experiencing the good. The *Divine Comedy* is a story of sacrifice, but the greatest sacrificial victim is Dante himself. He has to put himself to the sword, entering the realms of the dead to prove his commitment to his wounded love. But his sacred wounds already existed before him, for Dante follows a path already set as he is guided through the darkness and out into the light of sacrificial wisdom.

That love is borne of sacrifice is precisely the original conception of love that must be undone. Outliving the sacrificial image of thought means we must unravel the knots which bind us to the violence of an artificial love. We know that such love is foundational to the political order of things. We see it in the love that demands a securitization of the realm, the love that demands allegiance, the love that binds us into contractual arrangements, the love that needs to prove itself, the love that is forced to endure, the love that kills and massacres in return. Every great tyrant knows how to love their people in this way. They shower them with protections, they cover them with visions and claims of sacrifice so their contained love might learn to flourish. This has always been the source of our oppression, for its hold is suffocating and its kisses deadly. And still we put these tyrants on pedestals to look down upon us from lofty heights.

But what of memorialization? Are we not all guilty of playing sacred games when it comes to the memories of those we have lost? In resurrecting the memory of a loved one, especially when we continue their legacy and work, are we not turning them into a sacred object of devotion? This is only the case if we reduce them to a universal ideal, if we purify their memory and gloss over their complexities and fallibilities. The gravest injustice we can do to the dead is to make them untouchable. Such an act truly diminishes a life, rendering it sacred by denying its struggles and the mistakes it made, which, in the end, were what made it human. The most poetic memories are those which can without any warning open a wound in time, but a wound in whose name you'd hope no violence ever followed, a reopened scar to remind you that the world should and can be different. This is the sort of memory that passes love over, leaving it undiminished by the passing. This undiminished love is that which you'd give everything and ask nothing in return. It is a love that's carried on broken wings, a love without sacrifice or the violence of angels guarding it.

Returning to Dante, while he is renowned for giving us a vision of Hell on earth, we should not overlook the way he humanizes sacrifice and makes it accessible to the human mind. He makes sacrifice a learning process, which, guided by a metaphysical master, affirms the sacrificial idea of a life, which overlays the triangulation between victims, perpetrators, and witnesses with that of violence, justice, and love. But if Dante is the ultimate victim here, we are the eternal witnesses to this sacrificial tale. Dante provided the testimony so that we might carry it across the generations. And yet, while many have fallen into the depths of despair, their own personal Hell, there is no guarantee that we will return the same as we were.

So, what makes Dante endure this ordeal and subject himself to such personal sacrifice? Why was he not, like you or I perhaps would when asked to carry such a weight of suffering, consumed by the feeling that life is exhausting in the face of tremendous loss or its potential annihilation? The terrifying brilliance of Dante's journey could be explained fully if we recognized how its sacred claim was hidden even from its author. Might it not be the case that his journey's sacrificial demands were too unbearable even for him to consider? Surely we can

272 Into the Void

relate, for we too are continually witness to extreme violence, and we often fail to question the real source of our fears. With Dante as our guide, at best, we learn to tolerate the intolerable scenes of violence, but never to question the theater in which they take place. And, certainly, we never question what lies behind the sacrifice, behind the theological topographies—the absence of all meaning, the void that denies the very idea of the sacrifice. Our concept of humanism remains allegiant to these wounds of history; we painfully walk down the same treacherous paths, hoping for love and yet fearful of its presence (and eventual severance).

Dante's poetics are thus a continuation of the tragic, eliciting an allegiance to the sacrificial motif so that life may find meaning in response to the unbearable weight of suffering. But while we are overwhelmed by the persistence of the brutality and torture, the real violence is hidden in plain sight, like a perverse stowaway still ever marching onward while the masses are distracted by the spectacles of violence and the individual tales of wretchedness and suffering. There is no doubting that this violence is intimately felt. The politics of love, however conceived, could not be presented in any other way, especially when commanded by legions of those who have been, or will be, sacrificed. No claim to love, however artificial, however violent, could appeal to the naked light of reason alone. Sacred love needs to be viscerally felt, just as its wounds need to be painted in the most tremendous colors. It must continually wrap itself in sublime reverence, like a gilded church of old, we must learn again to be terrified by the infinite presence of what is always absent in the moment. And so, if there is a warning to consider, it is to be mindful of which poets from history are guiding us. We must ask what they are really forcing us to carry as we seek to lighten their unbearable load?

THE OPEN WOUND

The love that makes its appeal to the demands of the unbearable weight of history is no love at all. No daughter should have to feel the burden of a sacrifice carried out in her name. This is not a call for forgetting, but a call to break out of the sacred idea of love being the original wounding, inextricably bound to its tragic forebodings. But how can we instigate a more poetic account of history in terms of rethinking the ongoing struggle against the forces of nihilism and devastation? How can we finally make a break with the sacred and its violence?

Might we ever learn to reimagine a metaphysics that goes beyond the sacrificial pale and still gives meaning to life in the face of its absence?

It is here we might turn to the beautifully devastating account of insanity recounted by Leonora Carrington in her mediation from *Down Below*.[5] Carrington, like others who have journeyed into the void, finding eternal rescue in the passion of human creativity as a truly resistive energy, while exposing the insanity and violence of civilized domesticity and its modes of sedation, asks us to consider again and again through her doubts two very clear questions: What does it truly mean to eviscerate a memory, a life or an idea by exerting the material will to nothing? And why is art so important in affirming our existence by counteracting the nihilism of the void? Disappearance as also understood in Carrington's work is the evisceration of the creative act. It is the denial of a life and the surrendering to violence, such that what really disappears is the idea that the world can be different. It is a slaughtering of potential, the homicide of creation. While it has been tempting to see humanity as a universal subject, total in its unity, bound together by the trauma of realizing its collective endangerment, the poets of history have reminded us the opposite is true. Humanity lives and breathes through its creative expressions. It outlives the suffocations and forced disappearances, which it effects either through forced complicity or outright annihilation.

The poetic provides us with an aesthetic opening through which we can rethink and reimagine the world. The poetic is the storm that just might be capable of destroying those sacrificial tableaus, if only we can summon what remains yet to be discovered about the abstract in thought and apply it toward creative resistance. The poetic calling, as we might choose to listen, is a timeless reverie—a human connection to the ineffable—which, recognizing the intolerable nature of violence and the unbearable weight of human suffering, asks whether a different order for thinking the meaning of existence is possible. This demands a rethinking of the political imagination and its images of thought.

We might consider here once again Alexander McQueen's disdain for "throwaway images," or even think about it more fully in terms of "throwaway thoughts" and "throwaway relationships" marked by "throwaway love." Art as it is understood in relation to a truly creative rupture has an eternal future in the affirmation of its expression. As Timothy Morton has written, "Art is thought from the future. Thought we cannot explicitly think at present. Thought we may not think or speak at all."[6] This is where tragedy in art is useful to us as a critical resource. It asks us what stage of life we occupy.[7] And by recalling the tragic nature of our mortality, it presents us with a complex ambiguity, which, like lightning, devastates, but can also be the spark that ignites the human imagination. Tragedy leads us to the edge of that confrontation with mortal finitude, to "tremble at the edge of the abyss" and to seek out affirmation in the process.[8] But we cannot simply stop to gaze at the wound. And we must certainly be alert to the processes where the tragic becomes an untouchable object, something sacred and beyond all criticism. Moreover, we must avoid assuaging our shame by confiding in the sacred, however righteous or egalitarian it may appear.

Rothko has shown that the invisible can appear in lines and movements, through his use of color which is not merely representative but creates for the viewer a deep field of sensation which opens onto the abyss of despair. He forces us to concede and recognize that the violence is also immersive, for it allows no separation between its past and future. But this is not to be defeated. Neither is it to confront violence with a purer "non-violent violence" of whatever critical persuasion. Such orientations are merely a resurrection of the sacrificial by another more considered name. It demands instead a willingness to confront the intolerable depths of human suffering, to steer history in a different direction. This cannot be achieved by denial or through absolution, let alone by joining the chorus for some sacred melancholic lament. The pain of humanity needs to be felt. And it needs to be affirmatively resisted. This is why the transgressive witness must take that leap into the void. There is no alternative.

But what does it mean to truly feel the beauty and pain of the world's obscure beasts, coming face to face with their daemonic presence? How do we even begin to try to find tenderness in savagery, while staying alert to the brutalities of the most devastating angelic disfigurements? The angelic and the demonic—beings of Heaven and Hell—are after all fictions belonging to this world. Obscured, yet all too real, their ghostly presence fills the void, shapeshifting yet appearing with uncertain clarity, from a time within time. Still, the questions continue to appear: knowing the risks to our state of mind, does anybody really have the courage to willingly go there? Who dares to venture into this non-place? What might it mean to even suggest this journey without donning a hero's mantle? And how might we return without being defeated by pessimism after what we confronted, both in the void and after we emerged? We know that very few send back postcards from the void. It is more than uncertain. It is the unknown unknowns.

The politics of pessimism and the dialecticians of history are complicit in the unfolding drama of a history that remains wedded to the sacrificial model.

Nietzsche was right—we do need art to prevent us from dying from the truth. And this places it in direct conflict with hope. It's not that hope is too idealistic. Rather, hope is all too pessimistic. It only finds reasons in the yet-to-come, forgetting the poetics of past and present. Art is the counter to such hope. It offers us a resistance from the future in the present, drawing its energies from the past while instigating an affirmative movement from the abstract to the real. This is the very act of creation which positions itself against the pessimism of the defeated.

Art thus reveals the tragedy of hope—hope as a false promise, guided by visions of water lilies and Gardens of Eden. Art is the actualization of the affirmative conditions of reality that short-circuits the reductiveness of idealism, the living toward a possible future never that was except for now in its actualization. But we shouldn't idealize ourselves here. Art can undoubtedly speak to the pessimism of humanity as well; can also appear enslaved and defeated, as the motor of a history that merely objectifies and consumes the realms of all appearance. And yet, even the most pessimistic of artists (worthy of being so called) evoke the affirmative in their denial of any image of a future which is foreclosed for all eternity. Its message continues to outlive the investiture of human denials. Art, then, is not the fire. That belongs to the black sun that burns in the wilderness of the soul. Rather, art is the air that gives rise to the flame defiantly dancing in the wind—the unknowable force that dissolves pessimism before it succeeds at its effacement of the image, toward the image yet to come in all its poetic and brutally honest abstract realism.

The void is a spherical non-place that appears through an open wound in the fabric of history. It is made of permanently swirling forces; it has heights and depths, in which the life of the mind manifests itself as a battlefield of conflicting memories and actualizations of the conditions of the new. Carrying the dust of history—the remnants of everything that has met its ruin—these memories are always contained within an invisible aesthetic energy that silently screams, laughing at a future already in the making. From this perspective, what is aesthetic always precedes static and representational embodiments of crude figuration. But as critics might counter, when has any work of art ever stopped a bullet? Or to put it more starkly, where is the ethical demand for peace truly to be found? On the surface, nothing matters in the void except for the force of its untameable movements, which are capable of consuming anything at any given moment. Devastating our perceptions of an unforgettable past, these movements carry whatever remains of a promissory future toward the genesis of new lifeforms.

This is why both the creative and the destructive take their energies from the same chaotic rhythms. Both are made possible by overspills from the void of existence, from the absence that permits what is open to the abstract in thought, wherein the potential for all things to cease to exist is all too real. Such a condition overspills as it seeks to contain everything in potentiality and of nothingness complete—a swirling vortex of affirmation and denial, liberation and oppression, where poets and tyrants are found in a conflict far more brutal than the depicted fall of the rebel angels. At least Hell promised the continuation of a worldly existence, into a place where the soul lived on into whatever eternity constantly waited for its arrival, whereas the stakes here—in the void of humanity—are the aesthetics of appearance and disappearance, whether humanity is to have meaning or whether we are to vanish without a trace.

And yet we are all unwitting carriers of those undefeated traces of human disappearance. The truth of nihilism, in the end, is in the impossibility of its will to nothingness. This is perhaps the greatest of all human delusions: the belief that we can bring about our own extinction as if we had never existed in the first place. Everything that is seemingly forgotten remains, despite its own annihilation! History teaches us this much. This is why those who argue for a politics of forgetting have no politics of the visceral. Painful and traumatic experiences jump from bodies to bodies, across generational fields of feeling and shared human consciousness. Some wounds can be patched over, but others cut so deep they never heal. Just as the void forces forgetting and denial upon our disoriented human memories, creating the very conditions by which denial is further possible, it also echoes the silent screams of history, audible enough to those who can hear their sounds as they travel on the unforgotten wind.

Still there is always a warning we must heed. Those who consciously search for the disappeared are often defeated by the collapse of space and time, and are doomed to search every day with only the solidarity of those fortunate enough to still be alive and their shared memories of fading hope as their weapons. Meanwhile, those who return victorious from the void can find themselves living in another Hell on earth, marked in time by the same violent eruptions in the heavenly stars, falling back to earth like the burning Icarus who couldn't read the signs.

We might contrast the flight of Icarus with Yves Klein's solitary leap into the void. Critics may counter here that the image is nothing more than a fiction, an illusion. But let's not forget every grand claim to power has depended upon the mysticism of its excess—the untouchable myth from which all sacred objects emerge. Politics is a fiction, its myths integral to the continuation of sacred forms of violence. This is true whether we are talking about the myth of Gods, the myth of Nation or the myth of Humanity, which have all presented before us as sacred objects demanding allegiance and justifying violence in their names. Perhaps this is the real nature and origin of what economists call debt:—the idea that we owe our entire existence to an excessive claim, which can never be fully understood, and yet since we have been allowed to glimpse its presence, always we are required to pay.

Klein's work is a leap of the imagination,[9] a spontaneous act, which is resistive and transgressive—willing the void to appear, while refusing to accept the certainty of oblivion in the final act. Solitude in this regard (which Arendt herself always favored in the act of thinking) proves to be different from merely being alone. In solitude, one is always greater than one—always in the company of the poets of history who have sparked our imagination and opened our eyes to the primordial flame. This is the creativity of the void. Being alone, in contrast, is to be thrown into the darkness, to be cast out and held down by the immensity of being, in the company of no one and nothing except the terror. This is abstract nakedness. We might see Klein as being at the threshold between life and death, yet his expression is joyfully poetic. Separated from causality—the predicable claims of the nullifying mind—the image operates on the psychological plain, seeing the void as also a site for creation. The immense solitude and suspension of this peaceful composition, where the artist willingly goes into the void, is crucial here. As Bachelard observed in the *Poetics of Space*:

> Immensity is within ourselves. It is attached to a sort of expansion of being that life curbs and caution arrests, but which starts again when we are alone. As soon as we become motionless, we are elsewhere; we are dreaming in a world that is immense. Indeed, immense is the movement of motionless man. It is one of the dynamic characteristics of quiet daydreaming . . . In other words, since immense is not an object, a phenomenology of immense would refer us directly to our imagining consciousness. In analysing images of immensity, we should realize within ourselves the pure being of pure imagination. It then becomes clear that works of art are the by-products of this existentialism of the imagining being. In this direction of daydreams of immensity, the real product is consciousness of enlargement. We feel that we have been promoted to the dignity of the admiring being.[10]

Gaston Bachelard was always a far more compelling thinker of the void than Bataille ever dreamed to be. Bataille, in fact, was no dreamer at all, he merely sought to push the sacred over the edge. It is perhaps no concidence that Klein continually referred to the work of Bachelard.[11] Not only did the latter understand the importance of the elements, he also asked us to consider how absence is anything but empty space. Like the dust of history, the black void is not absent of meaning; it is the sum of all colors pushed together with such intensity it would take a truly poetic eye to appreciate its radiance. As Bachelard explains,

> In connection with the intuition of dust, one should also study the intuition of the void, for it is not difficult to show that it also is a quite positive one. In fact, upon reading the Greek philosophers, we become convinced that the entire polemic over the void amounts to either aiding or combating that intuition. But in any case, when we first encounter this basic intuition, the void poses problems from a metaphysical perspective by the very fact that it raises no problem from a psychological point of view. Such a polemical outlook is well suited to demonstrate that the void and dust are truly immediate and important facts of experience.[12]

Drawing upon Aristotle's original philosophical proposition, "if we are to believe the Pythagoreans, the void is originally found in numbers, for the void is what gives them their particular and abstract nature," Bachelard then goes on to write:

> In implementing rational necessities, all we did was fill space with reasoning, and we still have to make the characteristics produced by the immediate intuition of the void reappear . . . who does not see that positing metaphysical fullness amounts to attributing to it all the characteristics of the intuitive void? . . . Surely, no one has failed to object that, in fact, the experience of the void for the ancients as well as for common knowledge is obviously erroneous since all the early physical experiments are carried out in air, with an almost total ignorance of phenomena peculiar to the gaseous state. We should then concede that the direct intuition of the void corresponds in reality to the experience of a physical state that, in itself, is well determined although poorly known. But an error of thought or expression has nothing to do with the truth of an intuition. What must be called the tangible perception of the void is closely linked to a quite positive observation.[13]

Bachelard allows us to think more intuitively about this in a wonderful chapter in *Air and Dreams* concerning Nietzsche.[14] According to Bachelard, it is only when "Nietzsche comes near to the abyss" that he finds the "dynamic image of ascent"—or, to quote the work's protagonist, "To throw myself into your height, that is *my* depth."[15] Such verticality refers us to what Bachelard understood to be the dynamism of the imaginary, to consider the flight of the arrow bearing the lightning of all possible storms. In this regard, we can see that art is not simply concerned with presenting or transgressing the past; it smuggles the future back into the present to reimagine the poetic constellation of being.

And it is in this sense we might recognize why "imagination, more than reason, is a unifying force of the soul."[16] Taking place within the territory of the void, for a world that is beautiful before its true, the imagination appreciates that an "aerial life is not a flight far from the earth. It is an offensive against the heavens" armed with a "lightning that can be seen rising from the abyss toward the sky" to pierce the sun.[17] Or, to quote Bachelard as he quotes Nietzsche: "Downward from every height you've sunk. And in the depths still shine." Hence, Bachelard shows this battle within the heart of the void, the crucible which forges all creativity and annihilation, is being waged over the imaginary, the very attempt to affirm or negate the freedom of being: "If the image that is *present* does not make us think of one that is absent, if an image does not determine an abundance—an explosion—of unusual images, then there is no imagination."[18] Deleuze and Guattari both share this position, writing, "All sensation is composed with the void in compositing itself with itself, and everything holds together on earth and in the air, and preserves the void, is preserved in the void by preserving itself."[19]

Icarus, we might recall, was the son of Daedalus, the artful inventor of the labyrinth. The son's fate was determined by his hubris, and his failure to listen to his father's warnings. Daedalus gave his son the power of ascension, the ability to fly out of the prison—both physical and imagined—of the father's creation. Icarus was, however, seduced by the light of the sun, wanting to touch the untouchable, to feel its excess. Thus, he destroyed himself and, in the process, Daedalus's belief in the power of the arts. There is an important lesson here. Icarus's journey was already fated to end tragically, for the escape was cast within a scene of sacredness. And yet, the ultimate casualty is the art itself, which also gets burned by the sacred flames that ultimately destroy everything.

That is why the idea of the black sun is so compelling here and needs to be completely detached from its nihilistic or occultist connotations. What the black sun represents is more than some hollow or darkened land or indeed a mere eclipse or optical illusion of the light. The black sun is the center point in the ascension, the exit out of a vortex, which knows its dance doesn't always promise to scorch the flesh or the body of the earth. Within the territory of the mind, the black sun is the spot at which the labyrinth ends; the center point behind the pupil of the eye where consciousness seeps out into the world; the absent refrain between the realm of the imagination and the terrestrial plane; the inversion of light, through which the poet shows how to transgress the sacred and expose how every myth can be touched, its excess accompanied, and its fires befriended as the beholder of one's most intimate secrets.

The black sun reveals itself in the cosmic heights, through the rupture in the void itself, to open up the logics of space and time and illustrate how it is possible to return from the void and unsettle the sacred order of things. No doubt the black sun is a terrifying prospect to behold. Like its radiant opposite, it too, we can assume, expands over the course of its life, its mysterious power leaving us in awe of the violence and devastation it promises. But the black sun has no concrete surface. It is an opening into which the collision of universes provides a way to affirm what we have learned from the poets of history. And so, the more the black sun expands, the more it pulls all things from the depths of the vortex into which destructive and creative life has been thrown.

Biblical and apocalyptic overtones aside,[20] it's easy to understand why nihilists have sought to appropriate this symbol and connect it specifically to some death drive. Its energy and power are all too seductive. In turn, this also opens up a psychoanalytical space for relating its appearance to melancholia and depression in the face of the great black hole of absence.[21] Or, as Helene Cixous reminds us, "Dark is dangerous. You can't see anything in the dark, you're afraid. Don't move, you might fall. Most of all, don't go into the forest. And so we have internalized this horror of the dark."[22] And yet, even if it does unquestionably provide a potent symbol for those who give their allegiance to violence and despair, the black sun can also be seen as a sphere of creative wonderment, upon which all the poets of history have gazed to find their escape. We could invariably be drawn here to both Chagall's *Black Sun Over Paris* (1952) and Rothko's *Untitled* (1964-67) black-on-black triptych at the Rothko Chapel in Houston to recognize the radical ambiguity of the black sun's appearance, and to explain how it explicitly works against metaphysical certainty.

As Stanton Marlan explains of these latter paintings with acute resonance, "Rothko's attempt to paint this pivotal point between presence and absence was also an attempt to paint the void."[23] While the black sun may be associated with the death drive, that of individuals and of entire cosmos, more expressively it offers something beyond the negative, a true reach to attain the "unthinkable" in spite of the nihilism of the times. Indeed, while its banal appropriation by fascist movements has turned the black sun into something that appears to be unimaginative, often drawn out with uninspiring technical lines of articulation and kitsch icons of death, as artists such as Chagall and Rothko show, its creative potency has nothing to do with fascist regalia. Rather, it signifies the mystery of mysteries wherein absence itself is shown to be full of meaning, even if its territory cannot possibly be charted out linearly.

Fascists seek to map the black sun in order to throw life into its abyss with maddening repetitiveness. But the poets of history understand that its communicative flames, ignited by the ancestral flames of creativity, contain more depth in their singularities and feature more illumination in their unique dance than the fascists will ever know. This resonates with Morton's theorization on those dark ecologies, whose strange appearance evokes not depression, but a shimmering cloud of unknowing that takes us even further than the uncanny, culminating in a poetic counter with a tragic world that dazzles us with spectacles of violence and sparkles with nothingness. This is not to deny the melancholic wound, but to find reasons to believe in defiance of a world that seeks to continually annihilate through its sacred claims. Call it idealism if you will; a better term is the imaginary. But whoever said, fascists aside, the world was too full of ideas anyway?

Certainly, then, we will not find the answers to our predicament upon mountaintops, or by journeying to some idyllic retreat. Dante's and Nietzsche's climbs are just as spatial and solitary as the journeys of those seeking refuge in the Garden of Earthly Delights, which, like Eden, is colored by anticipation of obscure beasts and their violence-to-come. There is a need to cross over into the non-place, not to abstract oneself from reality, but immerse oneself fully in the intimate depths of life, to lose oneself in the joy of existence so that we might find reasons to believe in this world again. Hence, if life is burdened with the prospect of death, it is no longer sufficient to repeat the mantra that to philosophize is to learn how to die—especially if such a pessimistic concept of death owes to the suffering inherent to survival compounded by a fear of venturing into the void.

When asked whether he would prefer the torments of Hell to the possibility of annihilation, the artist Francis Bacon replied: "Yes, I would, because if I was in hell, I would always feel I had a chance of escaping. I'd always be sure that I'd be able to escape."[24] How might we approach the void with the same artistic sensibility? Maybe the answer can be found in rethinking what philosophy itself means as it is endlessly tasked with questioning and preparing for an impending death. As Paul Celan understood, what does it mean to look at life from the always and already present perspective of death? If religion is for people who fear Hell and spirituality for those who have been there, how might we learn to appreciate our own finitude and eventual return into the unknown by looking at life from the perspective of its passing? To rise into the depths of the black sun and feel the lightness of being in the presence of the poets of history? To learn to gaze back upon humanity and question the measure of its existence from the perspective of the void, the absence of absence? To acknowledge how the shame of being human stemmed from the violence of our sacred humanism, which has continued to preach enlightenment to the point of our extinction? And to look intently at the way the sacred has reappeared in secular places, and especially to critically question the violence behind all claims to a righteous or higher love? This asks serious questions of us about our lives, our present, and our ideas for the future, while we find ourselves hopelessly immersed in our tragic and yet wondrous condition.

The appearance of the black sun brings into question the sacred space into which it is so visibly positioned. We can imagine it like the Rothko Chapel, which has a poetic mediation at its blackened heart. This is the point at which we can depart from Julia Kristeva, who, although wanting to imagine a sun which is "bright and black at the same time"[25] by rethinking the poetic form and reimagining the decomposition and recomposition of signs, is nevertheless committed to rescuing the sacred. Despite her poetics—or we might say because of her particular poetic sensibility as it appears through the ontotheological moment in post-modernity—she still seeks some form of sacred meaning which, she holds, will reveal itself as the result of a tragedy so overwhelming that even the sun itself turns black. This sun is not a radiant star that somehow turns black, but the black as it appears in the original scene. The black sun is thus not an eclipsing of perception, but something so radically undecidable it denies any sacred meaning, despite the ways it's been violently appropriated for such ends or tied to a melancholic lament that calls out for another sacred object to appear. If the black sun so perturbs us, it is precisely because it appears on the horizon as the unthinkable event for a world in which all sacred objects have been undone and its dark poetic shadows liberated.

What has too often been eclipsed in perception and memory is not the radiant sun but the violence of our sacred light. What we might see as the dream of a secular life memorialized for all eternity in recognition of the wonder of its achievements, parted by the dream of total annihilation where the existence of a life vanishes without any meaningful trace, have proved effectively to be opposite sides of the same metaphysical vision, which emanates from sacrificial greatness. The greater the idea, the greater the violence carried out toward its resolution. Such has been the tragedy of the human condition. Guided by an artificial love— where love itself is the order of a politics that segregates and colonizes in the name of its protections and the authentic claim to rightfulness. This is a love that sacrifices that which is loved to prove of its existence; what remains is a body of thought violently shadowed by its own presence.

So just as we are carrying the traces of the disappeared, so we now also carry the void of humanity. We are the void, the inner territory that articulates a presence, and that which through both its suffering and its imagination goes beyond its own bodily form to shatter its own familial constructs. The void is the crack in the foundations that humanity creates for itself. But if the wound is made of flesh and bone, then the void belongs to the life of the mind as it turns to gaze toward that vortex of the sun. It is manifest in every emotional state as it appears to be earth-shattering—and by this we always mean life-shattering—in some exceptional form. The void is, however, important when beginning anew. If the exceptional is the outcome of the normalization of violence, while also being the name proper to that which transgresses the void into which life is violently thrown, our search for an art of the political sets us to reimagining a truly exceptional politics that goes beyond the sacrificial pale. Or, to put it another way, what would it mean to do justice to thoughts, words, and actions in the same way Rothko does intimate justice to the aesthetic field of human sensations?

THE COMEDY DIVINE

To reimagine humanity means to reimagine what humanism could mean after the death of liberalism. We have explored how liberalism could offer a reading of history as some natural unfolding into a universal state of enlightenment, bound to the sacralization of the victim. However, such an account of history would only trace its steps back to condemn the history of illiberal atrocities while affirming the righteousness of the liberal power's mission. But how might we learn to walk the same path back in time, so that that we might steer the future in a different direction? Is it possible to truly learn from history, adding to its complex layering with poetic reverie, to insist that the past can be just as open-ended as the future in terms of how we think, perceive, and relate to this world? Can we suggest that the very idea of humanism and, by extension, humanity can be completely undone so that they are unchained from the politics of sacrifice?

One possible way to think about this is through a final return to Dante. What would it mean to reread and rewrite this poem in reverse? What if we were to fabulate a new poetic image that begins at the final destination of sacred completion, then works its way from the metaphysical stars back down to the earthly depths? The "Comedy Divine," then, as a tale of the violence that begins with the ends of sacrifice, the metaphysical gift, which inverts the story so that it becomes one of witnessing the slow damnation of a man, revealing the divine violence at the heart of the comedy of existence. Without being too teleological, it would certainly be important to retain the cantos' numerical sequencing, albeit in the opposite direction. Rather than presenting itself as a natural and logical unfolding to a more elevated and emancipatory state of celestial wonderment, the Comedy Divine would become a countdown to desolation and the realization of our most animal state. We would in the process become less concerned with the triumphant circularity of the number three, in terms of both destination and theological symbolism, than with the singularity of the number one—the first cantica of our reimagined work would result in a solitary man left alone in the wilderness of own his thoughts. The more pessimistic could even imagine Dante walking in the dark forest for all eternity, trapped in the unforgiving void, incapable of putting into words the horrors he has seen, muted by the terror of divine violence and fully abandoning the metaphysical hope for a sacrificial life worthy of its place in Paradise. Thus, beginning the journey on the summit in Canto Thirty-Four of *Inferno*, so the Comedy Divine might begin:

> Now we went in, gazing one last time upon the stars.
>
> Some of the beauteous things that the skies above bear;
> Till I simply beheld through a round aperture
> We mounted up, he first and I the second,
>
> And without care of having any rest
> Now entered once more, to return to the abysmal world;
> The Guide and I into that hidden road

Our rewriting of this chapter, in which Dante descends into the Inferno, would certainly require a new and more critically astute guide. Virgil would not be up to this task; his poetics are too committed to the sacrificial in thought. Nietzsche, on the other hand, would at least understand the significance of the mountains and the descent into the abyss. And he would have enough critical fortitude to guide our willing traveler back into this wound in time. But who might we now meet on this journey? Rather than merely castigating individuals, what if we found Satan devouring the treacherous pillars of faith, hope, and reason themselves? Soon after, we would come upon the universal truth-tellers, feasting on one another's flesh in the frozen lake of Cocytus, home to the fraudsters of history. Beyond its shores, we would likely find Tony Blair seated on a chair in a barren wasteland, in a readaptation of Marina Abramovich's performance "The Artist Is Present." He has his eyes closed, then every minute he opens them to look upon the ghostly faces of every victim of war since the dawn of humanity. Blair's witnessing never ends as the victims give themselves over to this eternal return.

The further we descend, the torment of Ugolino della Gherardesca and his sons might be reimagined as "the ideologies of man" devour with schizophrenic pleasure the rotting brains of their pitiful and impotent forefathers. And what of these ideologies' principal architects, armed with their sacred claims? Let's imagine Dante led by Nietzsche to a square mirrored pit that has been dug into the ground, each of its sides fully covered. As they look down, they see four chairs whose corners are touching and facing outward in a cross formation. Bound to the seats we see Adolf Hitler, Winston Churchill, Joseph Stalin, and Harry Truman, whose heads are fixed frontwards so that they are forced to stare into the distance of themselves. They are comforted only by the presence of the others, the four of them ultimately alike in their thought processes.

But what of those whom Dante had moralistically condemned? What of the forest of suicides? Let us no longer add suffering to those who have already suffered too much in their mortal life—rather, let us now stand witness to the likes of Celan and Deleuze, who are joyfully leaping into the void, over and over, like children in their exhilaration. And what of Paolo and Francesca, the tormented lovers? Yes, they remain caught in the swirling winds that throw them into the skies above, but now they are looking into each other's eyes, staying true to their love that had long since denied the idea of sin, knowing they would do so for all time regardless of their punishment. Later scenes would be populated by every religious figure, at least to give Muhammad company. And it would be tempting to set aside a closed room where Jesus of Nazareth debates Judas Iscariot, mediated by Luis Borges, about who sacrificed the most? And as for Iphigenia, perhaps she will replace the ferryman Charon, the one who makes the treacherous journey possible to begin with, but now she carries across the River Styx a wearied Dante, sick from all the violence and suffering he has been forced to witness.

But Nietzsche would ultimately have to leave Dante at the gates of Hell and send him alone into the wilderness, for Nietzsche, too, is still allegiant to the sacred. And so, as our protagonist looks back at the entranceway into hopelessness, standing alone in the woods, he just might hear the voice of Beatrice telling him she never wanted him to have sacrificed so much, and she never wanted any violence associated with her name. And so, he calls out:

> Speak will I of the other things I saw there.
> But of the good to treat, which there I found,
> So bitter is it, death is little more;
>
> Which in the very thought renews the fear.
> What was this forest savage, rough, and stern,
> Ah me! how hard a thing it is to say
>
> For the straightforward pathway had been lost.
> I found myself within a forest dark,
> Midway upon the journey of our life

But the wilderness in this adaptation cannot be merely reduced to the solitary, pessimistic place identified above. Dante is no longer alone, isolated in his own mind. The wilderness into which Dante returns could alternatively be interpreted as alight with the poetic flames of history, carried across the unknowable and unbounded planes of existence, surrounded by a swirling vortex, the point of origin whose maelstrom does more than merely pull things into the depths of human despair to void them of all meaning and truth. Here he is back in the flow of becoming, freed from the sacred chains, gazing upon the black sun that demands its own ascension and whose laws have revealed themselves as snapshots of the past. Surely, he would know, the ground beneath his feet was precarious, and would quake with all the force of his first breath.

And Dante must now learn to wander the heights and depths of the wilderness, its unknown fiery paths whose memory renders oblivion oblivious. But, having willfully thrown himself into the void, he must also be open to the mystery of life without being tempted back by the sacred call, whose melancholic lament can still be heard in the distance. Far from being alone in this world, Dante must therefore find joy in the bewilderment of the wilderness, having already walked away from the light and seen the violence carried out in the light's name. Thus, the sacred binds that hold together the celestial with the infernal can be broken. Recognizing how sacred language all too easily calls for vengeance, Dante must confide in the fire of the wound, undoing his own humanism so the concept might be thought anew, opening his heart to the idea of a love without sacrifice, giving himself over while asking nothing in return. We can only imagine how the world might look with the liberation of this fire. Nothing lasts forever, including nothing itself.

Notes

FOREWORD: AN OBITUARY FOR THE LIBERAL

1. Friedrich Nietzsche, *The Birth of Tragedy: Out of the Spirit of Music* (London: Penguin, 1993), 32.
2. Sigmund Freud, *Beyond the Pleasure Principle* (Minneola, NY: Dover, 1991), 2.
3. Pierre Klossowski, *Sade My Neighbor* (Evanston, IL: Northwestern University Press, 1991).
4. Cited in Julia Kristeva, *Black Sun: Depression and Melancholia* (New York: Columbia University Press, 1989), 107.

PREFACE: ENCOUNTERING THE VOID

1. René Girard, *Violence and the Sacred* (London: Continuum, 2005).
2. Giorgio Agamben, *Homo Sacer: Sovereign Power and Bare Life* (Stanford, CA: Stanford University Press, 1998).
3. Walter Benjamin, "Critique of Violence," in *Reflections: Essays, Aphorisms, Autobiographical Writings* (New York: Shocken, 1986), 277–300.
4. Dante Alighieri, *Inferno* (London: Penguin, 2006).
5. Brad Evans and Julian Reid, *Resilient Life: The Art of Living Dangerously* (Cambridge: Polity Press, 2014).
6. Brad Evans and Henry A. Giroux, *Disposable Futures: The Seduction of Violence in the Age of the Spectacle* (San Francisco, CA: City Lights, 2015). On this see also Brad Evans and Henry A. Giroux, "Intolerable Violence," *Symploke* 23, no. 1–2 (2015): 197–219.
7. These conversations are freely available to access online via the *New York Times* forum The Stone and the Histories of Violence section of the *Los Angeles Review of Books*. An anthology that featured a selection from both has also been published. See Brad Evans and Natasha Lennard, *Violence: Humans in Dark Times* (San Francisco, CA: City Lights, 2018). A further collection is now also in production: Brad Evans and Adrian Parr, *Conversations on Violence: An Anthology* (London: Pluto Press, 2021).
8. The artworks and wider project can be viewed here: https://www.historiesofviolence.com/state-of-disappearance.

9. To engage with the full corpus of work in Agamben's tremendous series, see Giorgio Agamben, *The Omnibus Homo Sacer* (Stanford, CA: Stanford University Press, 2017).

10. Jean-Paul Sartre, *Being and Nothingness: An Essay on Phenomenological Ontology* (Abingdon, UK: Routledge, 2003).

11. On this, see "Introduction: from experience to economy," in *The Bataille Reader*, ed. Fred Botting and Scott Wilson (Oxford: Blackwell, 1997), 1–34.

12. Brad Evans, *Liberal Terror* (Cambridge: Polity Press, 2013); Evans and Reid, *Resilient Life*.

1. HUMANITY BOUND

1. On the importance of the painting to the history and development of the Western imaginary, see Marcia Hall, *Raphael's School of Athens* (Cambridge: Cambridge University Press, 1997).

2. An informative set of essays on the links between the Renaissance and humanism has been put together by Jill Kraye: *The Cambridge Companion of Renaissance Humanism* (Cambridge: Cambridge University Press, 1996). In terms of its opening onto the sacred, see Ingrid Rowland, *From Heaven to Arcadia: The Sacred and the Profane in the Renaissance* (New York: New York Review of Books, 2008).

3. This point on the violence of humanism is explicitly made by Jean-Paul Sartre in his preface to Frantz Fanon's *Wretched of the Earth*. As Sartre writes, "We must face that unexpected revelation, the striptease of our humanism. There you see it, quite naked, and it's not a pretty sight. It was nothing but an ideology of lies, a perfect justification for pillage; its honeyed words, its affectation of sensibility were only alibis for our aggressions." In Fanon, *The Wretched of the Earth* (London: Penguin, 2001), 21.

4. *Je Vous Salue, Sarajevo* (1993) is a short two-minute film produced and narrated by Jean-Luc Godard. It centers on the graphic photo of an execution of innocent civilians taken by U.S. photographer Ron Haviv in Bijeljina, Bosnia on March 31, 1992.

5. We might recall Franz Kafka's point that "The messiah will only come when he is no longer necessary; he will come only on the day after his arrival; he will come, not on the last day, but the very last." Doubtless, the importance of Jacques Derrida's thinking on this cannot be understated. For a purposeful set of essays on this, see Susan Gerlac and Pheng Chang, *Derrida and the Time of the Political* (Durham, NC: Duke University Press, 2009). Inspired by Derrida (along with Michel Foucault), Michael Dillon is another serious and astute thinker on the relationship between eschatology and time. See his essays, "Spectres of Biopolitics: Finitude, *Eschaton*, and Katechon," *South Atlantic Quarterly* 110, no. 3 (2010) 780–92; "Political Spirituality: Parrhesia, Truth and Factical Finitude," in *Foucault and the Modern International*, ed. P. Bonditti and F. Gros (New York: Palgrave, 2017), 79–96; and "Violences of the Messianic," in *The Politics to Come: Power, Modernity and the Messianic*, ed. A. Bradley and P. Fletcher (London: Continuum, 2010), 191–207.

6. As Nietzsche writes in section 822 of *The Will to Power*: "For a philosopher to say, 'The good and the beautiful are one,' is infamy; if he goes on to add, 'also the true,' one ought to thrash him. Truth is ugly. We possess art lest we perish from truth."

7. The idea that everything begins with language is a profoundly theological claim. As written in John 1:1: "In the beginning was the Word, and the Word was with God, and the Word was God."

8. I am borrowing here from Merleau-Ponty's conceptual language. See, in particular, Mauro Carbonne, *The Flesh of Images: Merleau-Ponty Between Painting and Cinema* (New York: SUNY Press, 2015).

9. The image of thought is a concept first put forward by Gilles Deleuze, *Difference and Repetition* (London: Continuum, 2004), 164–213. While apparent in many of his other writings, it also substantively appears in chapter 3, concerning the "conceptual persona," in his collaboration with Felix Guattari, *What Is Philosophy?* (New York: Verso, 1994), 61–84. For an excellent introduction and elaboration on this aesthetic idea, see Gregg Lambert, *In Search of a New Image of Thought: Gilles Deleuze and Philosophical Expressionism* (Minneapolis: Minnesota University Press, 2012).

10. Indebted to René Girard (though less anthropologically inclined and evidently more subtle in his thinking on overlaps between religion and secularism), Jean-Pierre Dupuy holds that it is only by harnessing the power of the sacred that we might save ourselves from the ravages of contemporary catastrophe and violence. Dupuy thus sees a world teetering ever closer to the abyss, since it is now almost bereft of the sacred (as properly conceived), and somewhat lacking in sacrificial claims. This is both political and personal. As he insinuates, those who are denied the sacred in life are forced to live with an "impossible love, a story of failed transcendence, swallowed up by the black hole of nothingness." Jean-Pierre Dupuy, *The Mark of the Sacred* (Stanford, CA: Stanford University Press, 2013), 19.

11. There are many volumes which have been inspired by the work of Arendt. In terms of her life and continued importance, I would recommend, Anne C. Heller, *Hannah Arendt: A Life in Dark Times* (New York: Amazon, 2015); Elizabeth Young-Bruehl, *Hannah Arendt: For Love of the World* (New Haven, CT: Yale University Press, 2004); and Dana Villa, *Cambridge Companion to Hannah Arendt* (Cambridge: Cambridge University Press, 2006).

12. Hannah Arendt, *Eichmann in Jerusalem: A Report on the Banality of Evil* (London, Penguin Classics: 2006). The original investigations, commissioned by the *New Yorker* in 1963, have been digitized and are available online here: https://www.newyorker.com/magazine /1963/02/16/eichmann-in-jerusalem-i.

13. Hannah Arendt, *The Origins of Totalitarianism* (New York: Harcourt, 1976), 459.

14. Arendt, *The Origins of Totalitarianism*, 229.

15. I have made this point earlier concerning both the changing biopolitical nature of liberal rule and its forms of ghettoization. Compare to chapter 5, "A New Leviathan," in *Liberal Terror*; and Brad Evans and Mark Duffield, "Bio-Spheric Security: How the Merger Between Development, Security and the Environment [Desenex] Is Retrenching Fortress Europe," in *A Threat Against Europe? Security, Migration and Integration*, ed. P. Burgess and S. Gutwirth (Brussels: VUB Press, 2011).

16. Jacques Derrida, *Paper Machine* (Stanford, CA: Stanford University Press, 2005), 103.

17. George Bataille, *The Tears of Eros* (San Francisco, CA: City Lights, 1989), 199.

18. For an accessible overview of the return to religious themes in continental philosophy, see Gregg Lambert, *Return Statements: The Return of Religion in Contemporary Philosophy* (Edinburgh, UK: Edinburgh University Press, 2016).

19. Brad Evans and Henry A. Giroux, "Intolerable Violence," *Symploke* 23, no. 1–2 (2015): 197–219

20.   One of the most explicit earlier treatments on this, which was also important in terms of proposing a new understanding of the sacred, was provided by Catherine Clement and Julia Kristeva, *The Feminine and the Sacred* (New York: Columbia University Press, 2001). It would subsequently be articulated in Simon Critchley, *The Faith of the Faithless: Experiments in Political Theology* (New York: Verso, 2014), and also in the work of John Caputo, who draws upon poetics and puts forward the idea of a "weak God": *The Weakness of God: A Theology of the Event* (Indianapolis: Indiana University Press, 2006). Further compelling mediations can be found in John Caputo and Gianni Vattimo, *After the Death of God* (New York: Columbia University Press, 2009); Jeffrey W. Robbins, *Radical Democracy and Political Theology* (New York: Columbia University Press, 2013); and Catherine Keller, *Political Theology of the Earth: Our Planetary Emergency and the Struggle for a New Public* (New York: Columbia University Press, 2018).

21.   See Caputo, *The Weakness of God* and Dupuy, *The Mark of the Sacred.*

22.   The most prominent in this regard would be Michael Waltzer, *Just and Unjust Wars: A Moral Argument with Illustrations* (New York: Basic, 2015). For an important critique of just war and how it links to liberal theology, see John Gray, *Black Mass: Apocalyptic Religion and the Death of Utopia* (New York: Penguin, 2007).

23.   On this, see chapter 2, "Insecurity by Design," in Evans and Reid, *Resilient Life*, 38–67.

24.   Richard Kearney's concept of anatheism is notable in this regard as a precise attempt to both reclaim and reimagine the sacred. Richard Kearney, *Anatheism: Returning to God After God* (New York: Columbia University Press, 2011). For a further set of lively debates on this and broader concerns with the sacred in contemporary life, see *Reimagining the Sacred*, ed. Richard Kearney and Jens Zimmerman (New York: Columbia University Press, 2015).

25.   Certainly, the most compelling thinker on tragedy currently is Simon Critchley, whose rich artistic insight allows for a further opening up into new thinking about mysticism and what it might mean with regard to insisting upon the need for a more poetic mediation in thoughtful and agreeable ways. See in particular Simon Critchley, *Tragedy, the Greeks, and Us* (New York: Pantheon, 2019).

26.   For detailed photographs of these works, including full panoramas of their positioning in the cathedral, see the artist's personal website at: http://www.judah.co.uk/works/great-war-commemorative-sculptures/.

27.   "Twin sculptures at St. Paul's Cathedral commemorate First World War Centenary," *Centenary News*: First World War 1914–18 (June 6, 2014). Online at: https://centenarynews.com/article?id=1698.

28.   https://www.stpauls.co.uk/news-press/latest-news/giant-white-crosses-remind-st-pauls-worshippers-and-visitors-of-the-horrors-of-warfare.

29.   In my earlier work I took up the idea of the event to question the links between insecurity and the unknown, and also to consider what constituted the conditions of the new. This was particularly in response to the politics of catastrophe. See chapter 6, "The Event Horizon," in *Liberal Terror*, 165–200.

30.   For an excellent brief introduction to this concept, see Mark Fisher, "What Is Hauntology?" *Film Quarterly* 66, no. 1 (2012), 16–24.

31.   Influenced by Benjamin, Derrida conceived of a "messianism without religion, even a messianic without messianism." Jacques Derrida, *Specters of Marx* (New York: Routledge, 2006), 74.

Concerning Agamben's messianic politics, see Catherine Mills, "Agamben's Messianic Politics: Biopolitics, Abandonment, and Happy Life," *Contretemps Online Journal of Philosophy* 5 (2004), 42–62; and Antonio Cimino, "Agamben's Messianism in 'The Time That Remains,'" *International Journal of Philosophy and Theology* 77, no. 3 (2016).

32. This point is well made by Charles Taylor in his book *A Secular Age* (Cambridge, MA: Harvard University Press, 2007).

33. The ambivalence of the sacred was duly recognized by Emile Durkheim: "Not only is there no clear border between these two opposite kinds, but the same object can pass from one to the other without changing nature. The impure is made from the pure, and vice versa. The ambiguity of the sacred consists in the possibility of this transmutation." This means that nothing is inherently sacred, but anything could become sacred within a symbolic order of things. However, as Durkheim further noted, the sacred must be beyond reproach; guarded by prohibitions (the sacrilegious), it belongs to something unique. Sacred things are "things set apart and forbidden." Seen this way, what is sacred is never self-evidently true. It is a construct that is part of a myth-making process of social constructivism. "The sacredness exhibited by the thing is not implicated in the intrinsic properties of the thing: It is added to them. The world of the religious is not a special aspect of empirical nature: It is superimposed upon nature." Emile Durkheim, *The Elementary Forms of Religious Life* (New York: Free Press, 1995), 448, 44, 35, 30. For a concise overview of Durkheim's theory and how it connects to Girard and Bataille, see Elisa Heinamaki, "Durkheim, Bataille and Girard on the Ambiguity of the Sacred: Reconsidering Saints and Demoniacs," *Journal of the American Academy of Religion* 83 (2015), 513–36.

34. Georges Bataille, *The Absence of Myth: Writings on Surrealism* (New York: Verso, 2006), 114–15.

35. On this, see my criticism of the State of Exception in *Liberal Terror*.

36. Bataille, *The Absence of Myth*, 115.

37. As Bataille wrote in his book concerning Inner Experience, "Only violence can bring everything to a state of flux in this way, only violence and the nameless disquiet bound up with it." We "cannot imagine the transition from one state to another one basically unlike it without picturing the violence done to the being called into existence through discontinuity." Georges Bataille, *Inner Experience* (New York: SUNY Press, 2014), 17.

38. Aeschylus, *The Oresteia: Agamemnon, The Libation Bearers, The Eumenides* (London: Penguin, 1979), 109.

39. It was precisely this doctrine of suffering that irked Nietzsche so much, especially the judgments inherent to it, which led him to pen his last and arguably most provocative text—*The Anti-Christ: Curse on Christianity* (1895).

40. On this, see George E. Michalson Jr.'s insightful critique *Fallen Freedom: Kant on Radical Evil and Moral Regeneration* (Cambridge: Cambridge University Press, 1990). I have developed upon this idea of the secular fall, and have added to its importance in the moralization of biopolitics in chapter 4, "On Divine Power," in *Liberal Terror*, 98–134.

41. I'm evidently borrowing from Agamben's terms here. See Giorgio Agamben, *The Time That Remains: A Commentary on the Letter to the Romans* (Stanford, CA: Stanford University Press, 2005).

42. As Sartre reminds us in his *Being and Nothingness*, "The flesh is the pure contingency of presence," 367.

43. Building upon Benjamin's earlier interest, Agamben offers a short essay on "Vortexes" in his book *The Fire and the Tale* (Stanford, CA: Stanford University Press, 2017).

44. The start point for this claim begins with Gilles Deleuze, *The Logic of Sense* (New York: Columbia University Press, 1990). It is also derived from the ideas of Brian Massumi and Erin Manning, *Thought in the Act: Passages in the Ecology of Experience* (Minneapolis: University of Minnesota Press, 2014); along with Erin Manning's *Always More Than One: Individuations Dance* (Durham, NC: Duke University Press, 2013).

45. This point is explicitly made by Deleuze in *The Logic of Sense*, especially in his brief yet compelling mediations on Lewis Carroll's *Alice in Wonderland*. There is certainly a strong case to be made for seeing Alice as a counter-sacred form of political subjectivity. She seems to hold nothing sacred and throughout the fable continues to give over to others while asking nothing in return.

46. On the importance of duration, see the profoundly important and influential work of Henri Bergson, in particular his timeless book *Time and Free Will*. In terms of purposeful introductions and applications of this thinking, see Suzanne Guerlac, *Thinking in Time: An Introduction to Henri Bergson* (Ithaca, NY: Cornell University Press, 2006); Jimena Canales, *The Physicist and the Philosopher: Einstein, Bergson, and the Debate That Changed Our Understanding of Time* (Princeton, NJ: Princeton University Press, 2015); and invariably Gilles Deleuze's wonderful introduction and rearticulation, *Bergsonism* (New York: Zone, 1991).

47. Wilhelm Reich, *The Mass Psychology of Fascism* (New York: Farrar, Straus and Giroux, 1998).

48. Joan Cocks, "Disappearance," *Political Concepts*, Internet Journal (2012). Online at: https://www.politicalconcepts.org/disappearance-joan-cocks/.

49. Gaston Bachelard, *Air and Dreams: An Essay on the Imagination of Movement* (Dallas, TX: The Dallas Institute, 2011).

50. See Jacques Rancière, *The Future of the Image* (New York: Verso, 2009).

51. As Adorno claimed, "The need to let suffering speak is a condition of all truth. For suffering is objectivity that weighs upon the subject . . . " Theodor Adorno, *Negative Dialectics* (New York: Seabury Press, 1973), 17-18.

52. Jacques Rancière, *Figures of History* (Cambridge: Polity Press, 2014).

53. Rancière, *Figures of History*, 49-50.

54. Edward Said, *Orientalism* (London: Penguin Classics, 2019), 68-72.

2. THE SACRED ORDER OF POLITICS

1. See in particular René Girard, *Violence and the Sacred* (London: Continuum, 2005), along with Walter Burkert, *Homo Necans: The Anthropology of Ancient Greek Sacrificial Ritual and Myth* Berkeley: University of California Press, 1983). For a useful collection of discussions on these authors, see Walter Burkert, René Girard, and Jonathan Smith, *Violent Origins: Ritual Killing and Cultural Formation* (Stanford, CA: Stanford University Press, 1987). For completeness, we should also recall again here Emilie Durkheim's contribution and the dichotomy she draws between the sacred and the profane, especially what this means for the cohesion of social orders. See Durkheim, *The Elementary Forms of Religious Life*.

2. The literature on the links between Mesoamerican culture and human sacrifice is exten-
    sive. While many of these works are deeply racist (notably written to reaffirm "savage"
    versus "civilized" tropes), for informative and objective historical accounts see Charles
    Editors and Ernesto Novato, *Huitzilopochtli: The History of the Aztec God of War and Human
    Sacrifice* (Ann Arbor, MI: Charles River Editors, 2019) and David Carrusco, *City of Sac-
    rifice: The Aztec Empire and the Role of Violence in Civilization* (Boston, MA: Beacon Press,
    2000). An informative set of essays committed to rethinking the subject has also been
    compiled by Vera Tisler and Andrea Cucina, *New Perspectives on Human Sacrifice and Body
    Ritual Treatments in Ancient Maya Society* (New York: Springer, 2007).

3. On the sacrifice of Dionysus, see Euripides, *Bacchae* (London: Penguin, 2014); Walter F.
    Otto, *Dionysus: Myth and Cult* (Indianapolis: Indiana University Press, 1995); along with
    Nietzsche's classical reading in *The Birth of Tragedy.*

4. See Saint Augustine, *The City of God* (Harmondsworth, UK: Penguin, 1984), 379.

5. On these points, see Douglas Hedley, *Sacrifice Imagined: Violence, Atonement and the Sacred*
    (London: Continuum, 2011).

6. Charles Taylor, *Philosophical Arguments* (Cambridge, MA: Harvard University Press,
    1995).

7. Emmanuel Levinas, *Totality and Infinity* (Pittsburgh, PA: Duquesne University Press,
    1969), 195.

8. On the importance of Cain and Abel and how their rivalry connects to the story of
    Genesis, see Leon R. Kass, *The Beginning of Wisdom: Reading Genesis* (Chicago: University
    of Chicago Press, 2003).

9. On this, see the lively exchange between René Girard and Walter Burkert in Robert G.
    Hamerton-Kelly, *Violent Origins* (Stanford, CA: Stanford University Press, 1987), 118–23.

10. Jacques Rancière, *Aisthesis: Scenes from the Aesthetic Regime of Art* (New York: Verso, 2013).

11. On the continued relevance of Greek tragedy and its relationship to violence, see Simon
    Critchley, *Tragedy, the Greeks, and Us* (New York: Pantheon, 2019); Emily Katz Anhalt,
    Enraged: Why Violent Times Need Ancient Greek Myths (New Haven, CT: Yale University Press,
    2017); Judith Butler, *Antigone's Claim: Kinship Between Life and Death* (New York: Columbia
    University Press, 2000); George Steiner, *The Death of Tragedy* (New Haven, CT: Yale Univer-
    sity Press, 1996); and Raymond Williams, *Modern Tragedy* (London: Vintage, 1966).

12. Girard, *Violence and the Sacred.* For a good collection of essays on the links between
    sacred violence and religious movements, see *Violence and the Sacred in the Modern World:
    Terrorism and Political Violence,* ed. Mark Juergensmeyer (London: Routledge, 1992).

13. Girard, *Violence and the Sacred,* 73.

14. Jacques Derrida, "Deconstruction and the Other," ed. R. Kearney, *Dialogues with Contemporary
    Continental Thinkers* (Manchester, UK: Manchester University Press, 1984), 117.

15. Girard, *Violence and the Sacred,* 83.

16. We might recall here Goethe's claim: "Within tragedy catharsis occurs through a form
    of human sacrifice, which may actually occur or through a benevolent deity be replaced
    by a surrogate, as in the case of Abraham or Agamemnon." Cited in Hedley, *Sacrifice
    Imagined,* 92.

17. Dupuy, *The Mark of the Sacred* (Stanford, CA: Stanford University Press, 2013).

18. Sigmund Freud, *Totem and Taboo* (London: Routledge, 1961).

19. On the enduring cultural legacy of the myth of Cain and Abel to the Western conscious-
    ness, see Ricardo J. Quinones, *The Changes of Cain: Violence and the Lost Brother in Cain and
    Abel Literature* (Princeton, NJ: Princeton University Press, 2014). Concerning its various
    interpretations and political meaning, see George M. Shulman, "The Myth of Cain: Frat-
    ricide, City Building, and Politics," *Political Theory* 14, no. 2 (1986): 215–38.

20. Carl Schmitt, *The Concept of the Political* (Chicago: University of Chicago Press, 1991).

21. Lars Östman, "The Sacrificial Crises: Law and Violence," *Contagion: Journal of Violence,
    Mimesis, and Culture* 14, no. 1 (2007): 97–119.

22. The importance of Antigone as a body loaded with political symbolism has attracted
    widespread interest from Hegel, Nietzsche, Heidegger, Lacan, and Derrida, as well as
    more recent exegesis from Slavoj Žižek, Judith Butler, and Bonnie Honig, to name a few.

23. Evans and Reid, *Resilient Life: The Art of Living Dangerously* (Cambridge: Polity Press,
    2014).

24. Critchley, *Tragedy, the Greeks, and Us*, 63–64.

25. Nicole Loraux, *Tragic Ways of Killing a Woman* (Cambridge, MA: Harvard University
    Press, 1987), 32.

26. Simon Critchley and Richard Kearney, "What's God? A Shout in the Street," in Kearney,
    Reimagining the Sacred, 170.

27. In terms of the links between Christ, the sacred, and the aesthetics of violence, I would
    highly recommend Richard Viladesau's trilogy of books, *The Beauty of the Cross: The
    Passion of Christ in Theology and the Arts from the Catacombs to the Eve of the Renaissance*
    (Oxford: Oxford University Press, 2006); *The Triumph of the Cross: The Passion of Christ
    in Theology and the Arts from the Renaissance to the Counter-Reformation* (Oxford, Oxford
    University Press: 2008); *The Pathos of the Cross: The Passion of Christ in Theology and the
    Arts—The Baroque Era* (Oxford: Oxford University Press, 2014).

28. Umberto Eco, *On Ugliness* (London: Maclehose Press, 2007), 49.

29. On this see Julia Kristeva, *The Severed Head: Capital Visions* (New York: Columbia University
    Press, 2012).

30. Georg Wilhelm Hegel, *Aesthetics: Lectures on Fine Art Vol. 1* (Oxford: Oxford University
    Press, 1975), 537.

31. See in particular Mary D. Garrard, *Artemisia Gentileschi* (Princeton, NJ: Princeton Uni-
    versity Press, 1989) and Andrew Graham-Dixon, *Caravaggio: A Life Sacred and Profane*
    (London: Penguin, 2011).

32. Georges Bataille, *Inner Experience* (Albany: State University of New York, 1988), 119.

33. David Sylvester, *Interviews with Francis Bacon* (London: Thames and Hudson, 1980), 46.

34. Milan Kundera, "The Painter's Brutal Gesture," in *Francis Bacon: Portraits and Self-Portraits*,
    ed. France Borel (London: Thames and Hudson, 1996), 16–17.

35. Ernst Van Alphen, *Francis Bacon and the Loss of Self* (London: Reaktion, 1992), 122.

36. For an excellent and detailed exposition on the importance of blood, see Gil Anidjar,
    Blood: A Critique of Christianity (New York: Columbia University Press, 2014).

37. Thomas Wright, *Circulation: William Harvey's Revolutionary Idea* (London: Vintage, 2013).

38. Gil Anidjar in his book, *Blood*, offers a particularly compelling argument for seeing blood
    as an element itself, which has been intrinsic to the development of Christianity and the
    modern state.

39. Giorgio Agamben, *Pilate and Jesus* (Stanford, CA: Stanford University Press, 2015), 2.

40. Agamben, *Pilate and Jesus*, 45.

41. Ricardo J. Quinones, *Foundation Sacrifice in Dante's* Commedia (University Park, PA: Pennsylvania State University Press, 1994).

42. Quinones, *Foundation Sacrifice in Dante's* Commedia, 134.

43. For accessible and concise histories, along with his position in respect to the Renaissance and past and contemporary European culture, see Peter S. Hawkins, *Dante: A Brief History* (Oxford: Blackwell, 2006); Marco Santagata, *Dante: The Story of His Life* (Cambridge, MA: Harvard University Press, 2013); and Giuseppe Mazzotta, *Reading Dante* (New Haven, CT: Yale University Press, 2014).

44. See Evans, *Liberal Terror* (Cambridge: Polity Press, 2013), 106–20.

45. On this, see Giorgio Agamben, *The End of the Poem: Studies in Poetics* (Stanford, CA: Stanford University Press, 1999).

46. Giambattista Vico, *The New Science* (London: Penguin Classics, 1999), 367–68.

47. See John Kleiner, *Mis-Mapping the Underworld: Daring and Error in Dante's Comedy* (Stanford, CA: Stanford University Press, 1994).

48. John Milton, *Paradise Lost* (London: Penguin, 2000), 9.

49. On this, see Ken Hiltner, *Milton and Ecology* (Cambridge: Cambridge University Press, 2003).

50. On the life and works of Goya, and how they connect directly to violence, see Stephanie Loeb Stepanek and Frederick Hehman, *Goya: Order and Disorder* (Boston, MA: MFA Publications, 2014).

51. Brad Evans and Jake Chapman, "The Violence of Art," in Evans and Lennard, *Violence*, 244.

52. Cited in Francisco de Goya, *The Disasters of War* (Minneola, New York: Dover, 1967), 1.

53. Friedrich Nietzsche, *The Gay Science* (New York: Vintage, 1974), 181–82.

54. Cited in Harald Wydra, *Politics and the Sacred* (Cambridge: Cambridge University Press, 2015), 2.

55. While the theological nature of the modern features in many of his writings, the most explicit treatment is given in Carl Schmitt, *Political Theology: Four Chapters on the Concept of Sovereignty* (Chicago: University of Chicago Press, 2006).

56. Ray Brassier, *Nihil Unbound: Enlightenment and Extinction* (New York: Palgrave Macmillan, 2007).

57. Friedrich Nietzsche, *Beyond Good and Evil* (London: Penguin, 2014) [maxim 146], 107

58. On this, see the BBC documentary *Goya Exposed with Jake Chapman*, directed by Ben Harding (London: BBC, 2016).

59. Stephanie Loeb Stephanek and Frederick Hehman, *Goya: Order and Disorder*, 29.

60. Zygmunt Bauman, *Modernity and the Holocaust* (Cambridge: Polity Press, 1991), 218.

61. For an excellent exploration of this, see Mary Coffey, *How Revolutionary Art Became Official Culture: Murals, Museums, and the Mexican State* (Durham, NC: Duke University Press, 2012).

62. Cited in Coffey, *How Revolutionary Art Became Official Culture*, 25.

63. Cited in Stuart Jeffries, "The Storm Blowing from Paradise: Walter Benjamin and Klee's *Angelus Novus*," *Verso Books* (blog), August 2, 2016, https://www.versobooks.com/blogs/2791-the-storm-blowing-from-paradise-walter-benjamin-and-klee-s-angelus-novus.

64.   On the life and works of Dix, see Philipp Gutbrod, *Otto Dix: The Art of Life* (Berlin: Hatje Cantz, 2010) and Michael Mackenzie, *Otto Dix and the First World War: Grotesque Humor, Camaraderie and Remembrance* (London: Peter Lang, 2019).

65.   Cited in Jackie Wullschlager, "Otto Dix: *Der Krieg*, De La Warr Pavilion, Bexhill, East Sussex, UK—Review," *Financial Times*, May 18, 2014, https://www.ft.com/content/abf66272 -dc49-11e3-9016-00144feabdc0.

66.   Susan Sontag, "Looking at War: Photography's View of Devastation and Death," *The New Yorker*, December 9, 2002, https://www.newyorker.com/magazine/2002/12/09/looking-at-war.

67.   Susan Sontag, *Regarding the Pain of Others* (London: Penguin, 2004), 29.

3. THE SHAME OF BEING HUMAN

1.   Judith Butler, "Hannah Arendt's Challenge to Adolf Eichmann," *Guardian*, August 29, 2011, https://www.theguardian.com/commentisfree/2011/aug/29/hannah-arendt-adolf-eichmann -banality-of-evil.

2.   Hannah Arendt, *Thinking Without a Bannister* (New York: Schocken, 2018), 201.

3.   Hannah Arendt, *The Origins of Totalitarianism* (New York: Harcourt, 1976), 293.

4.   Michael Shapiro, *War Crimes: Atrocity and Justice* (Cambridge: Polity Press, 2015), 15.

5.   Hannah Arendt, *Eichmann in Jerusalem : A Report on the Banality of Evil* (London, Penguin Classics: 2006), 268.

6.   Arendt, *Eichmann in Jerusalem*, 268–69.

7.   See in particular Agamben, *Homo Sacer: Sovereign Power and Bare Life* (Stanford, CA: Stanford University Press, 1998) and *Remnants of Auschwitz: The Witness and the Archive* (New York: Zone, 2002).

8.   Agamben, *Remnants of Auschwitz*, 51.

9.   Agamben, *Remnants of Auschwitz*, 61.

10.   Agamben, *Remnants of Auschwitz*, 13.

11.   On the biblical and earthly themes conveyed in this painting, see in particular Ziva Amishai-Maisels, "Chagall's 'White Crucifixion,'" *Art Institute of Chicago Museum Studies* 17, no. 2 (1991): 138–53.

12.   For useful introductions and key debates on the changing nature of international law with respect to crimes against humanity and legal institutions, see Shoshana Felman, *The Juridical Unconscious: Trials and Traumas in the Twentieth Century* (Cambridge, MA: Harvard University Press, 2002); Lawrence Douglas, *The Memory of Judgment: Making Law and History in the Trials of the Holocaust* (New Haven, CT: Yale University Press, 2001); and William Schabas, *Unimaginable Atrocities: Justice, Politics, and Rights at the War Crimes Tribunals* (Oxford: Oxford University Press, 2012).

13.   See Shapiro, *War Crimes*, 13–49.

14.   Mathias Enard, *Zone* (London: Fitzcarraldo, 2014), 80.

15.   Enard, *Zone*, 80.

16.   Enard, *Zone*, 82.

17.   Brad Evans, *Liberal Terror* (Cambridge: Polity Press, 2013).

18.   On this, see the 1997 essay by Subcomandante Marcos of the rebel Zapatistas, titled "The Seven Loose Pieces of the Global Jigsaw Puzzle," http://www.elkilombo.org/documents /sevenpiecesmarcos.html.

19. See Wilhelm Reich, *The Mass Psychology of Fascism* (New York: Farrar, Straus and Giroux, 1998).

20. This quote comes from Pierre-Andre Boutang's documentary *L'Abécédaire de Gilles Deleuze* (1996), in which Deleuze is talking about the letter "R" for resistance.

21. Theodor Adorno, *Minima Moralia: Reflections on Damaged Life* (New York: Verso, 2005), 36.

22. Gilles Deleuze, *Foucault* (London: Continuum, 2006), 76.

23. Gil Anidjar, "Survival," *Political Concepts: A Critical Lexicon* (internet journal), January 1, 2013, https://www.politicalconcepts.org/survival-gil-anidjar/.

24. These words were from Jacques Derrida's last interview before his death, which was published in *Le Monde* in August 2004. The interview would subsequently be published in book form—Jacques Derrida, *Learning to Live Finally: The Last Interview* (New York: Palgrave, 2007).

25. See in particular Primo Levi, *If This Is a Man* (London: Abacus, 1991).

26. Zygmunt Bauman, *Modernity and the Holocaust* (Cambridge: Polity Press, 1991).

27. *Concentrationary Imaginaries: Tracing Totalitarian Violence in Popular Culture*, ed. Griselda Pollock and Max Silverman (New York: I. B. Taurus, 2015).

28. On the political problematic of shame in Deleuze's work, for example, see Ian Buchanan, *Deleuzism: A Meta-Commentary* (Durham, NC: Duke University Press, 2000), 73–93.

29. On this, especially the appropriation of the "shame of being man," see Bernard Stiegler, *Symbolic Misery: Vol 1. The Hyper-Industrial Epoch* (Cambridge: Polity Press, 2014).

30. Simona Forti, *New Demons: Rethinking Power and Evil Today* (Stanford, CA: Stanford University Press, 2014).

31. Forti, *New Demons*, 40.

32. Forti, *New Demons*, 308.

33. Edward Said, "The One State Solution," *New York Times*, January 10, 1999. On this, see also *Blaming the Victims: Spurious Scholarship and the Palestinian Question*, ed. Christopher Hitchens and Edward Said (New York: Verso, 2001).

34. See François Laruelle, *General Theory of Victims* (Cambridge: Polity Press, 2015) and François Laruelle, *Intellectuals and Power: The Insurrection of the Victim* (Cambridge: Polity Press, 2015).

35. Among the most instructive critical volumes that map out this history and the changing nature of liberal rule are Mark Duffield's *Global Governance and the New Wars: The Merging of Development and Security* (London: Zed, 2001) and *Development, Security and Unending War: Governing the World of People* (Cambridge: Polity Press, 2007).

36. Robert Elias, *The Politics of Victimization: Victims, Victimology, and Human Rights* (Oxford: Oxford University Press, 1986).

37. Robert Elias, *Victims Still: The Political Manipulation of Crime Victims* (London: Sage: 1993).

38. David Campbell, "The Iconography of Famine," in *Picturing Atrocity: Photography in Crisis*, ed. Geoffrey Batchen et al. (London: Reaktion, 2010), 84.

39. Susan Sontag, *On Photography* (New York: Penguin, 1979). See also Susan D. Moeller, *Compassion Fatigue: How the Media Sell Disease, Famine, War, and Death* (New York: Routledge, 1999). It is worth noting that Sontag later questioned this notion in her essay in the *New Yorker*, "Looking at War." This is also something I've expressed a number of concerns about in Evans and Giroux, *Disposable Futures*.

40. On this, see in particular Luc Boltanski, *Distant Suffering: Morality, Media and Politics* (Cambridge: Cambridge University Press, 1999).

41. Luc Boltanski, "The Legitimacy of Humanitarian Actions and Their Media Representations: The Case of France," *Ethical Perspectives* 7, April (2000): 12.

42. On this, see *Violence and the Sacred in the Modern World: Terrorism and Political Violence*, ed. Mark Juergensmeyer (London: Routledge, 1992).

43. This argument is explicitly made by Durkheim in *The Elementary Forms of Religious Life* (New York: Free Press, 1995).

44. A point notably made by Susan Sontag in *On Photography*.

45. On this, see in particular, Lucy R. Lippard, *A Different War: Vietnam in Art* (Seattle, WA: Real Comet, 1990); Denise Chong, *The Girl in the Picture: The Story of Kim Phuc, the Photograph, and the Vietnam War* (New York: Viking, 1999); and Nancy K. Miller, "The Girl in the Photograph: The Vietnam War and the Making of National Memory," *JAC* 24, no. 2, Special Issue, Part 1: Trauma and Rhetoric (2004): 261–90.

46. Cited in Andrew Erish, *Col. William N. Selig, the Man Who Invented Hollywood* (Austin: University of Texas Press, 2012), 210–13.

47. For images from Ravelo's *Untouchables* series, see https://www.huffpost.com/entry/erik-ravelo_n_3900061.

48. The photograph of the exhibit is featured here: https://www.dazeddigital.com/fashion/article/16812/1/remembering-trayvon-devolution-of-the-hoodie.

49. David Theo Goldberg, *Are We All Postracial Yet?: Debating Race* (Cambridge: Polity Press, 2015).

4. A HIGHER STATE OF KILLING

1. In terms of Benjamin's continued relevance, I could do no better than to point to James Martel's trilogy of books: *The One and Only Law: Walter Benjamin and the Second Commandment* (Ann Arbor: University of Michigan Press, 2014); *Divine Violence: Walter Benjamin and the Eschatology of Sovereignty* (London: Routledge, 2011); and *Textual Conspiracies: Walter Benjamin, Idolatry and Political Theory* (Ann Arbor: University of Michigan Press, 2011).

2. Walter Benjamin, "Critique of Violence," in *Reflections: Essays, Aphorisms, Autobiographical Writings* (New York: Shocken, 1986), 277–300.

3. Benjamin, "Critique of Violence," 299.

4. We will deal with the importance of this frontispiece in chapter 6. See also Giorgio Agamben, *Stasis: Civil War as a Political Paradigm* (Edinburgh, UK: Edinburgh University Press, 2015), 19–44.

5. On this, and for an excellent engagement with divine violence more generally, see James Martel, *Divine Violence*.

6. Benjamin, "Critique of Violence," 297.

7. Benjamin, "Critique of Violence," 297.

8. Jacques Derrida, "Force of Law: The Mystical Foundation of Authority," in *Deconstruction and the Possibility of Justice*, ed. Drucilla Cornell, Michael Rosenfeld, and David Carson (New York: Routledge, 1992), 56.

9. See Giorgio Agamben, *Homo Sacer: Sovereign Power and Bare Life* (Stanford, CA: Stanford University Press, 1998).

10. Agamben, *Homo Sacer*, 105.

11. Giorgio Agamben, *Means Without End* (Minneapolis: University of Minnesota Press, 2000), 4.

12. Agamben, *Means Without End*, 8–9.

13. Judith Butler, "Critique, Coercion and Sacred Life in Benjamin's 'Critique of Violence,'" in *Political Theologies: Public Religions in a Post-Secular World*, ed. Hent de Vries and Lawrence Sullivan (New York: Fordham University Press, 2006), 201.

14. Butler, "Critique, Coercion and Sacred Life," 211.

15. Slavoj Žižek, *Divine Violence and Liberated Targets*, http://www.softtargetsjournal.com /web/Žižek.php.

16. See Domenico Losurdo, *Liberalism: A Counter History* (New York: Verso, 2011).

17. Michel Foucault, *Society Must Be Defended: Lectures at the Collège de France 1975–1976* (New York: Picador, 2003); Michel Foucault, *Security, Territory and Population: Lectures at the Collège de France 1977–1978* (New York: Palgrave Macmillan, 2007); and Michel Foucault, *The Birth of Biopolitics: Lectures at the Collège de France 1978–1979* (New York: Palgrave Macmillan, 2008).

18. Benjamin, "Critique of Violence," 277.

19. Carl Schmitt, *Political Theology: Four Chapters on the Concept of Sovereignty* (Chicago: University of Chicago Press, 2006), 36.

20. Martel, *Divine Violence*, 23.

21. John Gray, *Black Mass: Apocalyptic Religion and the Death of Utopia* (London: Penguin, 2011), 1.

22. John G. A. Pocock, *The Machiavellian Moment: Florentine Political Thought and the Atlantic Political Tradition* (Princeton, NJ: Princeton University Press, 1975).

23. Michael Dillon, "Lethal Freedom: Divine Violence and the Machiavellian Moment," *Theory and Event* 11, no. 2 (2008): 1–22.

24. On this, see in particular Mark Duffield, *Development, Security and Unending War: Governing the World of People* (Cambridge: Polity Press, 2007).

25. See Michael Dillon and Julian Reid, *The Liberal Way of War*; and Julian Reid, *The Biopolitics of the War on Terror: Life Struggles, Liberal Modernity and the Defense of Logistical Societies* (Manchester, UK: Manchester University Press, 2006).

26. I have explored these in more detail elsewhere. See Brad Evans, "Liberal War: Introducing the Ten Key Principles of Twenty-First-Century Biopolitical Warfare," *South Atlantic Quarterly* 110, no. 3 (2001): 747–56.

27. Dillon and Reid, *Liberal Way of War*, 42, 81, 88.

28. Steven Pinker, *The Better Angels of Our Nature: Why Violence Has Declined* (London: Viking, 2011).

29. Pinker, *The Better Angels of Our Nature*, 217.

30. John Gray, "Delusions of Peace," *Prospect*, September 21, 2011, http://www.prospectmagazine .co.uk/magazine/john-gray-steven-pinker-violence-review/.

31. See Gray, *Black Mass*.

32. For a detailed historical account of the relationship between the media and conflict, see Susan Carruthers, *The Media at War: Communication and Conflict in the Twentieth Century* (London: Palgrave, 2011). I have also dealt with this extensively in Evans and Giroux, *Disposable Futures*.

33. McCarthy makes this point in a film I codirected with Simon Critchley on the tenth anniversary of 9/11. See Brad Evans and Simon Critchley, "Ten Years of Terror," *Histories of Violence*, September 11, 2011, https://www.historiesofviolence.com/tenyearsofterror.

34. On this and its relationship to aesthetics, see chapter 17, "Female Torturers Grinning at the Camera," in Cavarero, *Horrorism*, 106–115.

35. On this, see the chapter on "The Origins of Myth and Ritual" in Girard, *Violence and the Sacred*, 94–126.

36. Simon Critchley, *Tragedy, the Greeks, and Us* (New York: Pantheon, 2019), 41, 46.

37. Giorgio Agamben, *The Fire and the Tale* (Stanford, CA: Stanford University Press, 2017), 6.

38. Agamben, *The Fire and the Tale*, 7.

39. Agamben, *The Fire and the Tale*, 59.

40. Agamben, *The Fire and the Tale*, 60.

41. Walter Benjamin, *The Origin of German Tragic Drama* (New York: Verso, 2009).

42. For a rich posthumous collaboration between the writer and the artist, see Walter Benjamin, *The Storyteller: Tales Out of Loneliness* (New York: Verso, 2016).

43. A version of this essay is available online here: https://www.marxists.org/reference/archive /benjamin/1940/history.htm.

5. THE DEATH OF THE VICTIM

1. Quoted in Oliver Laurent, "What the Image of Alyan Kurdi Says About the Power of Photography," *Time* magazine, September 4, 2015, http://time.com/4022765/aylan-kurdi -photo/.

2. The first quote comes in Susan Ager, "This Wouldn't Be the First Time a Child's Photo Changed History," *National Geographic*, September 3, 2015, http://news.nationalgeographic .com/2015/09/150903-drowned-syrian-boy-photo-children-pictures-world/; the second quote appears in Laurent, "What the Image of Alyan Kurdi Says About the Power of Photography."

3. Nicholas Mirzoeff, "Don't Look Away from Aylan Kurdi's Image," *The Conversation*, September 8, 2013, https://theconversation.com/dont-look-away-from-aylan-kurdis-image -47069.

4. Natasha Lennard and Nicholas Mirzoeff, "What Protest Looks Like," in Evans and Lennard, *Violence*, 91.

5. Ian Jack, "Can Images Change History?" *The Guardian*, September 4, 2015, http://www .theguardian.com/commentisfree/2015/sep/04/images-aylan-kurdi-syria?CMP=fb_gu.

6. See https://time.com/magazine/south-pacific/4066265/october-19th-2015-vol-186-no-15 -asia-europe-middle-east-and-africa-south-pacific/.

7. François Laruelle, *General Theory of Victims* (Cambridge: Polity Press, 2015), 1.

8. On this, see Domenico Losurdo, *Liberalism: A Counter History* (New York: Verso, 2011).

9. I am borrowing the terms here used by Henry Giroux. See in particular H. A. Giroux, *The Violence of Organized Forgetting* (San Francisco, CA: City Lights, 2014).

10. This claim is made to the point of monotony by liberal thinkers and politicians alike. For the most recent treatment on this, see Madeline Albright, *Fascism: A Warning* (New York: HarperCollins, 2018).

11. Geoffrey Hartman, *The Longest Shadow: In the Aftermath of the Holocaust* (Bloomington, IN: Indiana University Press, 1996), 3.

12. Jeffrey C. Alexander, *Trauma: A Social Theory* (Cambridge: Polity Press, 2012), 58.

13. Mark Duffield, *Global Governance and the New Wars: The Merging of Development and Security* (London: Zed, 2001).

14. For a detailed background on this, see William Shawcross, *Deliver Us from Evil: Warlords and Peacekeepers in a World of Endless Conflict* (New York: Touchstone, 2001), 83–123.

15. On the politics and devastating violence of this campaign, see Horace Campbell, *Global NATO and the Catastrophic Failure in Libya* (New York: Monthly Review Press, 2003); and Cynthia McKinney, *The Illegal War on Libya* (Atlanta, GA: Clarity Press, 2012).

16. While there are volumes dedicated to the idea of the liberal peace thesis, among the most celebrated works with deals with the successes of liberalism in regulating and minimizing violence remains Pinker's *The Better Angels of Our Nature*.

17. On this see Zygmunt Bauman, *Retrotopia* (Cambridge: Polity Press, 2017).

18. For a series of essays in which I deal with the violence of the post-9/11 world, see Brad Evans, *The Atrocity Exhibition: Life in an Age of Total Violence* (Los Angeles, CA: LA Review of Books Press, 2019).

19. The idea of technological supremacy was at the heart of the revolution in the military, with its idea of zero-casualty wars and the inspired shift toward what many called "network-centric warfare" (notably developed and promoted by the RAND Corporation and its principle advocates, John Arquilla and David Ronfeldt). However, the idea that advanced technology leads to "smarter and more civilized" violence has been in existence since the dropping of the atomic bombs on Hiroshima and Nagasaki, an act which invariably required a redemptive narrative (see chapter 7). For a compelling history of the more recent links between technology and war, see Antoine Bousquet, *The Eye of War: Military Perception from the Telescope to the Drone* (Minneapolis: University of Minnesota Press, 2018).

20. See Mark Duffield, *Development, Security and Unending War* (Cambridge: Polity Press, 2007).

21. David Kilcullen, *The Accidental Guerrilla: Fighting Small Wars in the Midst of a Big One* (London: Hurst, 2017).

22. For a considered history on the role of the mercenary, see Tony Geraghty, *Soldiers of Fortune: A History of the Mercenary in Modern Warfare* (New York: Pegasus, 2011). See also Sean McFate, *The Modern Mercenary: Private Armies and What They Mean for World Order* (Oxford: Oxford University Press, 2014).

23. Mark Duffield, "Risk-Management and the Fortified Aid Compound: Everyday Life in Post-Interventionary Society," *Journal of Intervention and State Building* 4, no. 4 (2010): 453–74.

24. Mark Duffield, *Post-Humanitarianism: Governing Precarity in the Digital World* (Cambridge: Polity Press, 2019).

25. James Vernini, *They Will Have to Die Now: Mosul and the Fall of the Caliphate* (London: OneWorld, 2019), 14.

26. Brad Evans and Henry A. Giroux, "Intolerable Violence," *Symploke* 23, no. 1–2 (2015): 197–219.

27. Adriana Cavarero, *Horrorism: Naming Contemporary Violence* (New York: Columbia University Press, 2007).

28. John Arquilla and David Ronfeldt, *In Athena's Camp: Preparing for Conflict in the Information Age* (Santa Monica, CA: RAND, 1997), 9.

29. René Girard, *Violence and the Sacred* (London: Continuum, 2005), 45.

30. Vernini, *They Will Have to Die Now*, 19.

31. Julia Kristeva, *The Severed Head: Capital Visions* (New York: Columbia University Press, 2012), 91.

32. Kristeva, *The Severed Head*, 104.

33. Catherine Puglish, "Caravaggio's Life and *Lives* over Four Centuries," in *Caravaggio: Realism, Rebellion, Reception*, ed. Genevieve Warwick (New Jersey: Associated Press, 2006), 26.

34. Mieke Bal, "Reading Art," in *Generations and Geographies in the Visual Arts: Feminist Perspectives*, ed. Griselda Pollock (London: Routledge, 1996), 26.

35. I am referring here to first image of Haines in this harrowing sequence: http://www.dailymail.co.uk/news/article-2754934/ISIS-release-video-claiming-beheading-British-hostage-David-Haines.html.

36. Evans and Giroux, "Intolerable Violence."

37. Oscar Wilde, *Salome: A Tragedy in One Act* (New York: Dover, 1967).

38. Bauman, *Retrotopia*.

39. On the debates surrounding this see Sergei Prozorov, "Why Is There Truth? Foucault in the Age of Post-Truth Politics," *Constellations* 25, no. 1 (2019): 18–30.

40. Amartya Sen, *Poverty and Famine: An Essay on Entitlement and Depravation* (Oxford: Oxford University Press, 1981).

41. Brad Evans and Zygmunt Bauman, "The Refugee Crisis Is Humanity's Crisis," in Evans and Lennard, *Violence*, 46.

42. On the history of political animality, see Jacques Derrida's two wonderful mediations, *The Animal That Therefore I Am* (New York: Fordham University Press, 2008); and *The Beast and the Sovereign: Volume 1* (Chicago, IL: Chicago University Press, 2011).

43. See Carl Schmitt, *The Nomos of the Earth in the International Law of Jus Publicum Europaeum* (London: Telos, 2006).

44. See Domenico Losurdo, *Liberalism: A Counter History* (New York: Verso, 2011).

45. The idea that the world is full was put forward and developed by Zygmunt Bauman in *Society Under Siege* (Cambridge: Polity Press, 2002).

46. See in particular Gilles Deleuze and Felix Guattari, *A Thousand Plateaus* (London: Continuum, 2004).

47. Lorsurdo, *Liberalism: A Counter History*.

48. Jef Huysmans, *The Politics of Insecurity: Fear, Migration and Asylum in the EU* (London: Routledge, 2006).

49. Bauman, *Society under Siege*, 112.

50. Zygmunt Bauman, *Collateral Damage: Social Inequalities in a Global Age* (Cambridge: Polity Press, 2011), 57.

51. See Brad Evans, *Liberal Terror* (Cambridge: Polity Press, 2013).

52. See, on this, Peter Sloterdijk, *In the World Interior of Capital: Towards a Philosophical Theory of Globalization* (Cambridge: Polity Press, 2013).

53. Brian Massumi, *The Politics of Affect* (Cambridge: Polity Press, 2015), 113–14.

54. In *The Oresteia*, for example, with the killing of Agamemnon we encounter the metaphor of the oceans as they connect to the flow of blood: "There is the sea, and who will drain

it dry? Precious as silver, inexhaustible, ever-new, it breeds the more we reap it—tides on tides of crimson dye our robes blood-red."

55. Peter Sloterdijk, *Terror from the Air* (Los Angeles, CA: Semiotexte:, 2002).

56. Bauman, *Society Under Siege*, 112.

57. On this, see Adam K. Raymond, "The Story Behind the Viral Photo of a Drowned Migrant Father and Toddler," *New York Magazine*, June 26, 2019, http://nymag.com /intelligencer/2019/06/the-story-behind-the-viral-photo-of-drowned-migrants.html.

58. This point was made in a *New York Times* report by Manny Fernandez: "A Path to America—Marked by More and More Bodies," *New York Times*, May 4, 2017, https://www .nytimes.com/interactive/2017/05/04/us/texas-border-migrants-dead-bodies.html.

6. A SICKNESS OF REASON

1. Jake Chapman, "Two Weddings and a Mass Grave," in *The Quarantine Files*, cur. Brad Evans (Los Angeles: LA Review of Books, 2020), https://lareviewofbooks.org/article /quarantine-files-thinkers-self-isolation.

2. There is no shortage today of literature on the importance of plagues to historical understanding. I would draw particular attention to William C. McNeill, *Plagues and People* (New York: Bantham, 1998).

3. See on this Robin Mitchell-Boyask, *Plague and the Athenian Imagination: Drama, History, and the Cult of Asclepius* (Cambridge: Cambridge University Press, 2008).

4. In the book of Job, we also see an allusion to the arrow: "The arrows of the Almighty are in me; my spirit drinks their poison; the terrors of God are arrayed against me." (Job 6:4)

5. L. Marshall, "Manipulating the Sacred: Image and Plague in Renaissance Italy," *Renaissance Quarterly* 47, no. 3 (1994): 495.

6. On this, see especially Laura Spinney, *Pale Rider: The Spanish Flu of 1918 and How It Changed the World* (London: Jonathan Cape, 2018).

7. Michel Foucault, *Abnormal: Lectures at the College de France 1974–1975* (London: Verso, 2003); and Michel Foucault, *Discipline and Punishment: The Birth of the Prison* (London: Penguin, 1978).

8. Foucault, *Abnormal*, xxiii.

9. Gilles Deleuze, *Foucault* (London: Continuum, 2006), 76.

10. See Foucault, "History of Sexuality," 133–60.

11. Albert Camus, *The Plague* (London: Penguin, 2002).

12. Camus, *The Plague*, 29.

13. Camus, *The Plague*, 30.

14. Slavoj Žižek, "Monitor and Punish? Yes, Please!" *The Philosophical Salon*, March 16, 2020, http://thephilosophicalsalon.com/monitor-and-punish-yes-please/.

15. Anastasia Berg, "Giorgio Agamben's Coronavirus Cluelessness," *The Chronicle of Higher Education*, March 23, 2020, https://www.chronicle.com/article/Giorgio-Agamben-s/248306.

16. Each of these were published online in the Italian journal *Quodlibet*. Translations for the first two essays can be found online here: https://www.journal-psychoanalysis.eu /coronavirus-and-philosophers/.

    For a translation of "A Question" (as personally requested by Agamben), see Adam Kotsko's website here: https://itself.blog/2020/04/15/giorgio-agamben-a-question/.

17. Simon Critchley, "Sorry to Disappoint (I Knew I Should Have Been a Hairdresser)," in *The Quarantine Files*, cur. Brad Evans (Los Angeles, CA: LA Review of Books, 2020), https://lareviewofbooks.org/article/quarantine-files-thinkers-self-isolation.

18. "On Security and Terror" was first published in the *Frankfurter Allgemeine Zeitung* (Frankfurt general newspaper) on September 20, 2001. It is now available online here at https://libcom.org/library/on-security-and-terror-giorgio-agamben.

19. Paul Virilio, *Speed and Politics* (Los Angeles, CA: Semiotexte, 2006).

20. Simon Critchley, "To Philosophise Is to Learn How to Die," *New York Times*, April 11, 2020, https://www.nytimes.com/2020/04/11/opinion/covid-philosophy-anxiety-death.html.

21. Jean-Luc Nancy's response, "Viral Exceptions," was originally published in *Antinomie*. It is also available translated here: https://www.journal-psychoanalysis.eu/coronavirus-and-philosophers/.

22. As Andrzej W. Nowak explained:

> Maybe Agamben doesn't know it, but when you die, you lose everything. It is a normal part of life that we sacrifice a part of our freedom to ensure our lives, because it is only when we live that we have the chance to take advantage of even limited freedom. Life is negotiation. Only death can afford to be uncompromising. That's why I think that Agamben's proposal is a necromancer's statement, which from the heights of its philosophical intransigence could only rule the Army of the Dead—because they do not enter into "bourgeois" compromises that protect life.

> Andrzej W. Nowak, "Philosophical Necromancy or Accelerationist Hope? A Response to Agamben," *LeftEast*, March 21, 2020, http://www.criticatac.ro/lefteast/necromancy-or-hope-response-to-agamben.

23. Giorgio Agamben, "No to Bio-Political Tattooing," *Le Monde*, January 10, 2004.

24. Marco D'Eramo, "The Philosopher's Epidemic," *New Left Review*, no. 122 March/April (2020): https://newleftreview.org/issues/II122/articles/marco-d-eramo-the-philosopher-s-epidemic.

25. See Kim Stanley Robinson, "The Coronavirus Is Rewriting Our Imaginations," *New Yorker*, May 1, 2020, https://www.newyorker.com/culture/annals-of-inquiry/the-coronavirus-and-our-future.

26. Saidiya Hartman, "The Death Toll," in *The Quarantine Files*, cur. Brad Evans (Los Angeles: LA Review of Books, 2020), https://lareviewofbooks.org/article/quarantine-files-thinkers-self-isolation.

27. Arundhati Roy, "The Pandemic Is Portal," *Financial Times*, April 3, 2020, https://www.ft.com/content/10d8f5e8-74eb-11ea-95fe-fcd274e920ca.

28. Agamben, *A Question?* Translated and published at the authors request here: https://itself.blog/2020/04/15/giorgio-agamben-a-question/.

29. Gilles Deleuze, *Difference and Repetition* (London: Continuum, 2004), 333.

30. D'Eramo, "The Philosopher's Epidemic."

31. Brian Massumi, "The American Virus," in *The Quarantine Files*, cur. Brad Evans (Los Angeles: LA Review of Books, 2020), https://lareviewofbooks.org/article/quarantine-files-thinkers-self-isolation.

32. Giorgio Agamben, *Stasis: Civil War as a Political Paradigm* (Edinburgh, UK: Edinburgh University Press, 2015), 29.

33. Agamben, *Stasis*, 38.
34. Mark Duffield, "Warfare on Welfare: The Global Rise of the Digital Workhouse," in *Amidst the Debris: Humanitarianism at the End of Liberal Order*, ed. Julian Fiori et al. (London: Hurst Press, 2021) [forthcoming].
35. Brad Evans and Gareth Owen, "The Crises of Containment," *LA Review of Books*, April 6, 2020), https://lareviewofbooks.org/article/histories-of-violence-the-crises-of-containment.
36. Paul Virilio, *City of Panic* (New York: Berg, 2005), 31.
37. On this, see Greg Evans, "Trump Supporters Likened to Zombies After Protesting Lockdown Rules," Indy (from the Independent), https://www.indy100.com/article/trump-supporters-coronavirus-lockdown-protest-ohio-zombie-memes-9469171.
38. Giorgio Agamben, "Medicine as Religion," trans. Adam Kotsko, May 2, 2020, https://itself.blog/2020/05/02/giorgio-agamben-medicine-as-religion/.
39. René Girard, *Violence and the Sacred* (London: Continuum, 2006).
40. On the life of Benjamin, see Howard Eiland and Michael Jennings, *Walter Benjamin: A Critical Life* (Cambridge, MA: Harvard University Press, 2014).
41. Walter Benjamin to Lisa Fittko, cited by Bernard Witte, *Walter Benjamin: Une biographe* (Paris: Le Cerf, 1988), 253.
42. On the final days of Benjamin's life see the chapter "A Heavy Black Suitcase," in *In Search of Lost Books: The Forgotten Stories of Eight Mythical Volumes*, ed. Giorgio van Straten (London: Pushkin Press, 2017).
43. Jacques Derrida, *Athens, Still Remains: The Photographs of Jean-Francois Bonhomme* (New York: Fordham University Press, 2010), 1.
44. Jacques Derrida, *Spectres of Marx*.
45. This point has been also made by Bracha Ettinger, who notes, "Think of Paul Celan's poetry, for me the source of inspiration. It forms the frontier of death in life, where life glimpses at death from deaths side, to paraphrase Jacques Lacan." Brad Evans and Bracha Ettinger, "Art in a Time of Atrocity," in Evans and Lennard, *Violence*, 113.
46. Simon Critchley and Jamieson Webster, *The Hamlet Doctrine: Saying Too Much, Doing Nothing* (New York: Verso, 2013).
47. Jacques Derrida, *Learning to Live Finally* (Brooklyn, NY: Melville House, 2011), 52.

7. ANNIHILATION

1. See Hannah Arendt, *The Origins of Totalitarianism* (New York: Harcourt, 1976).
2. On this, see the chapter "The Right to Have Rights" in Richard Bernstein, *Why Read Hannah Arendt Now* (Cambridge: Polity Press, 2018), 21–35.
3. Arendt, *The Origins of Totalitarianism*, 297.
4. Bernstein, *Why Read Hannah Arendt Now*, 27–8.
5. Bernstein, *Why Read Hannah Arendt Now*, 29.
6. Arendt, *The Origins of Totalitarianism*, 455.
7. Arendt, *The Origins of Totalitarianism*, 438.
8. Giorgio Agamben, *Homo Sacer: Sovereign Power and Bare Life* (Stanford, CA: Stanford University Press, 1998), 51.
9. Cited in Giorgio Agamben, *Remnants of Auschwitz: The Witness and the Archive* (New York: Zone, 2002), 44.

10.   Arendt, *The Origins of Totalitarianism*, 454, 455.

11.   Agamben, *Remnants of Auschwitz*, 38.

12.   See in particular J. M. Bernstein, "Intact and Fragmented Bodies: Versions of Ethics 'After Auschwitz,' " *New German Critique*, no. 97 (2006): 31–52.

13.   Primo Levi, *If This Is a Man* (London: Abacus, 1991), 103.

14.   Primo Levi, *The Drowned and the Saved* (London: Abacus, 1989), 63–64.

15.   For a considered and selected digital archive of Aldo Carpi's artwork, see http://www .corriere.it/reportage/senza-categoria/2015/aldo-carpi-il-pittore-deportato-salvato-dai -suoi-disegni-shoah-memoria.

16.   For a powerful collection of artwork from the concentration camps, including Carpi's sketches, and featuring a foreword by Primo Levi, see Arturo Benvenuti, *Imprisoned: Drawings from Nazi Concentration Camps* (New York: Skyhorse Publishing, 2016).

17.   Siân Miles, *Simone Weil: An Anthology*, ed. Siân Miles (New York: Penguin, 2005), 184–85.

18.   Cited in *Anatomy of the Auschwitz Death Camp*, ed. Yisrael Gutman and Michael Berenbaum (Bloomington: Indiana University Press, 1998), 371.

19.   Online at https://www.mp.pl/auschwitz/journal/english/170025,teetering-on-the-brink -between-life-and-death-a-study-on-the-concentration-camp-muselmann.

20.   Gilles Deleuze, *The Logic of Sense* (New York: Columbia University Press, 1990).

21.   A point explicitly made by Zgymunt Bauman in *Modernity and the Holocaust* (Cambridge: Polity Press, 1991).

22.   On the importance of the former especially see Ian Patterson, *Guernica and Total War* (Cambridge, MA: Harvard University Press, 2007).

23.   Harry Truman, "Statement on Hiroshima," August 6, 1945, http://www.atomicheritage .org/key-documents/truman-statement-hiroshima.

24.   Cited in Charles Pellegrino, "Ghosts of Hiroshima," *Asian Pacific Journal* 16, no. 21 (2012). Online at https://apjjf.org/2018/21/Pellegrino.html.

25.   John Hersey, *Hiroshima* (New York: Vintage, 1989), 51.

26.   See Robert Harriman and John Louis Lucaites, "The Iconic Image of the Mushroom Cloud and the Cold War Nuclear Optic," in *Picturing Atrocity: Photography in Crisis*, ed. Geoffrey Batchen et al. (London: Reaktion, 2012), 135–46.

27.   See Oh Jung, "Hiroshima and Nagasaki: The Decision to Drop the Bomb," *Michigan Journal of History* 1, no. 2 (Winter 2002).

28.   This point is made by Robert Jay Lifton and Greg Mitchell, *Hiroshima in America* (New York: Avon, 1995), 328.

29.   See on this Michael J. Shapiro, "Hiroshima Temporalities," *Thesis Eleven* 129, no. 1 (2015), 40–56.

30.   Peter Sloterdijk, *The Aesthetic Imperative* (Cambridge: Polity Press, 2017), 277.

31.   Henry Giroux, "Hiroshima and the Responsibility of Intellectuals: Crisis, Catastrophe, and the Neoliberal Disimagination Machine," *Thesis Eleven* 129, no, 1 (2015): 103–18.

32.   Cited in Stephen Graham, "Foucault's Boomerang: The New Urban Militarism," *Open Democracy*, February 14, 2013, https://www.opendemocracy.net/en/opensecurity/foucaults -boomerang-new-military-urbanism/.

33.   On this, see John Lawrence Tone, *War and Genocide in Cuba* (Chapel Hill: North Carolina Press, 2006).

34. Achille Mbembe, "Necro-Politics," *Public Culture* 15, no. 1 (2003): 11.
35. Torres Rivas, "Epilogue: Notes on Terror, Violence, Fear and Democracy," in *Societies of Fear: The Legacy of Civil War, Violence and Terror in Latin America*, ed. K. Koonings and D. Kruijt (London: Zed Books, 1999), 291.
36. Brad Evans and Allen Feldman, "Living with Disappearance," in Evans and Lennard, *Violence*, 295.
37. Jean Franco, *Cruel Modernity* (Durham, NC: Duke University Press, 2013), 195.
38. Franco, *Cruel Modernity*, 208, 209.
39. John Ross, *The Annexation of Mexico: From the Aztecs to the IMF* (Monroe, ME: Common Courage Press, 2002).
40. For an in-depth analysis of the violence and how it connects to cultural responses, see Nuala Finnegan, *Cultural Representations of Feminicidio at the US-Mexico Border* (London, Routledge: 2019).
41. On the plight of the forty-three students, see in particular John Gibler, *I Couldn't Even Imagine That They Would Kill Us: An Oral History of the Attacks Against the Students of Ayotzinapa* (San Francisco: City Lights, 2017) and Anabel Hernández, *A Massacre in Mexico: The True Story Behind the Missing Forty-Three Students* (New York: Verso, 2018).
42. Judith Butler, *Frames of War: When Is Life Grievable?* (New York: Verso, 2010).
43. Jean-Luc Nancy, *The Ground of the Image* (New York: Fordham University Press, 2005), 67-68.
44. Cited in Kaira M. Cabañas, "Ana Mendieta: 'Pain of Cuba, Body I Am,'" *Woman's Art Journal* 20, no. 1 (1999): 12-17.
45. See Laura F. Perez, *Eros Ideologies: Writings on Art, Spirituality, and the Decolonial* (Durham, NC: Duke University Press, 2019), 91-111.
46. Cited in Jane Blocker, *Where Is Ana Mendieta? Identity, Performativity, and Exile* (Durham, NC: Duke University Press, 1999), 34.
47. On this, see Brad Evans and Bracha Ettinger, "Art in a Time of Atrocity," in Evans and Lennard, *Violence*, 107-16.
48. https://en.wikipedia.org/wiki/Mizoch_Ghetto#/media/File:Naked_Jewish_women_wait_in_a_line_before_their_execution_by_Ukrainian_auxiliary_police.jpg
49. On this, see Brad Evans and Bracha Ettinger, "To Feel the World's Beauty and Pain," *Los Angeles Review of Books*, February 27, 2017, https://lareviewofbooks.org/article/feel-worlds-pain-beauty.
50. See Marissa Vignault, "The Porous Space of Bracha L. Ettinger's Eurydices," in *Contemporary Art and Classical Myth*, ed. Isabelle Loring Wallace and Jennie Hirsh (Abingdon, UK: Routledge, 2016), 111-35.
51. Cited in Christine Buci-Glucksmann, "The Eurydices," *Parallax* 5, no. 1 (1999): 99-102.
52. Evans and Ettinger, "Art in a Time of Atrocity," 111.
53. The artist's full portfolio can be viewed here: www.chantal-meza.com.
54. Fredric Jameson, *The Political Unconscious: Narrative as Socially Symbolic Act* (Ithaca, NY: Cornell University Press, 1981), 102.
55. These images are scaled-down versions of a much larger public work featuring two torn canvases, on display at the Benemérita Autonomous University of Puebla.

8. THE TRANSGRESSIVE WITNESS

1.   Theodor Adorno, *Negative Dialectics* (New York: Continuum, 2005), 358.

2.   A version of this catalog has been republished by Ostara Publications (2012).

3.   Brad Evans and Gottfried Helnwein "Confronting the Intolerable" in Evans and Lennard, *Violence*, 170.

4.   Gilles Deleuze, *Francis Bacon* (London: Bloomsbury, 2014), 43.

5.   Deleuze, *Bacon*, 6.

6.   Deleuze, *Bacon*. 41.

7.   Deleuze, *Bacon*, 14.

8.   Deleuze, *Bacon*, 42.

9.   David Silvester, *The Brutality of Fact: Interviews with Francis Bacon* (London: Thames, 1987), 82.

10. David Silvester, *The Brutality of Fact*, 23.

11. Jacques Rancière, *Figures of History* (Cambridge: Polity Press, 2014), 44.

12. Rancière, *Figures of History*, 45, 46.

13. Rancière, *Figures of History*, 48, 49.

14. Deleuze, *Bacon*, 43.

15. Gilles Deleuze, *Essays Critical and Clinical* (Minneapolis: University of Minnesota Press, 1997), 116.

16. Deleuze, *Essays*, 117–18.

17. A request was made to feature this image but was refused by copyright holders. This arguably further reveals the appropriation of Basquiat and his entire work, as it is heavily policed and commodified. On the life and works of Basquiat, see the biopic *Jean-Michel Basquiat: The Radiant Child*, directed by Tamra Davis (New Video: 2010). See also Leonhard Emmerling, *Jean-Michel Basquiat 1960–1988: The Explosive Force of the Streets* (London: Taschen, 2015); Eric Fretz, *Jean-Michel Basquiat: A Biography* (Santa Barbara, CA: Greenwood, 2010).

18. On the importance of Basquiat in the context of questions of power and subjectivity, see Anthony B. Pinn, "Why Can't I Be Both?: Jean-Michel Basquiat and Aesthetics of Black Bodies Reconstituted" (*Journal of Africana Religions* 1, no. 1 (2013): 109–32; Andrea E. Frohne, "Re-Presenting Jean-Michel Basquiat," in *The African Diaspora: African Origins and New World Identities*, ed. I. Okpewho, C. B. Davies, and A. A. Mazrui (Bloomington: Indiana University Press, 1999), 439–51; Sirmans Franklin, "In the Cipher: Basquiat and Hip-Hop Culture," in *Basquiat*, ed. Marc Mayer (New York: Merrell Publishers, 2016).

19. Basquiat's work would be subjected to similar criticisms, with people disparaging his style as "primitive" to "child-like." As the critic Hilton Kramer wrote, " 'Basquiat's efforts were distinguished only by the fact that he had learned how to apply its alphabet of primitive signs and symbols to a prepared canvas rather than to the defacement of public buildings . . . There is no point in belabouring the aesthetic poverty of the paintings that Basquiat was now producing to meet the demands which his handlers had so adroitly created. Suffice to say that they consisted of a raw, ungifted amalgam of graffiti art, children's art and the kind of 'primitivist' art that sometimes passes as imitations of Jean Dubuffet." Hilton Kramer, "He Had Everything but Talent," *The Telegraph*, 1997), https://www.telegraph.co.uk/culture/4707974/He-had-everything-but-talent.html

20.   The article by bell hooks was originally published as "Altars of Sacrifice: Re-Membering Basquiat," *Art in America* 81, no. 6 (1993): 68–75. It can now be found online at: https://www.artinamericamagazine.com/news-features/magazines/from-the-archives-altars-of-sacrifice-re-membering-basquiat/.

21.   Thomas McEvilley, "Royal Slumming: Jean-Michel Basquiat Here Blow," *Artforum* (November 1992): 96.

22.   See Phoebe Hoban, *A Quick Killing in Art* (London: Quartet Books, 1998).

23.   Brad Evans and Gayatri Spivak, "When Law Is Not Justice" in Evans and Lennard, *Violence*, 85.

24.   Brad Evans and Lewis Gordon, "Thinking Art in a Decolonial Way" *Los Angeles Review of Books*, June 3, 2019, https://lareviewofbooks.org/article/histories-of-violence-thinking-art-in-a-decolonial-way/.

25.   Michel Foucault, "The Masked Philosopher" in *Ethics: The Essential Works of Michel Foucault 1954–84*, ed. Paul Rabinow (London: Penguin, 2000), 323.

26.   Jacques Rancière, *The Emancipated Spectator* (New York: Verso, 2008), 97.

27.   From Jacques Rancière's commentary on Jaar's installation, "Theater of Images," in *Alfredo Jaar: La Politique des Images* (Lausanne, Switzerland: JRP/Ringier, 2008), 76.

28.   Griselda Pollock, "Introduction" in *Visual Politics of Psychoanalysis*, ed. Griselda Pollock (London: Bloomsbury, 2013), 2.

29.   Ronald R. Bernier, *The Unspeakable Art of Bill Viola: A Visual Theology* (Eugene, OR: Pickwick, 2014), 3.

30.   Jens Zimmerman, "Introduction," in Richard Kearney and Jens Zimmerman, *Reimagining the Sacred*, 3.

31.   Chris Townsend, *The Art of Bill Viola* (London: Thames and Hudson, 2004), 118.

32.   Bernier, *The Unspeakable Art of Bill Viola*, 6.

33.   Quoted in Townsend, *The Art of Bill Viola*, 75.

34.   John Walsh cited in Townsend, *The Art of Bill Viola*, 146.

35.   Giorgio Agamben, *Nymphs* (Kolkata, India: Seagull Books, 2013), 4.

36.   Agamben, *Nymphs*, 20.

37.   Agamben, *Nymphs*, 19.

38.   Agamben, *Nymphs*, 5.

39.   Brad Evans and Gottfried Helnwein, "Confronting the Intolerable," in Evans and Lennard, *Violence*, 161.

40.   For a full explanation of this, see the interview with Jake and Dinos Chapman, "Hitler Turning in His Grave," Louisiana Art Channel (2015), https://www.youtube.com/watch?v=WBvfgJWCoWA.

41.   Online at https://www.telegraph.co.uk/culture/art/3593618/Inspired-vandalism.html.

42.   Online at https://www.theguardian.com/artanddesign/2017/nov/17/chapman-brothers-reunite-francisco-de-goya-art-spanish-exhibition.

43.   Quoted in Mark Schwartz, *The Disasters of War* (New York: *MoMA* 4, no. 1 (January 2001): 10–13.

9. WOUNDS OF LOVE

1.   On the influence and work of Mark Rothko, see the brilliant Christopher Rothko, *Mark Rothko: From Inside Out* (New Haven, CT: Yale University Press, 2015). See also *Mark*

Rothko: Towards Clarity, ed. Sabine Haag et al. (New Haven, CT: Yale University Press, 2016).

2.   This was stated in a letter from Mark Rothko and Adolph Gottlieb to the art editor of the New York Times, June 7, 1943.

3.   Mark Rothko, Writings on Art (New Haven, CT: Yale University Press, 2006), 77.

4.   André Breton, Nadja (London: Penguin, 1999).

5.   Leonora Carrington, Down Below (London: NYRB Classics, 2017).

6.   Tim Morton, Dark Ecology: For a Logic of Future Existence (New York: Columbia University Press, 2016), 1.

7.   See Simon Critchley, Tragedy, the Greeks, and Us (New York: Pantheon, 2019).

8.   John Sallis, Crossings: Nietzsche and the Space of Tragedy (Chicago, IL: University of Chicago Press, 1991), 99.

9.   On this, especially how it connects to the void, see Pierre Restany, Yves Klein: Fire at the Heart of the Void (Putnam, CT: Spring Publications, 2005).

10. Gaston Bachelard, The Poetics of Space (New York: Penguin, 1964), 184.

11. On this see chapter 2, "Origins of the Air Grid" in Victoria Watson, Utopian Adventure: The Corvial Void (London: Routledge, 2012).

12. Gaston Bachelard, "The Metaphysics of Dust," Parrhesia 31 (2019): 27.

13. Bachelard, "The Metaphysics of Dust": 28-29.

14. Gaston Bachelard, Air and Dreams: An Essay on the Imagination of Movement (Dallas, TX: Dallas Institute Publications, 1998), 127-60.

15. Bachelard, Air and Dreams, 147.

16. Bachelard, Air and Dreams, 152.

17. Bachelard, Air and Dreams, 154.

18. Bachelard, Air and Dreams, 1.

19. Gilles Deleuze and Félix Guattari, What Is Philosophy? (New York: Verso, 1994) 165.

20. In the book of Revelation, for instance, we read: "When he opened the sixth seal, I looked, and behold, there was a great earthquake, and the sun became black as sackcloth."

21. Julia Kristeva, Black Sun: Depression and Melancholia (New York: Columbia University Press, 1989).

22. Helene Cixous, "The Laugh of Medusa," Signs 1, no. 4 (1976): 875-93.

23. Stanton Marlan, The Black Sun: The Alchemy and the Art of Darkness (Austin, University of Texas Press, 2008), 88.

24. David Sylvester, The Brutality of Fact: Interviews with Francis Bacon (London, Thames & Hudson: 1990), 200.

25. Kristeva, Black Sun, 13.

Index

INSURRECTIONS: CRITICAL STUDIES IN RELIGION,
POLITICS, AND CULTURE

Slavoj Žižek, Clayton Crockett, Creston Davis, Jeffrey W. Robbins, Editors

The intersection of religion, politics, and culture is one of the most discussed
areas in theory today. It also has the deepest and most wide-ranging impact on
the world. Insurrections: Critical Studies in Religion, Politics, and Culture will
bring the tools of philosophy and critical theory to the political implications
of the religious turn. The series will address a range of religious traditions and
political viewpoints in the United States, Europe, and other parts of the world.
Without advocating any specific religious or theological stance, the series aims
nonetheless to be faithful to the radical emancipatory potential of religion.

After the Death of God, John D. Caputo and Gianni Vattimo, edited by Jeffrey W.
   Robbins

The Politics of Postsecular Religion: Mourning Secular Futures, Ananda Abeysekara

Nietzsche and Levinas: "After the Death of a Certain God," edited by Jill Stauffer and
   Bettina Bergo

Strange Wonder: The Closure of Metaphysics and the Opening of Awe, Mary-Jane
   Rubenstein

*Religion and the Specter of the West: Sikhism, India, Postcoloniality, and the Politics of
   Translation*, Arvind Mandair

Plasticity at the Dusk of Writing: Dialectic, Destruction, Deconstruction, Catherine
   Malabou

Anatheism: Returning to God After God, Richard Kearney

Rage and Time: A Psychopolitical Investigation, Peter Sloterdijk

Radical Political Theology: Religion and Politics After Liberalism, Clayton Crockett

Radical Democracy and Political Theology, Jeffrey W. Robbins

Hegel and the Infinite: Religion, Politics, and Dialectic, edited by Slavoj Žižek,
   Clayton Crockett, and Creston Davis

What Does a Jew Want? On Binationalism and Other Specters, Udi Aloni

A Radical Philosophy of Saint Paul, Stanislas Breton, edited by Ward Blanton,
   translated by Joseph N. Ballan